ALAIN DU NAY
ANDRÉ DU NAY
ARPAD KOSZTIN

TRANSYLVANIA
AND THE
RUMANIANS

TRANSYLVANIA - FICTION AND REALITY

THE DACO-ROMAN LEGEND

1997

MATTHIAS CORVINUS PUBLISHING

HAMILTON - BUFFALO

FIRST EDITION

© MATTHIAS CORVINUS PUBLISHING

ISBN 1-882785-09-6

LIBRARY OF CONGRESS No.

97-68143

CONTENTS

PART

I

ALAIN DU NAY

AND

ANDRÉ DU NAY

TRANSYLVANIA

FICTION AND REALITY

1997

MATTHIAS CORVINUS PUBLISHING

HAMILTON - BUFFALO

THE PAST OF TRANSYLVANIA –
FICTION AND REALITY

by

Alain Du Nay & André Du Nay

PREFACE

I. – In his Foreword to Ştefan Pascu's *History of Transylvania*, published in English in 1990 by Dorset Press, Paul E. Michelson states that it expresses "the Romanian position on Transylvania", that "it is an interpretation and synthesis" and it is interesting for "what it shows us [the American reader] of Romanian historiography." Pascu published *Istoria Transilvaniei* (The History of Transylvania) also at the beginning of his career, in 1944. In both books, however, "we are given the history of Romania and Transylvania from the vantage point of a committed Romanian nationalist" – as correctly stated by Michelson, who also expressed his belief that Pascu's book "will not long remain unanswered."

The present book is an answer to this *History of Transylvania*.

However, an answer to Pascu's way of writing history has been already given before ours. David Prodan, Rumanian historian (1902–1992), has in his memoirs devoted considerable space to this topic. He accuses Pascu of superficial knowledge of important aspects of Transylvanian history, of anachronisms because of faulty knowledge of elementary facts, etc. (see *Appendix*, p. 235, with concrete examples). Thus, the contention that Pascu's *History of Transylvania* is "the Rumanian position" is no longer tenable – it is the position of the extremely nationalistic, chauvinistic way of writing history, and this has a long tradition in Rumania. However, we should remember those Rumanian historians who, around the turn of the century, and also in the period between the two World Wars, wrote very much differently (see p. 167). These scientists were largely ignored in Rumania during the long decades of Communist rule, in which an extremely nationalistic spirit dominated all political and cultural manifestations, particularly after 1970.

We depart to a large extent from the same considerations that are on the basis of Prodan´s critique. We go, of course, into more details and also point out the results of the chauvinistic spirit in which this text was written: too many important circumstances and events are described in a distorted way, which makes large parts of the text worthless. One might consider that our approach too is nationalistic, – or "the Hungarian position"– but this is not the case. We do not use vague formulations, nor truncated quotations or expressions which appeal to the reader´s emotions, and we do not omit important, relevant facts. All our arguments are easily checked and represent established knowledge. They derive to a large extent from Rumanian sources (as is also the case with E. Illyés´ and A. Du Nay´s books about the origins of the Rumanians, which we use extensively). Since we take up only topics which Pascu wrote about, we cannot even be accused of a biased selection of topics. This text was written in the spirit of traditional Transylvanian tolerance and cooperation, a spirit the peoples of this wonderful country – Rumanians, Hungarians, and Saxons – have developed during centuries of living together.

Our method was to quote relevant passages from Pascu´s *History of Transylvania* and then comment upon them. In many cases, this implied completion of the text with essential and highly relevant material. In this way, also the reader not familiar with Pascu´s book will receive a picture about the chauvinistic way of writing Rumanian history and, at the same time, about interesting aspects of the fascinating history of Transylvania.

We wish to express our hope that in the new international political situation, Rumanian historiography will return to the spirit of those historians and linguists who, before the Communist era, tried to find out as much as possible about the past of their own people, by scientific methods, and without regard to considerations other than science. Until then, it is essential that those who have read Pascu´s book – or other historical treatises written in the same spirit – also take part of the present answer.

II. – Virgiliu Ştefănescu-Drăgăneşti asserts that the Old Germanic loanwords in Latin and the Latin words in Old Germanic are the result of contact between "Daco-Romans" in former Dacia Trajana and the Goths who were living there. It is shown that this theory does not stand up to critical analysis. This treatise is another example of the biased way of writing history – in this case, the history of language.

III. – The third section of this volume shows an example of how and for what purpose the chauvinistic writing of history has been propagated among the common people of Rumania. Lăncrănjan's essay is a literary opus, with long sentences loaded with emotion. Its message is that only one of the three historical peoples living in Transylvania is autochthonous and has therefore the right to live there – the Rumanians. The other two folk groups are, according to this concept, late intruders (colonists or rude conquerors) into "ancient Rumanian lands". The text instigates the Rumanian people against particularly the Hungarian folk group in Transylvania. It is shown how Lăncrănjan falsified written texts in order to be able to show "the Hungarian" as an enemy of the Rumanian people.

IV. – In the *Appendix*, some passages from David Prodan's memoirs (Bucharest, 1993) are given, translated by the present authors. They describe Prodan's view about Ştefan Pascu as a historian; they do not need any commentaries.

*   *   *

We hope that these critical surveys of three Rumanian publications will contribute to the knowledge of Americans about south-eastern Europe – about its past, but also about its present. In the United States one single language has in a comparatively short time become the mother-tongue of an entire, huge country, and there is also a high degree of cultural uniformity. A citizen who has grown up there may therefore have great difficulties in understanding the many different peoples, their endevours, their problems and all the hostilities in south-eastern Europe. In contrast to America, there are a large number of different populations, each of which has its own specific history, culture and most of the time also its own language. The ages of these may be measured in a thousand years or even more, rather than in centuries. Each of them contributes to the cultural richness of this area.

After the second World War, Eastern Europe was left to colonial exploitation by the dictators of the Soviet Union, who also established Communist regimes there by force. The sinister consequences of this fact are not yet entirely known, but the devastation of material and spiritual values, the suffering, torture and death of millions of people during the decades of Communism are certainly without precedent in the history of mankind.

The fate of the peoples living in this area is still to a high extent dependent upon the good will of the Great Powers. Since the only super-power in the world is the US, it is essential that Americans study carefully the circumstances in order to be able to make the right decisions. Thinking in terms of large numbers and huge territories, i.e., as if south-eastern Europe were one single, homogenous area, is not appropriate. Similarly, favoring certain groups of people to the detriment of other groups would only result in continued unrest. It should be realized that the Paris Peace Treaty after the First World War was one of the causes of the Second World War, by unjust, short-sighted arrangements, such as the large-scale changing of frontiers without asking the populations affected, and the creation of new countries. Among other evil effects there was the Bosnian war, the direct consequence of the creation of Yugoslavia after the First World War. The creation of this artificial country, instead of a serious attempt at finding a fair solution to the hostilities between Serbs, Croatians, and Slovenes was a fatal mistake. It was aggravated by the incorporation by force of Macedonians, Albanians, Hungarians, Germans, Rumanians and other populations. The great differences and the animosity between Serbs and Croatians, for example, have been well known, but they were ignored by the decision-makers at the Paris Peace Conference. Similar problems – more or less serious hostilities – exist in other parts of the area. The only way of preventing instability and unrest is to **solve these problems equitably.** It is obvious that this can only be done by a thorough knowledge of the nature of these problems. Of course, most of this work is the duty of the peoples involved, but in the situation of a kind of power vacuum in south-eastern Europe, the contribution of the US and, of course, that of Western Europe, is of great significance.

Ştefan Pascu:
A HISTORY OF TRANSYLVANIA
Dorset Press, New York, 1990
A CRITICAL SURVEY

This book by Ştefan Pascu, born in 1914, former professor of the history of Rumania at Cluj University, treats the history of Transylvania from the Stone Age to 1920. According to the statement of the publisher, p. IV, it was

> originally published as *Voievodatul Transilvaniei*, in 2 Volumes (Cluj Editura Dacia, 1972, 1979). English Translation Copyright 1982 by Wayne State University Press [...] This edition published by Dorset Press, a division of Marboro Books Corporation, by arrangement with Wayne State University Press. 1990 Dorset Press.

According to the cover text, "this volume is an abridgment of [...] Pascu's two-volume *Voievodatul Transilvaniei*", and in the Note on the Translation, it is stated that it "presents a synthesis of Ştefan Pascu's *Voievodatul Transilvaniei*, materials drawn from his other works, and passages written specifically for English-language publication." However, both regarding its contents and its size, it is most like *Ce este Transilvania?* [What is Transylvania?], Edit. Dacia, Cluj, 1983, a history of Transylvania. Its size is about a quarter of the first two volumes of *Voievodatul Transilvaniei*.[1] (Between 1972 and 1989, Pascu published four volumes of this book.) He published a *History of Transylvania* already in 1944, in Blaj, Rumania.

Unfortunately, there are too many serious faults in the text, pure mistakes as well as assertions based upon preconceived ideas rather than facts. It is very important that these be clearly shown, because otherwise the reader of Pascu's book will get an entirely wrong picture of the history of Transylvania. Our method of showing this is **to quote a statement by Pascu and then analysing it.** In a lesser number of cases, we summarize what Pascu says. Certain topics require a more detailed presentation. We use the relevant literature, to a large extent works written by Rumanian authors. Although written in the same spirit and showing similar faults as the English text, *Voievodatul Transilvaniei* will be referred to quite frequently, because it contains important details necessary for the understanding of several events and circumstances but omitted in the English text.

* * *

Pascu, p. XIX: **Introduction.**
Pascu starts with a description of the geography of Transylvania "as the name

---

[1] It contains 317 pages, *Voievodatul Transilvaniei* 576+614=1190, and there is more text on each page of these two volumes than on the pages of this volume.

is generally used". This usage has become general indeed, but it must be pointed out that other areas, which do not belong to Transylvania proper, are included: part of the Banat, the plains between the Munții Apuseni (Transylvanian Alps) and the Hungarian frontier from Arad to the region of Satu Mare (Hungarian Szatmár, German Salzmarkt), Maramureş and Crişana (Hungarian Máramaros and Körösvidék, respectively). In other words, it is the territory given to Rumania at the Paris peace treaty in 1920.

In the law about the annexation of the territories in question, passed by the Rumanian House of Deputies and the Senate on December 29, 1919, referring to the decision of the meeting of Rumanians in Alba Iulia on November 18, 1918, four different territories are specified:

> The decrete-law No. 3631 of December 13, 1918, about the unification of *Transylvania, Crişana, Satmar, and Maramureş* with the old Kingdom of Rumania is ratified and given the status of a law [1] (emphasis added to the names of the territories).

For the sake of brevity, and in order to follow the general usage, the designation *Transylvania* will be used to signify all these territories also in the present book.

Pascu, p. XX:
> Modern Transylvania is the creation of the indigenous Romanians and those peoples – Hungarians, Szeklers, Gemans, and Serbs – who have lived alongside them and helped to shape an unusually rich and complex cultural heritage. The Romanians, a synthesis of the Dacian and Roman peoples, have always constituted an absolute majority of the Transylvanian population.

These sentences contain two major assertions which belong to the main themes of Pascu´s book and, consequently, also of this critical survey. We abstain from commenting on them here and point out only that they are among the many assertions Pascu makes without giving any material evidence. The origins of the Rumanians and their settlement in Transylvania are vast and complex problems, treated recently in English by A. Du Nay and E. Illyés.[2]

---

[1] The original is found at Bucharest State Archives, Presidency of the Council of Ministers Fond, file 19/1919, f.31; reproduced for example in *Mărturii ale trecutului. Album de documente* [Evidences of the Past, Album of Documents], Bucharest, 1981, ed: Ionel Gal, Director General of the State Archives, p. 237 (see also below, map 14, p. 163).

[2] E. Illyés, *Ethnic Continuity in the Carpatho-Danubian Area*, East European Monographs, No CCXLIX, Boulder, Columbia University Press, New York, 1988; we refer to the 2nd, revised edition, Hunyadi Öcs. Mk., Hamilton, Ontario; Struktura Press, 1992, pp. 219 - 221. – Elemér Illyés, 1919 – 1989, historian; born in Torja, Transylvania, lived from 1942 in the West. He published articles and books on the past and present of Transylvania; the monograph mentioned here, as well as *National*

Frequent references will be made to these monographs. To arrive at a sound understanding of these problems, much more data are needed than are given by Pascu in this book – and, unfortunately, also the correction of very many of his statements.

Pascu, p. XXII:

... the Romanian people were aware of the Roman origin of themselves and their language long before any scholarly discussion, Romanian or foreign, of the subject.

Pascu refers to the Italian Humanist Flavio Biondo, who in the year 1453

knew of their Roman origin from the Romanians themselves, as well as from the evidence of their language...

The problem is who these Rumanians were: educated people or the common people, peasants and shepherds? Pascu does not give more details here but in *Voievodatul Transilvaniei,* volume IV, p. 364, one may read:

...the proof that the Rumanian language was used in writing is also confirmed by Flavio Biondo, who wrote in 1453 to Alfonso, the king of Sicily, that the coastal Dacians [*dacii ripensi*] or Vlachs (Romanians) declare their Roman origin as an honour and are proud of it, something which is seen from their speech, so that what they uttered according to the custom of their people had the scent of a peasant Latin, little grammatical.

Poggio Bracciolini wrote: *...rusticam male grammaticam redoleant latinitatem.* This does not imply that the speakers whom Bracciolini met were peasants. It is rather the first mention in a document of the observation that the Romance languages (in this case, Rumanian), developed from *popular* Latin ("Vulgar Latin"), not from classical Latin known from the grammars.

The Humanists in the 15th and 16th centuries visited monasteries and the court of the voivode in Muntenia, where the Rumanian language was used in writing and where also the similarity of Latin and Rumanian was known.

This was in the period of the renaissance, the revival of art and letters under influence of classical (Greek and Roman) models. Interest for the Latin language was therefore very high, but there were no sufficient data nor sound methods (systematic and critical research of the sources) of historical or philological investigation. Beginning with Poggio Bracciolini (1380-1459), Italian humanists explained the existence of a language in south-eastern Europe which was very similar to Italian, by simply assuming that the speakers of this language were the descendants of Trajan's soldiers. Francesco della Valle wrote

---

Minorities in Romania, Boulder, 1982, also published in the German langauge, are his most important works. – André Du Nay, *The Early History of the Rumanian Language,* Edward Sapir Monograph No 3, Jupiter Press, Lake Bluff, Illinois, 1977; and André Du Nay, *The Origins of the Rumanians,* Matthias Corvinus Publishing, Toronto–Buffalo, 1996.

4

in 1532, in his notes about a visit at the monastery Dealu near Târgovişte, that the language of the Vlachs is similar to Italian and if you ask them why, "they explain that they came in Antiquity from Rome" (*dicono esser venuti anticamente da Roma*). Such statements suggest a learned source, because a popular tradition would be about Oriental people, Greeks, etc. – not exclusively about Rome, from which only a very small part of the population of Dacia Traiana came.

An attempt has also been made to prove the existence of a popular tradition about Roman ancestry on the basis of the designation *rumîn* "Roman" but this is very dubious indeed.

Istoria Romîniei, 1960, discusses the question (pp. 797-799: "What does tradition tell us?") and mentions the Anonymous Chronicle of Ţara Românească (*Letopiseţul Cantacuzinesc*) which tells us about a late settling down (*descălecare*), but states that the rest of the Rumanian and foreign chroniclers were always convinced of the Roman origin and of the continuity in Dacia of the Rumanian people. "Tradition" is here defined as the contents in scholarly works, not as a conviction or belief among the masses of people.

Beatrice Daicoviciu gave a more detailed survey of what learned men in Western Europe wrote, between the 15th and the 18th centuries, about the Rumanians. Most of them stated that Rumanian is a Romance language, and many have also expressed their belief that it is a continuation of Latin once spoken in Dacia Traiana. Regarding the question of a popular tradition, nothing certain may be said (and only the tradition regarding Latinity is discussed):

> Regarding the knowledge among Rumanians about their Latinity, this is more difficult to document. Since the documents were written in chancellaries by scholars (thus, in learned places), an alien influence may always be suspected, and it is very difficult, if not impossible, to find out whether the masses have had a knowledge about Latinity.[1]

1. PRE-ROMAN TRANSYLVANIA (pp. 1 – 15)

Paleolithic and Neolithic Man
Pascu, pp. 2 – 3:

---

[1] Beatrice Daicoviciu, "Mărturii apusene despre latinitatea şi continuitatea românilor (sec. XV – XVIII)"[Western testimonies about Latinity and continuity of the Rumanians (15th– 18th centuries], in *Acta Mvsei Napocensis*, V, 1968, p. 204. A presentation of this problem is also given by Lajos Tamás, *Rómaiak, románok és oláhok Dácia Trajánában* [Romans, Rumanians and Vlachs in Dacia Traiana], Budapest, 1935, pp. 89-106; cf. also Elemér Illyés, *Ethnic Continuity in the Carpatho-Danubian Area*, Boulder, 1988; 2nd revised edition Struktura Press, Hamilton, 1992, pp. 32-37.

Human settlements from the Neolithic period have been discovered throughout Transylvania. Artifacts that have been unearthed include hand-shaped ceramics of quite good quality, axes drilled for hafting, small iron objects, gold ornaments, and fired clay tablets with archaic script. The creators of these treasures were the indigenous tribes, though there were certain influences from southeastern Europe and even Asia Minor.

The Neolithic period lasted from around 5.500 to 1.800 B.C. The first 2.000 years of this epoch are named the early Neolithic. On the basis of the material remains, different cultures have been established. The Neolithic cultures spread in Rumania from the territories north of the western part of the Black Sea and Asia Minor.[1] The map given by Berciu (p. 35) shows the Hamangia culture covering the western coast of the Black Sea (eastern Bulgaria, Dobruja, and southern Bessarabia (the Moldavian Republic);[2] the Criş culture covered eastern Hungary, the southern part of the area between the Danube and the Tisza, the Banat, northern Serbia and Bulgaria, parts of Transylvania, and Moldavia (Moldova) "this culture expanded eastwards as far as the Bug valley where it came into contact with the Bug culture" (p. 39); the Linear Pottery culture existed in the area along the middle course of the Mureş and the upper course of the Olt in Transylvania, and in Moldavia (Moldova).

The Middle Neolithic (3.500 - 2.700 B.C.)

Also in this period, the material remains show anything but a unitary picture in the territory of present day Rumania. The Tisza culture covered the area east of the river Tisza including the north-western parts of present day Rumania; Transylvania shows the Turdaş culture, with the exception of the east, where remains of the Boian culture were found, as also in most of Moldavia (Moldova) and eastern Muntenia. The shores of the Black Sea and Dobruja were dominated by the Hamangia culture; southern Muntenia by the Vădastra culture, also found in Bulgaria; and western Oltenia and the Banat by the Vinča culture, which extended to these areas from present day Serbia.

The late Neolithic (2.700 - 2.000/1.800 B.C.)

The late Neolithic in the Carpatho-Danubian region and south-east Europe is distinguished by its magnificent painted ware, the designs of which are executed in various colours or

---

[1] D. Berciu, *Romania before Burebista*, London, 1967, p. 37.

[2] The provinces of Rumania are shown on map 14, p.163. Historical *Moldova* (Moldavia) is situated between the Eastern Carpathians and the river Pruth. East of the present day frontiers of Rumania, between the Pruth and the Dniester, there is *Basarabia* (Bessarabia). When Bessarabia was a part of Russia and later of the Soviet Union, it was by the Russian officials called Moldavia and Rumanian spoken there the "Moldavian language" - part of a policy aimed at making the land more Russian. Today this country is called the Republic of Moldavia, which should not be confounded with Moldavia, Rum. Moldova, the province of Rumania west of the Pruth.

in graphite.[1]

The Tisza culture covers about the same area as in the Middle Neolithic. In most of Transylvania, the Petreşti culture is found, with the exception again of the east, where the Cucuteni culture extends from Moldavia (Moldova), the Moldavian Republic, and the Ukraine. In the Banat and northern Serbia, remains of the Vinča culture prevail; in Oltenia and south of it in parts of the Balkan peninsula, the Sălcuţa culture is found and in most of Muntenia and in Dobruja, the Gumelniţa culture, which also covers eastern Bulgaria.

Pascu, p. 4. **The Bronze Age**

> Bronze Age civilization was established throughout the Romanian territories by the efforts and intelligence of the Dacian population, the branch of the great Thracian people north of the Danube.

Pascu quotes Bogdan Petriceicu Haşdeu,[2] in whose opinion

> the Thracians and the Dacian tribes were the ancestors of the Romanian people – that is, they constituted the ethnic substratum of Romania.

Also during this period (2.200 B.C. – 1.100 B.C.), the territory of present day Rumania was covered by many different human cultures. We refer, for the sake of brevity, only to D. Berciu, *Romania*, London, 1967. The map on p. 69 shows the tentative chronology of the Bronze Age in Rumania. The whole country is divided into six large areas, which are further divided; thus, Transylvania is divided into four areas (Southeast, Middle, Southwest, and West; and Maramureş is treated separately).

The assumption of a single population (Dacian or any other specific, uniform people) is thus not warranted by the archeological finds.

The Iron Age (after 1200 B.C.)
Pascu, p. 8:

> Alongside the indigenous population north of the Danube, foreign peoples now began to settle. (The Illyrians, Scythians, Celts, and Bastarnae are mentioned.)

The first mentioning of a population of Getae is from the year 514 B.C. in Dobruja (Herodotos). They are described as a branch of the Thracians. On the basis of a statement by Strabo, to the effect that the Getae spoke the same language as the Dacians, certain authors have assumed that these were the same

---

[1] Berciu, 1967, p. 56.

[2] Bogdan Petriceicu Hasdeu, 1838–1907, was a poet, an author, a playwright, a historian, a philologian and a folclorist.

people. However, this is dubious; as stated by C. Poghirc, for example:

> Strabo's affirmation about the Dacians speaking the same language as the Getae (VII, 3, 13) is of no greater value than the assertion of Italian travellers in the Rumanian countries in the 16th century about Rumanian being a dialect of Italian.[1]

Pascu, p. 12:

> ...reconstructions from modern Romanian words of Dacian origin prove that the Dacians spoke a dialect of Thracian. [...] Experts estimate that over 160 Dacian words are preserved in Romanian; these are mostly words denoting everyday life and social relations. [...] Many Dacian river names have also been preserved – for instance, *Donaris* (Rom. Dunăre "Danube").

It is a widespread belief in Rumania that the substratum of the Rumanian language was Dacian and that there are Dacian words in modern Rumanian. This is taught in the schools, in some textbooks of history in a totally misleading way: 4 – 5 examples of "Dacian words" are given alongside 3 or 4 words of Slavic origin, so that the student is led to believe in a powerful Dacian and a less distinct Slavic influence upon Rumanian vocabulary. Rumanian linguists, however, have shown that this is wrong.

The "Dacian river name *Donaris*" did not exist, it was created by modern philologists in order to explain Rumanian *Dunăre*. The origin of the ending *-re* is unknown and there are not even plausible hypotheses to solve this question.[2] The Danube between the Iron Gate and the Black See was in Antiquity also called *Istros*. This name was not preserved in any language spoken today. The absence in the Rumanian language of an inherited Roman name for this great river is not compatible with the theory of an ancient home-land of the early Rumanians along ("on both shores of") the lower Danube. They must have lived once at a considerable distance from the Danube. In contrast, the Rumanian language has preserved ancient toponyms in northern Greece, such as Sărună, Lăsun, Flărină. – The ancient names of the largest rivers north of the lower Danube were transmitted to Rumanian by Slavs and Hungarians (cf. below, p. 65).

In the practical absence of Dacian words with known senses, the investigation must be made with Thracian words, which are preserved mostly in Greek or

---

[1]*Istoria limbii române* [The History of the Rumanian Language], red. I. Coteanu, vol. II, Bucharest, 1969, p. 318, note 2.

[2]Cf., for example, G. Schramm, "Der rumänische Name der Donau", *Dacoromania*, 1, 1973, pp. 228 – 236; G. Vékony, Dákok, rómaiak, románok [Dacians, Romans, Rumanians], Budapest, 1989, pp. 237-238. – A. Rosetti, *Istoria limbii române*, definitive edition, 1986, p. 217, considers that the Rumanians borrowed this name from Slavic, as shown by certain sound-changes.

8

Latin texts. I.I. Russu has compiled them; [1] his list contains 196 words with more or less certain or assumed senses. If the substratum of Rumanian would be Thracian ("Thraco-Dacian"), there would be some chance that a number of these Thracian words are found among the substratum-words of modern Rumanian. Among these 196 Thracian lexical elements, there are seven for which a Rumanian substratum word exists: male goat; child; big; hamlet; tendril, stem; joy, and fence. Not a single of these have the same form in Thracian; although in two cases a connection between the two languages has been proposed: the Rumanian word *mare* "big" has been connected with a part of compound Thracian personal names such as *Berimaros, Karsimaros*; and Rumanian *gard* "fence" was suspected to be connected with Thracian names of towns: *Gordion, Manegordum*. Since we do not know the sense of any Thracian personal name or placename, these remain only hypotheses. The same may be said about attempts at explaining Rumanian substratum words from Thracian (and in three cases Dacian) lexical elements and placenames. This does not in itself exclude the possibility of Dacian words in Rumanian; it must be stated, however, that known facts do not support this assumption.

The Rumanian scholar I.I. Russu pointed out this:

> ...the Thracian language had not (as far as we know today) any exclusive phonetic feature, existing only in our autochthonous words and totally unknown in other Indo-European languages; the Thraco-Dacian language of the satem type had the same phonetic system as had Illyrian, and shared very many elements with other languages of the satem type (Iranian, the Baltic languages, Slavic). Therefore, if we possessed data indicating that the ethnic-social basis of the territory of Romanization in Moesia, Dacia, etc., was Illyrian, Iranian, or Balto-Slavic, one could admit the possibility of such an origin for the autochthonous Rumanian words, although it is little probable that one may reckon with such a possibility. [2]

Russu has been vehemently criticized for this statement [3] but no critic can alter the facts. The assumption of a Dacian ethnic basis for the Rumanian people

---

[1] I.I. Russu: *Limba traco-dacilor* [The Language of the Thraco-Dacians], 1967, pp. 138 – 143.

[2] I.I. Russu, *Etnogeneza românilor* [The Ethnogenesis of the Rumanians], Bucharest, 1981, pp. 115 – 116. (I.I. Russu, 1911 – 1987, philologist, who conducted research into the ancient languages spoken once in South-East Europe (Illyrian, Thracian, etc.), as well as the Latin and Greek inscriptions found in the territory of present day Rumania. (Indoeuropean languages are divided into two large groups: in contrast to the *centum languages*, Ancient Indo-European *k* changed to *s* or *sh* in the satem-languages; *satem* "hundred" in Avestic.)

[3] Cf., for example N. Gudea: "Cîteva observaţii şi note critice cu specială privire la partea istorică a monografiei *Etnogeneza românilor* de I.I. Russu [Some Remarks and Critical Notes with Special Reference to the Historical Part of *Rumanian Ethnogenesis* by I.I. Russu]; in *Acta Mvsei Napocensis*, XX, 1983, pp. 903–916.

and language is based only upon the fact that the territory where Rumanian is spoken today coincides partly with the territory of the former Dacians. **The available linguistic material does not confirm this theory** – on the contrary: it makes possible that the substratum of Rumanian – or, the ethnic basis of the Rumanian people – is, for example, Illyrian.

The essential feature of those pre-Roman words in the Rumanian language is that the majority of them exist also in Albanian. This indicates close relations between the ancestors of the Rumanians and those of the Albanians. Pascu's description of these words is misleading: many of them denote "everyday life", but the specific life of **shepherds** living in high mountains. Words pertaining to shepherd terminology and the life in a mountainous territory of forests are the largest semantic group among these lexical elements, indicating the main occupation of the ancestors of the Rumanians (cf. Illyés, 1992, pp. 211 - 249; Du Nay, 1996, p. 83).

2. ROMAN RULE AND DACO-ROMAN CIVILIZATION (pp. 16 – 35)

Political, Economic, and Military organization

Pascu, p. 16:

> The conquered territories included what is now the Banat, Transylvania except the northwestern section, Oltenia, Muntenia, Dobruja, and southern Moldavia; these areas were integrated into the Roman Empire as the peripheral provinces of Dacia and Lower Moesia.

This description suggests that Roman Dacia corresponded approximately to present day Rumania. There are also maps in circulation on which these frontiers of the province are shown. However, this is not correct.

Istoria Rominiei [The History of Rumania], Bucharest, 1960, p. 350 – 352 gives the following account of the frontiers of Dacia Traiana:

(To Roman Dacia belonged, mainly according to the series of Roman *castra* built along the *limes*) ..."the Banat, most of present day Transylvania and Oltenia, where the Roman rule has everywhere left numerous and certain traces". Later, it is mentioned that the western part of the Banat (a region of marshes)

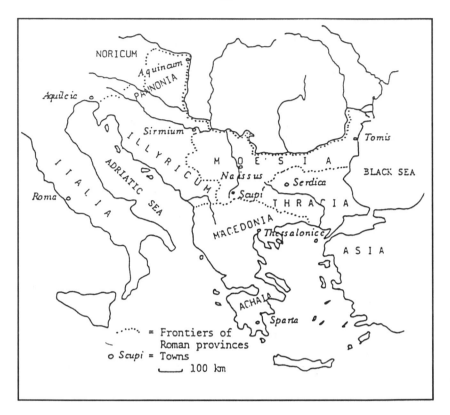

Map 1. – The south-east European provinces of the Roman Empire in the first century AD.

probably was not colonized by the Romans. IR 1960 (pp. 351–352) also stated explicitly which areas did **not** belong to the Roman Empire:

> Thus, the province of Roman Dacia did not include present day Crişana, Ţara Oaşului and Maramureş, and east of the Carpathians, entire Moldavia and Muntenia as far as to the Olt, with the exception of a short time, about a decade, when this last mentioned territory belonged to Moesia Inferior.

A Roman settlement on the southernmost border of Moldavia was described,

11

but otherwise, the above definition is accepted by most Rumanian historians.[1] Of the territory of present day Rumania, at most 40% belonged to the Roman Empire, (actually somewhat less, because not the entire Banat was part of the province; the territory between the river Olt and the *limes transalutanus* belonged to the Empire only between 200 and 245 A.D., cf. Du Nay, 1996, map 1, p. 14; *Istoria Rominiei,* see above). But the former Roman territory should be compared with the entire territory where Rumanians are living today: thus, including the Moldavian Republic and parts of Bucovina. Then, it is seen that the territory of Dacia Traiana was less than 40% of the present day Rumanian territories (taking also into account that the population in the Szekler territory and in several other areas in Transylvania is not Rumanian). Thus, even if they would have originated from the Roman population of Dacia Traiana, the Rumanians must have migrated later to about two thirds of the area where they are living today.

Pascu, p. 17 – 19:

> The miners entered a kind of contract with the state in its capacity as owner of the mines. These contracts were written on wax tablets, of which a large number have been found in the Bihor Mountains, where the richest gold- and silver-mining operations were located. There were mines at Alburnus Maior (modern Roşia), Abruttus (modern Abrud), and Ampellum (modern Zlatna), which was also the headquarters of the mining administration.

1. The placenames: Roman Ampellum is now called Zlatna, derived from a Slavic word with the sense of "gold". Thus, between the Romans and the Rumanians, there were Slavs, who named the settlement in their own language; Rumanian Zlatna is borrowed from Slavic. The name Ampellum may have survived in the river name Ompoi, Ampoi (Hungarian Ompoly); however, Rumanian Ompoi was borrowed from Hungarian or Slavic (Latin *amp-* would in Rumanian have changed to *ămp* > *imp-*, cf. Latin *campus* > N. Rum. *cîmp*, *quando* > *cînd*, etc.).

---

[1]See the maps given by *Istoria Rominiei,* 1960, pl. XII (facing p. 348); Protase, 1966, fig. 27, p. 64; E. Condurachi, C. Daicoviciu, *The Ancient Civilization of Romania,* London, 1971, p. 253, *Dacoromania,* 1973, p. 149-161; Protase *Autohtonii* 1980; Du Nay, 1996, map 1, p. 14. – Among maps published in the West which show the correct frontiers of Roman Dacia, we mention *The Collins Atlas of World History,* Guild Publishing, London, 1987; first published in France under the title *Le Grand Livre de L'Histoire du Monde,* Hachette, Paris, 1986, editor Pierre Vidal-Naquet; p. 61.

12

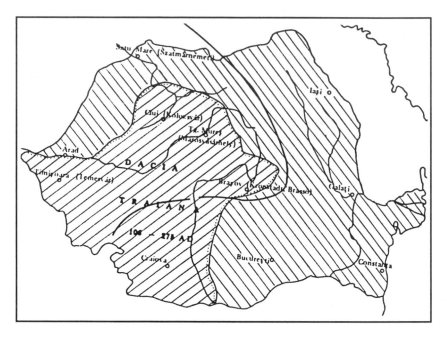

Map 2. The relation between the area of Dacia Traiana and present day Rumania. The area occupied by the Roman Empire is less than 40% of the territory of Rumania. (Cf. also the explanation about the frontiers of Dacia, map 3, p. 15).
(From Du Nay, *The Origins of the Rumanians,* 1996, p. 203.)

*Abruttus is "assumed, but not attested".[1] The name of *Abrud* (Hungarian *Abrud-bánya*) is first mentioned in a document from 1271: *terra Obruth, Abruth*; in 1320, *Obrudbania* is written. – *Abritus* (in some texts, *Abrittus, Abruttus*) is documented on inscriptions found in Razgrad, a town in north-eastern Bulgaria, thus, a settlement with this name existed in Moesia Inferior.[2] It is not impossible that Abrud derives from this name, but it cannot be inherited, because Latin *-b-* disappeared in Rumanian in this position: Latin *februarius, febrarius* >

---

[1] C. Suciu, *Dicţionar istoric al localităţilor din Transilvania* [Historical Dictionary of the localities of Transylvania], Bucharest, vol. I: 1967, p. 23; (vol II: 1968).

[2] Cf., for example, V. Pârvan, *Dacia,* translated from the French by R. Vulpe; 5th edition, Editura ştiinţifică, Bucharest, 1972, pp. 150, 221–222.

Rumanian *făurar*.[1] The *a* > *o* change occurred probably in Slavic and this form was originally borrowed by the Hungarians. In Hungarian, *o* changed in the 14th century to *a;* thus, Rumanian Abrud cannot have been borrowed (from Hungarian) earlier than in the 14th century.

2. Some data about the wax tablets give an idea about life in that remote mining area: these were found in the 19-th century, mainly walled up in pits. They contain commercial agreements, contracts of work, trading of slaves. The people here were very poor – a miner could earn during half a year his bread for one year. In the CIL, III, 25 documents are published, with clearly readable names of 68 free men. Only six of these may with certainty and another 10 – 12 with some probability considered to have been Roman citizens.[2] Most of the people here were thus peregrins, mainly from Illyricum, where they also worked in mines. The first document was written in 139 AD and the last in 167, the year of the Marcomann invasion into the province. In a document from 167, the society for burial is declared dissolved, apparently because most of its members (33 out of 50) have left Alburnus Maior.

Thus, mostly peregrins from the Balkan Peninsula worked in the region of the gold mines for some decades: the wax tablets known today comprise only 28 years, but even if we assume that they were there already before the first wax tablet was written (Dacia was occupied in 106 AD), this period of time was at most sixty years long. In 167, the Marcomann invasion extinguished this society.

Pascu, p. 19:
...Dacian religious beliefs were infused with Roman deities, creeds, and customs. Progress was made in sciences such as astronomy and medicine. These and other effects eventually produced a thoroughly mixed Daco-Roman civilization. Pascu, p. 26:
[The Dacians] ... did borrow from the Roman colonists a few customs of a broadly Roman-provincial type unknown to them before the conquest: tombs with a burnt grave and a coin for Charon, the ferryman for the dead, are definitely attested on Dacian territory from provincial times. Furthermore, the well-known phenomenon of *interpretatio Romana* – the worshipping of non-Roman deities under Roman names – certainly occurred in Dacia as in other provinces.

The question of religious life in Roman Dacia is very complex and cannot be treated reasonably in a few sentences. If it is necessary to characterize it briefly, then quite a different statement would be adequate. For example:

---

[1] ILR 1969, p. 143.

[2] E. Pólay, *A dáciai viaszostáblák szerződései* [The Contracts on the Wax-tablets from Dacia], Budapest, 1972, p. 69 – 71.

...in the [urban] centers of Dacia, with a population formed by so many heterogenous elements, as was Sarmizegetusa, Apulum [...] etc., was found and will be found in the future an extraordinarily large number of inscriptions and monuments which truly reflect this bizarre mosaic of religious conceptions and beliefs.[1]

Many assumptions have been made about Dacian gods hiding behind the Latin names of several gods, for example *Liber*. These have been proved wrong; thus, *Liber* appears very often also in Pannonia and even in Dalmatia.[2] There existed religious syncretism in Dacia, but the gods worshipped there were (besides Roman), Greek and Oriental, as shown for example by D. Tudor: *Oraşe, tîrguri şi sate în Dacia Romana* [Towns, Market places, and Villages in Roman Dacia], Bucharest, 1968. Tudor gives in this book a very thorough account of the religious life in the province, of which we mention that of Apulum, where almost all of the cults practised in Dacia existed (p. 159). *Aesculapius* and *Hygea* were by some investigators considered to have been protectors of Apulum. Those who worshipped Mithras (an Oriental deity) have left in this town about 60 monuments of stone with inscriptions or sculptures and probably 3 cult buildings (p. 161). The domination of Eastern cults is to a large extent explained by the fact that Dacia was occupied by the legions *Macedonia V* and *Gemina XIII,* whose soldiers originated from present day Syria and Palestina. But gods from Carthago, Paphlagonia (Little Asia), from Galatia (Little Asia), from Palmyria; Cimistenus from Bitinia (p. 164), and many others were worshipped there.

> In large groups or as isolated elements, these colonists brought the gods of their homeland to the heart of Dacia. Their great number and the similitudes of the cults hastened the relgious syncretism in Apulum, between these national gods and the official Roman gods. This process of syncretism is found especially with the gods brought here from the Orient, which held a large place in the Pantheon of Apulum. They made a real assault with the aim of conquering the"religious market" of the town.[3]

The detailed description given by Tudor contains only one single deity possibly syncretized with a Dacian one:

> As a singular deity, *Diana mellifica* ("producer of honey") appears. She would be syncretised with a Dacian one and her epigraphic dedication reflected the richness in bees of Roman Dacia (p. 165).

---

[1] C. Daicoviciu, *Dacica. Studii şi articole privind istoria veche a pămîntului românesc* [Dacica. Studies and articles on the ancient history of the Rumanian Land], Bibliotheca Mvsei Napocensis, Cluj, 1969, p. 201.– C. Daicoviciu, 1898 – 1973, was a historian and archeologist, "an impassioned research worker and a very good connoisseur of the Antique Era" (*Enciclopedia istoriografiei româneşti* [The Encyclopedy of Rumanian Historiography], Bucharest, 1978, p. 117).

[2] Daicoviciu, 1969, p. 201.

[3] Tudor, 1968, p. 165.

15

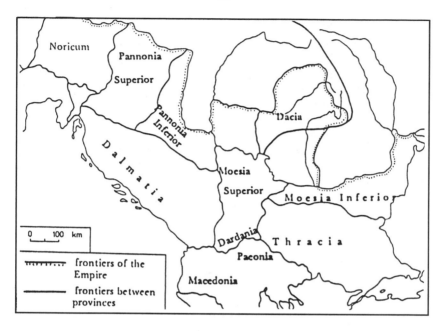

Map 3. – The Roman provinces in southeastern Europe between 106 – 275 AD. (From: A. Du Nay, *The Origins of the Rumanians*, 1996, p. 14.) The frontiers of Dacia Traiana are given according to general consensus.[1] In reality, the territory of Roman domination north of the lower Danube was smaller. It is not quite certain that the entire area shown on the map was occupied in 106 AD. The organization of *Dacia Superior* and *Inferior* in 119 and the division of the province into *Dacia Porolissensis, Apulensis,* and *Malvensis* in the years 158 – 168 AD may suggest a gradual extension of the frontiers during several decades. The *limes transalutanus* was built around 200 AD and the area between this *limes* and the Olt was under Roman rule only between 200 and 245 AD.[2] Only the mountainous part of the Banat belonged to the Empire: Roman military stations and civil settlements exist only there.[3]

---

[1] Cf., for example, *Istoria României. Compendiu,* 1974, p. 45; Protase, *Problema continuității în Dacia în lumina arheologiei și numismaticii,* 1966, p. 156; Condurachi & Daicoviciu, *The Ancient Civilization of Romania,* 1971, p. 253.

[2] Tudor, "Romanizarea Munteniei" [The Romanisation of Muntenia], *Apulum,* XII, 1974, p. 114.

[3] Tudor, *Orașe, tîrguri și sate in Dacia romană* [Towns, market-places and villages in Roman Dacia],1968, p. 55; Tudor also mentions that this part of the Banat was part of Moesia Superior, as judged by the frequent finds of epigraphic material with the name *Legio IV Flavia.*

16

Also Pascu aknowledges indirectly the lack of Dacian deities in the religious syncretism found in Dacia (p. 21):

> Roman deities, however, such as Jupiter, Diana, Venus, and Mithras, "the invisible Sun"— brought by the Romans from the East – became more and more prevalent as time passed, especially east of the border between Noricum and Pannonia.

One should add, that *interpretatio Romana*, in which an **indigenous** god appears under a Roman name, occurred in most other Roman provinces; cf., for example Protase (referring to Fr. Drexel, W. Schleiermacher, G. Behrens and other authors):[1]

> In many parts of the Empire, including Italia, Hispania, Gallia, Germania, Britannia, there are numerous, certain attestations to the fact that the indigenous deities were, under Roman rule, worshipped for a long time under different forms, with their own names, alongside those of the Greco-Roman Pantheon or even fused with them, while in Dacia Traiana not a single name of a Geto-Dacian god which was continued to be worshipped by the autochthons is known. Here, everything is hidden under the Greco-Roman religious forms.

Thus, the fact is that **no Dacian gods were worshipped in Dacia Traiana.** Given the importance of religion in the society in question, this fact reduces considerably the probability of the development of a "thoroughly mixed Daco-Roman civilization" in that province.

Regarding the "coin for Charon", about 20 coins of bronze were found, each in a tomb (at Soporu de Cîmpie, Sighişoara, and Obreja, Protase, 1980, p. 129). This Greco-Roman custom was imitated by many other populations of contemporary Europe, which, living outside the Empire, never adopted the Latin language, for example in eastern Preussia; and also in Moldavia, where coins were found in tombs of the Carps.[2]

On p. 20, Pascu states that, in order to analyze the importance of the Roman conquest of any given indigenous population, "we need to know to what extent the people adopted the conquerors' language, thought, and culture", and that "we must provide concrete analyses of the specific historical conditions affecting one or another Romanized people."

One can only agree with this, but, unfortunately, not much of these principles is realized in Pascu's text.

---

[1] D. Protase, *Autohtonii în Dacia* [The Autochthons in Dacia], I, Bucharest, 1980, p. 252.

[2] G. Bichir, *Cultura carpică* [The Carpic culture], Bucharest, 1973, p. 132.

Pascu p. 21:
> The peaceful coexistence between Roman and native forms can be observed in place names, dress, customs and manners, and language as well. Latin inscriptions – roughly 3.500 of them, an impressive number considering the extent of the Roman provinces – maintained both Roman and native names for generations.

Of these, dress, customs and manners are not sufficiently specific and will not be discussed here. (Roman influence upon these is shown by most of the people of Europe of the period in question.)

The question of the **placenames lacks in the following discussion given by Pascu.**

More than 3.000 inscriptions may be considered an impressive number. However, these inscriptions were rather different from those made in other Roman provinces, south of the lower Danube. There, inscriptions usually reflect the everyday life of the local population, while in Dacia, they are mostly of an official character:

> In the inscriptions found in Dacia, mostly acts of administrative and religious character are reflected, or the public and private manifestations of the army. It is only on rare occasions that the sincerity and the kind of speech of the ordinary citizen or of the slave permeates through them [1]

Then there is the question whether local Dacians raised inscriptions. One may assume that many of them appear under Latin names, but it is still astonishing to find that the proportion of Dacian or Thracian names on these more than 3.000 inscriptions is only about 70, thus less than 3%. This is really an insignificant number from which, moreover, should be extracted an unknown number of names which belonged to Thracians, coming from the provinces south of the Danube.

Thus, the inscriptions provide no evidence to strengthen the assumption of a (peaceful or otherwise) coexistence between Romans and Dacians.

Pascu p. 23:
> The process [of Romanization] was fastest and most thorough in the section along the Danube – dotted with towns, rural settlements, and military installations for legions and auxiliary troops – and in areas with urban and military concentrations in the interior. Regions where rural life predominated were affected less, but by no means untouched.

One glance at the map of South-East Europe in the period in question shows that most of the territory of Dacia Traiana belonged to "regions where rural life

---

[1] H. Mihăescu, *Limba latină în provinciile dunărene ale imperiului roman* [The Latin Language in the Danubian provinces of the Roman Empire], Bucharest, 1966, p. 278; quoted in Du Nay, 1996, p. 206.

predominated". The **southern** shores of the Danube were really dotted with towns, etc. But these towns belonged to Moesia Inferior, where a total of 28 Roman towns existed for several centuries. North of the lower Danube, there were, as Pascu also states, 11 towns. This is not a large number, and it should be added that these towns were not situated in a homogenous area, but spread from the south (Sarmizegetusa) through the valley of the Mureş – Apulum and Brucla – then further to the north, Potaissa, Napoca, and Porolissum.

To this comes, that the Rumanian language lacks very many inherited Latin terms that designate urban culture. The majority of Latin words existing in most Romance languages (panromanic words) but **lacking in Rumanian** "regard technical terms of the different professions and, in general, words which presuppose notions of a certain level of material culture."[1] Also the changes of meaning in Rumanian of certain Latin words indicate that the ancestors of the Rumanians were a typical rural population: *meridies* "middle day" to mean "the place where the cattle rest at midday" (Rum. *meriză*); *turma* "unit of the Roman cavalry; 30 men" to "flock" (Rum. *turmă*); *minor* "to rise, to menace" to "drive, urge on, goad" (Rum. *mîna*) etc.[2]

D. Protase, one of the chief archeologists in Rumania, who has devoted a large part of his scientific work to the study of Roman Dacia, believes also that the towns did not take part in the development of "Daco-Romans":

...in contrast to Italy and the western provinces, where some oppidan or urban centres of the autochthons continued to develop into veritable Roman towns, in Dacia, the more important autochthonous settlements and oppidan centers ceased to exist after the Roman conquest. All of the towns of Traian's province have been created after the Roman colonization from civilian or military settlements, having only borrowed the names of the ancient Dacian settlements: Sarmizegetusa, Apulum, Potaissa, Napoca, Porolissum, Drobeta, Dierna, etc. In Dacia, there was no Daco-Roman urbanistic development.[3]

Thus, besides the relatively short period of Roman domination (about 170 years), another circumstance diminishes the probability of the creation of "Daco-Romans:" the lack of a "Daco-Roman urbanistic development".

Pascu, p. 23:

In order to provide a clearer, more exact understanding of the Romanization of Dacia, it is necessary to repeat a well-known general fact: the Dacian population north of the Danube was subject to Roman influence long before the beginning of Roman rule.

---

[1] *Istoria limbii române* [The History of the Rumanian Language], red. I. Coteanu, Bucharest, 1969, vol. II, p. 126.

[2] Du Nay, 1996, pp. 54 - 55.

[3] Protase, 1980, p. 252.

19

Some examples from Rumanian historical literature of the thesis that Romanization in Dacia started already before the occupation of the territory by Trajan in 106 AD: In an album of documents, published in 1981 by the Management of the State Archives and the Council of Socialistic Culture and Education, with the Foreword written by Ştefan Ştefănescu, Correspondent Member of the Academy of the Socialist Republic of Romania, a Latin inscription: DECEBALUS PER SCORILO found at Grădiştea Muncelului (near ancient Sarmizegetusa), is commented as follows:

> I-st century A.D. Inscription engraved on a jar discovered at Sarmizegetusa, attesting to the fact that DECEBAL was the son of Scorilo. The presence of this inscription in Latin proves that the Romanization process was started even before the Dacia conquest.[1]

On the same vase there are two stamps, with the description DECEBALVS, and PER SCORILO, respectively. The meaning of this text is not clear, *per* may be Thracian *per, par-* "son"; it appears in Albanian family names: Lef Përdoda, Geg Përgega, etc.[2]

Also in *Istoria României, Compendiu*, 1974, "the adoption of the Latin culture and language" is asserted to have started already when the Roman occupation reached the lower Danube, in the era of Emperors Augustus and Tiberius (1st century B.C. – 1st century A.D.).[3]

However, other Rumanian historians abandoned these unfounded theories. Radu Vulpe (born in 1899, archeologist and historian of the Antique Era) quotes Pârvan, *Getica*, p. 724.[4]

> The occidentalization of the Getians was started in the 4th century B.C. by the Celts and intensified, from the 2nd century on, by the Romans; it could only lead to one single result: in the very moment when the Romans deifinitively took the role of civilisers from the Celts, exposing even these, from Gallia to the estuary of the Danube, to the Roman way of life, Dacia was perfectly prepared to become Roman. The Romanization of Dacia was shown anthropo-geographically already from 1000 B.C., when the Villanova culture prevailed also over the entire Carpathian area. The Celts have, however, transmitted also the material elements of the Greco-Italic culture. And the Romans drew the conclusions: ethnographical as well as spiritual ones.

---

[1] *Mărturii ale trecutului. Album de documente.* [Evidences of the Past. Album of Documents], ed. Ionel Gal, Bucharest, 1981, p. 26.

[2] Popović, I, *Geschichte der Serbokroatischen Sprache,* 1960, p. 82.

[3] Ş. Pascu (red.), *Istoria României. Compendiu* [The History of Rumania. Compendium], 3rd edition, Bucharest, 1974, p. 70.

[4] In Pârvan, *Dacia,* 5th edition, 1972, Bucharest; notes of the translator, note 273, p. 203.

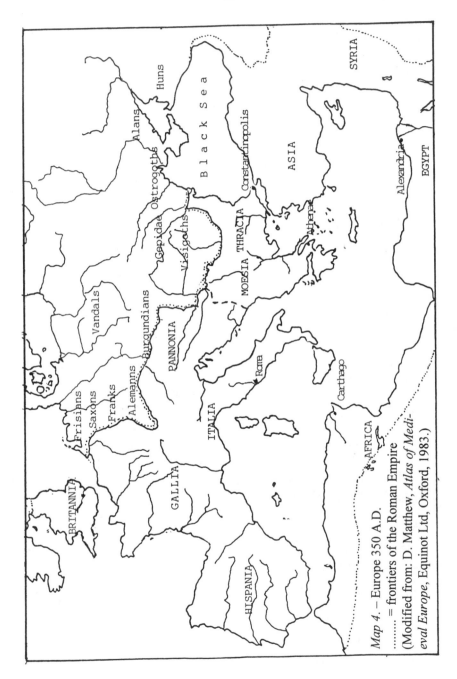

Map 4. – Europe 350 A.D.
.... = frontiers of the Roman Empire
(Modified from: D. Matthew, *Atlas of Medieval Europe*, Equinot Ltd, Oxford, 1983.)

To this, Radu Vulpe, who translated Pârvan's work to Rumanian from French and commented it, gave the following commentary:

> It is clear that Pârvan refers only to the process of Occidentalization which prepaired the later success of Romanism in Dacia, and not to a Romanization of this country before Trajan, as some of the thoughtless and superficial critics of *Getica* have thought in the past. Also for Pârvan, as for all specialists of ancient history, the Romanization of Dacia could not have taken place but after the conquest.

Also D. Protase (1980, p. 238) expressed his opinion that the assumption of Romanization in Dacia before 106 AD, put forward by some representatives of Rumanian historical literature, is wrong.
Pascu, p. 23:

> Thus the ground was prepared for the smooth, rapid acceptance of Roman culture, technology, and customs, and of the Latin language.

The decisive difference between introducing to a human society new technologies and customs, on the one hand, and the abandonment of the language spoken by the population on the other, is smoothed over by Pascu. Commerce, merchants, craftsmen and advisors travelling and working in Dacia, construction techniques, manufactured goods, coins, are given as evidence for preparation of Romanization (Pascu, p. 23). But these could at most have had the effect that some Latin loanwords entered the language of the Dacians. Some other phenomena – also given as factors of preparation for the Latin language in Dacia – such as the supervision by populations serving the Empire of certain areas in Muntenia, or military raids, cannot be considered at all as factors of Romanization or to have had any cultural influence whatsoever.[1]

Pascu, p. 24:

> In any case, the total military and civilian population that migrated to Dacia was certainly very large. [...] Thus, even in Trajan's time, the influx must have reached 500.000, which represents an increase of something like 50 percent over the preconquest population. – It is important to emphasize that the overwhelming majority of the newcomers to Dacian lands were Latin-speakers, lived according to Roman customs, and actively spread Roman culture among the original inhabitants.

That a large number of people migrated to the new province is obvious. But there are important aspects which do not appear from Pascu's description:
Although probably many of the newcomers spoke Latin, it is certain that Latin was not the mother-tongue of a large part of them. It seems not possible to

---

[1] Illyés, 1992, pp. 80–81.

determine how many people had Latin as their mother-tongue and how many spoke other (Greek, Illyrian, Oriental, etc.) languages. The following facts found in a thorough analysis made by D. Tudor, 1968, about the situation in Apulum, may throw some light upon the problem:

Municipium Aurelium Apulense was first mentioned in 180 A.D. According to inscriptions, "a powerful nucleus of Roman citizens existed there, who were colonized there officially (*consistenses*), from whom the *decuriones* for the communal council were recruited..."

Tudor states (p. 168) that "The onomastic study of the inscriptions shows that the great majority of personal names was Roman. There existed, however, also important contingents of *nationes* who came here by colonization and with the army."

He mentions 8 Illyrian, 10 Thracian or Dacian, 12 Oriental, and 10 Celtic names. There were Greeks as well as Hellenized Oriental or Balkan people. Greek names were "very numerous" (63 are given) and 11 inscriptions were written in the Greek language. They include votive altars devoted to the gods of health, to Athene, to Iupiter Sardendenos, to Mithras, Mater Troclimene; stamps upon bricks and vases, etc. "They contain personal names (often Roman or Oriental), of soldiers and civilians, very little affected by Romanization."

... "in Apulum, people wrote and spoke the Greek language much more than in any other town of Dacia, because of the great influx there of a large number of Greek, Oriental and Hellenized Balkan people" (Tudor, p. 169).

The association of the Augustales was powerful in Apulum, and its most splendid period of time was during the reign of the Severes (Septimius Severus ruled between 193 and 211 A.D.), ... "when many liberated slavs and rich peregrins belonged to it" (Tudor, p. 155). Tudor gives 11 non-Roman names of these people (p. 156). Also the "list of names of brick-making soldiers in Apulum is very rich, especially in Greco-Oriental names" (p. 158).

> The geographical and economic position of the town has drawn to it many merchants, some of whom exported goods to other provinces. Those known today from inscriptions were all Oriental people... (Tudor, p. 159).

Pascu, p. 25:
> The Roman authorities' insistence that the indigenous population be integrated with Roman society corresponded to the Dacians' own wishes.

Pascu does not mention how the Dacians expressed this wish. Given the scarcity of written documents about Dacia Traiana, it is possible that documents from which evidence for this assumption could be found were not preserved. But there is ample evidence in historical records as well as in material finds, that uprisings by some subdued elements were common in Roman Dacia; the

23

proportion of Dacians among them is not possible to elucidate. The fact remains that Roman domination was not appreciated by all of the inhabitants.

There are epigraphic attestations (in a note, CIL, III, 1448 is given)to that in the towns and villages of Roman Dacia, a poor population was successively formed, by liberated slaves, and impoverished colonists from other parts of the Empire. Later, important groups of barbarians were colonized from the territories outside the province, who had certain obligations.[1]

IR 1960 gives an account of the many attacks by barbarians, among them, free Dacians, from the territories beyond the frontiers, often at the same time with uprisings: in 143, 156–157, 167, and during the epoch of Commodus (180–192). In the first part of the third century, social unrest continues, as well as the attacks by the barbarian populations. This is indicated by numerous hoards of coins buried in that time. "In fact, here we find the fight between the exploited poor of the villages and the landowners, who, together with the enriched veterans seek shelter in the towns or start the exodus to the south of the Danube".[2]

Thus, the relationships between the Romans and the Dacians who were living outside Dacia Traiana were not friendly – something which does not fit well with the theory of their Romanization after the Romans had abandoned the province.

Pascu, p. 26:
After having asserted that, at the end of Roman rule in Dacia, the Dacians did use Latin instead of their mother-tongue:
the indigenous population was thoroughly assimilated, linguistically and otherwise, during the 170 years of Roman rule. It had become Daco-Roman
Pascu considers it necessary to affirm that after the Roman withdrawal in 271–274 A.D.,
Romanization of the territories north of the Danube did not cease, instead continuing in new forms through the sixth century.
This is not quite logical; – if the Dacians were, also linguistically, "thoroughly assimilated", i.e., they became "Daco-Romans", what means "continuing Romanization"? One gets the impression that Pascu himself is not quite sure about the "thorough Romanization of the Dacians" and feels therefore the need of strengthening it. Anyway, Pascu enumerates here the following circumstances: propagation of Christianity, continuing economic and cultural ties with the territories south of the Danube, the maintenance of economic life based on the Roman monetary system (i.e., the use of Roman coins); the return of Roman-

[1] *Istoria Rominiei* [The History of Rumania], red. C. Daicoviciu, Bucharest, 1960, p. 427.

[2] IR 1960, p. 434.

24

Byzantine rule north of the Danube under Constantine the Great and Justinian; and bridgeheads maintained north of the Danube. – Nothing of all this belongs to circumstances which significantly affect the language of masses of people.

Pascu, p. 28:
> Today over one hundred settlements are known in Transylvania alone where traces of the Dacian culture of the second and third centuries A.D. have been found. Recent investigations have also unearthed many more of the rural communes where the Dacian population continued to live. Of the more important ones we may cite Caşolţ and Slimnic in southern Transylvania and Lechinţa de Mureş, Obreja, and Noşlac in central Transylvania; Dacian funeral installations have been discovered in these settlements and in others. Finally, archeologists have discovered many settlements where the Roman and Dacian cultures coexisted in perfect harmony.

1. The assumption of Dacians living together with Romans in the same settlement is mainly based upon finds of pottery of the Dacian type. However, it was not the Dacian pottery of superior quality – this disappeared completely in the time of the conquest – but more primitive forms, made by hand.[1] It is difficult to determine, whether a vessel found in a settlement from the 2nd and 3rd centuries was made in those centuries or earlier. Most (about 90%) of the pottery is of the Roman style, and this type of pottery appears immediately after the conquest, without any transitional period. All this gives the impression that the Roman colonists lived in these settlements according to their customs, producing also pottery of their own. The small amount of primitive Dacian pottery, 10% of all, does scarcely warrant the statement of the "Dacian and Roman cultures coexisting in perfect harmony".

2. The assumption that Caşolţ (Hung. Hermány, German Kastenholz) etc. were Dacian settlements prevailed earlier in Rumania – see, for example, *Istoria Romîniei*, 1960. p. 391, or *Istoria României*, Compendiu, 1974, p. 50. However, it is now abandoned by Rumanian archeologists.

3. **The settlements show a discontinuity of a very high degree:** According to Protase, 1976, and 1980, 58 settlements in the province are assumed to have been inhabited by both Romans and Dacians. The material finds indicate that most of them were founded after the Roman conquest and existed only during the Roman domination: in 54, no signs of life may be detected after the seventh decade of the 3rd century. Of the remaining four, two (at Archiud [Erked], Bistriţa county, and at Mugeni [Bögöz], Harghita county) were not ancient settlements but were founded at the end of the Roman domination in Dacia Traiana. They all were abandoned already during the 4th century. Only one

---

[1]Cf. Protase 1980, pp. 157–165; Illyés 1988 and 1992, p. 89.

25

settlement shows signs of life from the 2nd century B.C. to the 4th century (at Şura Mică [Hung. Kiscsűr, German Kleinscheuern], Sibiu county [Szeben megye, Altland]), and one: Obreja (Obrázsa), Alba county, was inhabited from the mid-second century A.D. to about 370.[1] One could argue that the inhabitants of those 54 places may have settled after the Roman retreat in other parts of Dacia, although there are no indications of this. This hypothesis would be reasonable if only a (smaller) part of the settlements showed discontinuity. But the disappearance of a so high number of the settlements indicates much more probably radical changes in the demographic situation: the inhabitants disappeared – were either killed or left the territory.

Pascu p. 28: **Daco-Roman civilization in the Age of Migration**

> The withdrawal of the Roman army and administration from the province of Dacia did not mean that the Daco-Romans abandoned their lands.

This assertion is bolstered in the following by a series of arguments. As we have seen, material evidence is not sufficient to prove the emergence of "Daco-Romans" – on the contrary, several circumstances make it very questionable indeed. Some of the inhabitants of Roman Dacia may, however, remained there; the question is then who they were, how many they were and how far can their existence in the area be traced? It is known, for example, that a number of Latin-speaking peasants remained in Noricum after the Roman withdrawal, there are even lists of names of them; but they eventually disappeared, being assimilated into the surrounding, mostly Germanic population. Assimilation was the ultimate fate also of the Latin-speaking population of England after 410 A.D., and there, several Latin elements in placenames survived, such as *castra* in Man*chester*, Lan*caster*, *colonia* in Lin*coln*, *vicus* in War*wick*, etc.[2]

General assumptions, such as "there is no historical evidence that an entire people has ever left its home in the face of invasion", or that "the territories south of the Danube were neither more peaceful nor safer than those to the north" (p. 28), etc., have not much relevance. However, the material evidence put forward in favour of the assumption of "Daco-Romans" living north of the Danube after the second half of the 3rd century should be examined.

Constructions and tombs in Sarmizegetusa, Apulum and other towns: even if we assume that these were made by a Latin-speaking population, it must be

---

[1] See Table II, p. 94, in Illyés, 1992.

[2] Cf., for example, Du Nay, 1996, p. 209.

emphasized that they disappeared latest towards the end of the 4th century (the Hunnish invasion), when all signs of life were extinguished in the former Roman towns. Other material finds, such as two Roman pottery kilns, Christian artefacts, etc., may have been made, imported and used by any other population: the Goths or the free Dacians, the Carps. The Goths were Christian in the 4th century and bishop Ulfila preached, according to the sources (Auxentius Durostorensis, see below), both north and south of the Danube, in the Gothic language as well as in Latin. Latin inscriptions on two or three artefacts do not prove that they were imported by a Latin-speaking population, – such objects were also found in far away territories, where no Romanization was ever possible. Many of them were simply stolen from churches by barbarian soldiers who served some time in the Roman army. The Swedish archeologist M. Stenberger (*Det forntida Sverige* [Ancient Sweden], Stockholm, 1971, p. 371, describes a vessel with a Latin inscription found in Norway, east of lake Mjösa, and another vessel and two swords with Latin inscriptions found in Sweden. The inscription on the vessel found in Sweden is as follows: APOLLONI GRANNO DONUM AMMILIVS CONSTANS PRAEF TEMPLI IPSIVS VSLLM ("To Apollon Grannus was this gift given by his chief of temple Ammilius Constans"; the so called Apollo Grannus vessel).[1] Stenberger states that these vessels must have been brought to Scandinavia by plundering soldiers.

Pascu, p. 31:
> ...the Visigoths left traces primarily of their material culture, such as the great find at Sîntana de Mureş in central Transylvania and the burial grounds at Spanţov and Tîrgşor, south of the Carpathians on the Muntenian plain.

Pascu does not mention that the Sântana de Mureş culture (approximately between 270 A.D. and the end of the 4th century) was a complex of material remains stretching from Ukraine southward into areas of present day Rumania, among them also (especially northeastern and central) Transylvania. Its ethnic character was mainly Old Germanic, containing many elements of Roman provincial material culture – the Goths, as most of the barbarians, were strongly influenced by Roman culture and civilization.

The Goths lived in Transylvania for about a century (from the end of the 3rd to the end of the 4th century;) the Gepidae, another Old-Germanic people, for more than two centuries (from the early 5th century to the end of the 7th). Many settlements and tombs of the old-Germanic populations were found, showing that they not only ruled the territory but were living there. For a century, between the

---

[1] Du Nay, 1996, p. 222.

27

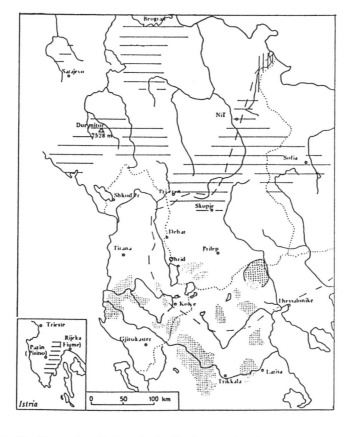

Map 5. The Rumanian dialects in the Balkan peninsula.

Northern Rumanian   Arumanian

||| placenames
                                             of N.Rum. origin

Istro-Rumanian ≡   Meglenitic

the frontiers of the Bulgarian language   — — —

The area of Istro-Rumanian is shown according to a map by Puşcariu, that of the
Arumanians and the Meglenites, after a map by Weigand and Puşcariu, the
frontiers of the Bulgarian language after a map by Conev. All maps are given in
A. Rosetti, *Istoria limbii române,* 1968.
(From: Du Nay, *Origins of the Rumanians*, 1996, p. 121.)

mid-5th and the mid-6th century, the eastern part of the Carpathian basin, including Transylvania, was called *Gepidia*.[1]

More recent Rumanian publications assume that Gepidae were living together with "Daco-Romans" in the same settlements in Transylvania (for example at Moreşti and at Porumbenii Mici; Pascu p. 31–32). Earlier, the coexistence of Old-Germanic peoples with "Daco-Romans" was generally denied because of the lack of Old-Germanic loanwords in the Rumanian language. Those historians who now assume such a symbiosis, should explain this phenomenon. However, Pascu does not even mention the linguistic problem.

Pascu, p. 32:
> As archeological research continues, new proofs of the nature of Daco-Roman civilization come to light. Roman coins of the fourth and fifth centuries, the great majority of bronze and a few of silver, have been discovered throughout the area. Bronze money reflects the humble socioeconomic status of its Daco-Roman users; the migrating peoples used only gold and silver coins. A more significant proof is furnished by the hoards of coins discovered at several Transylvanian sites: at Sarmizegetusa; in the Banat at Orşova and Răcăjdia; at Hunedoara; near Tîrgu Mureş; in the northeast near Dej, and in other places.

It is an old assumption of Rumanian archeologists that bronze coins, i.e., coins of a lower value, must have been used by "Daco-Romans", since they are assumed to have been a poor population. Pascu re-iterates this view, disregarding some important facts: bronze coins were most abundant along the Roman *limes*, where small scale commerce flourished. Most of them are, in South-East Europe, found in Oltenia and in the Banat along the Danube. Many bronze coins from the 4th century were found between the Timiş and the Mureş rivers, where Sarmatian Iazyges were living in that period.[2] – In Transylvania, such coins are numerous also beyond the territory which once belonged to the Roman Empire; in present day Crişana, at Cipău in the valley of the Mureş, where a group of free Dacians were living, as well as in the Olt valley, populated at that time by the non-Roman people of the Sf. Gheorghe culture. Bronze coins which date from the 4th century were also found in the extra-Carpathian territory of Rumania – in Moldavia and on the plains of Muntenia.[3] Thus, finds of bronze coins cannot be used to determine the ethnic character of their users.

The **hoards** of Roman coins are similarly non-specific and cannot be used to

---

[1] Illyés, 1992, p. 141.

[2] Cf. Protase, 1966, p. 197: "In the Banat, where the Iazyges have abundantly and for a long time used the Roman coins, the ethnic attribution of the monetary material is possible only taking into consideration the archaeologic surroudnings in which it appears".

[3] Cf. Illyés, 1988, p. 124, with references.

prove a special people in the places where they were found. (It may be added that most of these hoards were found long ago, mostly in the 19th century, they were partly plundered, descriptions about the exact place of find and other important circumstances are often lacking.)

Pascu, pp. 32 – 34:

> The Daco-Roman population also passed on through the ages the most important Latin words and concepts pertaining to religious life: *creştin* (Lat. *christianus* 'Christian'), *cruce* (Lat. *crux* 'cross'), *Dumnezeu* (Lat. *Dominus Deus* 'Lord God'); *înger* (Lat. *angelus* 'angel'); *biserică* (Lat. *basilica* 'church'). The last of these is maintained only in Romanian and the Rhaeto-Romance dialects spoken by a small group in Switzerland; the name for a house of worship in all other neo-Latin languages derives from a Greek word, *ecclesia* (Ital. *chiesa;* Fr. *église:* Span. *iglesia;* Port. *igreja).* In Albanian, too, the word for church *(chesa)* been borrowed from Greek; this would also be the case in Romanian if the Daco-Romans had actually retreated south to the Balkan Peninsula.[1]

Pascu gives here some examples of the Rumanian religious terminology of Latin origin. Since these terms show the sound changes of Late Latin, they must have been adopted by the ancestors of the Rumanians very early, in the 4th – 6th centuries.[2] There is no evidence in favour of the assumption that they were transferred in Dacia Traiana, by Christian missionaries. The Christianization of the ancestors of the Rumanians occurred in the Balkan Peninsula, where a very rich and powerful religious life is attested during the late centuries of the Roman Empire. More important is that Pascu forgets to mention a second group of Rumanian religious terms: those **of Greek origin.** Du Nay, 1996, (p. 113) mentions eight such terms which are also found in Bulgarian, and six of them also in Albanian. (The similarities between these three languages are very great, cf. Balkan Linguistic Union.) Greek lexical elements were thus borrowed by Rumanian, which invalidates Pascu's argument in connection with the word *biserică.* This word was otherwise used in the entire area of East Latin:

> *Basilica* is preserved in the Rumanian, Dalmatian and Albanian languages, which proves that it was a popular and widely spread word.[3]

Pascu forgets a third group of the Rumanian religious terminology – in fact, the largest one, those **borrowed from South Slavic** (most of them are originally Greek terms). Rumanian obtained them from Middle Bulgarian, a direct

---

[1]Rum. *cruce* < Latin *cruce(m);* Rum. *Dumnezeu* < Latin *Domine Deus* (vocative!) (note of the present authors).

[2]Du Nay, 1996, p. 111-112.

[3] Haralambie Mihăescu, *Limba latină în provinciile dunărene ale Imperiului roman* [The Latin Language in the Danubian Provinces of the Roman Empire], Bucharest, 1960, p. 277; Du Nay, 1996, p. 112.

30

continuation of Old Slavic, and "the majority of these words were transferred to Rumanian after the period of Old Slavic (Old Bulgarian), respectively, after the 11th century..." [1] These words pertain to all aspects of Christian religious life, including 1) fundamental notions of the Christian religion: e.g., *duh* "soul, spirit", *rai* "Paradise", 2) bad ghosts, pagan gods: *diavol* "devil; naughty boy", *idol* "(statue of a) pagan god", 3) names of the saints: *sfînt* "saint", *mucenic* "martyr"; 4) church hierarchy: *sobor* "gathering, meeting; synod;" *patriarh* "patriarch", *mitropolit* "metropolitan /bishop/", *popă* "priest", *ctitor* "founder, benefactor"; 5) monastery life: *stareţ* "Father Superior", *călugăr* "monk", *pustnic* "hermit, anchorite, recluse"; 6) very many words pertaining to the building of the church, clothes of the priests, cult objects: *mănăstire* "monastery", *metoh, metoc, mitoc* "small monastery, subordinated to a larger one", *oltar* "altar, communion table", *potcap* "cap used by priests and monks", *icoană* "icon", *mir* "sanctified oil used at the ritual; myrrh", 7) the religious ceremony, the main books: *slujbă* "religious service", *psalm* "psalm", *molitvă* "prayer used by the priest at certain circumstances, such as baptizing or for sick people", *cazanie* "sermon; book with sermons".[2]

The Rumanians encountered a Slavic population in the territories north of the lower Danube, but they cannot have taken such a large number of words, pertaining to the entire field of the Christian religion, from them. Not even the Bulgarian domination over Muntenia and southern Transylvania in the 9th century is sufficient to explain such a powerful impact. It presupposes a stable church and state organization (and this existed in Bulgaria during the 10th – 12th centuries), as well as sufficient time. Together with a series of terms referring to state organization, the large group of Rumanian religious terms of Bulgarian origin indicates that the ancestors of the Rumanians lived, during the time in question, in close contact with the Bulgarians, in the Bulgarian state.[3]

There are also Rumanian religious terms which testify to contact with Albanian.[4]

---

[1] G. Mihăilă, *Studii de lexicologie şi istorie a lingvisticii româneşti* [Studies of Lexicology and the history of Rumanian Linguistics], Bucharest, 1973, p. 126.

[2] Ibid., pp. 127–132; a total of 79 words are given.– Some of these terms gave rise to everyday Rumanian expressions and sayings, such as *metoh, metoc, mitoc > mitocan* ´cad; boor, churl, lout´; *a unge pe cineva cu mir şi cu tămâie (din creştet şi până în tălpi)* fig. ´to heap exaggerated praises on somebody who does not deserve it´. – Cf. also Du Nay, 1996, p.114.

[3] A. Du Nay, 1996, pp. 114 - 115.

[4] Ibid., p. 106.

31

Pascu, p. 34:

> Thus, the Daco-Romans were chiefly an agricultural people, and only to a much lesser extent craftsmen and miners. [...]
> Again we see proof of the continuity of the Daco-Roman civilization north of the Danube, for Romanian *jude* "judge" is derived from Latin *judex*, and Romanian *oameni buni și bătrîni*, roughly "wise old men", has its origin in Latin *homines boni et veterani*.

Much has been written about the occupation of the early Rumanians. Ovid Densusianu, for example[1] considered that the Rumanians were "in the first place a people of shepherds," and Capidan agreed. Rosetti, discussing the question, notes: "The affirmation is certainly exaggerated".

> The Rumanians were in those ancient times shepherds and peasants. It must be stated, however, that their agriculture was rudimentary, practised in the mountains, with the hoe, probably mostly by women, the elderly and children. The crop they grew was the millet, which had the advantage of a short vegetation period: between May and July.[2]

It is an enigma why Pascu asserts that the N. Rum. word *judeca* "to try (a case), to pronounce a judgment upon", inherited from Latin (*judicare*), (it exists also in the dialects only spoken south of the Danube; cf. Arum. *ǵudicu*) "proves the continuity of the Daco-Roman civilization **north of the Danube**"? This fact is in accordance with the Latin origin of the Rumanian language and does not prove anything else. It is a Panromanic word,[3] cf. Italian *giudice*, French *juge* "judge", etc. – Also this theory has been put forward long ago, cf. A. Sacerdoțeanu, in the volume: *Unitate și continuitate în istoria poporului român* [Unity and continuity in the history of the Rumanian people], Bucharest, 1963, p. 123:

> (the Rumanian word *judeţ* "county", connected with Latin *judex* "judge") ...started as a juristic institution and, preserving this quality, became also the main administrative institution of the Rumanian people. By this, the Roman system is continued.

In the first Rumanian texts, from the 16th and 17th centuries, *judeţ* is used in the senses of "judgment; place where justice is made, tribunal; judge, chief, prince; chief of the municipality"[4] and on Slavonic maps from the 14th – 15th centuries, it means "rural functionary who has juridic attributions".[5]

---

[1] *Păstoritul la popoare romanice* [Shepherding in the life of the Romance populations], Bucharest, 1913, p. 16, quoted by Rosetti, 1986, p. 576.

[2] Rosetti ILR 1986, p. 380.

[3] ILR, II, 1969, p. 112.

[4] Ovid Densusianu, *Histoire de la langue roumaine*, ed. V. Rusu, Bucharest, 1975, pp. 756 – 757.

[5] Rosetti, A., *Istoria limbii române*, definitive edition, Bucharest, 1986, p. 749.

Pascu, p. 34:

Although the empire no longer had direct authority over them, the "barbarian" territories still belonged to the Roman sphere of influence. This can be seen from the political organization of village communes into groups now known as "popular Romanias"; after the term coined by the great Romanian historian Nicolae Iorga.

Pascu does not give any reference regarding the basis of the term "popular Romanias" and there is no record on such "village communities" of "Daco-Romans" in the period Pascu talks about here (around the 6th – 8th centuries A.D.). In *Voievodatul Transilvaniei*, vol. I, p. 33, Pascu affirms:

VILLAGE COMMUNITIES. – The society was organized in village communities, in the valleys of the rivers and in the natural depressions. Such communities existed probably [*vor fi existat*] and were led by judges, patrons, and *cnez*-es, helped by "good and old men" in the valley of the Cerna, in the depression of Mehadia, in that of Nerei, in the valley of the Caraş, in the depression of Caraşova, in the valley of the Bîrzave, in the depression of Bozovici, in the depression of Caransebeş, in the valley of the Timiş, in the depression of Buziaş, in the lowland of Timişoara, along the left shore of the lower part of the Mureş, etc., etc., all in the Banat voivodate. This is the explanation of the existence, until late in the Middle Ages, of numerous Rumanian Banat-districts, of which some – about 7 – 8, had great privileges, others, about 15, had no privileges. It is the explanation of the semi-autonomous organization of the Banat during the entire Middle Ages.

We quoted the entire passage, because it reveals how Pascu argues. The large mumber of "village communities" is impressive. The reader must be very prudent to find out the real situation. How is all this documented? It appears that it is simply **not documented at all,** everything written here is sheer assumption! This appears in the text also, but in only three words: "*vor fi existat*" - i.e., **"they probably existed".** The later, documented Rumanian districts, beginning with the 14th century, were not the continuation of these early village communities – since they are only imaginary – it is the other way around: the documented Rumanian organizations are used to suggest that Rumanian village communities already existed there several centuries earlier.

In *Voievodatul Transilvaniei*, vol. I, Pascu continues the enumeration of these imaginary village communities in Crişana (13 village communities, all with names), in Transylvania (12), in Maramureş and surrounding areas (9), in the eastern Carpathians (12), in the depression of Bârsa (5), in Făgăraş and surroundings (7), and in Zarand (10). It must be stated again, that not a single of these is documented, all "existed probably". In the English translation, this "probably" ("*vor fi existat*") is omitted.

3. THE EMERGENCE OF THE ROMANIAN PEOPLE (pp. 36 – 41)

Pascu, pp. 36-37:

> The evolution of the Romanian people and their language thus began to reach completion, and the new forms to emerge more clearly, until in the seventh and eighth centuries we see a qualitative change: the Daco-Roman population becomes the Romanian people, and their language, so-called Vulgar Latin, becomes Romanian. [...]
> ...the Romanians have never called themselves Wallachs or Vlachs, but rather *Romani* or *Români*. Likewise, they have never called their own political formation Wallachia, but Romania or Țara Românească ("Romanian country").

There are no written documents about the ancestors of the Rumanians in those centuries. From the language it may be concluded that they lived under the entire period of Late Latin (4th – about 8th century A.D.) in close contact with the other Neolatin populations, in the area of East Latin. Until the end of the 10th century, the Rumanian language was largely unitary: *română comună* (common Rumanian) or *străromână* (ancient Rumanian). After the 10th century, four dialects developed: Northern Rumanian, now spoken mainly north of the lower Danube and in the Timok area of Serbia; Istro-Rumanian, on the Istrian peninsula; Arumanian, spoken in southern Macedonia and northern Greece, and Meglenitic, to the north-east of the Arumanians.

The Rumanians called themselves *rumîni* – this world derived from Latin *roman(us)* according to the sound-laws of Rumanian (Latin unstressed *o* > Rumanian *u;* Latin *a* in front of a nasal > *ă* > N. Rum. *î*). The designation has nothing to do with Dacia; also a Romanized population on the Balkans may have called themselves Romans.[1] The designation *"Țara Românească"* (=Muntenia, by foreign authors called Wallachia) was not used before the 15th century; the territory in question was during the Middle Ages called *Terra Transalpina* or *Ungrovlachia.*[2] This term appeared for the first time in the Church hierarchy, as a title of some dignitaries of the Church: *mitropolitul Ungrovlachiei.* As late as in 1406, the Rumanian voivode Mircea the Old (1386 – 1418) called himself in a document, among other titles, the ruler of "the entire country of Ungro-Vlachia" – which is identical with what today is called Țara Românească.[3]

---

[1] The term *rumîn* was, in Muntenia and Moldavia, for centuries used as a synonym of *șerb, iobag* "serf, villain", cf., for example, *Istoria României. Compendiu,* 1974, p.159.

[2] Treml, *Ungarische Jahrbücher,* 8, 1928, p. 32.

[3] The document, written in Slavonic, is found in *Archivele Statului* [State Archives], Bucharest, historical section 11. – Reproduced for example in *Mărturii ale trecutului. Album de documente* [Evidences of the Past. Album of Documents], ed. Ionel Gal, Bucharest, 1981, p. 55.

Pascu, p. 37:

> (Priscus Panites, an envoy of the Byzantine emperor to the "court of Attila," wrote that as he travelled north of the Danube he was able to communicate with the local populace, who spoke a language he called "Ausonic," a Romance language.)

Much has been written about the statement of Priscus Panites, who travelled in the court of the Hunnish king Attila:

> ...the Scythians are a mixed people and besides their barbarian language, they try to speak the language of the Huns or of the Goths or of the Ausonians when some of them have to do with Romans.[1]

The editors of *Fontes Historiae Dacoromanae* state in the introduction that

> for us, the indication of Priscus that this language (Ausonian) served for the understanding with the Romans, and not with the Byzantine Greeks is sufficient. It was thus a Romance language, probably Latin spoken in the Romanized area of the Danube valley (the Moesia-s, the Dacia-s and Pannonia...) (p. VIII).

The reasoning is not quite logical, because the other two languages which the Scythians used, according to Priscus, in contacts with the Romans (Gothic and Hunnish) are not Romance languages. Moreover, Latin spoken south of the lower Danube in the 5th century was essentially not different from the Latin spoken in other areas of the Empire, there was in any case no need to designate it otherwise than simply Latin.

Pascu, p. 37:

After having asserted that Arianism contributed to the "revitalization of Latin culture in the Daco-Roman areas", Pascu continues:

> This is shown, among other ways, by the fact that Bishop Wulfila used Latin when bringing his Arian-tinged Christianity to the "Goths." Since the actual Goths did not know Latin, Wulfila had to have been preaching not to them, but to the Daco-Romans.

This theory is also quite old; it may be read for example in an article written by Constantin Daicoviciu in 1941 (in *Dacica*, 1969, p. 525):

> Their Christianity, preached by Wulfila and other missionaries, is, rightly, connected with the Christian Daco-Roman population in the area of the lower Danube, for to whom would Wulfila have preached in the Latin language if not to these?

---

[1]*Fontes Historiae Dacoromanae* II, Bucharest, 1970, p. 264.

The life of bishop Wulfila (or Ulfila) has been described by Auxentius Durostorensis, who lived south of the lower Danube and became bishop in Durostor around the year 380 A.D. At the beginning of this text, the author writes:

"Having made all this and similar things, [living] for 40 years in the bishopric, he preached, by Apostolic grace in the Greek, Latin, and Gothic languages." In a note to this text, the editors of the *Fontes Historiae Dacoromanae,* II, 1970, p. 111, remark: "His preaching in three languages and especially in Latin attests to the continued presence of a Latin-speaking population north of the Danube."

However, reading further in the text, it appears that Wulfila was initially bishop over the Goths. Auxentius Durostorensis recounts that Wulfila was 30 years old when he became bishop over the Goths (*in gente Gothorum de lectore triginta annorum episkopus est ordinatus*); "to lead and improve, to teach and to build in spirit the people of the Goths" (*ut regeret et corrigeret /et/ doceret et aedificaret gentem Gothorum*); "this saint, by the decision and order of Jesus Christ, led, according to the Evangelic, apostolic, and prophetic directory the people of the Goths" (*iste sanctus ipsius Cristi dispositione et ordinatione ... agentem ipsam gentem Gothorum secundum evangelicam et apostolicam et profeticam regulam emendavit...*).

Wulfila preached among the Goths for seven years; then a persecution of Christians was started in that territory and Wulfila was forced to settle, with a part of his congregation, south of the Danube, in the Roman Empire: "Living with his people in the territory of the Romans, he preached, besides those 7 years, another 33 years the truth..." (*Degens cum suo populo in solo Romaniae absque illis septem annis triginta et tribus annis veritatem predicavit...*).

Thus, Auxentius Durostorensis states clearly that Wulfila preached first among the Goths (this is in fact three times re-iterated in the text; and without any mentioning of "Daco-Romans"); then he was forced to settle in the Roman Empire and preached there for another 33 years – of course, also in Latin.

Pascu, p. 38:

> The developing language [*romåna comunå*] was enriched by a few Slavic and Greek lexical elements, but its syntax and morphology was not at all affected by other languages, and the grammatical structure of modern Romanian is purely Romance.

How much the Rumanian language was affected by Slavic appears from any textbook of the history of this language. The ancestors of the Rumanians lived for several centuries in symbiosis with South Slavs. As stated by I. Nestor:[1] "La

---

[1] Revue roumaine d´histoire, III, 1964, pp. 383–423, quoted by A. Rosetti, *Istoria limbii romåne* [The History of the Rumanian Language], Definitive edition, Bucharest, 1986, p. 268.

36

dernière étape de formation du peuple roumain (entre le VIe et le Xe siècle) a revêtu, la caractère d'une symbiose protoromano-slave." Rosetti, in his discussion of the powerful Slavic influence upon Rumanian, states:

> Rumanian presents in its structure non-Romance elements (which we will examine in the following pages), which are only explained by the Slavic languages and by the contact between these two languages.[1]

A large part of the religious terminology as well as that pertaining to state organization derives from Bulgarian. In English, the Slavic impact upon the Rumanian language is presented in Du Nay, 1996, pp. 98 – 111.

Pascu, p. 38:

> The Bratei culture, the creation of the Daco-Roman people, is known from finds all over Romania: at Bratei, Ciumeşti, and Moreşti in Transylvania; at Costişa and Monoaia in Moldavia; and at Ipoteşti and Stolniceşti in Oltenia and Muntenia.

(Ipoteşti is in Moldavia [Moldova]). A monograph about the Bratei culture – the cemetery Nr. 1 at Bratei from the 4th - 5th centuries – was published in 1973 by Ligia Bârzu.[2] A presentation of this cemetery in English may be found in Du Nay, 1996, pp. 166 - 169. It appears that many elements in this cemetery are also found in the *Sântana de Mureş* culture, as well as in the *Sf. Gheorghe* culture, in southeastern Transylvania. There are also material finds characteristic of the Dacian sites: pieces of pottery made by hand, for example the Dacian censer (*căţuia*). There are large quantities of animal bones in this cemetery, which is not the case in Roman or Illyrian cemeteries, but is characteristic of Dacian tombs at Porolissum–Salca. The funeral rite of ritually burned cavities is found in Pannonia, Moesia, and Illyricum. Objects of glass were all imported, mostly from Pannonia. There are no signs of commercial contacts between these peoples and the Roman towns along the lower Danube.[3] According to Ligia Bârzu, the "Daco-Roman heritage" consists in this cemetery in the first place of large quantities of big vessels of supply. They are, however, not of the Roman type; and are also found among the material remains of the Sîntana de Mureş culture.

---

[1] Rosetti ILR 1986, p. 268.

[2] Ligia Bârzu, *Continuitatea populaţiei autohtone în Transilvania în secolele IV - V (cimitirul 1 de la Bratei)* [The Continuity of the Autochthonous Population in Transylvania in the 4th – 5th Centuries (the cemetery Nr. 1 at Bratei)], Bucharest, 1973.

[3] Bârzu, 1973, p. 95.

There are very many foreign elements in this burial site and even several Rumanian archaeologists consider it non-Roman. (It must be remembered also that the material remains found here show that the cemetery was not in use during the Roman epoch but only thereafter, from the beginning of the 4th century.) Gheorghe Diaconu denied the "autochthonous character" of the Bratei culture mostly because of the funeral rites[1] and Kurt Horedt stated in *Siebenbürgen im Frühmittelalter*, Bonn, 1986, p. 65, that the burial ground at Bratei is Slavic and cannot be connected with a Romance population.

Material remains of Roman origin or made after the Roman style are very numerous in most European territories in the epoch in question. As we have seen, such remains are found in the *Sântana de Mureş* culture as well as in the cemetery at Bratei. After the 5th – 6th centuries, this influence diminished and disappeared eventually entirely. The cultures enumerated by Pascu on pp. 38 – 41: *Ipoteşti-Cândeşti-Ciurelu; Sărata-Monteoru-Balta Verde; Suceava-Şipot,* also contain material imported from the territory of the former Roman Empire, although in general much less than earlier cultures. The material remains dated to the 6th – 10th centuries are characteristic of Avars, Gepidae, and Slavs.

Some remarks are necessary as regards the enumeration by Pascu of Rumanian words with the apparent aim of demonstrating a) that the early Rumanians (in Pascu's terminology: "Daco-Romans") were mostly peasants and b) that Rumanian is a Romance language: "Modern scholars unanimously accept the Latinity of the Romanian language"(p. 40).

The last-mentioned statement is obvious, although Pascu exaggerates the Latinity of Rumanian. Rumanian lacks considerably more Panromanic Latin words than any other Romance language.[2] Pascu also fails to mention the extremely powerful South Slavic impact upon Northern Rumanian.

The terminology pertaining to agriculture does not prove that the early Rumanians were mainly peasants. The large number of words pertaining to the shepherd way of life among the substratum words indicate that they were mainly shepherds, who also practised some relatively primitive agriculture.

Pascu, p. 39:

> The Romanian word for "village" itself – *sat* – is from Latin *fossatum* "area surrounded by moats or ditches"; likewise, when such villages formed a "popular Romania", it was known to the common people as *ţară* " country", from the Latin term *terra.*

---

[1] *Studii şi cercetări de istorie veche şi arheologie* [Studies and Investigations in Ancient History and Archaeology], 30, 4, 1979, p. 550.

[2] ILR, 1969, p. 123. Words existing in all Neolatin (Romance) languages are called "Panromanic words"; there are, of course, exceptions – each Romance language lacks a smaller or larger part of these words. The number of such exceptions is highest in the Rumanian language .

Latin *terra* "earth; land (in contrast to sea); country e.g., *terra Gallia, terra Italia*" was inherited by Rumanian (Northern Rumanian, Arumanian and Meglenitic): cf. N. Rum. *ţară* "land, country". The notion of a Rumanian *ţară* in the sense Pascu refers to above is not attested during the Middle Ages. Modern N. Rumanian *sat* "village", in the 16th century, *fsat,* was **not** inherited from Latin. Latin *fossatum*[1] "(small) settlement with a ditch around"(abstracted probably from terms such as *locus fossatum, pagus fossatum*) was borrowed by the Albanians: *fshat* (the loss of the first vowel occurred thus in Albanian) and then transferred from Albanian to Rumanian. The sense of "village" exists only in these two languages. In Arumanian, the first vowel is preserved: *fusáti, fusắţi* because the Arumanians borrowed this word from Greek (cf. New Greek φουσατο "army" < Latin *fossatum).*[2] The intimate relationships with Albanian belong to those facts which contradict the assumption that Rumanian is the descendant of Latin once spoken north of the Danube. The ancestors of the Albanians lived mainly east of Albania, in Macedonia and in parts of Serbia.[3]

---

[1] Rosetti, 1986, p. 182.

[2] Matilda Caragiu Marioţeanu, *Compendiu de dialectologie română (nord- şi sud-dunăreană)* [Compendium of Rumanian dialectology (nord and south of the Danube)], Bucharest, 1975, p. 259.

[3] The first mention of Albanians in documents is from 1079 A.D. and refers to the territory between Ochrida and Thessalonike, and to Epirus. In present day Albania (in its northern part), they were for the first time described in the 13th century. The analysis of placenames and geographical names suggests that they lived, during the first centuries of Roman conquering on the Balkan peninsula, (also) in the northern part of present day Albania; according to Georg Stadtmüller, the center of the ancient Albanians was the area of the river Mati. There are a number of ancient Albanian geographical names in Albania, for example the river Bunë (cf. Albanian *buenë, bujenë* "inundation"), or Šar Planina, from Greek Σκάρδος, with the typical *sk* > *š* sound change. Most of the ancient geographical names in Albania do not, however, show Albanian features, and very many are of Slavic origin. Moreover, in the Albanian language, the sea-terms and words concerning fishing are predominantly of foreign (Greek, Venetian, Turkish or Slavic) origin. It is therefore probable that the Albanians are not indigenous in entire Albania. In any case, there is plenty of evidence to show that they lived east of their present country. The archaic sound pattern of a number of Greek loanwords (for example *bretëkë* "frog", from Greek βρωταχος) suggests that they lived in contact with Greeks. A large number of placenames in Macedonia and parts of Serbia show typically Albanian features: Štip, from Greek Αστιβος shows the disappearance of initial *a-* as well as the *s* > *š* change; Naissus > Niš, Petrus > Petruša are further examples; Ochrida, cf. Greek Αγχις, shows *n* > *r* after a velar consonant, etc. It is significant that, in contrast to Rumanian, there are Latin loanwords in Albanian which show a very ancient sound pattern, from the 1st century B.C.: Lat. *cingula* >Albanian *qingëlë; vetus, veteris* > *vjetër* etc. The Romance languages have inherited these words from Vulgar Latin, thus N. Rumanian *chingă* ´belly band, saddle girth´, from **cingla; bătrân* ´old´ from *veteran,* etc. – Cf. I. Popović, *Geschichte der Serbokroatischen Sprache,* 1960, pp. 79-85; G. Stadtmüller, *Forschungen zur albanischen Frühgeschichte,* 1966; A. Rosetti, *Istoria limbii române,* 1986, pp. 195-197.

Pascu, p. 40:

> ...the Romanian people and language evolved in the strongly Romanized regions along the Lower Danube (where there were about forty Romanized, Latin-speaking towns) and in Dacia north of the Danube, where Latin was likewise spoken in towns, military camps, mining centers, and craftsmen's *collegiae*. Summarizing the formation of the Romanian people and their language, one may say that the process proper began with the Romanization of the population north of the Danube in the second to fourth centuries; at the heart of it were the two main ethnic elements, Dacian and Roman.

It is right that the the northern part of the Balkan peninsula was strongly Romanized. One should add that Latin was spoken there during five to six centuries, that there was a rich Christian religious life for several centuries, and a numerous Latin-speaking population also in the countryside. Many Latin placenames were preserved (borrowed by the Slavs), and dozens of Northern Rumanian names of villages and geographical names were also borrowed by the Slavs when they, beginning with the 6th – 7th centuries, populated the peninsula. In Dacia Traiana, "Latin was likewise spoken" – but the situation there was totally different: eleven towns, only 170 years of Roman domination, no placenames preserved and not a single geographical name was inherited from Latin. In that territory, there is no evidence of the development of a Romanized indigenous population. It is obvious that Pascu´s assertion: [the formation of Rumanian] "began with the Romanization of the population **north** of the Danube" is baseless.

4. EARLY MEDIEVAL CIVILIZATION (pp. 42 - 64)

The Dawn of Feudal Society.
Pascu, p. 42:

> The civilization of the eighth and ninth centuries in Transylvania was a direct continuation of that of the preceding period. Known as the Romanian Dridu civilization, after the place in Ţara Românească where the most extensive remains have been found, the society was created by the Romanian people and retained its original character everywhere they lived. It developed in the eighth century as the indigenous ethnic element consolidated following the assimilation of the first wave of Slavic peoples;...

In *Istoria României, Compendiu*, Bucharest, 1969, p. 106, the following is stated about the Dridu-culture:

> The term "Dridu culture" is not correct, since the material remains of this type are more numerous and better represented on the territory of Bulgaria, where this culture also has been formed. It is an **early Slavic culture** (or, better, **Slavo-Bulgarian**) culture and its

spread north of the Danube is caused by influences from the south as well as by the temporary extension of the first Bulgarian kingdom over some north-Danubian areas. With more success could be sustained, we believe, the Ancient Rumanian or Rumanian character of the so called *Bucov* culture in the hilly area of northern Muntenia [emphasis in the original].

This view is expressed also by Constantin Daicoviciu in an article from 1967 (in *Dacica*, 1969, p. 552), and earlier even by Ştefan Pascu (e.g. in 1968):

> ...we agree with the view of academician C. Daicoviciu and of other investigators, according to which it [the Dridu culture] was in the 9th century mostly spread by the Bulgarians, as it is also proved by its geographical distribution.[1]

This culture extended in time from the 8th to the 11th centuries and covered, besides Bulgaria, parts of present day Rumania and beyond, to the river Dniester.

It was characteristic of Rumanian historiography during the Communist era that concepts were changed radically without any decisive new discovery or evidence. Thus, in the 3rd edition of *Istoria României. Compendiu*, published in 1974, (after the death of C. Daicoviciu,) the above passage is changed to the following:

> The material culture of the type Dridu reflects an ethnic as well as a socio-economic reality of the various human communities in the Carpatho-Danubian geographic space. Also the Ancient Rumanian or Rumanian character of the so called *Bucov* culture may be sustained, in the hilly area of northern Muntenia, where some details characteristic of the Rumanian population have been discovered. Thus, as regards pottery, alongside the Slavic and the south-Danubian type, also pottery burned red appeared, made on a wheel with fast rotation, derived from the provincial Roman pottery of the 4th – 5th centuries and specific to the Rumanian population.[2]

The first version states clearly that the Dridu culture is Slavic (Bulgarian). In the second version, it is not said explicitly that it is now considered Rumanian (it is a culture "of different human comunities in the Carpatho-Danubian area"). The word "also" in the next sentence (which refers to the Bucov culture, considered Rumanian), is thus not logical, because it contradicts the previous sentence – but may suggest for the superficial reader that also the Dridu culture is Rumanian.

---

[1] Ş. Pascu, M. Rusu, P, Iambor, N. Edroiu, P. Gyulai, V. Wollmann, Şt. Matei: "Cetatea Dăbîca" ["The fortress at Dăbîca"], *Acta Mvsei Napocensis* V, Cluj, 1968, p. 174.

[2] IR Compendiu, 1974, p. 88.

Pascu, p. 43:

> These communities had earthen fortresses, as, for example, in Arad (Vladimirescu) in southwest Transylvania and in Moreşti and Dăbîca in central and northeastern Transsylvania...

A detailed description of the fortress found at Dăbâca (Hungarian Doboka) was given by Ş. Pascu, M. Rusu et al. in 1968.[1] The material remains indicate Slavs, Hungarians and Petchenegs (Patzinaks). In favour of the assumption of a Rumanian population here, the authors give the following reasoning:

> So far no fortresses of the type that exist at Dăbîca have been reported or investigated in the plains of the Tisza or in Pannonia (inhabited by Moravian Slavs and Hungarians), therefore, those discovered in Transylvania must be attributed to the local Rumanian-Slavic population, their aim having been military, as the centres of formations first of *cnez-es*, later of voivodes (p. 180).

This is a weak argument for the Rumanian character of this type of fortresses. It is invalidated by the fact that similar earthen fortresses from the same time were found in the Hungarian plain. The construction of the fortress of Dăbâca started in the second half of the 10th century by the Hungarians.[2]

Pascu, p.43:

> In this period new Slavic tribes, more numerous and better organized than those of the seventh century, settled on Romanian territory. Their influence was correspondingly more substantial, but it was felt primarily in the Romanian vocabulary. [...]
> The Slavs also transmitted some influences from the Bulgarian kingdom, which has been established in 686 after the Bulgars settled south of the Danube in the Byzantine Empire.

As we also have seen above, Pascu tries to play down the tremendous Slavic impact upon the Rumanian language. To describe it as "some influences from the Bulgarian kingdom" does not correspond to reality. The South Slavic influence upon the Rumanian language presupposes very different circumstances from those that prevailed north of the lower Danube in the 8th – 10th centuries, with

---

[1] "Cetatea Dăbîca" [The fortress at Dăbîca], in *Acta Mvsei Napocensis*, 1968, pp. 153 – 202. The passage quoted here is found on p. 180. (The correct spelling of this name is now, after the spelling reform introduced in the early 1990's, Dăbâca.)

[2] Illyés, 1992, p. 190.

a relatively scanty Slavic population, not yet Christianized.[1] In the 9th century, Bulgaria ruled over southern Transylvania, but from the 10th century on, Hungarians occupy its valleys and its central areas, and Petchenegs invade the extra-Carpathian territories. Most of the South Slavic influence was exercised on Northern Rumanian after this period, i.e.,during the 11th – 13th centuries. Thousands of Slavic words were borrowed, and also the phonetics and morphology of the language were affected. The Slavic influence gave the superstratum of Rumanian, as for example the Frankish language was the superstratum of French.[2]

Pascu, p. 43–44:

> At the beginning of the tenth century, yet another foreign people, the Magyars, entered Transylvania. Their penetration of Transylvania was similar to other expeditions which these tribes undertook in western Europe and Byzantine Empire after settling in Pannonia in 895-96. The Magyars, of Finno-Ugric origin, had left the region of the northern Ural Mountains around the end of the ninth century, in response to pressure from other tribes. Under the leadership of "Duke" Arpad, they settled first in Pannonia and later in the Tisza plain. They found these new territories, inhabited by Slavs, Romanians, and others, insufficient for grazing their herds, which was their principal occupation in their new home. They undertook expeditions of conquest in order to expand their pasture lands and to obtain Transylvania's underground riches – especially salt, which was an absolute necessity for them, but which Pannonia lacked. After they have accomplished these goals, the majority of the tribesmen withdrew from Transylvania. Only a few remained among the indigenous population, which explains why, in all of Transylvania, definite traces of the tenth-century Magyar population have been discovered only in Cluj, Biharea-Oradea, and Siclău-Arad [sic] (from the early tenth century), and at Gîmbaş and possibly at Lapodea [sic] near Aiud (later in the century).

(Rightly: Şiclău [< Hungarian Sikló]; Lopadea [< Hungarian Lapád]).

This description of the Hungarians' early settlement in Transylvania, as well as that of the history of the Hungarians before they occupied the Carpathian basin is false: originally a population speaking a Finno-Ugric language, the Hungarians lived for many centuries north of the Black Sea, where they came into close contact with Turkish tribes. From there, they migrated, pushed by the Petchenegs, to the Carpathian basin towards the end of the 9th century.

At several places in Transylvania, definite traces of a Hungarian population have been found – cemeteries, as mentioned also by Pascu, buildings, churches, and fortifications. These were situated in the valleys of the rivers and in the

---

[1] Cf., for example, C. Daicoviciu (red.), *Istoria României* [The History of Rumania], 1960, p. 753: ..."most of them [the Slavs living in the territory of present day Rumania] have maintained their old religion, as shown by the cemeteries in which the pagan rite has been retained (Satu Nou, Castelu) up to the 9th century inclusive."

[2] Cf. Du Nay, *The Origins of the Rumanians*, 1996, pp. 98 - 111.

Transylvanian basin, where circumstances were suitable for agriculture and the raising of animals. From those centuries there is not a single trace of a Rumanian population in Transylvania. As it will be seen below, the early placenames of the territory are Slavic, Hungarian and German; **the first Rumanian placename there appeared in the 13th century.**

Pascu, p. 45: **Political organization**
p. 46:

> In fact, Romanian society in the ninth to eleventh centuries was marked by a considerable degree of political organization. There is evidence that communes in river valleys and natural basins all over Transylvania had formed alliances called *knezates* and *voivodates*. Knezates were smaller and less important than the voivodates, which were also popularly known as *ţări*, "countries." [...]
> The most important of the written sources is the chronicle known as the *Gesta Hungarorum*, the late twelfth-century work of a certain *P. magister, Belae regis notarius* (Master Peter or Paul, secretary to King Béla – probably Béla III). This chronicle is complemented and confirmed in various ways by other Magyar chronicles...

Pascu, pp. 46 – 48:

> According to the *P. magister* chronicle, when the Magyar tribes invaded at the beginning of the tenth century, most of Transylvania was organized into three great voivodates (or "duchies," to translate the Latin terminology of the various sources): Crişana, under the voivode Menumorut [...] .the Banat, under the voivode Glad [...] and Transylvania [...] This voivodate was led by the Romanian (*Blachus*) voivode Gelu, whose subjects included both Romanians and Slavs (*Blachi et Sclavi*).

Pascu, p. 48:

> These political units were certainly "countries" like the many other *ţări* into which the Romanian lands were divided at the time. Written sources mention Ţara Românilor (Bolohovanilor) and Ţara Cîmpulungului Moldovenesc in the northeast...

(the names of a total of 21 such "countries" [properly speaking:districts] follow, 12 in the extra-Carpathian territory of Rumania and 9 in Transylvania).

Investigating the evidence of what Pascu asserts here, one finds that it is boiled down to a few, unconfirmed statements in the *Gesta Hungarorum*. An analysis of this chronicle is given among others by Illyés, 1992, pp. 11 - 32, with a summary of the entire chronicle as well as the English translation of the passages referring to eastern Hungary and Transylvania; cf. also Du Nay, 1996, pp. 215 - 219 . Here, we will only discuss some of the most conspicuous errors in Pascu's text, referring otherwise to the above analyses.

　　1. Those "Romanian districts"(*ţări*)[1]　which Pascu enumerates are not recorded in written sources to have existed in the period in question, the 9th –

---

[1]Rumanian *ţară* as used here by Pascu means "district; surroundings of the governorship of a castle or of the center of an estate".

10th centuries. Thus, also the assumption that "there were unquestionably other *ţări* as well, but these would not have been mentioned by the chronicles if they had nothing to do with the Magyar tribes on their expeditions in search of minerals and pastures" (p. 48) is baseless.

2. According to the *Gesta Hungarorum*, Gelu was "*quidam Blachus;*" but neither Menumorut in Crişana nor Glad in the Banat are described to have been Rumanian: the former is said to have been Kazar, "with a Bulgarian heart" (*bulgarico corde*), and the second, a "Cuman". This is not stated by Pascu, and so he "includes" also these territories into the Rumanian territories, as if the *Gesta* had done the same: "For example, the anonymous notary of King Béla III describes the chieftains of the Romanian groups in Crişana, the Banat, and Transylvania proper" (p. 51).

3. A large Rumanian necropolis near Alba Iulia from 8th – 9th centuries is asserted to have been found recently (p. 48), but no reference is given about it. Since Slavs were living in the territory in those times, it would be essential to give the reasons why this necropolis is considered Rumanian.

The rest of this chapter – about accumulated wealth in the towns by the Rumanian voivodes, social stratification, etc., is not documented, or, there are indications about the material culture, but nowhere is it confirmed that the people here were Rumanians.

Pascu, p. 53:
The Eleventh and Twelfth Centuries
The Romanian political units consolidated territorially, militarily, and politically.
Pascu, p. 54:
[The prince of the Transylvanian voivodate] ...was Gyla, whose name perhaps derives from a Hungarian word meaning an army commander and high judge, of from the name of a Petcheneg tribe living in southeastern Transylvania. The center of Gyla's expanded voivodate was at Bălgrad, near Alba Iulia, a fortress town built of earth, wood, and stone. [...]
Such were the circumstances at the beginning of the eleventh century, when the Hungarian king Stephen I and the aristocrats of his court began to look toward neighbouring lands, the home of Romanian farmers and herdsmen, miners and craftsmen. The changes that had occurred in Magyar society were the most important reason for the expansionist policy. [...] Stephen eventually won.

Pascu's assertion about the consolidation of "the Romanian political units" is baseless. Such units did not exist in the 11th century. No written document mentions Rumanians in Transylvania in that period and archeological finds as well as the river names and the placenames of the territory contradict Pascu's assumptions.[1] Here, we only point out the circumstance that the popular Rumanian name of present day *Alba Iulia* (Hungarian *Gyulafehérvár)* was derived from Slavic: *Bălgrad.* The first part of the modern official name of this town is a translation from Hungarian or Slavic and the second part *(Iulia)* was borrowed from Hungarian *(Gyula).*

Hungarian *gyula* had in the period in question the sense of "high commander, chieftain".[2] After the Christianization of the Hungarians, it became a personal name and through this, a name of settlements. There is in eastern Hungary the town *Gyula,* in Maramureş the village *Giuleşti,* Hungarian *Máragyulafalva,* first mentioned in 1349: *villa Gylafalva, Gyulafalva* (near Sighetul Marmatei), *Giula,* Hungarian Kolozsgyula, first mentioned in 1307: *terra seu possessio Gyula* (near *Gherla), Coasta* or *Giulatelec,* Hungarian *Gyulatelke,* first mentioned in 1318: *villa Gyulatelke* (near *Gherla), Fîntînele* or *Gialacuta,* Hungarian *Gyulakuta,* first mentioned in 1332: *sacerdos de Kulakuta,* 1335: *Gulacuta,* near Tg. Mureş, and *Giuluş,* Hungarian *Gyulas,* first mentioned in 1413 (later than the other names with *Gyula): poss. Gyulatelke, Gyulastelke,* (near *Târnăveni).[3]* It is obvious that these names are old, with first mentionings (with one exception) in the 14th century, and that all were borrowed by the Rumanians (in various forms: *Giula, Giala[cuta], Giula[telec], Giuleşti);* the present day Rumanian names were given by 19th century intellectuals or by officials.

Thus, *Gyula* was a Hungarian chieftain, who had built up his own power and was able to defy his relative, the Hungarian king Stephen I. The independence of Transylvania in that period was not caused by a non-Hungarian population but by struggle for power between Hungarian leaders. King Stephen I determined to make all his country Christian and integrate it into Christian western Europe.[4]

---

[1]Cf., for example, Du Nay, *The Origins of the Rumanians,* 1996.

[2]Before their Christianization, the Hungarians´ highest chief was the *kende;* a kind of a sacral king, who almost never showed himself for the people. The real chief was the *gyula:* the commander of the army and the highest judge. After the Christianization, *gyula* was no longer a dignity but became a personal name.

[3]Suciu, I, 1967, p. 279.

[4]The Hungarian kings of the Árpád-family used to give certain parts of the country already in their lifetime to their heir, i.e., their eldest son. These "little kings" or petty monarchs, ruled over the territory in question preparing themselves for the duties of a king. Thus, for example, king András II made his son Béla (later king Béla IV) the petty monarch of Transylvania, where he ruled for ten years. Other names for this dignity were *bán* ("ban, governor or viceroy")and *kormányzó* ("governor, regent"), and only later *vajda* ("voivode"). This word was by the Hungarians as well as by the Rumanians borrowed from Slavic. Its original sense in Slavic was "high commander of the army". The designation *bán* was then mostly used for the ruler of Szörény and Croatia, and *vajda* for the regent of Transylvania.Later, also others than the king´s son were appointed *vajda.*

46

Pascu, p. 55:

> The Magyars, unsuccessful until the end of the eleventh century in their attempts to reenter Transylvania, called the area Ultrasilva, Ultrasilvana, Transilvana, Erdeelu, and Erdeleu– which means, both geographically and politically, the land "beyond the forest," "beyond the woods".

Indigenous populations all over the world have their own name for themselves and for the land they are living in. The Rumanian name for Transylvania was borrowed from Hungarian: *Ardeal*. It is first mentioned in a document from 1432, in the form *Ardeliu* (stated also by Pascu, although not in the English translation but in *Voievodatul Transilvaniei*, I, p. 22). This form derives from Hungarian *Erdély* (the *e* > *a* change in Rumanian borrowings from Hungarian is demonstrated by many examples: Hungarian *egres* > Rumanian *agriș* ("gooseberry"), Hungarian *Egyed* > Rumanian *Adjud,* etc.[1] This is still the popular name of Transylvania, used by the people; "Transilvania" is a coined word, taken from the Latin translation of *Erdő-elü* > *Erdély* "beyond the forest". In the documents, the name of this territory is first mentioned in its Latin translation: *Ultra silvam ad castrum quod vocatur Turda...*(1075 A.D.), then, in 1111, the chief assigned for the territory by the Hungarian king is mentioned: *Mercurius princeps Ultrasilvanus*. This form is used also by Rogerius, prebend of Nagyvárad (Oradea) in his description of the Tartar invasion in 1241: *Ultra Silvam, Ultrasilvanus episcopus*. However, in the *Legenda Sancti Gerhardi,* written in the first half of the 12th century, we find *Partes Transsilvanae,* and beginning with the 14th century, this name is used generally in the documents.[2]

The first mention in a written text of the Hungarian name is in Anonymus' *Gesta Hungarorum*, from the end of the 12th century: *siluam igfon que iacet ad erdeuelu* (chapter 11; cf. Illyés, 1992, facing p. 17; cf. also pp. 335 – 336), in modern Hungarian: *erdő-elve* "beyond the forest," from which the present form developed: *Erdély*.

The assertion by Pascu (in *Voievodatul Transilvaniei* I, p. 21) that "the Hungarian name of Transylvania is nothing else than a translation of the Latin name," is thus wrong. There were no Romans to give this name to the territory, and the Hungarian population could not, of course, give a Latin name to any territory (see also below, *Appendix*). They called it *Erdő-elve* and this was translated by the learned people who wrote the documents for the Hungarian kings; in that time, it was general usage to write official documents in Latin. Not even Pascu pretends that *Transilvania* was a name used by "Daco-Romans".

[1]Illyés, 1992, p. 336.

[2]These data are given by Ș. Pascu in *Voievodatul Transilvaniei* I, pp. 19–22.

47

The German name of this territory is *Siebenbürgen*. *Septem Castra* appears in the documents beginning with the 13th century; from the 14th century, the following forms are recorded: *Simburg, Simburk, Sibenburg, Sybenburg, Syebenpurg, Sebinburgen, Sebinburgin, Sibenpurgen.*[1] The Teutonic Knights settled in south-eastern Transylvania (in Burzenland, Hung. Barcaság, Rum. Ţara Bârsei) by King Andreas II at the beginning of the 13th century, erected (1211-1225) seven castles there: German Marienburg, Hung. Földvár, Rum. Feldioara; Heldenburg (Heltven), Höltövény, Hălchiu; Schwarzenburg, Feketehalom, Codlea; Eulenburg, Bagolyvár, (there is no Rumanian name because no settlement developed around this castle); Rosenauer Burg, Rozsnyóvár, Râşnov (today part of Braşov); Törzburg, Törcsvár, Bran; and Kreuzburg – Thell (name of the castle and of the settlement, respectively, Keresztvár – Nyén, Teliu (only the settlement has a Rumanian name).

Pascu, p. 55:

Nevertheless, Magyar control of Transylvania was made difficult by local resistance. The Magyar kings therefore sought to win over the leading groups among the indigenous population, and in certain regions they also established colonies, first of Magyars and later Szeklers, Saxons, and lastly Teutonic knights.

p. 56:

Finally, when Magyar authority took in the southeastern corner of Transylvania at the beginning of the thirteenth century, the Szeklers were settled there, alongside the indigenous population. There they remain today.

p. 57:

As with the territories settled by Szeklers and Saxons, so with the lands granted to the Teutonic knights: they were already inhabited by an indigenous Romanian population, as is shown by place names and the remains of a few fortified settlements mentioned in contemporary documents.

It is only on rare occasions that Pascu refers to a documentation of his assertions. He re-iterates that there was, in the 10th century, an "indigenous Romanian population" in practically the entire territory in question, without giving any evidence. In the above passages, Pascu refers to **placenames and fortified settlements** (in Barcaság, Rum. Ţara Bârsei, German Burzenland), but does not mention a single placename. One may ask: what is found in the documents about these settlements and what are those placenames that indicate "indigenous Rumanians" in the area in question?

The assertion made by Pascu that the Barcaság was "already inhabited by a Rumanian population" when the Teutonic knights were settled there, is entirely

[1] *Voievodatul Transilvaniei*, vol. I, p. 22; referring to *Chronici Hungarici compositio saeculi XIV*, chapter 26; *Chronicon Monacense*, chapter 9, etc.

groundless, as shown by the following analysis of the placenames there:

Documents from the first part of the 13th century tell us about *terra Blachorum et Bissenorum* situated probably in parts of present day *Făgăraş* (Hungarian *Fogaras*). The Teutonic knights were settled in the *Barcasăg*, and possibly a small part of *Fogaras*. One of their chief fortresses was at present day *Feldioara;* the ruins of this are still visible in the village. The name has no sense in Rumanian and is obviously the borrowing of Hungarian *Földvár* "earthen fortress". The nearest villages are *Hăghig, Araci*, and *Rotbav*. The names of two of these were transferred to Rumanian from Hungarian and that of the third from German, as shown by the following: *Hăghig* derives from Hungarian *Hídvég* ("bridge abutment"), first mentioned in 1332: *sacerdos de Hydueg. Araci* was by the Rumanians earlier called *Arpatac* (the form *Araci* is of a late date) derived from Hungarian *Árapatak* (Hung. *patak* "brook"). *Rodbav* derives from the German name of this village: *Rotbach;* a parallel name-giving with the Hungarians, who have *(Szász)Veresmart* (Hungarian *veres* "red" and *mart* "[river-]bank"). – This is the case also of the other villages in the area: their Rumanian names were borrowed either from Hungarian or from German. Towards the north-west, there is Rum. Cloaşterf, from German Klossdorf, shortened from Nikolausdorf. The sound pattern of this placename indicates also approximately in which period it was adopted by the Rumanians: while the Hungarian name of this village: Miklóstelke, contains the name corresponding to German Nikolaus, the Rumanian name is based only on the shortened German form, which necessarily must be a later development. This indicates that the Rumanian population arrived to this place quite late, i.e., after the settlement of both the Germans and of the Hungarians. – Not a single placename of Rumanian origin is found in the entire area and all those 18 names of villages known in the 13th – 14th centuries were borrowed by the Rumanians – which proves that they settled among Hungarians, as well as among German and Walloon settlers. Even the Petchenegs have left a placename in the area: *Talmács* (Rumanian *Tălmaciu,* German *Talmesch, Talmatsch*) first mentioned in 1318: *Tholmach.*[1]

---

[1] Along the relevant part of the river Olt, the following villages were known in the 13th – 14th centuries: *Talmács,* 1265, of Petcheneg origin; *Galt* (on the place of present day *Ungra,* Hungarian *Ugra:* 1211: *indagines castri Noilgiant,* 1222 *Noialt,* 1325 *Galt,* 1850 *Ungra,* 1854 *Szász-Ugra*), from Walloon-French *noiale galt* "forest of nut-trees"; *Venice,* present day Rumanian *Veneţia de Jos,* Hungarian *Alsóvenice,* 1235 *Venetia, sacerdos de Venetiis,* from Italian *Venezia; Kolun,* present day Rumanin *Colun,* Hungarian and German *Kolun,* 1322 *villa seu poss. Colonia,* 1494 *Kollen,* from German *Köln – Colonia.* These names were given by the settlers from western Europe and borrowed, as shown by the Rumanian names, by the Rumanians, who must have settled there after the 12th century, when the first German and Walloon settlers came to the area. The rest of the village names are Hungarian: *Szakadát* (1306), *Földvár* (1322), *Fogaras* (1291), *Halmágy* (1211), *Miklósvár* (1211), *Hídvég* (1332), *Árpás* (a river name in 1223 and the name of a villages in 1390), *Szombathely*

49

Pascu, p. 57:
Social Changes in the Twelfth and Thirteenth Centuries

The indigenous aspects of feudalism were maintained throughout the country in the Middle Ages, although most strongly in the peripheral areas. The *ţări* so often mentioned in the sources of the time – Ţara Bîrsei, Ţara Făgăraşului, Ţara Haţegului, Ţara Severinului, Ţara Oaşului, and Ţara Maramureşului, which completely surround Transylvania – are in fact the old autonomous Romanian political units, alliances of communes.

p. 59:

...judgements at law were based on ancient custom, traditional land rights, or Romanian law (*jus valachicum*), which the authorities were compelled to recognize;...

The sources of the time (12th – 13th centuries) do not mention a single one of these *ţări*; they appear in documents much later. The origin of their names, not discussed by Pascu, will be presented below, p. 83 (see also table 2, pp. 84-86). Here, we only mention that they all are borrowings.

Silviu Dragomir described the Vlach shepherds living in the central parts of the Balkan peninsula during the Middle Ages. One of their characteristic features was a great mobility: "They try to flee from one landlord to the other, using the paths of shepherds they know very well. Good pastures and favourable living conditions were always decisive."[1] These migrations resulted in the spread of this population to almost all parts of the Balkan peninsula, to many areas north of the Danube, as far as to Moravia, Poland, Ukraine and other areas north of the Black Sea; some groups of Vlachs reached even the Caucasian mountains.

The Vlach shepherds had, during the Middle Ages, special obligations and rights. This "*jus Valachicum*" originated from the Balkan peninsula. The Vlachs in Serbia belonged to the king, or, later, to the monasteries. In many cases they only paid their metayage (*dijme*) for grazing in the forests of the monastery. It was in these circumstances, in medieval Serbia, that the *jus Valachicum* developed, on the basis of the special occupation, cattle breeding, of the Vlachs:

Their situation became more clearly defined when the Serbian lords started to make laws concerning them. Such laws or statutes were made at first for the Vlachs of the monasteries of Studenica and Milosevo. These were not preserved to our age. Their obligations are, however, clearly shown by the so called "law of the Vlachs" [*lege a vlahilor*], found in the *hrišov* of Banja and in two of Czar Dušan's donations, those from Vranje and Prizren. We may say that they [the Vlachs] in general provided all the

---

(1291), *Betlen, Sárkány, Debren* (1235 *Debran*, mentioned by Suciu, II, 1968, p. 315 among villages that no longer exist); *Kormospatak, Héviz*, and *Doboka*. All these Hungarian names were borrowed by the Rumanians.

[1] Silviu Dragomir, *Vlahii din nordul peninsulei Balcanice în evul mediu* [The Vlachs in the north of the Balkan peninsula in the Middle Ages], 1959, p. 172.

products of grazing, that they had to occupy themselves with the breeding of all kinds of cattle and also with all kinds of transports.[1]

This *jus Valachicum* followed the Vlachs everywhere in their wanderings, as far as to Poland:

> The special character of the Rumanian villages in Poland was given by the *jus Valachicum*, which states certain norms: *cnez*-es in front of a village, a special jurisdiction, the economic obligations; the *cmet* [peasant] had the right to be treated according to the *jus Valachicum* also in case he moved to another village, etc. Thus, the "Vlach right" had an economic part and a juridical one; it could not be violated; it was brought from the country of origin. In the course of time, however, it decreased until it disappeared, together with the Rumanians, in the large mass of the Northern Slavs.[2]

In Poland, the Vlachs protested against those who "dared to interfere and violate the recognized privileges of the Vlachs", as stated in a document from the year 1447.[3]

The country of origin of these special Vlach law appears from studies of the early Vlachs living in the Balkan peninsula. In Serbia, numerous documents (*hrišovs*) were preserved, written by kings and noblemen during the 12th to 15th centuries.

> In the *hrišovs* of Prizren, the obligations of the Vlachs, who were subject to the king, are stated. These were not too heavy: each of them had to give each year, out of 50 sheep, one sheep with a lamb and a cow; and each second year a horse. They owned, thus, even horses, but their chief obligation was the *quinquagesima*. This must have been an ancient custom because we find it, with certain changes, also among the Daco-Romans and among the Vlachs living in Croatia.[4]

One must add, however, that this "jus Valachicum" did not imply a kind of a local autonomy or a developed juridical system; in eastern Hungary and in Transylvania, the *quinquagesima ovium* was practiced: the immigrating Vlachs were initially no regular serfs on the estates, only tolerated shepherds, without any juridical status. To be permitted to graze their sheep on the territory of the estates, they were obliged to also graze the sheep of the estate and to give each year a female sheep with her lamb out of fifty sheep. The landlords had to pay

[1] Dragomir, 1959, p. 122.

[2] Ş. Meteş, *Emigrări româneşti din Transilvania în secolele XIII - XX* [Emigrations of Rumanians from Transylvania in the 13th – 20th centuries], Bucharest, 1977, 2nd edition, p. 30.

[3] Meteş, p. 30.

[4] Dragomir, 1959, p. 122.

taxes to the king according to the number of Vlachs living on their territory.

The documents which mention Rumanians in the first decades of the 13th century

The earliest documentary mention of Rumanians (Vlachs) in Transylvania refers to the year 1210 AD. It is a deed of gift by king Béla written in 1250 and mentions an army made up by Szeklers, Saxons, Petchenegs and Vlachs *(Olacis)*, sent in 1210 by king Endre II to the help of the Vlacho-Bulgarian emperor Assen. It is stated that these Vlachs were shepherds living in the area of Hermannstadt (Rumanian Sibiu, Hungarian Szeben), and were frontier guards of the Hungarian king.

L. Tamás[1] has collected all the documents that mention Vlachs in Transylvania in the 13th century. These are, besides that from 1250 mentioned above, the following:

1. In a document from 1222, the Teutonic knights are given by the Hungarian king Endre II the privilige not to pay customs when transporting salt through the territories of the Szeklers or the Vlachs (*cum transierint per terram Siculorum aut per terram Blacorum*). These Vlachs were living in the vicinity of Kerc (Rumanian Cârţa, German Kerz).

2. King Endre II confirmed in 1223 the ownership of a land of the monastery at Kerc, a land taken from the Vlachs (*terram quam prius eidem monasterio contuleramus exemptam de Blaccis*). It is questionable whether the Vlachs living here were a sedentary population, since no Rumanian placenames are mentioned in this document. Out of those five names mentioned, Olt and Kerc are of unknown origin and three are Hungarian: *Eguerpatak, fagus Nogebik*, and *rivulus Arpas* – indicating a sedentary Hungarian population.

3. King Endre II defined in 1224 the privileges and rights of the Saxons, in the *Diploma Andreanum*. This was for the Saxons the same as was only two years earlier for the Hungarian population the Golden Bull (*Aranybulla*). In the *Diploma Andreanum*, also the right to use a forest of the Petchenegs and the Vlachs was included (*silvam Blacorum et Bissenorum cum aquis usus communes exercendo cum praedictis scilicet Blacis et Bissenis*). This forest was probably in the high mountains in the area of Kerc.

In the period before the Tartar invasion (1241), these four documents mention Rumanians, all of them living along the southern border. They were most probably shepherds serving the Hungarian king as frontier guards. In these early documents, they are consistently called Blaccis, Blacis.

---

[1] Lajos Tamás: *Rómaiak, románok és oláhok Dácia Trajánában* [Romans, Rumanians and Vlachs in Dacia Traiana], Budapest, 1935, pp. 191 – 197.

Documents in which Vlachs are mentioned after the Tartar invasion (1241) until the end of the 13th century:

1. King Béla IV gave the territory of Szerém to the Saint Johns' knights of Jerusalem in 1247 "with the knezates of Ioan and Farcaş up to the river Olt, without the area of the knezate of voivod Lynioy" and Cumania "without the territory of Seneslav, voivode of the Vlachs." These areas between the lower Danube and the southern Carpathian mountains belonged earlier to the Cumans and the Tartars but were now under the reign of the Hungarian king. This document is the first one in which Vlach (Rumanian) knezates are mentioned in these territories.

2. King Béla IV gives to his son the land called Szék, which is situated *inter t(erras Olacorum de Kyrch, Saxonum) de Barasu et terras Siculorum de Sebus* – areas depopulated by the Tartar invasion: *vacua et habitatoribus carens remanserat.*

3. King Béla IV confirms in 1256 the rights of the archbishopric of Esztergom (Hungary), among other things *in decimis percipiendis regalium proventum ex parte Siculorum et Olacorum, in pecudibus, pecoribus et animalibus quibuslibet, exceptis terragiis Saxonum, sed ex parte Olacorum etiam ubique et a quocumque provenientium, in regno Hungariae persolvi consuetorum.* It appears from this document that the Rumanians in question were not a sedentary population.

4. In the year 1260, King Ottokar II records his victory over King Béla IV to the Pope, and relates that in the Hungarian army, also Cumans, Szeklers, Petchenegs and other peoples, and also Vlachs (*Valachi*) were fighting. It is not stated where these Vlachs came from.

5. King Béla IV records the incomes of the archbishop of Esztergom in 1262, which includes the tenth paid by the Szeklers and the Rumanians after cattle (*de pecudibus et pecoribus exigendis ab Olacis et Siculis idem archiepiscopus percipiet decimam partem*).

6. In 1291, in a royal jurisdiction, King Endre III gives back Fogaras (Rumanian Făgăraş) and Szombathely to a certain Ugrin. The document refers to neighbouring Vlachs who, besides Szeklers and Saxons, have made a testimony (*Saxonibus, Syculis et Olachis*).

7. In 1292, King Endre III allows Sándor, from the family Ákos, to colonize Vlachs in three villages in the county of Hunyad (Hunedoara) and to keep them there. The names of these villages were: *Elye, Zad* and *Fenes.* They all are Hungarian: *Elye,* today *Marosillye,* first mentioned in 1266: *villa Helya,* in 1292: *terra Elye,* borrowed by Rumanian in the form of *Ilia; Zad,* first mentioned in 1292: *Zad,* in 1468: poss. Zadya; the Rumanian name, a tautology, appears for the first time in a document in 1733: *Guraszáda,* today: *Gurasada* (Hungarian *szád* "mouth; the opening of a valley"; Rumanian *gură* has the same sense).

Fenes is not preserved as the name of a settlement. Here, it is documented that at the end of the 13th century, Vlachs were settled in Hungarian villages.

8. In 1293, King Endre III orders that all Vlachs (Rumanians) who are living on estates of the aristocracy or on any other kinds of estates (*universos Olacos in possessionibus nobilium vel quorumlibet aliorum residentes*) must be returned to his estate Scekes. The only exception was the chapter of cathedral of Gyulafehérvár (Alba Iulia), to whom it was permitted to keep 60 families of Vlach bondsmen (*sexaginta mansiones Olacorum libere et secure valeant commorari*) on his estates in Fylesd and Enud. This indicates that the number of Vlachs living permanently on the territory of the Hungarian kingdom in this period (end of the 13th century) must have been quite low.

9. In 1294, Rolandus, the voivode of Transylvania concludes an armistice with the defenders of the fortress Fenes in Bihar county, and promises them to defend them against bondsmen of the bishopric, as well as against his own Hungarian and Rumanian bondsmen (*ab omnibus siue Vngarys siue infra indagines Solumus siue extra constitutis*).

As it appears from the Latin quotations, in the documents written in and after the mid-13th century, the Rumanians no longer are called *Blaccis,* but *Olacis* (<Hungarian *oláh* – the original name of the Rumanians in the Hungarian language; as is the designation *olasz* for the Italians.[1] The designation *román*, used today, was introduced much later, in the 19th century.)

Thus, contrary to what Pascu asserts (p. 57), neither the placenames nor the documents indicate anything of the kind of Szeklers and Saxons settling in areas "already inhabited by an indigenous Romanian population." This evidence **proves,** to the contrary, **that Rumanians settled, during several centuries, around and in settlements in which Hungarians or Saxons were living. In several cases, the sound pattern of the placename also indicates the approximative period in which the first Rumanians came to the settlement in question** (for example German Nikolausdorf > Hungarian Miklósfalva, later Klossdorf > Rumanian Cloaşterf).

In these documents written in Latin, the designation *terra* is used for all kinds of land (there is not only *terra Blachorum,* but also *terra Siculorum,* and *terra*

---

[1]This word was originally the name of a Celtic tribe in Old German; later it became to signify "Latin". It was borrowed by the Slavs: South Slavic *vlah,* plural *vlasi.* The Hungarians borrowed the plural: *olasz* "French, Walloon; Gallicus", from the 16th century on, also "Italus". Probably from another Slavic language, the Hungarians borrowed *vlah* in the singular. As shown by the documents, this word was adapted to Hungarian in the 13th century: *oláh.*

Saxonum), it is also used as a synonym for *villa* (*terra seu villa*) and does not imply a local organization on a certain territory, as Rumanian *ţară* was used later (after the 14th century). Pascu's assumption of "autonomous Romanian political structures," p. 59, is therefore baseless. The mentioning of *terra Blachorum* in Făgăraş in the document from 1222 does not imply, as Pascu asserts (p. 60), that "...the free peasants were organized into the so-called Country of the Romanians (*Terra Blachorum*; mentioned in 1222)"...

Outside Transylvania, south of the Carpathian mountains, several Rumanian cnezates are mentioned, for the first time, in the mid-thirteenth century. These were the beginnings of the later voivodates in Oltenia and Muntenia.

The Hungarian kings organized the country in counties (German *Komitat*, Hungarian *megye*, Rumanian *judeţ*), they built fortresses (*castrum regale*). They needed people who served in the fortresses, as well as soldiers to defend the borders from the incursions of Petchenegs and later of Cumans and Tartars.

It was mentioned above that the king gave often the reign over Transylvania – or the eastern part of the country – to his son, whose dignity was initially called *kiskirály* "petty king", *bán* "ban, governor" and, later, *vajda* "voivod". The voivods – later not necessarily the son of the king – have often become powerful lords and could also defy the king, but this was not because of a Rumanian population was living there. In those times, the king had the power and he exercised it in eastern Hungary through the voivod. In *Voievodatul Transilvaniei*, I, p. 147 – 148, Pascu mentions some of the voivods, for example *Gyula* (in 1201 and 1214); in 1212 – 1213, the office of the voivod was occupied by the archbishop of *Kalocsa* (a Hungarian town along the Danube), although he probably did not really exercise it. Most of the voivods were Hungarian, as judged by their names.

Parallel with the organization of the counties, the Church was organized.

Pascu, p. 61:

> The most powerful Romanian communes, however, were those in Ţara Maramureşului in northern Transylvania, which managed, by steadfast struggle, to resist the coming of feudalism until the middle of the fourteenth century.

The Rumanians living there had a special status which followed from their history, as stated by Jancsó:

> Ancient Russian chronicles tell us that King Ladislaus the Cuman [Kun László] asked in 1284 – 1285 for help in Rome and in Constantinople against Tartar incursions. Constantinople sent strong help – a number of Vlachs – from the area of the river Ibar in present day Serbia. These Vlachs, together with the Hungarians, defeated the Tartars in the upper valley of the river Tisza. Since they did not want to return to their lands, the king

55

settled them in Máramaros (Maramureș).[1]

Pascu, p. 61– 62:
> Yet other towns appeared following the colonization by various groups in the twelfth and thirteenth centuries at the royal fortresses at Cluj, Satu Mare, and Timișoara, through the development of the economically well-situated villages of Brașov, Sibiu, Bistrița, Sighișoara, Mediaș, Sebeș, and Orăștie...

"Various groups"? The most important founders of towns were Germans.

Pascu, p. 62:
The Tartar Invasion
p. 64:
> In order to reorganize the region, Béla IV put out a call for new colonists, offering substantial privileges to those who accepted his offer.
>
> [The peasants] rose up against their oppressors, refused to pay taxes [...] or settled in other areas, even south and east of the Carpathians, where they lived with other Romanians, their own people.

These two statements about circumstances in the same century contradict each other. It was exactly after the Tartar invasion that large numbers of Rumanians settled in Transylvania, because the terrible destruction there resulted in vast, depopulated areas. (The number of the soldiers in the army of the Tartar chief, Batu, is estimated to more than 600.000.) The oppression of the peasantry was a reality in later periods, and usually more brutal in Muntenia and Moldavia than in Hungary. Ș. Meteș, who published a book about "Rumanian emigrations from Transylvania from the 13th to the 20th centuries"[2] does not mention – in spite of its title – a single case of a Rumanian having emigrated in the 13th century to Muntenia or Moldavia. The single emigration of Vlach shepherds he knows about is to southern Poland, to the region of the rivers Dunajec and Poprad. This took place after prince Boleslav married Kunigunda, the daughter of the Hungarian king Béla IV, to whom he gave, in 1257, the territory of Sandets. It may be mentioned that Vlach shepherds wandered with their sheep across practically the entire Balkan peninsula, southern Hungary, northern Hungary (the Slovak area), the territories north of the Black Sea, reaching as far as the Caucasus. This way of life is explained by their main occupation.

---

[1] Benedek Jancsó, *Erdély története* [The history of Transylvania], Cluj-Kolozsvár, 1931, p. 61. The Ancient Russin Chronicle of Nestor is a rich source regarding the early contact between the Hungarians and the Russians.

[2] Ș. Meteș, *Emigrări românești din Transilvania în secolele XIII – XX* [Emigrations of Rumanians from Transylvania in the 13th to 20th centuries], 2nd edition, Bucharest, 1977, p. 22.

56

5. THE TRANSYLVANIAN VOIVODATE (pp. 65 – 72)

Pascu re-iterates (p. 65) his assertions about the assumed "resistance from the Romanian population" against the institutions of the Magyar feudal state and that the knezates, voivodates and districts were "deeply rooted indigenous institutions" from which the Transylvanian voivodate arose. These questions were discussed above.

Pascu, p. 66:

> Transylvania and the Kingdom of Hungary remained two separate countries.

p. 67:

> The autonomy of the Transylvanian voivodate and its orientation toward Moldavia and Țara Românească can be explained further by the fact that all three regions were ethnically homogenous.

Pascu refers to the 19th century Hungarian historian Sándor Szilágyi. The assertion is based upon the frequent struggles for power between the king and the nobility, or the king and the prince, who, although he was given his position by the king, secured often as much power for himself as possible. The authority of the king declined strongly in the second half of the 13th century, because of weak kings. (Most conspicuous among these princes were the son of King Béla III, Stephen, and prince Roland Borsa, in the second half of the 13th century, cf. Pascu, p. 66.) This situation was usual in the Middle Ages in all European countries. It is important to emphasize that the struggles were fought between the highest chiefs: the king, the prince, and some powerful members of the nobility. In those times, the nationality or the language of the people had no significance, it was the social position that counted.

According to political law, Transylvania was never before the mid-16th century a country separate from Hungary. After the battle at Mohács in 1526, when the Hungarian army was defeated by the Turks and king Lajos II died, Transylvania became a principality, dependent to a certain degree on the Turkish empire but with its own ancient laws, administration and own (Hungarian) princes. It was never occupied by the Turkish army. Its status was thus in sharp contrast to the Rumanian principalities, which were Turkish pashalics for several centuries.

Pascu, p., 67:

> Most of the people in Moldavia and Țara Românească were Romanian, as were a majority of those in Transylvania. Of the approximately 550.000 inhabitants of Transylvania on the eve of the great Tartar-Mongol invasion of 1241, roughly 65 percent were Romanian and 35 percent Hungarian, Saxon, Szekler, or of other groups.

The reader may believe this or not. No references, no documents are given, only a theory based upon false premises (see below, p. 58). One is forced to turn to *Voievodatul Transilvaniei*, and there, the following information is found:

The demographic situation in the 13th century is discussed in detail in vol. I, pp. 152 – 159 and 228 – 229; and in vol. II, pp. 331 – 332. Pascu uses available documents and literature, and makes certain assumptions. The number of 550.000 inhabitants was arrived at by assuming a population density of 5 per square kilometer (the entire intra-Carpathian territory of present day Rumania is 102.000 square kilometers). This estimation is based upon the assumption of 20 houses – 60 people – in a village in the 12th century, an increase to 25 houses and 75 people per village in the first part of the 13th century, and 635 settlements (*Voievodatul Transilvaniei*, vol. I, p. 159). The population density in Hungary at the same time is estimated to 8 – 10 inhabitants per square kilometer (*Voievodatul Transilvaniei*, vol. II, p. 332). These estimations may be more or less correct, but it seems to be difficult to get more exact data.

But how did Pascu arrive at the proportion of 65% Rumanians? A study of the entire material used to elucidate the population density (see above), shows that **there is not a single reference to the nationality** of the population! Pascu thus asserts a Rumanian majority in Transylvania on the eve of the Tartar invasion **without even an attempt at an analysis of the available data (documents, placenames, etc.).** As it will be shown below, **the number of Vlachs in Transylvania during the first half of the 13th century was very low, in fact, negligible.**

It is very important to point out this, because after the Tartar invasion, the number of the Rumanians in Transylvania increased rapidly. To be able to understand the history of the following centuries, it is necesary to bear in mind that the territory had practically no Rumanian population in the first half of the 13th century.

Pascu, p. 67:

> Thus, by 1300 the population of Transylvania presumably had returned to the level of sixty years earlier. This population, however, may have been even more heavily Romanian, since fewer Romanian lives were lost during the invasion and the number of Romanians grew more rapidly afterwards.

Here, Pascu reveals two important circumstances: the Rumanians were in those days primarily shepherds, living in the high mountains. The invading Tartars, a people used to the plains north of the Black Sea, evaded these also because there was much more to plunder in the valleys and the plains. And after the invasion, when very large areas became depopulated, the Hungarian king made efforts to bring in new people in those areas – it was in that period that the number of the Rumanians began to increase more significantly.

58

Pascu, p. 67–68:
> On the basis of records of papal tithes for the years 1332 – 37, we can determine for Transylvania as a whole the approximate ratio of the Catholic population (Hungarian, Saxon, and Szekler) to the Orthodox (Romanian), since only the former were subject to papal tithes. The records show 950 Catholic parishes, and since at this time there were approximately 3.000 settlements in Transylvania (more than 2.550 are specifically mentioned in documents up to 1350), roughly 2.000 contained no Catholic parish.This in turn means that either those settlements had no Catholic inhabitants or too few to constitute a parish, and it therefore follows that 2.000 settlements were entirely or very largely only Orthodox. In other words, more than 65 percent of the inhabitants of Transylvania were Romanian, or, rarely, Ruthenian – and less than 35 percent were Catholic Hungarian, Szekler, or Saxon.

Pascu forgets that in that time, as also today, to most of the parishes, one or two affiliated churches (outparishes) belonged which had no priest (but may have had a church). Therefore, the total number of Catholic settlements could have been well above 2000. However, the number of settlements in the period in question in Transylvania was probably lower than 3000.[1] The number of Catholic churches in the same period is estimated to at least 2000.[2] Thus, the testimony of the papal tithes suggests a predominantly Catholic population.

Pascu, pp. 70 – 71:
In the description of the development of the towns, Pascu mentions several German words – *Bürgermeister, Hann*; also the German proverb about legal freedom in the towns is quoted in the original language. This gives an idea about the great role of the Saxons in the building of the towns in Transylvania – as also in many other territories of Central and Eastern Europe. Similarly, Pascu mentions Alba Iulia (pp. 70–71) as "the bishopric in central Transylvania" without giving the information that it was a Catholic bishopric.

After the Tartar invasion, the Hungarian kings changed their earlier methods in defending the borders. The fortresses at the place of the central settlements (county capitals) were not effective against invasions; the construction of new fortresses in strategically important places, e.g. at the estuary of rivers, or even in remote, mountainous areas started. The king gave an estate only with the condition that the new owner obliged himself to build such fortresses.These then needed people around them. Here was the chance for a population of shepherds: the habitat suited perfectly for the Vlach shepherds, who were settled in many

[1] According to I. Kniezsa, 1331 settlements were recorded up to 1350 A.D.; cf. "Keletmagyarország helynevei" [The Placenames of Eastern Hungary] in *Magyarok és románok* [Hungarians and Rumanians], vol. I, ed. J. Deér & L. Gáldi, Budapest, 1943, p. 158, quoted by Illyés, 1992, p. 331.

[2] Á. Kosztin, *A dákoromán legenda. Keresztény kultuszhelyek Erdélyben* [The legend of the Daco-Romans. Christian places of worship in Transylvania], Budapest, 1989, p. 81.

areas around these fortresses and could continue their age-old occupation in the high mountains. Instead of imaginary nationalistic aims, based upon the superiority of Latin culture and the assumed ancient existence in the territory, the spread of the Vlachs in Transylvania during and after the 14th century is explained by this socio-economic circumstance. During the following decades and centuries, they spread gradually to the villages in lower regions, the valleys of the rivers and also to central Transylvania (Hungarian Mezőség, Rumanian Câmpia Transilvaniei).

However, the process was prolonged and gradual, going on for centuries. The documents show that colonization was actively promoted by the authorities of the Hungarian state. Thus, from 1495:

> ...the King as well as the voivodes, barons and other officials who rule those frontier areas [are] calling them and giving the Vlachs their guarantees (*ad vocationem et assecurationem regie maiestatis ac vaivodarum, baronum et ceterorum officialium ista confinia regni tenentium*).[1]

The colonized Vlachs paid the typical Vlach tax: the *quinquagesima ovium*, i.e., one sheep and a lamb after 50 sheep. Only Vlachs paid this kind of tax in Serbia as well as in Hungary. They did not pay taxes in agricultural products, since their agriculture was of the primitive type, for their own needs only.[2]

It must be emphasized also here that all these colonizations occurred entirely according to the customs of the period; the aim was economical. As pointed out for example by I. Iordan, *Nume de locuri,* 1952, p. 251, "Considerations about nationality (which were not possible in those times) had nothing to do in this problem, which was a pure 'affair' of the ruling class" (Iordan, discussing the situation in Muntenia, refers here to the creation of new villages in general in those times).

The leaders of the Vlach shepherds on the Balkan peninsula had several names, such as *celnik* (the most usual), *sudce, premikjur, knez, vladika, katunar*; in Hungary, they were only called *kenéz*. This is a designation of Slavic origin, and the Hungarian authorities used it since a long time for the leaders of the Slavs living in the kingdom. In Rumanian, there is *cneaz (*plur. *cneji),* borrowed from Slavic, but the Rumanians borrowed also the Hungarian form, as shown by the word *chinez*, used occasionally even today. The Hungarian authorities, by acknowledging them as *kenéz*-es, confirmed them in their role as leaders. Initially, a *kenéz* was "a locator; the settlers of the Vlach shepherds and serfs

---

[1] Köpcczi, 1986, p. 313.

[2] Ibid., 313.

60

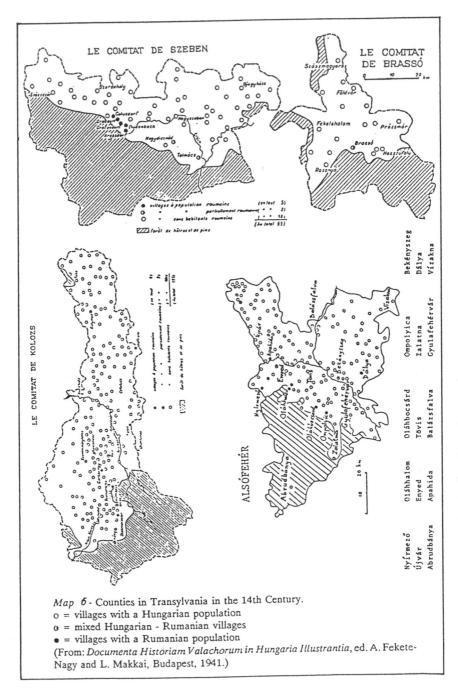

Map 6 - Counties in Transylvania in the 14th Century.
o = villages with a Hungarian population
o = mixed Hungarian - Rumanian villages
● = villages with a Rumanian population
(From: *Documenta Historiam Valachorum in Hungaria Illustrantia*, ed. A. Fekete-
Nagy and L. Makkai, Budapest, 1941.)

61

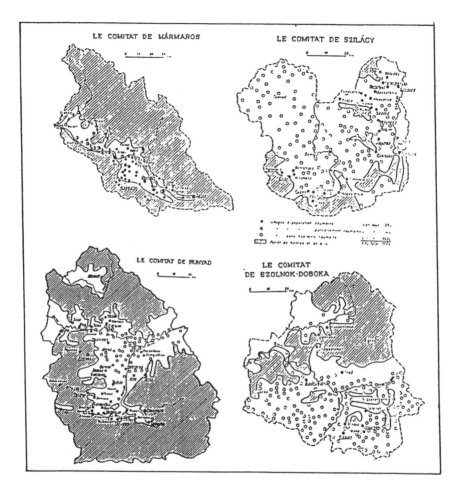

Map 7. – Counties in Transylvania in the 14th century. (For explanation, see map 6.)

who moved from Muntenia and Moldavia to the estates of the Hungarian noblemen in Transylvania". They were thus intermediators between the landlords and the serfs. Later, they received, for their services, certain rights and even own estates and many of them also were taken up into the nobility (for example the Jósika-family in Karánsebes [Caransebeş]). As shown by a number of villages around the mountain fortresses which were in the 14th – 15th centuries ruled by Rumanian *cnez*-es and have Rumanian names of Slavic origin, the chiefs of the fortresses gave these villages to the Rumanian *cnez*-es, who were more suitable for military services than the Slavs.[1] It were most probably also these *cnez*-es who, discovering that agriculture gave more stable incomes, disposed more and more people under their rule to pursue agriculture. To assure a stable, sedentary population, the chiefs of fortresses accorded a certain **juridical status,** including tax exemptions for new villages (*villa libera*); such villages were on both sides of the Carpathians called by a Slavic designation *ohaba* or *slobozia*. Later, when a number of *cnez*-es have risen into the Hungarian nobility, they received estates also on the basis of exemplary conduct in battle; this implied the right to inheritence of these villages, which were called *uric* (from Hungarian *örökbirtok*). The *ius keneziale* was synonymous with the hereditary ownership of the "free villages".[2]

The testimony of the river- and placenames

Pascu does not give any data about the river names and the placenames of the territory in question, although he mentions the importance of the placenames (p. 57). The reader not familiar with four different languages: Slavic, Hungarian, German, and Rumanian, may have difficulties in understanding the real situation. It is, however, indispensable to give an idea about this aspect, since the river- and placenames represent a most important part of the facts we have regarding those early centuries, from which the documentary attestations are scarce. The question is discussed by Illyés, 1992, pp. 291 - 336, and Du Nay, 1996, chapter VI. We give here a short description of the main facts.

In *Voievodatul Transilvaniei*, vol. II, pp. 473 – 494, Pascu states (pp. 473 – 474) that

> ...the placenames are more stable than those of persons, they are less exposed to the changes of fashion. Therefore, Dacian and Latin names have been preserved up to the present day. Especially names of rivers. Toponymy is also an additional argument for the continuity of the Rumanian people on the territories where these names have been preserved, north of the Danube and in the Carpatho-Danubian-Pontic area...

[1] Köpeczi, 1986, p. 315.

[2] Ibid.,p. 316.

[...]
those who have preserved the word which characterizes the basic settlements, the villages, from Latin *fossatum* (settlement surrounded by ditches) have never abandoned these settlements in order to migrate to other territories and to return, after centuries, exactly to those areas from which they have departed.

Pascu also affirms that some villages were given new names by the authorities. Then, the microtoponymy of the villages, i.e., the names of small hills, brooks, fields, is "mostly Rumanian in Transylvania," and Pascu asserts that this proves the priority of the Rumanians there.

Pascu, *Voievodatul Transilvaniei* II, p. 477:
> The toponymy of Transylvania was, in the Middle Ages, exposed to a pressure from the authorities with the aim to change it. The most often used method for this aim was the translation or changing of the toponymy. In other cases, one has only put to the Rumanian names of villages the suffix *"falva"* (village) or *"háza"* (house)...

Examples are: Rumanian *Mărul* was changed to *Almafa* "apple-tree", *Mestecăniş* to *Nyires* "group of birch-trees", *Câmpulung* to *Hosszúmező*"long field", etc. Direct borrowings: Rum. *Luncă* "waterside, river meadow" > Hung. *Lonka, Mesteacăn* "birch" > *Mesztákon*. Among Pascu's examples of putting a suffix to a Rumanian name one finds *Harnicsháza* – from Rumanian *Harniceşti, Bukurfalva* – from Rumanian *Bucur*, etc.[1]

Pascu mentions also villages which have names in two or three languages; parallel namegiving (pp. 477 – 478). Finally, about the microtoponymy:
> Based on the thorough analysis of the toponymy of Rumania, the specialists have arrived at the conclusion that this is in 80% of Rumanian origin *(Voievodatul,* II, p. 478).

Pascu then gives a large number of placenames, divided into categories (those based on apellatives, personal names, social circumstances, etc.) for each county (pp. 479 to 494).

Most of these placenames are of Rumanian origin, but they appeared for the first time in the documents quite late, **in the mid-14th century or later.** A few of these settlements were recorded in the 13th century with a Hungarian name. Pascu puts in this list erroneously also names of settlements which the Rumanians borrowed from Hungarian also in later periods. Thus, Rumanian *Căuaci* was, in 1405, mentioned as *Kovachfalva. – Căuaci* has no meaning in the Rumanian

---

[1] Pascu refers here to E. Petrovici, "Toponimia ungurească în Transilvania medievală" [Hungarian toponymy in Medieval Transylvania], in *Transilvania*, 1943, 74, nr. 1. – It should be pointed out that these are not suffixes but words meaning "house", "village", etc. in the genitive form, for example Bukurfalva "the village of Bukur".

language and it is obvious that this name was borrowed from Hungarian: *kovács* "smith". The same is the case with *Aghireş* from Hungarian *Egrespatak* "gooseberry-brook", *Giulacut,* Hungarian *Gyulakuta* "the fountain of Gyula", *Hăşmaş,* Hung. *Hagimas* (Hungarian *hagyma* "onion"), *Sarsig* Hung. *Sarzeg* (Hungarian *sár* "mud", *szeg* "small area, corner"), etc.

The word of Latin origin, **not** inherited in the Rumanian language but borrowed from Albanian (Alb. *fshat* > Rum. *fsat,* later *sat*) was discussed above, p. 38. The theory presented in *Voievodatul Transilvaniei* ("those wo have preserved the word *fossatum* did never abandon these settlements") is thus based on faulty knowledge of the history of the Rumanian language.

A general survey of the question of the placenames

Pascu's treatment of this question shows the following flaws:

1. Instead of investigating the totality of placenames, or at least a representative part of them, he choses arbitrarily those which agree with his theory.

2. He does not take into account the **chronological** aspect of the problem.

3. He ignores the significance of the **sound pattern** of the different names. In the majority of cases, these indicate the source of the name, from which important conclusions may be drawn about the situation in ancient periods, especially concerning the relations between different populations.

4. Pascu´s theories about the authorities giving new names to villages and about the significance of microtoponymy are not acceptable.

5. The absence of an analysis of the river names.

In *Voievodatul Transilvaniei*, vol. II, pp. 31 – 54, Pascu reproduces maps of six Transylvanian counties, without mentioning that they were taken from *Documenta Historiam Valachorum in Hungaria Illustrantia,* Budapest, 1941. These maps show the villages existing in the 14th century, giving also the ethnic character of their population – Hungarian , Rumanian, or mixed, (but without their names; cf. above, maps 6 and 7, pp. 60–61). All these maps together demonstrate that in that century, in the Transylvanian basin, the Székely and the Saxon districts, on the plains west of Transylvania, only Hungarian and Saxon villages existed. Rumanian villages were found in Maramureş (Máramaros), (and there, they were in the majority), in Caraş-Severin (Hungarian Krassó-Szörény), also in a majority but to a lesser degree. But also in counties which later became mostly Rumanian, there were more Hungarian than Rumanian villages in that period: in Făgăraş (Fogaras), 10 out of a total of 15, in Hunedoara (Hunyad), Hungarian villages are in the majority in the valleys and most of the Rumanian villages were in the area of high mountains around Hátszeg (Haţeg).

It is a well-known fact that no ancient or Roman placename was preserved north of the lower Danube – in sharp contrast to the territory south of the river.

North of the Danube, only the ancient names of the large rivers are extant. In the territory in question, there is Rumanian *Mureş,* Hungarian *Maros,* German *Mieresch; Someş, Szamos; Olt, Olt. Alt;* and the name of the rivers *Criş,* Hungarian *Körös.* The ancient names are: *Samu(s)* – first mentioning in a Hungarian document in 1231: *Zomus. Mureş – Maris* (Herodotos), later *Morisos, Marisus, Marisia –* Hungarian *Moris* (1044, *S:t Gellert Deliberationes); Olt – Aloutas* (Ptolemaios), *Alutus* (Peutinger-tablets), *Aluta* (Jordanes), in Hungarian documents *Alt* (1211) and *Olt* (1233). The Rumanian forms cannot have been inherited from Latin, since in that case they would show **Sames,* **Mares,* and **Alut.* The *a* > *o* change must have occurred in another language – most probably Slavic, and was from that language transferred to Rumanian.[1] The origin of the river-name *Ompoi* was described above, p. 11.

The ancient names of all other rivers in the territory in question are unknown.

Tributary of:	Hung>Rum	Sl>H>R	Slavic >Rum	H>Rum or Sl>Rum	German> Rum
Szamos	16	5	1	5	0
Maros	12	2	1	7	0
Olt	13	0	0	0	3
total	41	7	2	12	3

Table 1. The origins of the river names in Transylvania. (Szamos = Rum. Someş, Maros = Mureş, Olt = Olt.) Of unknown origin are 1 of the tributaries of the Szamos and seven of those of the Olt. These may be of Turkish origin.

Table I shows the names of rivers that flow through at least 3 villages, tributaries of the *Szamos* (Rumanian *Someş*), *Maros (Mureş),* and *Olt.* It appears that, as shown by the sound patterns, most (at least 48)of the Rumanian names of rivers were borrowed from Hungarian. Of these, 41 are original Hungarian names and seven were borrowed by Hungarian from Slavic. In 12 cases, the sound pattern of names of Slavic origin does not give any indication about the direct source of the Rumanian name (Hungarian or Slavic). There are two cases of certain Rumanian borrowings from Slavic. The Rumanians have also adopted three names of rivers from German.

---

[1] Köpeczi, 1986, p. 248.

Not a single of these 65 river names is of Rumanian origin.

The theory was put forward (Puşcariu[1]) that if the name of a river in the highest mountains, i.e., its beginning, is Rumanian, then this proves that Rumanians were the original population in the area, because earlier the entire river must have had that (Rumanian) name and it was only later that the Rumanians borrowed the name given by newcomers or by the authorities.

The translation of Latin names by Slavs was usual in the Balkan Peninsula. Thus, the name of a village in Dobruja is recorded on an inscription found there: *Petra* (cf. Latin *petra* "stone"). This village is now called *Camena* – a name of Slavic origin, the translation of *Petra*. In this environment, hypotheses of the kind Puşcariu has put forward could be discussed but north of the Danube, where there is not a single example of such a translation (Puşcariu was forced to give the example from Dobruja, in lack of such cases north of the Danube), they are of no value.

In the north of Transylvania, most of the river names of Slavic origin were borrowed in a sound pattern which indicates that they were handed down to Rumanian by Hungarian; in the south, there are a number of direct adoptions by Rumanian from Slavic. Taking into consideration all the rivers of some length (those which flow through at least 3 villages) in Transylvania, Kniezsa found 153 names. Of these, 39 are of Slavic origin, of which 10 are the tributaries of the Danube, all of which were probably tansferred to Rumanian directly from Slavic. Another 3 tributaries of the Danube have names of Hungarian origin, which were transferred to Rumanian directly from Hungarian. In the rest of the intra-Carpathian areas of present day Rumania, 29 river names of Slavic origin remain. Out of these, 8 were transmitted to Rumanian by Hungarian (for example Slavic *Trescava* > Hungarian *Torockó* > Rumanian *Trăscău* (not *Treascava),* Slavic *Lovina* > Hungarian *Lóna* > Rumanian *Luna,* etc.). In 7 cases, the sound pattern of the Rumanian name shows a direct borrowing from Slavic, for example: Slavic *Vrbova* > Rumanian *Gârbova* (the Slavic word means "willow", borrowed by the Hungarians in the form of *Orbó*); Slavic *Trnava* > Rumanian *Târnava,* etc. In the remaining 14 cases, the sound patterns of the names are comaptible with borrowing from both Slavic and Hungarian.[2]

---

[1] S. Puşcariu, "Le rôle de la Tranylvanie dans la formation et l'évolution de la langue roumaine", in *La Transylvanie,* 1938, p. 41.

[2] Illyés, 1992, pp. 318 - 319.

The Hungarian placenames

The names of eight Hungarian tribes that settled in the Carpathian basin in the 10th century were recorded by the Byzantine Emperor and scholar, Constantine Porphyrogenitus. These names became later placenames, and the distribution of such placenames indicates therefore the earliest Hungarian settlements (mostly in the 10th century). A difference between Transylvania and the plains of eastern Hungary is revealed in this respect: In the territory of the plains including the Banat, such names are frequent: Kniezsa records 16 of them (quoted by Illyés, 1992, p. 329). Only three of them are extant in Transylvania (all in its northern part): *Keszi* > Rumanian *Chiseu* in *Satu Mare* county, *Jenő* > Rumanian *Ineu* in *Dăbâca* county and *Keszü* > Rumanian *Chesău* in Cluj county. As shown by the sound pattern of the Rumanian forms, all were borrowed by the Rumanians.

The form of a number of Hungarian placenames indicates that they were given **in the period from the end of the 11th to the middle of the 13th century:** personal names or the names of different ethnic groups without a suffix or with the suffixes -*d* or -*i*. The use of a personal name alone, without a suffix, as a placename is specific to the early Hungarians and is not found among the Slavs, Germans or Rumanians. The personal names may be Christian or from the pre-Christian era, and are, besides Hungarian, – Turkish, Slavic, or German. The names with the suffix -*i* are also very numerous: a personal name + *i: Tamási, Kovácsi;* name of dignitaries: *Apáti* (*apát* "abbot"), *Püspöki* (*püspök* "bishop"), name of a population: *Németi* (German), *Csehi* (Czech), *Horváti* (Croatian) etc. (a total of 19 such place names are listed by Kniezsa (quoted by Illyés, 1992, p. 330). Placenames created with the suffix -*d* are: *Bánd, Bencéd, Diód, Koppánd, Peterd,* etc.

These names are numerous over large areas of Transylvania and of course also on the plains west of it. The language of the personal names as well as the names of the various populations give an indication about the different peoples that lived during this period, from the end of 10th to the middle of the 13th century, in the area. As shown by the above enumeration, there were, besides Hungarians, – Turks, Slavs (Croatians, Czechs, Russians), Germans, and Petchenegs. Thus, before the mid-thirteenth century – the Tartar invasion – **there is not a single one among these placenames which would suggest a Rumanian population in the area.**

This does not exclude the possibility of Rumanians, although it argues strongly against a significant number of them, because very many placenames are involved and the chances are great that all populations of some significance in the area left some traces in these early Hungarian placenames. Kniezsa has also determined the number of names of settlements mentioned in documents in the 13th century and the proportion of Hungarian, Slavic and Rumanian among them. His list contains a total of 511 placenames in the entire intra-

Carpathian area of present day Rumania. Of these, 83% are of Hungarian origin, about 10% derive from Slavic and 0.6% – 3 – are of Rumanian origin.[1]

In the 12th century, compund placenames appeared with (1) name + (2) -laka, - népe, telke, -ülése, -soka and in the 13th century also -háza, -falva; i.e., house, ground plot, village, etc. in the genitive.

It is not earlier than in the mid-14th century that Rumanian placenames appear in more significant numbers: the first of these are found in Hunyad (Hunedoara) county: Tămăşasa (in 1341), Râu de mori (in 1359) and Rea (in 1360). It is also in Hunyad county and about the same period that the first Rumanian placename was borrowed by the Hungarians: Râuşor (Rumanian râu "brook") > Hungarian Rusor (1377), Nucşoara (Rumanian nuc "walnut") > Hungarian Nuksora (1394: Noxara).

Among settlements mentioned in the first half of the 14th century, 36 (4.4%) have names of Rumanian origin (out of a total of 820) and in the following half century, their number increases to 76 – 4.3% out of a total of 1.757 names of settlements.[2]

Pascu (Voievodatul, II, p. 457 – 473) enumerates a large number of villages whose names attest to the nationality of their inhabitants: Saxons, Croatians, Russians, Szeklers, Hungarians, Rumanians, etc. He states that the attribution "Vlach" appears in 80% of these, which should prove that the Rumanians were the majority population.

This is, however, erroneous. It must be stated, first of all, that the proportion of 80% is true in later centuries, perhaps in and especially after the 14th, when the village names with "Olah" were very numerous. In the 13th century, however, they were rare. To name a settlement according to the nationality of its inhabitants is only necessary and meaningful if the nationality is different from that of the surrounding territory. There are many villages designated "Saxon", "Croatian", "Russian", etc. but, beginning with the 14th century, the largest number of villages thus distinguished are Oláh – "Vlach". This means that in a number of cases, Croatians, Russians, etc. settled in a territory inhabited by people of other ethnicity, but Rumanians settled in a much higher number of cases among non-Rumanians. These non-Rumanians were most often Hungarians, who gave the name "Oláh" to the newcomers, and also Saxons: "Walachendorf." In many cases, two villages with the same name appear, distinguished by the adjectives Oláh (Rumanian) and Magyar (Hungarian), respectively; and in the Saxon areas, Szász (Transylvanian Saxon).

---

[1]Illyés, 1992, p. 331.

[2]Ibid.

The first appearance of a village name in the documents of the Hungarian state gives an indication about the existence in a certain period of the village in question. The time elapsed between the establishment and the first mention of a settlement varies. It depends upon several circumstances – one of which is, as also stated by Pascu, the establishing of feudal relations with the settlement in question. Of course, there are other factors, and one should also reckon with the fact that not all documents were preserved to us. A few data have no value in themselves, but a large number of a certain type of names appearing in a certain era may give valuable information. The colonization of the German (Saxon) population in Transylvania gives a possibility to test this hypothesis, i.e., to get an idea about how reliably and how soon the names of new villages were recorded in documents. It is known that the Saxons were invited by King Géza II. and started to come around 1150; their colonization lasted about one century, going on also after the Tartar invasion. The colonization of the Saxons must have resulted in several settlements with the attributive of "Saxon". How is this reflected in the documents, i.e., do such names appear in them and how long after the period in which the Saxons were colonized? We use the list of placenames which include the name of a nationality, given by Pascu in *Voievodatul,* II, pp. 457 – 468.

The decisive period is the 13th century, because this was in and immediately after the period of the Saxon colonization. In that century, there are 9 names of settlements mentioned in the documents (in Pascu's list) in which "Saxon" or the names of other populations from Western Europe appear. The first one is from 1215: *Aldorf,* (German *Wallendorf,* with Walloon settlers) in the area of Bistriţa; followed by *Silivaşul Săsesc* (<Hungarian *Szász-szilvás,* from Hungarian *szilva* "plum" and *szász* "Saxon") in Solnoc-Dăbâca; in 1238 Saxons are mentioned in the district of Orăştie; and in 1248 in county Alba. In 1269, there is *Nemty* (Hungarian *német* "German") in Solnoc-Dăbâca; in 1290: *terra Sospatak,* 1503: *poss. Zazwelgye,* Hungarian *Szászvölgye,* Rumanian *Valea Sasului,* in the county of Târnava; in 1291, *terra Saxonum* – (translated by Pascu as *Pământul saşilor*). From 1292, Saxon villages are mentioned in counties Alba and Cluj. – Thus, in most of Transylvania proper, the settlement of Saxons is reflected in the names of villages found in the documents of the period of colonization and some decades later. – In the same century, the presence of Russians is indicated by the names of four villages, all at the end of the century, in counties Bihor, Cluj and in the Saxon area. The attribution *Székely* "Szekler" is found in two cases, in counties Bihor and Trei Scaune, and that of *Magyar* "Hungarian" in one, in county Alba, where they are mentioned together with Vlachs.

What is the situation with the villages designated *Oláh* "Vlach"?

Their total number in the 13th century is seven. The first of them is from the year 1252 (*terra Olachorum*) in the region of Braşov, the southern frontier-area, the rest is from the end of the 13th century: *Olahtelke* in 1294, also in the region of Braşov, *Elye,* Vlach and Hungarian, in 1292 – 1350 in the county of Hunedoara, *Olahgorbó* from 1292 in county Cluj, *Olah Scekas* from 1293 – 1294 in county Alba and a mentioning together with Hungarians is from the county Bihor, from 1294 – 1397.

This situation must be compared with that in the following 14th century, when there are a number of indications of Slavs, Germans, Turkish peoples, but the number of villages called *Olah* "Vlach" shows an enormous increase. Only in county Bihor, several dozens of such names are given in Pascu's list for the 14th and the 15th centuries. This great difference as compared to earlier periods can only be explained by the creation of new settlements mostly by Vlachs. It is also in the 14th century that a significant number of Rumanian placenames appear (after only 3 in the preceding century), as well as the first Hungarian borrowings of placenames from Rumanian (see above). It was in those centuries that the number of Rumanians became significant in Transylvania.

An analysis of the sound pattern of a group of place names

More historical conclusions may be drawn from an analysis of the **origins** of the placenames. For the sake of brevity, we take only those villages which in the 13th century were indicated to have Rumanian inhabitants. Are their names of Rumanian origin?

In Hunedoara, there are the villages *Elye,* one Hungarian and one Rumanian in 1292 – 1350. The Hungarian name was adopted by the Rumanians: *Ilia,* mention is made of "Rumanian villages which belong to *Ilye"*. In county Alba, *Olahlapod* is mentioned from 1299, borrowed by Rumanian in the form of *Lopadea.* In the county of Cluj, there is 1292 *Gorbo Walachalis,* today *Gârbăul¹ Român,* and in Bihor county, *ungaris sive olahis infra indagines Solumus, valahi de Solmus* are mentioned, i.e., Hungarians and Rumanians living in the village named *Solymos* (Hungarian *sólyom* "falcon"), Rumanian *Şoimuş.* The word *şoim* is Rumanian (of Hungarian origin, appearing in documents from the second half of the 15th century). However, *-uş* in this name cannot be a suffix, *Şoimuş* is a borrowing of Hungarian *Solymos.* The two mentions in the area of Braşov are: in 1252, *terra Olachorum de Tyrek* and in 1294: *terra seu villa Tohou <=Tohan> alio nomine Olahteleky.*[2] Tohan probably derives from the language of the Petchenegs, while the origin of Tyrek is uncertain.

---

[1] From Hungarians *Gorbó,* (< Slavic *Gъrbova*); as indicated by the absence of the Slavic ending *-ova* in the Rumanian name.

[2] Suciu, II, 1968, p. 199.

Thus, out of seven names of settlements in which the documents from the 13th century tell us about Rumanians, the origin of five may be determined. **All these Rumanian names were borrowed from Hungarian.**

The arguments against the obvious conclusions to be drawn from these data are of no value. The assumption that the authorities re-named a number of Rumanian villages is based upon present day circumstances. Aspects of nationality or language were in those times of no importance, the economic and political interests of the nobility and of the king (the state) decided the policy. The struggle for power was waged not between different nations but between more or less powerful lords. But there is also more direct evidence against the above argument: if the practical absence of Rumanian village names before the Tartar invasion and their low number also during the following century was caused by the policy of the Hungarian authorities, then this policy must have been strongest during the 10th – 13th centuries and then gradually decreasing. This is very unlikely. Even more important is the recording of the Slavic place-names: Out of 511 names of settlements recorded in the 13th century, about 50 are of Slavic origin – if the Hungarian policy was to re-name non-Hungarian villages, why did they not re-name also the Slavic villages?

Pascu also asserts that the microtoponymy has more historical significance than the placenames and the names of the rivers. This is true to some extent, but it should be taken into account that the names of very small brooks, fields, small hills, the properties of the individual peasants, etc., are much less stable. Pascu gives the proportion of Rumanian microtoponymy in entire Rumania: 80%, but this figure is irrelevant for Transylvania. If a village was devastated by invading Tartars or Turks, and re-populated by Rumanians, it is obvious that these newcomers could not have been told the names of all the surroundings, although they probably knew the name of the village itself. But also a gradual change of the inhabitants may in the long run led to the loss of the original microtoponymy, since these names, used by a restricted number of people, are much more unstable than the names of settlements or of rivers.

As was shown above, there is no example of Hungarians borrowing a Rumanian placename before the end of the 14th century. What is the case with the Germans, who settled in several areas of Transylvania between the mid-12th and the second half of the 13th century? They were a population speaking a language different from all those spoken in the territory and their settlement was going on in a fairly short period of time. They were bound to borrow river names and placenames in large numbers from the population they found in their new places.

In the list of Pascu *(Voievodatul* II, pp. 457 – 468), no answer is found to this question. There are German names: *Reusdorf, Reussen, Walachendorf, Dettschpien*; and Hungarians: *Orozfalw, Olah Egres* > Rum. *Agrişul Românesc;*

72

Olahzentmiklos > Rum. *Sînmiclăuşul Român; Zaazkyzd* > Rum. *Saschiz,* etc.
A general survey and a summary of the problem is given by Illyés, 1992, pp.
332 – 333.[1] The majority of the placenames in the Saxon areas are of German
origin. This suggests that the statement found in several documents, asserting
that these territories were *terra deserta et inhabitata* ("desert and uninhabited
area") is not entirely wrong. Several German names were also borrowed by
Hungarian as well as by Rumanian: German *Burgberg* "mountain where the
fortress stands" > Hungarian *Borberek* (popular etymology: *bor* "wine", *berek*
"riverside coppice, grove"); the Rumanians borrowed this German name in the
form of *Vurpăr*. German *Katzendorf* > Rumanian *Caţa;* German *Kaltwasser*
"cold water" > Rumanian *Calvasăr* (Hungarian by parallell namegiving:
Hidegvíz "cold water"); German *Weidenbach* > Hungarian *Vidombák* >
Rumanian *Ghimbav;* German *Rotbach* > Rumanian *Rotbav;* German *Weisskirch*
> Rumanian *Viscri,* etc.

Thomas Nägler determined the origin of a total of 242 placenames in all areas
in which Transylvanian Saxon dialects were spoken in the 20th century. He
found 140 names of German origin (58%), 16 were from Hungarian (6.6%), and
8 were from Slavic (3.3%); 78 (32.2%) were of unknown origin.[2] There are no
early German placenames borrowed from Rumanian.[3]

Thus, on the territory of the Transylvanian Saxons, who settled there in a well-
defined period (between approximately 1150 and the end of the 13th century),
**there is not a single early example of Germans having borrowed a
Rumanian placename.**

Conclusions to be drawn from the study of the river- and place-names

The data shown by the river names and the placenames exclude the possibility
that Rumanians lived in Transylvania before the Slavs and also before the
Hungarians and the Saxons. One wonders how it is possible at all that this

---

[1]Based mainly upon *Urkundenbuch zur Geschichte der Deutschen in Siebenbürgen,* vol. I, 1191–
1342, compiled by Franz Zimmermann and Carl Werner (Hermannstadt: 1892); Thomas Nägler, *Die
Ansiedlung der Siebenbürger Sachsen,* Bucharest, 1979; István Kniezsa, "Keletmagyarország
helynevei" [The Placenames of Eastern Hungary], in: *Magyarok és románok* [Hungarians and
Rumanians], József Deér, László Gáldi (eds.), Budapest, 1943; Coriolan Suciu, *Dicţionar istoric al
localităţilor din Transilvania* [Historical Dictionary of the Localities in Transylvania], Bucharest, vol.
I, 1967, vol. II, 1968.

[2] Thomas Nägler, *Die Ansiedlung der Siebenbürger Sachsen,* Bucharest, 1979, pp. 174–179.

[3] István Kniezsa, "Keletmagyarország helynevei" [The Placenames of Eastern Hungary], p. 139;
in: *Magyarok és románok* [Hungarians and Rumanians], ed. J. Deér & L. Gáldi, Budapest, 1943. (In
recent times, the Saxons use a number of Rumanian placenames instead of their original names,
e.g., Reschinar, from Rumanian Răşinari, instead of Städterdorf, etc.)

hypothesis has been put forward. In fact, even Rumanian scholars have expressed their doubts. Thus, for example, E. Petrovici stated the following as regards entire Rumania:

> The contradiction between the Romance character of the Rumanian language and the non-Roman, in the first place Slavic, but also Hungarian, Cumanian, etc. origin of the old toponymy on the territory of the Rumanian language cannot be solved, I think, other than by assuming that the Romance language (Rumanian) spread over a territory where mostly Slavic was spoken.[1]

This was said only 7 years after the war, in an era when the propagation of the importance of the Russians and of the Slavs in general was the official policy in Rumania, and the glorification of I.V. Stalin had reached its apogee. In spite of great ambitions, I.V. Stalin's contribution to linguistics was not very brilliant, and the fact that the above statement was made in a meeting where this was praised decreases its value. Rosetti, quoting it, added that it "does not correspond to our opinion". However, in the following section Rosetti discussed the situation in different areas in the extra-Carpathian territories of Rumania, and stated that in large areas of Rumania "the Rumanian-speaking population has settled over a relatively sparse Slavic-speaking population," referring again to E. Petrovici ("comunic. acad. E. Petrovici").[2] This suggests that Rosetti did not entirely oppose the idea and that Petrovici has sustained his opinion even later. It is characteristic of the situation in Rumania during the 1980-s that this entire section is omitted in the definitive (1986) edition of Rosetti's *History of the Rumanian Language*.

The river names and the placenames in Transylvania, as well as early documents indicate that the Rumanians appeared at the beginning of the 13th century in some areas of the high mountains (the southern Carpathians) which were partly uninhabited, partly inhabited by a sparse population of Slavs and Hungarians. After the Tartar invasion in 1241 – 1242, the Rumanians were colonized initially around royal fortresses in the frontier region of the high mountains, a habitat which perfectly suited for this population of shepherds. Probably beginning in the late 13th century, they were settled also in villages inhabited mostly by Hungarians, but also by German and Walloon settlers who

---

[1] E. Petrovici, "Învățăturile lui I.V. Stalin cu privire la știința limbii și sarcinile lingviștilor din R.P.R." [The teachings of I.V. Stalin about linguistics and the tasks of the linguists of the R.P.R.], in *Problemele științelor sociale în dezbaterea Academiei R.P.R.* [The problems of the social sciences in the debate of the Academy of the R.P.R.], March the 21– 25th, 1951, Bucharest, 1951; quoted by Rosetti, ILR 1968, p. 288.

[2] Rosetti, 1968, p. 289.

74

were invited by the Hungarian king in the period between the mid-12th and the late 13th century. In several parts of southwestern Transylvania, they lived for some time in symbiosis with the Slavs they found there.

6. THE LATE MIDDLE AGES (pp. 73 – 95)
Pascu, p. 73:

> [In the 14th to the 16th centuries, Transylvania] became an increasingly autonomous element in the Hungarian kingdom, through the consolidation of its own political and administrative institutions and because of its role in blocking the expansion of the Ottoman Empire.
>
> ...
>
> Transylvanian autonomy was manifested primarily in the consolidation of the voivodate.

Pascu describes the history of Transylvania from the period of the Dacians on as if it had been an autonomous unity, on the basis of the Roman and Dacian, later Daco-Roman and Rumanian people and the traditions and political institutions of these "autochthonous populations". This is totally wrong: there are no reports about Daco-Romans and archaeological finds, in any case after the 3rd century A.D., do not indicate the existence of such a population. From the 10th century on, Transylvania was populated by Hungarians and belonged to the kingdom of Hungary. As was shown above, the Rumanians appeared there in the 13th century.

Until this point, Pascu's way of presenting events and circumstances resulted in a totally distorted description of history: the arguments for the existence and continuity of "Daco-Romans" are by far not sufficient and an analysis of all relevant facts excludes this theory. (Moreover, there are also circumstances which indicate **where** the Rumanian language and people developed.) The theories about a Rumanian population in Transylvania before the 13th century do not stand up for a critical analysis in the light of available documents, as well as of the river- and placenames. These theories are mainly constructed by projecting the situation in the 14th – 16th centuries back three to four centuries earlier. Here, there was no question of "interpreting" the past, since this notion implies some truth left, even if interpreted in a subjective way.

From the 14th century on, Pascu's selective presentation gives also, in general, a false picture of the history of Transylvania, although it is now possible to apply Roberts' statement: "the historian is the organizer and interpreter of the past, not merely its recorder" (Paul E. Michelson, in the Foreword to Pascu's *History of Transylvania*, p. XI).

If a history textbook from the former Czechoslovakia writes a half sentence

75

about János Hunyadi, who "temporarily stopped the Turkish conquest of Hungary," [1] this is not wrong, although it may scarcely be considered good history-writing. Similarly, if Pascu re-iterates in this chapter several times the "increasing autonomy" of Transylvania, this is not false, but Pascu's description is still misleading since he suggests that the causes of this are to be sought in the Rumanian – different from the Hungarians – population of the territory.

The princes of Transylvania were assigned by the Hungarian king, and were mainly Hungarians – as it appears also from the enumeration of the names of several princes from that period: Toma Széchenyi, the Lackfis, the Csákis, Ladislaus of Losoncz (Pascu, pp. 73 – 74). They were most of the time the son of the king or noblemen from Hungary west of Transylvania, who had their estates in central or western Hungary and some of them also stayed mostly outside Transylvania (in such cases, the vice-voivode ruled there).

Pascu, p. 75:
> In 1442, when Iancu of Hunedoara, the son of a family of Romanian knezi from southern Transylvania, ascended to the position of voivode, the country was in a unique position. It constituted a kind of center of gravity for Ţara Românească and Moldavia in their efforts to create a powerful anti-Ottoman bloc.

The origin of the family of *Johannes Hunyad* or *Johan Hunyad* – to use the name which appears in a German text given by Pascu on p. 79 – is not entirely clear. According to certain sources, the oldest known members were the Serbian princes (*cnez*-es) Radoslav and Serb who, as many of the other *cnez*-es, were settling Rumanians into Hungarian territory.[2] His father, Vojk, was a knight in the court of the Hungarian king Sigismund, who gave him in 1409 the castle of Hunyad in south-western Transylvania, as a recognition for his services and his bravity. Vojk's wife, the mother of Johannes (János), was a Hungarian woman and János was their first son. He was for a short time the captain of Ujlaki, the *ban* of Macsó, and served as a soldier on the estates in southern Hungary of the Serbian reigning prince Brankovič. In 1428, he became the knight of king Sigismund and married Horogszegi Szilágyi Erzsébet, whose father was his colleague in the service of prince Brankovič. In 1433, he followed king

[1] *Csehszlovákia története: Tankönyv a középiskolák második és harmadik osztálya számára* [The History of Czechoslovakia. Textbook for the 3rd and 4th grade of the middle-schools], Bratislava, 1966; 80, 186-187; quoted by I. Deák in *The Hungarians. A Divided Nation*, red. Stephen Borsody, Yale Russian and East European Publications, 1988, p. 306.

[2] *A történeti Erdély* [Historical Transylvania], red. M. Asztalos, Budapest, 1936, p. 211.

76

Sigismund to Italy and stayed with him until the death of the king in 1437. [1] In 1439, king Albert made him the *ban* (local ruler) of Szörény (Severin), and under the next king, Ladislaus I (I. Ulászló), he became the captain of Nándorfehérvár (today Belgrade) and in 1440, the voivod of Transylvania.

Pascu, p. 75:

> The year after the loss [at Varna in 1444], Iancu's alliance turned defeat into a fine victory, again with support by Ţara Românească. It is therefore not surprising that this great military leader overcame the opposition of the Hungarian nobility and was chosen governor of Hungary, establishing himself as the true ruler of the Hungarian kingdom.

János Hunyadi fought several battles with the Turks and after the battle at Varna (1444), he was elected member of the Hungarian government of seven men. He was extremely popular in the entire Hungary, and among all social classes, and also abroad, especially in the Balkan peninsula. After the lost battle with the Turks at Varna on November 10th, 1444, when king Ladislaus (Ulászló) died in the plague, Hunyadi was forced to flee. He reached Muntenia, and was put into prison by the voivode Vlad Dracul. Only after the Hungarian noble order threatened Vlad Dracul with war did he release Hunyadi.[2] In 1446, László, the son of king Albert, was elected the Hungarian king, and because he was only a child, Hunyadi was appointed governor until the king had reached his majority. Hunyadi drove away voivode Vlad Dracul and made Dan to voivode. Dracul then attacked, with Turkish assistance, voivode Dan, but Hunyadi defended him successfully. However, voivode Dan did not show worthy of Hunyadi's confidence: in 1448, Hunyadi started another Balkan offensive against the Turks, but was defeated, because of the treason of voivode Dan, at Kosovo Polje.

It is obvious that the assertion: Hunyadi "overcame the opposition of the Hungarian nobility" gives a fundamentally false picture of János Hunyadi. He was **"the idol of the Hungarian middle nobility."**[3] He was a Hungarian leader and hero, whose main concern was to secure his country, Hungary, from the attacks of the Turks. The core of his army were always the Transylvanian Hungarian and Szekler soldiers. The Serbian historical songs call him *Szibinyányi Jánk* (in Hungarian spelling) or Johan the Szekler; and also the popular legends of Moldavia (Moldova) use this name. In the Arumanian historical songs he is called *Iencio Ungurul* (John the Hungarian) as well as *Iencio Secuiul* (John

---

[1] The data about János Hunyadi are taken mainly from *Erdély története* [The History of Transylvania], B. Jancsó, Cluj-Kolozsvár, 1931, pp. 75 – 80.

[2] B. Jancsó, *Erdély története* [The History of Transylvania], Cluj-Kolozsvár, 1931, p. 76.

[3] *Erdély rövid története* [A Short History of Transylvania], red. B. Köpeczi, Budapest, 1989, p. 201.

77

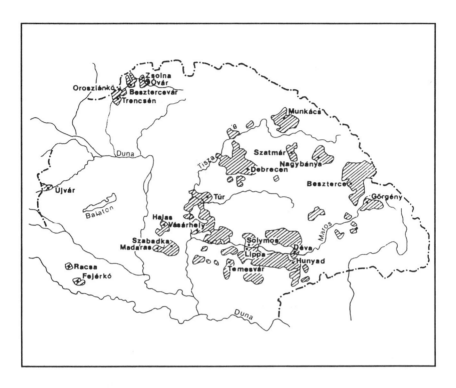

Map 8. – The estates of János Hunyadi in 1456. (From J. Held, "Hunyadi János pályája" [The Vocation of János Hunyadi], in *História* [History], Budapest, XV, 1, 1993, p. 14.)

the Szekler).[1]

He was also one of those Hungarian nobles who possessed the largest number of castles and estates. In 1446, his private possessions in Hungary amounted to 28 castles and fortresses, 57 towns, about one thousand villages and 2.354.000 hectares of land. Most of this was east of the river Tisza (Theiss) and in Transylvania[2] (see *map 8*). He used this enormous wealth to the maintenance of

---

[1] Jancsó, 1931, p. 77.

[2] *A történeti Erdély* [Historic Transylvania], red. Miklós Asztalos, Budapest, 1936, p. 212; J. Held, "Hunyadi János pályája"[The Vocation of János Hunyadi], *História*, (Budapest), XV,1, 1993, p. 14; Ştefan Pascu, *Voievodatul Transilvaniei*, vol. III, p. 57: map showing the estates of Hunyadi, after L. Elekes.

an army, providing a significant part of the material necessities in the fight against the Turks.

The description given by Pascu about the policy of János Hunyadi and the fight against the Turks in the 15th century (pp. 75 – 78) is extremely subjective. The presentation of Hunyadi as a Rumanian hero whose aim was to achieve a unity of Transylvania, Muntenia and Moldavia, is baseless and anachronistic. Pascu, p. 75:

> Under Iancu's leadership, a much closer unity was forged among the three Romanian countries, since he in fact controlled them.

p. 76: [about János Hunyadi's successfull fight against the Turks in 1456.]

> thanks to the support of the great masses of peasants, Romanian knezi, burghers, and petty nobles and to the fact that the clear object of the struggle was to defend and strengthen the cooperation among the peoples of southeastern Europe and the interrelations of the three Romanian lands.

The expression "the three Romanian lands", of which one is Transylvania, is often used by Pascu. This is wrong. Transylvania was in the period in question not a Rumanian land. It was not Rumanian, neither **legally**: it was part of the Hungarian kingdom and was ruled by lords chosen by the Hungarian kings; nor **historically**: as we have seen, before the 13th century, there is no evidence whatsoever of any Rumanian settlement there, and even from that century, only three Rumanian villages are known. It was not Rumanian as regards **its population**: this was mainly Hungarian (including the Szeklers) and German; the Rumanians were, although increasing in numbers, in the minority. If one asks when the number of the Rumanians reached that of the other nationalities together (i.e., 50% of the population), this was around the year 1700. However, this does not imply that the territory was then a "Rumanian land." Transylvania was and is also today, with a Rumanian majority, a territory in which different ethnic and linguistic groups are living, as in so many areas in southeastern Europe.

János Hunyadi controlled the voivodes of Muntenia and Moldavia, as did the Hungarian kings since they organized their territories in the 13th century, – they were in other words the vassals of the Hungarian king. These voivodes have, of course, wanted to become independent and had to balance between three powers: Hungary, Poland, and the expanding Turkish Empire. On many occasions, they fought together with the Turks against Hungary. In 1438, an army of Turks, Rumanians and Serbs attacked Transylvania across the Iron Gate, and their leader was Vlad Dracul, voivode of Muntenia. They plundered and devastated Szászsebes (Rumanian Orăştie), Gyulafehérvár (Alba Iulia) and Küküllővár

(Cetatea de Baltă) and left, according to contemporary sources, with 70.000 prisoners.[1] As mentioned above, p. 76, János Hunyadi was in 1444 put into prison by Vlad Dracul, and in 1448, the Turks won the battle at Kosovo Polje, to a large extent because of the treason of voivode Dan of Muntenia. At the beginning of the rule of king Mathias, Vlad Țepeș made a raid into the Barcaság (Rumanian Țara Bârsei), devastating also the suburbs of Brassó (Rumanian Brașov). He believed that the Saxons were hiding a pretender of his voivodate; it was on this occasion that he ordered a number of Saxons be impaled in front of a church, while he ate breakfast.[2] Pascu does not mention this, although the event is shown on the jacket illustration of his book: "Vlad the Impaler at breakfast, surrounded by spiked burghers. A Strasbourg woodcut of 1500."– Another cause of this incursion was probably that Țepeș wanted to punish the Saxon merchants of Sibiu and Brașov who did not respect his orders to restrict their trade in the peripheric marketplaces. The aim of this order was, of course, to protect the interests of the Muntenian merchants.[3]

Vlad Țepeș was destituted by the boyars surrounding him, because of his extreme cruelty, and his younger brother, Radu, was made voivode. Without any supporters, Țepeș was forced to flee. In the hope of getting help from king Mathias, he fled to Transylvania. However, voivode Ștefan of Moldavia obtained a letter written by Țepeș in Rășinari to the Turkish Sultan, saying that he would help him to occupy Transylvania if the Sultan put him back as voivode in Muntenia. Ștefan sent this letter to king Mathias, who then arrested Țepeș and kept him im prison for ten years.[4] According to Istoria României. Compendiu, 1974, p. 131, this letter was a forgery made by the Saxons, who wanted to revenge the incursion of Țepeș some years earlier. However, this textbook states that it was not only the nobles who were dissatisfied with Vlad Țepeș: "His too harsh methods have estranged also the masses, who hade hoped much from the voivode opposed to the boyars."

The characterization of Vlad Țepeș by a Rumanian textbook of history is not without interest:

A complex and contradictory personality, Vlad Țepeș has been denigrated by some because of his coarse character and not sufficiently balanced temper. Others have praised his heroism in defending the country and because of his efforts to put an order in a society in anarchy. These are beyond doubt merits which cannot be contested or underestimated, since his actions have delayed the establishment of Turkish domination

---

[1] Erdély rövid története [A Short History of Transylvania], red. B. Köpeczi, 1989, p. 200.

[2] Jancsó, 1931, p. 81.

[3] Istoria României. Compendiu [The History of Rumania. Compendium] red. Ștefan Pascu, 3rd edition, 1974, p. 131.

[4] Jancsó, 1931, pp. 83– 84.

over the Rumanian lands by more than three quarters of a century.[1]

It is relevant for the relations – as we have seen, by far as friendly as Pascu pretends – between Transylvania and the Rumanian voivodates, that at about the same time, the Moldavian voivode Ştefan plundered the county of Háromszék (Rumanian Trei Scaune). His aim was to force the prince of Transylvania to hand over voivode Petru Aron, whom Ştefan drove away.[2]

Pascu, p. 76:
> In 1479, the Transylvanian armies, led by the voivode Istvan Báthory and by Pavel Chinezul (Paul the Knez), count of Timişoara and a descendant of Romanian knezi, won a great victory at Cîmpul Piîuii [sic]. [3]

Pascu does not mention some important facts in this connection: The son of Vlad Ţepeş, Vlad Ţepeluş, joined a Turkish army and was fighting in this battle together with the Turks, against the Hungarian army led by István Báthori, and Pál Kinizsi, the prince of Temeşvár (Timişoara), called by Rumanian historians "Paul Chinezul".[4] Kinizsi's origin was of practically no significance in the period in which this man was living. On the other hand, the fact that a voivode of Muntenia fought on the side of the Turks against Transylvanian armies is of great significance. The princes of Muntenia and Moldavia fought for their own power, against the Turks, against Hungary, and – against one another.

In the late 14th and the early 15th century, both Poland and Hungary tried to get control over the estuary of the Danube. Without going into details of this

---

[1] *Istoria României. Compendiu,* [The History of Rumania. Compendium], M. Constantinescu, C. Daicoviciu, Ş. Pascu (red.), Bucharest, 1969, p. 160; in the 3rd edition (1974), red. by Ş. Pascu, p. 132.

[2] Jancsó, 1931, p. 81. – Without going into details, we quote here a description in a recent essay by H.-R. Patapievici, which gives a good idea about the conditions in those times: "According to Bolintineanu, 'the Rumanians are more cruel against each other than the Turks are against them'. This austere sentence generalizes something which only a few people know today, namely a similar observation attributed to Ştefan cel Mare [Stephen the Great] [..]. which says that 'the Muntenians are for us as are the Turks' (in a speech addressed to his people in Bistriţa, on 20 June, 1473). I don't think that this is a metaphor. The animosity between the Moldavians and the Muntenians is richly proved by both parts. Typical for the relations of Ştefan with the Rumanians on the other side of the Milcov [i.e., in Muntenia] are armed encroachment and plundering. Ştefan plunders the Rumanians with the same sentiments with which he robs the Szeklers, without making any 'patriotic' distinction between them." H.-R. Patapievici, *Politice,* Bucharest, 1996, p. 74.

[3] Right: Câmpul Pâinii, Hungarian Kenyérmező; at the river Mureş, near Orăştie (Hungarian Szászváros).

[4] *A történeti Erdély* [Historical Transylvania], red. M. Asztalos, 1936, pp. 215 and 219.

question, we quote only Şerban Papacostea about János Hunyadi: "After a series of Hungarian and Polish actions and counter-actions, Iancu de Hunedoara installs a Hungarian garrison in Chilia, securing thus what was the main aim of his actions in Moldavia"[1] The same author reveals (p. 908) in this connection also the fighting between the two Rumanian voivodates in the 15th century:

> In the place of Hungary, which was now occupied on other fronts, Ţara Românească comes to the scene with claims on Chilia, which led to fierce battles between those two Rumanian countries, until the Turks, in 1484, occupied the estuary of the Danube.

The expanding Turkish Empire caused great concern in 15th century Europe and efforts were made to throw back the Turks. At the same time, Catholic leaders endeavoured to unite the Eastern Orthodox Church with the Catholic Church. An agreement was reached in 1439 in Florence, where the union of the two Churches was proclaimed and the Catholic Powers promised military action against the Turks. Between 1440 and 1444, king Vladislav I reigned in both Hungary and Poland, and the two powers started an offensive against the Turks, in which the chief military leader was János Hunyadi. In the year 1443, the anti-Ottoman coalition won great victories, but in the following year, it was defeated at Varna, where also king Vladislav died.

János Hunyadi started then a new attack against the Turks, in alliance with the Albanian leader George of Castrioti (whose Turkish name was Skanderbeg), but they were defeated at Kosovo Polje in 1448.

János Hunyadi contributed substantially to the culture of Transylvania: the Catholic Cathedral of Gyulafehérvár (Rumanian Alba Iulia) had an addition built on, receiving its present day shape. Hunyadi built the churches in Magyarorbó, Szentimre, and Tövis (Rumanian Gârbău, Sântimbru, and Teiuş), and he financed much of two churches in Kolozsvár (Cluj).[2] All these were Catholic and, consequently, Hungarian or Saxon.

The description given by Pascu about the **Economic Development** (pp. 78–84) is largely adequate, but here too, as in discussing the development of the towns, one must add a clear indication about the nationality of those who introduced and practiced the trades. Of course, this aspect was of no great importance in the age in question, but it is not insignificant that the economic

---

[1] Şerban Papacostea, "Relaţiile internaţionale în răsăritul şi sud-estul Europei în secolele XIV–XV." [The International Relations in the East and South-East of Europe in the 14th–15th centuries], in: *Revista de Istorie*, Bucharest, 34, 5, (May, 1981), p. 908.

[2] Jancsó, 1931, pp. 79 - 80.

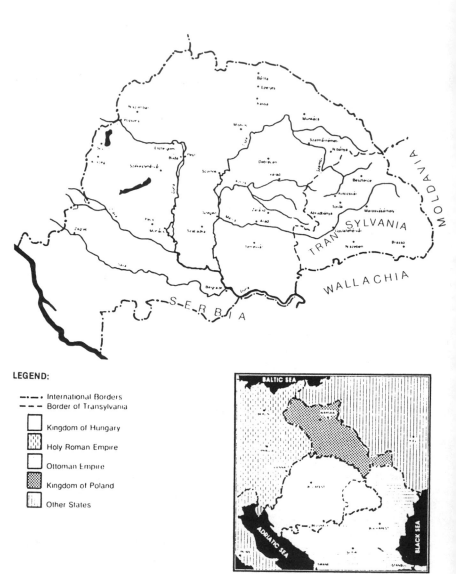

Map 9. – Hungary and Transylvania in the 15th century. (From: *Transylvania. The Roots of Ethnic Conflict*, ed. J.F. Cadzow, A. Ludanyi & L. J. Elteto, Kent State University Press, 1983, p. 39.

development in general was led by people who immigrated from Western Europe, particularly by Germans. The only hint at this in Pascu's text is the following, but even this is misleading:

> The workers were mostly local people, either freemen or serfs, though some were imported from Germany and Slovakia. Since the foreign workers had more experience, they were used for the more demanding tasks (p. 81).

All industry, commerce, even more developed viticulture – in general, all trades except agriculture and the raising of animals – were introduced into Transylvania by Germans (Saxons, later Swabians, Walloons, etc.).

Social Stratification (p. 84).

Pascu, p. 84 – 86:

> There was still a free Romanian peasantry as late as the fifteenth century, in Ţara Făgăraşului, Ţara Haţegului, Ţara Maramureşului, and the Banat...[...] At least two things explain the survival of these autonomous Romanian communities: first, the authorities' desire to involve the local population in defending the frontiers against Turkish assaults; and second, the close relations between the Transylvanian Romanians and the Romanians on the Muntenian and Moldavian slopes of the Carpathians.

As pointed out above, the Rumanians living in the above-mentioned areas were brought in by "the authorities" – i.e., the Hungarian kings, with the main aim to defend the frontiers, beginning with the second half of the 13th century. No organized Rumanian areas existed there before the 14th-15th centuries, as Pascu's expression "survive" would suggest.

These frontier districts were the first to be populated by Rumanians and are since that time the most purely Rumanian areas in Transylvania. One would believe that the names of these "*ţări*" are Rumanian. But are they? Pascu does not give any information about this question.

The name of the Banat derives from the designation of the territory between 1716 and 1778 in the Latin language: *Banatus Temesiensis* and this was borrowed by German, Hungarian, Serbian and Rumanian. *Făgăraş* derives from Hungarian *Fogaras*. The etymology from Rumanian *fag* "beech" has been proposed, but is not acceptable. The first mention is from 1291: *Fogros*. It was possibly a personal name; in any case, the original word in two syllables developed into a word with three syllables in Hungarian: *Fogaras*. This name was borrowed by the Rumanians: *Făgăraş*, and the Germans: *Fogarasch*. – *Haţeg* has no sense in Rumanian; it derives from Hungarian *Hátszeg*, in 1276/91: *Hatzak*. Hungarian *hát*: (approximately) "ridge of a hill" and *szeg* "corner, angle, nook". – *Maramureş:* from Hungarian *Máramaros,* which was originally the name of a small river: 1231/1397: *Maramors.* The etymology of this name is not

84

clear; it may be connected with Indoeuropean *mori "sea".[1]
Thus, not a single of those Rumanian *țări* has an original Rumanian name.

The origins of the names of "the more significant Rumanian districts" in the 14th century

However, a few names have no decisive significance, and the above mentioned names may happen by chance to be of Hungarian origin. For reliable conclusions, it is necessary to investigate a larger number of areas inhabited by Rumanians. We take the map facing p. 220 in *Voievodatul Transilvaniei*, vol. I: "The politico-administrative organization of Transylvania in the 14th century." It appears that no Rumanian villages of any significance existed in Central and Eastern Transylvania. In other areas, the map shows small, round patches of "the more significant Rumanian districts," of a diameter of about 10 kilometers or less. These are, from the North towards the South, shown in the following table:

Name of "Rumanian district"	First mentioned (year, name)	Actual Hungarian name	Etymology
Medieș	1271: villa Megyes	Aranyosmegyes	Hung. arany "golden" + meggy "morello"
Ardud	1216: Erdowd	Erdőd	Hung. erdő "forest"
Rodna	1235: Rodna	Radna	Sl. *ruda "or"
Crainimăt	1264: villa seu terra Querali	Királynémeti	Hung. király "king" német "German"
Chioar	1349: Kouray 1378: Kewar	Kővár	H. kő "stone" vár "castle"
Suplac	13th cent: Zeplac	Széplak	H. szép "beautiful" lak "home"

[1] These data were taken mainly from Suciu, vol. I,1967; and vol. II, 1968; and Lajos Kiss, *Földrajzi nevek etimológiai szótára* [Etymological Dictionary of Geographical names], Budapest, 1978. – These same sources were mainly used also for the names in the following presentation of Rumanian villages in the 14th century.

Valcău (today Văleni)	1213: villa Vulchoi 1291-94: Wolkou	Magyarvalkó	Czech vlkov "wolf"
Calata	1213/1550: Kalatha	Kalota	Sl. Kalota
Beiuş	1270: Belenjes	Belényes	H. bölény "bison"
Abrud	1271: terra Obruth	Abrudbánya	Abruttus? transmitted by Hungarian or Slavic
Izv. Crişului	1075: Crys	Körös	Ancient name, cf. Greek Krisos
Capâlna	(detached fr Ginta 1552)	Kápolna	Hung. kápolna "chapel"
Hălmagiu	1390: Halmag	Halmágy	Hung. halom "hill" ágy "valley"
Ciuci	1334: Chuch	Maroscsúcs	H. csúcs "top"
Ribiţa	1417: Ribiţa (Cyrillic letters)	Ribice	Sl. ribica "little fish"
Dobra	1387: Jwfiw	Jófő, Dobra	Sl. dobra, H. jó "good"
Deva	1269: Dewa	Déva	Hung. pers. name
Hunedoara	1265 Hungnod	Hunyad(vár)	" + vár "castle"
Haţeg	1276/91: Hatzak	Hátszeg	H. hát "ridge" szeg "angle, corner" (?)
Streiu	1453 Strigfalva	Zejkfalva	Sl.?
Amlaş	1309: Omlas	Omlás	Hung. omlás*
Comiat	1547: Komját	Komját	Czech komnata "room"

Lugoj	1334: sacerdos de Lucas	Lugos	Sl. lug "swamp, bog; grove"? personal name?
Caransebeş	1290: Karansebes	Karánsebes	Sl. pers. name + H. sebes "fast"
Sebeş	1245: Malembach 1300: Sebus	Szászsebes	H. szász "Saxon" + sebes "fast"
Bârzava	1471: Bozova	Berzova	Serb. brza "fast"
Caraşova	1333: Karasov	Krassóva	Old Turk. *qara suy "black water"
Almaj	1407: poss. Almas	(Nagy)almás	H. alma "apple"
Mehadia	1323: Myhald	(Mihályd)	Hung. pers. name + d
Iladia	1223: poss. regalis Elyad	Illyéd	H. pers. name + d

Table 2. – The origins of the names of the "more significant Rumanian districts" (Pascu) in Transylvania in the 14th century.
* Rum. Amlaş < Hungarian *omlás* "crumbling soil; eroding hill or mountain".

Out of these 30 names (mostly of villages), 16 (or 17) are of Hungarian origin, and 7 derive from Slavic; one contains a Slavic personal name and Hungarian *sebes*; one derives from Turkish. Two are ancient names handed down by Slavs, and the etymologies of three (or two) are uncertain. At least 21 were borrowed by Rumanian from Hungarian. Not a single of these 14th-century villages in which (also) Rumanians lived in that period and which later became the most characteristic Rumanian areas in Transylvania has an original Rumanian name.

The 10 Saxon territories given on this map (as also those given on a similar map in vol. III, p. 394) have German names, some of which were borrowed by the Rumanians; in other cases, they borrowed the Hungarian name.

The eight Szekler territories have all original, Hungarian names, of which five are on the map listed in their Rumanian form (borrowed from Hungarian) and three in their original, Hungarian form.

Although Pascu's map *(Voievodatul...,* I, facing p. 220) shows 30 "Rumanian districts" and only 10 Saxon and 8 Szekler territories, it clearly indicates the low

87

number of the Rumanians in the 14th century. The Saxons and the Szeklers lived in administrative organizations called *szék,* which included areas of different extension, with a number of villages and towns. What Pascu calls "districts" of the Rumanians were in reality mostly single villages. Rumanian districts were created from the 15th century on, around royal fortresses built along the southern frontier in Hátszeg (Rumanian Haṭeg), Krassó-Szörény (Rumanian Caraş-Severin) and Fogaras (Rumanian Făgăraş). It was king Ladislaus V in the mid-15th century who united the two first-mentioned territories into one administrative unit.[1]

Antifeudal Uprisings
Pascu, p. 93 (about the peasant revolt in 1437–1438):

> By this time the revolt involved large numbers of Romanian and Hungarian peasants from all over Transylvania...

Pascu gives the names of the leaders of the peasant revolt in Rumanian – in the English text: "Gheorghe Doja, a Szekler peasant" (in the 16th century), Pavel of Voivodeni, Anton the Great of Buda. This may be accepted, under the condition that it is made clear for the reader that these names were translated by the author and that all of them were Hungarian named Dózsa György, Vajdaházi Pál, Budai Nagy Antal. This lastmentioned name is translated in a misleading way; "the Great" used to be applied to strong leaders, political or military, but in this case Nagy (Hungarian *nagy* "big, great") was simply the family name of the person, a common name among Hungarians even today. The only Rumanian peasant leader was Mihail the Romanian from Vireag.

More important is the question of the numbers of Rumanians among the revolting peasants. The social circumstances suggest that the proportion of Rumanian peasants who took part in this uprising was less than their proportion in the entire territory: It is true that the Catholic Church was, in the 15th century, able to impose the tithe on those of Orthodox faith, as stated by Pascu on p. 89, but only in the case of those peasants who were living on the estates of the Church, and there were very few Rumanians among such peasants. Those of them who were settled on the estates of the nobles, did not pay the tenth but the *quadragesima* (1/40). Most of them lived in this time under the rule of their *cnez*es and voivods. Except those (few) who were living on the estates of the Church, the Rumanians had thus no reason to revolt against the nobility.[2]

---

[1] Jancsó, 1931, p. 88.

[2] Ibid., p. 71.

The peasantry was by king *Nagy Lajos* (Ludwig the Great) in 1365 taken from the rule of the officials of the king (*ispán*) and put under the nobles' jurisdiction. In the first decades of the following, 15th century, the nobles deprived the peasants from the right of free moving. Moreover, the Transylvanian bishop, George Lépes, was in those times in constant conflict with the Saxons and somewhat later also with the nobles because of the tenth. This was increased, and, moreover, Lépes required it to be paid in new money of a higher value. The payment of this was, because of increasing economic burdens and general poverty, but also as a consequence of Hussite ideas, denied by entire villages. The Church did not take into consideration the poverty but fought fiercely against Hussitism, giving harsh punishments. Many priests left their parishes; the Church authorities closed many churches and denied religious services. These were shortly the causes and the background of the revolts.

Lépes tried to force also the Saxons to pay a tax, but, being aware of their rights and privileges, they locked the doors of their towns and did not let in any tax-collector.

7. TURKISH SUZERAINTY (pp. 96 – 129)

Pascu, p. 101:

> ...the diet of this period represented the interests of the privileged classes and the high clergy. It excluded the common people, the Orthodox religion, and the most numerous group, the Romanians. Since the Romanian peasants were not one of the three constituent nations of the country, they were excluded from political life, and after 1437 they were doubly oppressed – socially and as an ethnic group – by the privileged nations. [...] But like the diet, these assemblies [of the Szekler and Saxon seats] included only the Szekler leaders and the Saxon elite. The peasantry was not represented and did not benefit from their acts.

As shown above, the Rumanians were not the most numerous group in that time. Not even in the following century were they more than about 280.000 = 29% out of an estimated total population of 950.000.

The passage quoted above contains a contradiction. On the one hand, it is stated that the diet excluded, among others, "the common people", and also in the Szekler and Saxon territories, the peasantry was shut out from sharing in the power. On the other hand, Pascu affirms that the Rumanians were "doubly oppressed – socially and as an ethnic group." The real situation is – something which logically follows also from Pascu's text – that the peasants were excluded from power, without regard to their nationality, Rumanians as well as Hungarians. In feudal society, this was the situation in Europe. This situation implied of course that – as stated also by Pascu, p. 87, – the Rumanian *cnez*-es and voivodes who became ennobled, in many cases also embraced Catholicism and married into noble Hungarian families, became part of the Hungarian nobility.

It is a general belief in contemporary Rumanian historiography that the *Unio Trium Nationum* at Kápolna (Rum. Căpâlna) in 1437 was a kind of a pact of the Hungarian, Szekler and Saxon nations against the Rumanians. This is wrong, because it does not take into account the political system of the period in question: **feudalism.** It was not the nationality but the social-economic situation of a man that decided his status. Feudalism was a kind of democracy of the nobles and based on the concept of subsidiarity. People with the same social status (the nobles) were equal and had equal rights. (In contrast, in the Rumanian voivodates, the boyards [the nobles] were the serfs of the voivod.) Those who did not belong to the nobility, the peasants etc. – without regard to their language or nationality – were not included in this system. It is very important to emphasize these historical facts because the concept of projecting the present circumstances back into the past, asserting anti-Rumanian contracts etc. where they did not exist, gives a totally false picture of history. In south-eastern Europe, this is not only the concern of historians or intellectuals in general but affects social life, also by generating hatred against the non-Rumanian folk groups, particularly the Hungarians, among the Rumanian public.

Michael the Brave
Pascu, p. 104:

> Uninterrupted cultural and economic links among the three Romanian countries; [...] ancient political ties, which had been strengthened in the face of the Turkish threat; and a common language, customs, and traditions meant that Romanians on both sides of the Carpathians were actively aware of their ethnic identity. It was this ethnic awareness that paved the way for Michael the Brave's attempt in 1599 – 1600 to unite Moldavia, Transylvania, and his own country under a single ruler.

Feudal society was very different from society in later periods and especially from that of the 20th century democracies. In South-Eastern Europe, the incursions of the Tartars and later the Turkish expansion caused an almost constant state of war. To this comes the fight between the central power (the state) and more or less powerful local leaders. The princes sent to Transylvania by the Hungarian king sought often to seize as much power in their hands as possible, and this was the case with practically all local potentates in the period in question in Europe. The ruling aristocracy, including the high clergy, strove for as much economic gain as possible. To this aim, they needed manpower and settled actively on their estates whoever they found. The nationality, language, and culture of the settlers did not count; it was the function they were expected to fullfill that decided the colonisations. Thus, the Vlach shepherds, who were willing to serve as frontier gards around royal fortresses were welcome, as well as the German and Walloon merchants and craftsmen, who settled in towns, and peasants who were acquainted with superior methods of agriculture. Although the Turkish menace was perceived as a common danger for all, and many successfull battles were fought against the Turkish army, especially in times of strong leaders, as János Hunyadi, the fight for power between the different voivodes went on almost constantly.

To throw some light on these questions, we give a survey of the circumstances about Michael the Brave's role in Transylvania.

To the background of Michael's occupation of Transylvania in 1599 belongs the weakness of government there during the reign of Sigismund and later of András Báthori and the absence of political leadership after the death of this last named prince; as well as the discontent of the Szeklers with the Báthori family. In 1562, they were deprived of their old freedom and rights. In 1595, they were promised to regain them after the successfull battles fought by Prince Sigismund Báthori in Muntenia, in which 20.000 Szekler soldiers played a decisive role. However, Báthori did not keep his promise and sent troops to the Szeklerland, who killed the Szekler leaders and devastated much of the country.

When Michael invaded Transylvania, he sent a message to the Szeklers, declaring that he was the representative of emperor Rudolf, and his aim was to expel voivode Endre Báthori. The major part of the Szeklers then revolted against their elite, expelling or killing some of them, and joined Michael in his camp at Bodza (Rumanian Buzău). Out of those 36.000 soldiers in Michael's army, one third were Szeklers. A smaller part of the Szeklers – those of Aranyosszék and Marosszék – joined the Transylvanian voivode Endre Báthori. The battle was fought near Hermannstadt (Rumanian Sibiu), at Schellenberg (Rumanian Şelimbăr) and ended with the victory of Michael, who then marched into Alba Iulia.

He summoned a diet, where he declared that he came to Transylvania on the mandate of king Rudolf, as his governor. The nobles proclaimed their loyalty to Rudolf and to his governor, Michael. Michael used in Transylvania the following signature on official documents: "Michael, voivode of Muntenia, the councillor of His Majesty the king and emperor, his Transylvanian governor, the military chief of his troops in Transylvania and the annexed territories".[1] His first decree introduced something entirely unknown before in Transylvania: the *Legământul lui Mihai* ("binding [to the earth] by Mihai"), which he earlier enacted in his own country, Muntenia. By this, also the Transylvanian Rumanian peasants became deprived of their right of free moving: every peasant shall be the *rumân*, i.e., the

---

[1] Jancsó, 1931, p. 121.

serf, of his lord for ever.[1]   Michael retained the political system of Transylvania (according to *Istoria României. Compendiu*, 1974, p. 160, "in order to assure the collaboration of the nobles"). Some boyars from Muntenia joined the diet and a lord from Muntenia became the councillor also of Transylvania. In *Istoria României. Compendiu*, 1974, p. 160, the following conclusion is drawn from this and some other measures of Michael, such as the giving away of estates in Transylvania to boyars from Muntenia, placing Rumanian boyars in the front of a number of fortresses and as judges in certain towns: "These are facts which illustrate the plans of political unification and of successively introducing a Rumanian administration in Transylvania".

Michael, who knew the Hungarian language fairly well, sent his proposals to the diet in Hungarian, and the diet made its resolutions, as before, in Hungarian. Michael wrote his letters to the Saxons, and discussed with the representatives of king Rudolf in Hungarian. Official documents were also under his time issued in Latin. The statement of Pascu: "Romanian was used in official acts in addition to Latin and Hungarian" (p.105) is not entirely wrong, although with the significant addition that documents pertaining to Transylvania were only issued in Latin or in Hugarian and never in Rumanian; this language was only used in documents regarding Muntenia.[2]   Michael did not show any sign of having the aim of liberating the Rumanians in Transylvania and this was not even expected of him. Even Rumanian historians have stated this fact:

> He could not reckon with any support from our peasants, who were bondsmen, although it is only upon such support that he had been able to build in Transylvania a durable Rumanian rule.[3]

In fact, even Pascu gives a hint on this:

> The social classes who had an interest in centralized power – the towndwellers and the peasants – had been neglected (p. 107).

The reign of Michael in Transylvania was too short and all conclusions regarding his aims for the future can only be hypothetical. However, the general

---

[1] "Michael abolished the free right of moving of the peasants, enacting that they shall be bound to the earth (1595 – 1596)." ... The peasants were transformed to "serfs whom it was possible to give away, to change, to sell, according to the interests of the boyars. This measure, which established that the peasant, 'who shall be *rumân* for ever, where he is', was, by its consequences, a serious blow for the peasantry. The movements provoked by the 'binding' have weakened Michael's power" (*Istoria României. Compendiu*, 1974, p. 159).

[2] Jancsó, 1931, p.122.

[3] Nicolae Iorga, *Istoria românilor* [The History of the Rumanians], p. 177, quoted by Jancsó, 1931, p. 122.

situation in Europe at that time was very different from that in the 19th century, with emerging national states. Also Pascu states (p. 107) that the boyars of Ţara Românească were opposed to the union of their voivodate with Transylvania (because they feared the growth of central power); and the Moldavian voivod was also unfriendly towards Michael. To this comes that Michael took no interest whatsoever in the Rumanian peasants of Transylvania, and also lacked their support. Thus, nothing remains of the idea of a kind of Great Rumania in 1600, based on the "unity of the Rumanian language and people," as it is claimed today. On the contrary, Mihai was a man of his own (feudal) age and his activity excludes the thought of a national hero who fights for the interests of the Rumanian people, the Rumanian nation, as it is defined today.

Pascu does not even mention the most thorough and scholarly study on Michael written by Petre Panaitescu (*Mihai Viteazul,* Bukarest, 1936). Panaitescu showed that Michael was supported by and came to power with the help of the boyars of Oltenia and consequently served **them** in the first place. He also emphasized Michael´s fight against the Turks. In Panaitescu´s opinion, Michael occupied Transylvania not because of a desire to create Great Romania but mainly for military reasons and in order to gain more power.

Pascu, p. 107:

> The union of the three Romanian countries under a single leadership was an achievement of enormous importance in the history of the Romanian people, since it marked the first time that the territories inhabited by Romanians formed a political and administrative unit.

The occupation of Transylvania by voivode Michael the Brave for one year, four centuries ago, has a significance today only for those politicians who need a historical confirmation, a historical anchorage for the present situation, when Transylvania belongs to Rumania.

Pascu, p. 107

Successors to Michael the Brave

The title of this section suggests a natural continuity from Michael the Brave to the following princes of Transylvania. It is necessary to point out that the princes of this country were Hungarians; Michael the Brave succeeded to seize power there for a very short time – one year – **he was not elected as a voivod;** the representatives of the three Transylvanian nations considered him only as the governor of Emperor Rudolf; it was only he who called himself voivod of Transylvania. The following princes had different aims and led very different policies.

93

Pascu, p. 108 (about prince Gabriel Bethlen, 1613 – 1629):
> Thus, he developed the idea of creating a Protestant Kingdom of Dacia incorporating Transylvania, Moldavia, and Ţara Românească. Bethlen sought support for his plan from Cyril Lukaris, the patriarch of Constantinople, whom he asked for help in converting the Romanians to Protestantism.

Neither in the correspondence of Bethlen, nor in the writings of Bethlen's chroniclers are there any traces of a plan about the forcible conversion of the Orthodox population to Protestantism. Pascu's above assertion serves a similar aim as his statements about Michael the Brave: to suggest that there was a tendency also from the Hungarian part to unite Transylvania, Muntenia and Moldavia in one single country. In the historical sources, there is no evidence of this. – The aims of Gabriel Bethlen may be summarized as follows: (1) he wanted to create prosperity in Transylvania by re-building and furthering its economy after the devastations by Michael and by the Austrian army that followed Michael's assasination some years earlier and (2) to strengthen the international status of the principality in the period of the religious wars.

Pascu writes only one and a half page about Gabriel Bethlen – one of the most significant princes of independent Transylvania – and two and a half pages about Michael the Brave. Even of this short text, a large part discusses Bethlen's preoccupation with Muntenia and Moldavia. Gabriel Bethlen took part in the thirty-years war on the side of the Protestant powers, against the Habsburgs. Bethlen strengthened the general European opinion of the age about Transylvania as the country of religious freedom, of the freedom of conscience, where everyone persecuted for his belief could find a refuge. Transylvania was under his reign a country of the same importance as any one of the western powers; Bethlen's court at Gyulafehérvár was similar to that of king Mathias in the second half of the 15th century. He succeeded to get the Saxons and the Szeklers to take part in strengthening of the central power (especially the Szeklers had to pay high taxes).[1] The Szeklers were his best soldiers. He was able to prevent the incorporation of Transylvania into the Turkish empire, as were Muntenia and Moldavia. Industry and commerce prospered and developed in the Saxon towns and also in agriculture, new methods were introduced. Bethlen's reign is characterized by law and general security. Bethlen also supported the Churches and founded a number of schools. It was also during the reign of Bethlen that the constitutional organization of Transylvania was entirely created. Thus, 12 counsellors were elected from the three accepted nations (the Hungarians, Szeklers and the Saxons), these were responsible to the parliament; in important matters, the prince was obliged to require the opinion of this council. The

---

[1]Jancsó, 1931, p. 146.

94

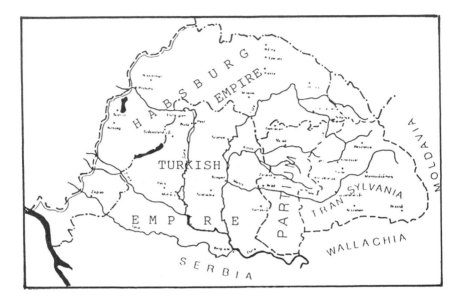

Map 10. – The Principality of Transylvania between Ottomans and Habsburgs, 1606. (From: *Transylvania. The Roots of Ethnic Conflict*, ed. Cadzow, Ludanyi, & Elteto, Kent State University Press, 1983, p. 88.)

Parliament was called each year by the prince. Laws were made in the Latin language until the year 1564; from 1565, in Hungarian. This language was also used in the debates. (The Saxons spoke German at their separate national meetings, but Hungarian in the debates.) Beside the prince and the state council, there was the chancellor, the president of the state council and the council of the prince.

The war led by Rákóczy György II against Poland was a disaster for Transylvania. Its army was defeated and almost totally annihilated; Tartar and Turkish troops invaded and devastated the country. As always in such situations, the Hungarian population suffered most, since they were mainly living in villages and towns in the valleys, while the majority of the Rumanians were quite safe in the regions of high mountains.

The consequence of the defeat was that "Ottoman rule was strengthened," as is also mentioned by Pascu (p. 112).

Pascu, p. 111:
>The new prince of Ţara Românească, Mihnea III, was meanwhile putting together a bold plan to bring back the time of Michael the Brave.

About Mihnea III, Giurescu gives the following account:

Mihnea III [...] is one of the most peculiar and interesting figures of our history; [...] he was a stranger – the chronics of the country call him"Greek usurer [money lender]", the son of Iane Surdul, but asserted to be related to the rulers of the country, the son of Radu Mihnea. As also Radu Mihnea, he lived among the Turks, but as soon as he came to power, he turned against them and made war, with the same result. He had qualities: he was a poet, a learned man, calligrapher, knew the Turkish, Arabic, Greek, Latin and Rumanian languages. He chose as a model Michael the Brave, and changed his name, in order to be similar to him; he used to say. "I, Michael Radu voivode". After the uprising against the Turks, he was forced to leave the throne; he died at Satu Mare in 1660. [1]

Pascu op 113.

The Renaissance and Reformation in Transylvania

Pascu does not mention that Zsuzsánna Lórántffy, the widow of György Rákóczy I, the ruler of the castle of Fogaras, founded 39 Rumanian elementary schools in Fogaras (Rum. Făgăraş) on the territory of her own estate. She also founded the high school in Sárospatak, which then became the third center (after Nagyenyed and Gyulafehérvár) of education in Transylvania. Comenius (Jan Amos Komenský), the Czech Humanist and pedagogue had taught there for some years, as well as in Gyulafehérvár.

The Latin school Pascu mentions on p. 115 at Cotnari was not founded by Johannes Sommer but by the Moldavian voivode Despot vodă (in 1562).[2]

Pascu, p. 114:

[The ideas of European renaissance] ...are to be found in the humanistic culture of the sixteenth and seventeenth centuries in Romanian territory in general and in Transylvania in particular. [...] The great humanistic scholar of Romanian origin, Nicolaus Olahus...

Transylvania was not, as pointed out above, a Rumanian country; Nicolaus Olahus was, although of Rumanian origin, a Hungarian humanist. The ideas of the renaissance in Transylvania were spread by Hungarian and Saxon educated men. A significant difference between Transylvania and the Rumanian countries Muntenia and Moldavia in this respect was that the Hungarians and the Saxons, who in the 16th and 17th centuries were in the majority, have adopted the ideas of the Reformation, while the Rumanians did not. *Oláh Miklós* (his name translated to Latin was *Nicolaus Olahus*), was the son of a family of Muntenian boyars, but born in Hermannstadt (Nagyszeben, Sibiu). He was educated to be

---

[1] C.C. Giurescu, D.C. Giurescu, *Istoria românilor din cele mai vechi timpuri pînă astăzi* [The History of the Rumanians from ancient times to the present], Bucharest, 1975, p. 437.

[2] Giurescu, 1975, p. 390.

96

a Catholic priest and became the archbishop of Esztergom (Hungary). He considered himself as a *Hungarus* (Hungarian); and in his writings, he showed himself to be a member of the Hungarian ruling class. His main themes were: the state of Hungary, the Hunnish king Attila, and king Mathias.[1]

Pascu, p. 117:
> Coresi [...] published some thirty-five books in Romanian and Slavonic to disseminate the Orthodox creed.

Pascu neglects here an important circumstance: a very important principle of the entire Reformation movement in Europe was that all peoples should have the opportunity to hear and to read the Gospel in their mother-tongue. It was in this spirit that Transylvanian Saxon and Hungarian learned men, nobles, and town officials founded printing offices in which religious books in Rumanian for the use of the Orthodox priests could be produced. They invited learned Rumanians (mostly to Brassó [Braşov, Kronstadt]) for the purpose of printing such texts. The first Rumanian book in print was the Lutheran Cathechism printed in Cyrillic letters (*Catehismul luteran*, 1544), translated on the initiative of Saxon Reformators. These reformators noticed that the language of the lithurgy in the Rumanian Orthodox churches was Ancient Slavonic, which not only the people but even many priests were unable to understand. This they considered to be an obstacle for the progress of general education among the Rumanian population. They wanted, therefore, to introduce the mother-tongue in the Rumanian Church as they did with German and Hungarian. The great reformator in Brassó was *Honterus,* who converted the town's Saxon population in a very short time from Catholicism to Lutheranism. It was the Saxon judge[2] Lukács Hirschel, who called deacon Coresi to Brassó and commissioned him to print, in the town's printing establishment, religious books in Rumanian. Also the Saxon mayor of Braşov, Hans Benkner (Johannes Benknerus), who had a paper industry, supported Coresi.[3] Coresi worked in Brassó, Bolgárszeg (Şcheii Braşovului, the Rumanian quarter of the town) for 23 years and printed 35 books. In that period, this was an exceptionally high achievement, made possible by the generous help given by the Saxons: they paid the manual workers necessary in the printing process, provided the stock of printing types, etc.

The Lutherans and the Calvinists (Saxons as well as Hungarians) wanted in

---

[1] *Erdély története* (The History of Transylvania), red. Béla Köpeczi, Budapest, 1986, II, p. 513.

[2] Jancsó, 1931, p. 104.

[3] Giurescu, 1975, p. 387.

general the printing of religious books in the Reformed spirit, but Coresi fullfilled these desires only partially.

A printing office was created in the 1640-s also in Gyulafehérvár, under the direct supervision of the prince, with the aim of publishing religious books in Rumanian. It functioned until 1689 and published three Calvinist Catechisms in the Rumanian language in 1640, 1644, and 1656.[1] Also books according to the Orthodox confession were printed there.

Coresi printed in 1559 *Întrebare creștinească* [Christian Question], in the spirit of the Reformation. Called *Catehismul Bîrseanu*, it is identical with the *Catehismul Marțian*, a manuscript translated in Máramaros (Maramureş). However, the majority of the books published by Coresi were in the Orthodox tradition. His language was that of northern Muntenia and Rumanian spoken in southern Transylvania.

Palia de la Orăştie (1582) was the work of 5 Rumanian scholars, who made the translation not from "the Jewish, Greek, and Serbian languages to Rumanian", as it is asserted in the preface, but from a Hungarian source, to which another, written in Latin, was added. The Hungarian model is *Pentateuchon* printed by Gáspár Heltai in 1551 in Kolozsvár (Cluj), and the Latin model is a corrected edition of the Vulgate, similar to that published in 1573 by Luca Osiander in Tübingen. In several cases, the use of a Slavonic model cannot be denied. The translation and the printing of this book was paid by the Hungarian baron Miklós Forró of Háporton.

"The translation of the Hungarian text was made *ad litteram*, the turns of the phrase and the order of words of the original were preserved."[2] There are also a large number of words, morphological and syntactical elements borrowed from Hungarian.

Most important were these texts for Rumanian culture: as stated for example by Giurescu, in them "the beginnings of our literary language" are to be found.[3]

The Hungarian and Saxon protestants wanted to spread Reformation among the Rumanians, but not by coercion. This appears from their policy of publishing religious books in Rumanian: as shown above, they did not prevent those in the Orthodox spirit. By the synod in Debrecen, it was determined that a dean was to be chosen among the Reformed Rumanians, who should supervise and see to it

---

[1] *Istoria literaturii române. Folclorul. Literatura română în epoca feuadală (1400 – 1780)* [The History of the Rumanian Literature. The Folklore. The Rumanian Literature in the Period of Feudalism], 2nd edition; red. A. Rosetti et al., Bucharest, 1970, p. 316.

[2] *Ibid.*, pp. 294 – 295.

[3] Giurescu, 1975, p. 387.

98

that the Rumanian Orthodox priests should convert out of conviction and not in order to attain freedom.

Pascu p. 115:

The Transylvanian population was more strongly affected [than by the ideas of Hussitism] by the teaching propounded by Martin Luther in the early sixteenth and by John Calvin in the mid-sixteenth century.

The Transylvanian population referred to here were Saxons and Hungarians; the Rumanians did not join the Reformation movement.[1]

The university founded in Kolozsvár (Cluj) in 1581 by the Jesuits was also a Hungarian institution, the predecessor of the Báthory-Apor Seminar.

Pascu, p. 118:

It is a great step from the Romanesque stone churches of the twelfth to the fourteenth centuries in Țara Hațegului to the Gothic churches of the fourteenth and fifteenth centuries in the cities of Transylvania.

This statement contains an obvious error and blurs the real situation as regards the building of churches in Transylvania. No Rumanian church is known from the 12th and most of the 13th century. In the 12th century, Catholic churches (Hungarian and Saxon) were built in Arad (1139), Kolozsvár, and Nagyszeben; but already a century earlier, in the 11th century, Catholic churches were built in Gyulafehérvár and Nagyvárad.[2]

The first Orthodox church is that in Demsuș (county of Hunyad): it was built in the last years of the 13th century. In the same period were the Orthodox churches in Hátszeg (Hațeg) and Hunyad (Hunedoara) built by Rumanian *cnez-es:* at Sînta Maria Orlea, Strei, Nucșoara, and Gurasada.[3] Thus, Orthodox churches started to be built about two centuries later than the Catholic churches. Also the churches built in the 14th to the 15th centuries, which Pascu mentions (p. 118), at Cluj, Brașov, Sibiu, Sebeș, and Sighișoara, were all Catholic. The first Orthodox churches in these cities were built much later: in Cluj – 1796, in

---

[1] An article in English about the Reformation movement in Transylvania may be read in *Transylvania. The Roots of Ethnic Conflict,* ed. J.F. Cadzow, A. Ludanyi & L. J. Eltetö, The Kent State University Press, 1983, pp. 61–70: "Reformation Literature and the National Consciousness of Transylvanian Hungarians, Saxons, and Rumanians", by Louis J. Elteto.

[2] Árpád Kosztin, *A Dákoromán legenda. Keresztény kultuszhelyek Erdélyben* [The legend of the Daco-Romans. Christian cult-places in Transylvania], Budapest, 1989, p. 74.

[3] Giurescu, 1975, p. 338–339.

Braşov – 1495; in Sibiu, a church was bought at the end of the 19th century.[1]

It is sometimes assumed that the Rumanians did erect churches earlier than in the late 13th century, but these were of wood and did not survive.[2] There is, however, no evidence of this neither in written sources nor in archeological finds. Also, one should remember that even in Muntenia and Moldavia, Orthodox churches were not being built before the 14th century.[3] In Muntenia, the monastery at Snagov, the voivode's church at Curtea de Argeş (Hungarian Argyas), were among the first ones to be built (in the 14th century); the bishop's cathedral at Buzău was built in 1500 on the territory of the former Catholic Cumanian bishopric of Milcov (Hungarian Milkó), the voivode's church at Piteşti in the 17th century. In Moldavia, the earliest Orthodox cult places are the monastery at Vînători-Neamţ, from 1375, and the church at Siret, from 1384.

Pascu, p. 120;

> [The representatives of late Humanism and early Enlightenment]... were desk-bound schoolroom humanists, no longer at the forefront of cultural change. Albert Szenczi Molnár, for example, though a learned linguist and notable poet, was not a fighter, but a scholar detached from the social disarray;...

Albert Szenczi Molnár was not "a scholar detached from the social disarray". He was an ardent preacher of the Reformation movement, an intellectual of great significance. He translated 150 David-psalms into Hungarian which gave the Rumanians the impetus to translate into Rumanian the Book of Psalms. He also translated the psalms of the French Huguenot poets, Theodore Bèze and Clément Marot. Szenczi was also the chief corrector of the Bible translation into Hungarian by Gáspár Károli; this translation became the basis of the Hungarian literary language. – Similarly, it may hardly be said about János Rimay that he was "contemplative and pessimistic."

Mihail Halici was, as Pascu writes, a notable poet – he was the first Rumanian to compose songs of love known today. He adhered to the Reformed religion and corresponded only with Hungarian Humanists. He wrote his songs in Rumanian, with a Hungarian spelling, for example: *Kénték dé drágoszté* (correctly : *Cântec de dragoste*).

Pascu, p. 121 (about folk poetry) :

The theme of Hungarian Clement the Mason *(Kőműves Kelemen)* and

---

[1] Kosztin, 1989, p. 74.

[2] Giurescu, 1975, p. 338.

[3] Kosztin, 1989, p.76.

Rumanian Master Manole *(Meşterul Manole)* is common, but it is a European wandering theme of folk poetry. That folk poetry played an important role in spreading the tradition of the people's struggle in Transylvania is an old Marxistic theory but has little substance.

Pascu, p. 122: **Social and Economic Developments**
p. 124:
> ...noblemen who had fled from territories occupied by the Turks and the Habsburgs settled in Transylvania. These newcomers, taking advantage of the political struggles that were dividing the principality, soon acquired large estates and filled powerful offices.

There were very few families of nobles in Hungary who did not have part of their estates and relatives in Transylvania or in the Partium. Thus, most of them did not acquire new estates but came to their own. In this context it is important to point out that many Rumanian families have, in Transylvania, received estates and were ennobled by the Hungarian kings. The earliest were the Drágffy-s (in Máramaros [Maramureş]) and the Jósika-s (in Karánsebes [Caransebeş]); then there are the families Moga, Nopcsa, etc; about Nikolaus Olahus, see above, pp. 95-96. The Rumanian origin of these families is known and acknowledged by Hungarian historiography, as is the Slovakian origin of the Draskovics-, Reviczky-, and Mednyánszky-families or the Croatian or Serbian origin of the Zrínyi-s, the Lazarevics-s and the Jaksics-s.

Pascu, p. 125:
> There were many causes for the impoverishment of the peasantry but exploitation by the feudal lords must certainly be counted as the most important.

The feudal exploitation of the peasants may be condemned today, in a democratic society. A historical approach to the problem, however, has to take into consideration the socio-economic situation in Europe in the period in question. Then it will be seen that the exploitation of the peasants was general; peasant uprisings occurred from time to time almost everywhere. In the Rumanian voivodates, the peasants were exploited in a much higher degree than in Hungary. A quotation from *Descriptio Moldaviae* by Dimitrie Cantemir (1673 – 1723) gives some idea about the degree of exploitation:

> [However] ... without regard to ethnicity, the peasants are obliged to work for their lords continually (*dominorum suorum operis assidue incumbere tenentur*); there is no given measure as regards how much they have to work (*nullus illis quo operentur modus dictus est*); it depends upon the lord to call him to work as many days as he wants. The lord is not supposed to take the money or the animals of the peasants and if a peasant finds a treasure of great value, the lord has no part of it; and if he should take it, he would be condemned by the court to give it back to him. If the lord, however, would want

to do an injustice, he beats him fiercely until he gives him spontaneously anything he wants.[1]

It was forbidden by law to kill a peasant. But the lord was permitted to sell a peasant within the village in which the peasant was born; only in case the lord had sold the entire farm, had he the right to sell a peasant outside his birthplace. In a note to this, the editors of the 1973 edition of Cantemir's work remark that this was not always so, there were cases of peasants having been sold also without a farm.

> The peasant pays as much tribute as the lord requires and this tribute is not defined or limited. (*Tributi tantum solvit, quantum exiderit princeps, nec ullus ei praescribitur modus vel terminus.*) – In one word, I would say that of all those wo are in the world who work in agriculture, the most miserable are the Moldavian peasants, if the richness of the soil did not help them out of poverty. [2]

As a comparison, in Transylvania, the *robota* (urbarial work for the landlord) was in the 17th century fixed to two days in one week.[3]

One of the main causes of this exceptionally bad situation of the peasantry was that the Rumanian principalities were degraded into Turkish pashalics. Thus, a similar misery prevailed in Muntenia. Turks appointed voivodes mainly from members of families of boyars, who intrigued against each other and paid increasing amounts of money to the Sultan and the high officials of his court in order to be chosen. This, and some other circumstances, such as foreign influence, resulted in very frequent changes of voivodes. Thus, for example, between 1521 and 1633, the number of voivodes in Muntenia was 32, none of whom reigned for more than 10 years, the mean having been 3½ years. This caused a severe discontinuity in all spheres of life: the high officials were to be changed at each change of the ruler, legal processes were re-opened, the gifts one voivode made to the boyars were to be re-inforced by his successor, as well as the ranks in society of the boyars. This state of affairs resulted of course in anarchy, especially when all these changes recurred each second or third year. "The Rumanian principalities were Turkish estates, which the Sultan, this careless and ignorant owner, auctioned in almost each year to the most predatory, thoughtless and ignorant lessees."[4]

---

[1] Dimitrie Cantemir, *Descriptio Moldaviae*, ed. Acad. RSR, Bucharest, 1973, p.298.

[2] Ibid., p. 300.

[3] *Istoria României. Compendiu*, 1969, p. 209.

[4] D. Drăghicescu, *Din psihologia poporului român* [On the Psychology of the Rumanian People], Bucharest [1907], Editura Albatros, 1996, p. 222.– Writing about history, Drăghicescu refers to 19th century Rumanian historians, particularly to A.D. Xenopol (1847-1920).

The tribute paid to the Turkish empire was, according to the treaty of submission during the reign of Mircea cel Bătrân (1386-1418) fixed to 3.000 ducats (*galben*-s), but increased enormously during the following centuries: for example, in the early 17th century, Moldova paid 58.000 ducats. But these yearly tributes were not the only way of extracting money from the Rumanian pashalics. Beside the regular tribute, several other payments increased their economic burdens in a much higher degree. The largest of these were the gifts, i.e., payments in money, gold, etc. made by the pretenders of the throne to the Turks. Thus, for example, Mihnea (voivode between 1577 and 1583 and 1585 and 1591) paid 600.000 ducats to the Sultan and 100.000 ducats to the *beg* (ruler) of Greece.   Many of the boyars in the Rumanian principalities were of non-Rumanian origin (especially Bulgarian, and also Greek), but even the Rumanian boyars despised the peasant, the *rumîn,* which was synonymous with slav. "A real abyss existed always between the boyars and the *rumîn*-s."[1] The moral decadence of the boyars made it easy for the Turkish empire to exploit the two principalities. After having given some examples, Drăghicescu concludes:

"The entire sad history of our nation is full of such cases of sellings [treacheries for money], treacheries, intrigues and discords by the boyars" (p. 236). "These plots and treacheries of the boyars continued throughout the 17th, the 18th, and part of the 19th century, leading to extreme degradation and humiliation of the country.." (p. 237). The relation between the Rumanian boyars and the peasants in these centuries is described by Drăghicescu as follows: "The deep distinction that always existed between the class of boyars and the peasantry is shown by the merciless persecutions, the methodical plunderings exercised by the boyars among the peasants. Having on their side the voivode and in their possession all the powers of the state, the boyars have in all times succeeded to secure that the necessities of the country, the payments, the tribute with all the inhuman taxes which the Turks squeezed out of the country, always fell only on the peasants. They have always evaded to contribute to these sacrifices" (p. 239).

The ruling class in Muntenia and Moldavia adopted the oriental life style of the Turkish lords: they had innumerable servants, they copied the oriental clothings, the idleness and carelessness, doing nothing else than lying on an ottoman and eating, drinking coffee and smoking a Turkish pipe 7 - 8 feet long.[2]

Although the history of Muntenia and Moldavia does not belong to the theme of this book, we considered it necessary to give some idea of the conditions in

---

[1]Drăghicescu, 1907 (1996), p. 231.

[2]Ibid., chapter VIII, pp. 258-275.

the Rumanian principalities, because the picture depicted by Pascu is embellished and wrong. Contrary to what Pascu pretends, it is obvious that the peasantry (Hungarian and Rumanian) lived under much better, more human conditions in independent Transylvania than beyond the Carpathians, in the Turkish pashalics.

8: TRANSYLVANIA UNDER THE HABSBURGS (pp. 130–149)

Pascu p. 131 –132:
(In the period in question, Transylvania was considerably larger than its historical territory; it included also several counties in Northern Hungary, with the towns Kassa, Munkács, Késmárk, Bártfa and Eperjes.)

The Austrian rule entailed in Transylvania a powerful counter-Reformation. The aim was to annihilate the vigorous Protestant atmosphere which characterized Transylvania at that time. Caraffa was called "the executioner of Eperjes". In the last few years of the 17th century, 40 Protestant priests were taken as galley-slaves;[1] a large number of Protestant churches and schools were confiscated. In spite of this persecution, areas with Reformed and Unitarian congregations survived in Transylvania. Least persecuted were the Lutherans, most of whom belonged to the Saxon population.

The Banat was under Turkish rule, between Hungary, Transylvania, Serbia and the Turkish empire, an area where large troops were moving in all directions and exposed to very severe devastation; most of its earlier inhabitants were killed or driven away. It was liberated from Turkish rule at the turn of the 17th century. As also mentioned by Pascu (p. 135), it was declared crown property. The *Neoacquistica Commissio* was a commission set up by the Austrian government to ensure the non-Hungarian majority in the Banat which would make it easier to govern it from Vienna. Thus, this territory was populated by settlers from Austria, Germany and some other Western European countries, (Pascu p. 141: "German, Italian, French, Spanish, and Bulgarian colonists were brought in to populate the region and given the most fertile land.") However, somewhat later, large groups of Rumanian refugees from Muntenia infiltrated the territory; the Austrian authorities were unable to send them back. The Hungarians were largely excluded from acquiring land there. It was during this time that the ethnic diversity of the Banat developed.

In the context of the religious turmoil, a very important fact should be

---

[1] They were after several years liberated by the Dutch admiral Michael Ruyter.

104

mentioned: **At the diet of Torda, in 1568, religious freedom – the freedom of conscience – was made law,** at the same time when fierce battles between the different religions were fought in Western Europe. Four confessions: Catholic, Lutheran, Calvinist, and Unitarian received legal guarantees to freely develop their faith (*received religion,* Latin: *recepta religio*). The Orthodox faith was not among these, it was, however, an *accepted religion (Latin: acceptata religio).* This meant that although the rights of those who adhered to this religion were not coded in law, they were *de facto* treated in the same way as the believers of the received religions. Thus, the distinction was mainly formal.

Pascu, p. 133:
> In the schools of Blaj, the center of the new Greek Catholic faith, generations of young people from all over Transylvania were educated without regard to differences of religion, as were many from Ţara Românească and Moldavia.

This is not correct. Students who wanted to study at this school were subject to a very severe procedure of selection. They were to have been ethnic Rumanians; all were originally Orthodox and were converted to Greek Catholicism. Those who aimed at becoming priests, were supposed to belong to the Basilite branch of Greek Catholicism. This was not required of those who wanted to become teachers. Blaj was a school of high standards; a very differentiated network of the Rumanian education was developed there. It is only natural that students from Muntenia and Moldavia were sent there, since in those principalities, teaching for cantor and teacher was going on only at some of the large monasteries.

Pascu, p. 134:
> Rákóczi called on nobles and commoners alike to join the struggle against the Habsburg rule, promising exemption from taxes and *robota* to those who responded.

Rákóczy did not promise such things.

The struggle, started by Ferenc Rákóczy II, was essentially the struggle of Hungarians against the Habsburgs; of course, many Slovaks, Ruthenians, and also a smaller number of Rumanians took part in it. Geographically, its centre was in Northern and North-Eastern Hungary. It had also some connections with social problems, but it was not, in the first place, a social movement. Thus, there is little substance in the assertion of Pascu: "The movement began to take on the appearance of a social rebellion..." (p. 134). Members of the petty nobility, as well as those who had lost their land and had become peasants, were now able to excel in battle; – and Rákóczy made many of them noble. Such a legendary figure was Tamás Esze. The Hungarians were organized in a society of estates, but these numerous acts of ennobling of individuals on the basis of military excellence show that this society was not rigid, there were many opportunities for people for social mobility.

The rebellion of the Szeklers at Madéfalva (Rumanian Madefalău, Cic-Matefalău, later changed to Siculeni) was put down by the Austrian army, as stated by Pascu (p. 138); a large number of Szeklers emigrated to Moldavia, where their descendants are still living.

9. THE DAWN OF THE MODERN ERA (pp. 150 – 181)

Pascu, p. 153:

> The "Transylvanian School" developed the ideas of the great seventeenth-century chroniclers from Moldavia and Ţara Românească, in particular those of Dimitrie Cantemir, a humanist and pre-Enlightenment scholar and prince of Moldavia. The representatives of the school focused their ideas and their scholarly and political work on the most important questions: the origin, continuity, and unity of the Romanian people. Their zealous defense of their cause occasionally led them to exaggerations – for example, they asserted that the Romanian people were of purely Roman origin, and the Romanian language purely Latin. Some of their ideas, however, were entirely correct, as they sought to demonstrate the continuity of the Daco-Roman people in Dacia, the ethnic unity of the Romanian people, and the Romanian people's right the their own national life. [...]
> The fruit of all scholarly work of the Transylvanian School was the foundation for the Romanian national movement.

This passage and particularly the last sentence shows how intimately ideas about the past were connected with politics. This was not unique for the Rumanian nation; in the 18th and the 19th centuries, when the nations in the modern sense of the word were born in Europe, historical theories laid down the fundaments of political action in many countries. In Rumania, the theses of the Transylvanian School have still in our days a very strong influence upon historical thinking. And still, there were great Rumanian scholars who noticed the risk of distorting the truth when political aims are pursued. Thus, Ovid Densusianu stated in the preface to his *Histoire de la langue roumaine,* 1901, (p. 26, ed. B. Cazacu et al., 1975) that patriotism will for a long time to come keep back the Rumanian researchers to seek and to tell the truth, although "the real patriot is not he who falsifies the facts and deceives himself". Also Iorgu Iordan remarked, in the context of research about the placenames, that those who see the placenames as testimonies in a cause of national interest, are disposed to see

106

such testimonies where they do not exist.[1]   One of the chief protagonists of the Transylvanian School was Petru Maior (1756–1812). His *History of the Origins of the Romanians in Dacia* was published in 1812 in the Hungarian capital Buda. Pascu reproduces the title page of this publication (p. 167), on which one may read (in Cyrillic letters) that it was written by "Petru Maior de Dicio-Sînmartin", i.e., Hungarian Dicső-Szentmárton. (This town in Transylvania was later renamed and its Rumanian name today is Târnăveni.)

Pascu p. 161:
...the uniform distribution throughout Transylvania, except for the Szekler seats, of villages inhabited by Romanians...

Besides the Szekler seats, including *Aranyosszék* (south of Kolozsvár [Cluj]), the population was predominantly non-Rumanian in many other areas; for example in the Saxon territory, with many purely Saxon villages; in Kalotaszeg, west of Kolozsvár (Cluj). Also in the Partium, and in the lowlands of Eastern Hungary, the overwhelming majority of the population was Hungarian.

Pascu, p. 168:
Many of the peasants who had left thought of returning, accompanied by Moldavian and Muntenian peasants. A few even seem to have put these thoughts into action.

There is no evidence in written texts, or in oral tradition, of connections between peasants in Transylvania and in Muntenia or Moldavia. This appears also from the cautious formulation by Pascu: "many ... have **thought of** returning"... but only "a few seem to have put these thoughts into action". The situation of the peasantry was also in this period much more difficult in Muntenia and Moldavia than in Transylvania.

As mentioned above, Dimitrie Cantemir described the severe exploitation of the peasants in Moldavia in the 17th century. Their situation became even worse in the 18th century. From *Istoria României în date* [The Chronological History of Rumania], Bucharest, 1971, we reproduce the following short statements:

1741, September – 1744, July. – The unbearable taxation policy practised by Mihai Racoviţă in Muntenia provokes the flight in masses of the population.
1746, March 1.– Constantin Mavrocordat, the high clergy and the boyars decide to liberate from serfdom the Rumâns who fled, if they return to the country.
August 5. – Constantin Mavorcodat abolishes *rumânia* (the binding to the earth); the serfs are liberated only as regards their person, the land remaining the property of the lords

---

[1]I. Iordan, *Nume de locuri româneşti în RPR* [Rumanian Placenames in the Peoples´ Republic of Rumania], Bucharest, 1952, vol. I, p. VII.

and the monasteries.[1]

Mavrocordat made a "Constitution" in 1741,

favourable to the boyars and the clergy; who were no longer obliged to pay taxes to the voivode. The numerous taxes paid by the peasants were concentrated in one, to be paid in money, in four parts. Statute labor was retained and extended to peasants who were settled by agricultural agreement at some estates ...[2]

The boyars of Ţara Românească and Moldavia, wishing to increase their incomes by all means, helped also by the Fanariots, have, in the 6th and 7th decades [of the 18th century] abolished the regulations of C. Mavrocordat, when these no longer served their interests, required of the peasants a much larger quantity of labour by the introduction of the *nart* (norm of daily work impossible to achieve under normal conditions). The result was the strengthening of discontent and intensification of the peasant and urban rebellions: flight within and outside the country, a large number of complaints to the voivode, refusal to work and refusing other obligations, the revolt of the poor population in Bucharest and Iaşi, helped by the peasantry living in the surroundings.[3]

The Fanariot period (from 1711 in Moldavia and from 1716 in Muntenia, until 1821), was the darkest period in the history of the Rumanians, in which the population was exposed to an extremely harsh exploitation. Greek merchants living in the quarter of Constantinople named Fanar paid large sums of money to the Turkish state in order to be named voivodes in Muntenia and Moldavia. Arriving in the voivodates, they imposed enormous taxes, which masses of peasants were simply unable to pay. Flight outside the country was in three main directions: from Moldavia to Russia, from Muntenia to the neighbouring areas of Bulgaria and Serbia, and to Transylvania and the Banat; this last mentioned area was the most important.[4] During the war in 1738, and after the expulsion of the Turkish troops, large numbers of Rumanian peasants fled to the Banat, who hid in the forests and the reeds. Later, they successively took many abandoned lands into possession. Most of them, however, cleaned new lands on which they initially were allowed by the landlord to live without any obligations. However, these lands were later made the property of the landlords and the Rumanians became their serfs. In the 1730-s, a count showed in the Banat only 25.000 people, mostly seminomadic Rumanians and Serbs. Between 1741 and 1744, during the reign of Mihail Racoviţa, about 15.000 Rumanian families

[1] *Istoria României în date* [The Chronological History of Rumania], ed. C.C. Giurescu, Bucharest,1971, p. 151–152.

[2] IR Compendiu, 1969, p. 241.

[3] Ibid., pp. 241–242.

[4] Jancsó, 1931, p. 212 – 213.

108

abandoned Muntenia, many of which settled in the Banat. Racoviţa was expelled by the Turks and followed by Constantin Mavrocordat, who continued the exploitation of the peasants; during his reign, the number of families paying taxes dropped from 146.000 to 35.000. The flight of the Rumanian peasants to the Banat continued and it was impossible to halt it, in spite of orders from Vienna. The result of the immigration in masses was that the number of the Rumanians in historical Transylvania increased from 250.000 in 1700 to 547.000 in 1761 and to 787.000 in 1784.[1]

D. Drăghicescu, in his book published in 1907 in Bucharest, writes about the life of the peasants in Muntenia and Moldavia in the 19th century:
"How were the peasants able to pay all these taxes? Very bitterly. There are still old men who can tell us what they saw in their early childhood. They have paid, because the magistrates, the agents and the farm hands of the age invented tortures and sufferings which could have served as examples even for the Spanish Inquisition. It is said that the servants of the landlords put large trunks of tree on the abdomen of those who could not pay their tributes so that they were suffocated; or that they hanged them in the smoke above the hearth, or they burned them and mutilated them with hot iron-chains. Constantin Golescu wrote around 1820: 'I assert that there were people, who, because they were unable to pay a certain amount of money, were hanged with their head downward in pigsties which then were put on fire'".[2]

Pascu, p. 164: **The Uprising of 1784**
pp. 169 – 170:
> The clear national consciousness is attested in numerous contemporary references to the rebels' intention of expelling the nobility from the country and replacing the foreign administration with a Romanian one.

Pascu makes efforts to show that the peasant uprising towards the end of the 18th century in Transylvania was a consciously Rumanian, national action. There are newspaper reports of Rumanians "thinking" of calling Muntenian peasants for help, people speak about plans to unite Transylvania with Muntenia, etc. That Horea would have said "I die for my nation" (Pascu, p. 170) is not probable – Horea had not the conscience of a nation (in the modern sense of the word) and may have used such words as *norod, neam,* or *popor* (old words for "people"). It is not plausible that Horea would have uttered a similar statement at all; this

---

[1] Jancsó, 1931, p. 213.

[2] Drăghicescu, [1907] 1996, p. 390. – Constantin Golescu (1777-1830) was the author of the first Rumanian narrative of a journey. He travelled in Western Europe and comapared in his narrative the conditions there with those in his own country, Muntenia.

was probably attributed to him by later authors.

Among the Rumanian peasants, the belief of a righteous, generous emperor was widespread; they believed that Joseph II has made laws to ameliorate their situation but the landlords did not keep them. Horea travelled to Vienna and received encouragement from Joseph II in 1784.

The concept of the nation in its modern sense **started to develop** in that period; *Istoria României. Compediu,* 1969 (p. 268), also eager to find a national character to the peasant revolt of 1785, gives the following account:

> **The struggle of the Transylvanian Rumanians for political rights**
> The social and at the same time national character of the revolt of Horea demonstrates the fact that the process of formation of the Rumanian nation was in progress, and, parallel with this, the transformation of ethnical conscience to national conscience.

The revolt led by Horea, Cloşca and Crişan was not a conscious, premeditated action. The peasants did not struggle for political rights but revolted against some concrete grievances. The centers of the revolt were the marketplaces. The holders of the right to have an inn interdicted the peasants to sell their own spirits. This was a severe blow for them, since the selling of spirits was one of their most important source of income; they naturally revolted. To this comes, that at the same time, an imperial clerk deprived the peasants of the area, the Transylvanian Alps (Munţii Apuseni) of their right to the forests. This was another important source of income for them, since they made and sold many kinds of vessels and other products of wood. The Orthodox priests and the leaders – Horea, Cloşca, and Crişan, – incited the people against the Hungarian landlords, and masses of furious peasants killed all men they encountered on the estates; the Orthodox priests baptized their wives and children according to the Orthodox faith; in other cases even women and children were killed. Several towns and villages were devastated.[1] The Orthodox priests baptized also those

---

[1] In 20th century Rumanian historiography, the extreme horror of this peasant rebellion is generally ignored or denied. However, in a book about Horea´s revolt published in 1884 in Bucharest (Nicolae Densuşianu, *Revoluţia lui Horea,* pp. 163-171), one may read: "In their fury, they [the peasants] did not spare the women nor the children of their lords, and they executed their feudal lords in the same way as they executed also those who did not possess any serfs. The revolution was not only against the nobles but against all Hungarians."
"In every place where the troops of peasants marched, nothing of the houses of the nobles remained but ashes or depressing ruins. Thus, the remains of this horrible war of extermination, although covered by the new ruins of the years 1848-49, are still extant in the county of Zărand."
(Quoted by Drăghicescu, [1907] 1996, p. 351.)

few Hungarian petty nobles who joined the rebellion, which caused that most of these left the movement. This is an early sign of the fact that the rise of the Rumanian national sentiment was in a high degree connected with the Orthodox Church.

As pointed out by Joseph Held,[1] the long-range consequences of the uprising were very serious. Those Rumanians who led the revolt – predominantly not peasants but Orthodox priests, village teachers and other intellectuals, whose number increased in the following decades – transferred their hatred to all Hungarians, regardless of class. This tradition was certainly an important factor in the 19th century, when the intolerant, chauvinistic attitude became dominant in Rumanian politics, defeating those who wanted cooperation and peaceful coexistence.

As an immediate consequence of this uprising, the emperor issued a document in August 22, 1785, by which he abolished the personal servitude and the binding to the earth of the peasants. These have received the right to marry according to their own wish, to study all kinds of trades and professions, as well as to dispose of their goods.[2]

About the *Supplex libellus Valachorum*

A Memorandum written by Rumanians living in Transylvania was presented to Emperor Leopold II in 1791.

Pascu, p. 178–179:

> Written by Iosif Meheşi, a high official at the Transylvanian Aulic Chancellary, in collaboration with the most learned Romanians of the time, it made several proposals for reforms. 1) That the Romanian nation should be restored to its rightful position next to the Hungarian, Szekler, and Saxon nations...

The writers of the *Supplex* defined the "nation" **in its modern (ethnical) sense;** for them, it comprised all Rumanian-speaking individuals. The Transylvanian diet was composed of representatives of the three "nations" of Transylvania – **according to the feudal definition:** the Hungarian nobles, the Szeklers, and the Saxons, not including the serfs. The *Supplex* did not take notice of the juridical status of Transylvania, which was based upon the *Diploma Leopoldinum* from 1691, revised in 1699 and 1701. This recognized the laws of St. Stephen and of all the following Hungarian kings, as well as the laws of in-

---

[1] Joseph Held, "The Horea-Cloşca Revolt of 1784-85: Some Observations", p. 93 – 107; in: *Transylvania. The Roots of Ethnic Conflict*, ed. J.F. Cadzow, A. Ludanyi, L.J. Elteto, The Kent State University Press, Kent, Ohio, 1983.

[2] *Istoria României. Compendiu*, 1969, p. 267.

dependent Transylvania. The *Supplex* may have been right in questioning the feudal order, pointing out its obsolence and demanding the same rights for all inhabitants – thus, for all serfs. But instead of this, it demanded privileges for all Rumanians. Therefore, the diet could only refer to the fact that the Hungarian serfs are in the same situation as the Rumanian serfs.[1]

The writers of the *Supplex* argued that the Rumanians were earlier one of the (feudal) nations, referring to a sentence in the treaty between the three nations and the peasants concluded at Bábolna in 1437. About one of the peasant leaders, Pál Vajdaházi, it is stated: *vexilifer Universitatis regnicolarum Hungarorum et Valachorum huius principatus Hungariae* (the standard-bearer of the universality of the Hungarian and Rumanian inhabitants in this province of Hungary). From this text, the authors of the *Supplex* drew the conclusion that before the treaty concluded in 1437, the Rumanians also were a Transylvanian nation, but were deprived of this by the treaty, which was concluded in order to oppress them.[2] This is, however, obviously a false reasoning: the word *universitas* refers also to the Hungarian serfs, who did not belong to the Hungarian feudal nation, they were also "outside the fortifications of the Constitution". *Universitas* in this document means the entirety of the peasants (all of the peasants) who concluded the contract with the nobility.[3] Also other sections of this treaty refer to the Rumanians always together with Hungarian serfs and never with Hungarian nobles.[4]

All this was clear for the diet and made the practical rejection of the *Supplex* natural; according to the laws of the feudal order.

The affirmed continuity in Transylvania of the Rumanians was the other argument for the demands included in the *Supplex*. The authors asserted that the *Gesta of Anonymus* proved that the Hungarians found a Rumanian population when they settled in Transylvania in the 10th century.[5] At that time, this problem was not yet solved; the necessary data to decide it were not yet collected. Today, we know that the theory of Roman – Rumanian continuity north of the lower Danube is false.[6]

---

[1] István Kocsis, *Történészek a kereszten* [Historians on the Crucifix], Budapest, 1994, p. 292.

[2] Benedek Jancsó, *Erdély története* [The History of Transylvania], Cluj-Kolozsvár, 1931, p. 71.

[3] Idem.

[4] Kocsis, 1994, p. 294 – 295.

[5] For a description, with the relevant passages in English translation and a critical discussion of Anonymus' text see Illyés, 2-nd edition 1992, pp. 11 – 32.

[6] Cf., in English: Du Nay, A., 1977, 1996; Illyés, F., 1988, second edition 1992; in Hungarian: Kosztin, Á., *A dákoromán legenda. Keresztény kultuszhelyek Erdélyben* [The Legend of the Daco-Romans. Christian Cult-places in Transylvania], 1989; Vékony, G., *Dákok, rómaiak, románok*

112

The third argument was the large number of the Rumanians in Transylvania – which was correct and frightened the Hungarian nobles.

Chapter 10.
NATIONAL CONSCIOUSNESS AND THE REVOLUTION OF 1848 (pp.182-208)

Prelude to the Revolution   p. 182 – 191.
Pascu p. 182:

> *Linguistic unity* is evident in the fact that Romanian has been a single language ever since it developed, in the seventh and eighth centuries, in the entire area inhabited by the Romanian people. It never had dialects in the strict sense of the word, but only slight local variations...

The 7th and 8th centuries belong to the period of Late Latin. New, Romance languages, different from Latin, appeared later, after about 800 A.D. Common Rumanian (*româna comună*) was quite unitary up to around 1000 A.D. After that period, two main dialects developed: 1. Northern Rumanian (Daco-Rumanian), with Istro-Rumanian, and 2. Arumanian, with Meglenitic. The cause of this must have been the separation of the speakers of Common Rumanian – a part wandered southward: the Arumanians, and another migrated towards the north-east: the Northern Rumanians. The sub-dialect of Northern Rumanian, Istro-Rumanian, is now spoken in a few villages on the Istrian peninsula. Pascu ignores the dialects and writes only about Northern Rumanian. It is this dialect which shows a remarkable unity, having only what may be called sub-dialects.[1]

Pascu's description of the prelude to the revolution, i.e., of the two decades before 1848 is one-sided; it refers almost exclusively to the development of the Rumanians' demand for more rights and, finally, the creation of an independent Rumanian state. But the revolution of 1848 in Europe was something else. The uprising in Paris in February 1848 (Pascu p. 191) started a series of uprisings throughout Europe. People wanted freedom from imperial suppression, etc.

The reformist movement started in Hungary in 1825, when emperor Franz I convoked the Hungarian diet and opened it with the following words: *Animi meo carissimi Hungari! Iuncti fuimus, iuncti sumus, et iuncti semper manebimus,*

[Dacians, Romans, Rumanians], Budapest, 1989.

[1]Du Nay 1996, pp. 119 - 131.

donec mors nos separabit.[1] These solemn words uttered by the emperor served to captivate the young Hungarian reformist generation.

The Hungarian count *István Széchenyi* wrote several books about the need of reform in most of the sectors of society: not only politics, but also economics and education needed thorough reforms, and Széchenyi showed the way of achieving this. He also offerred large amounts of money of his own for example to the establishment of the Hungarian Academy of Sciences, he took the initiative of building bridges across the Danube in Budapest, etc. His ideas were widely spread in Hungary; in Transylvania, Miklós Wesselényi worked in a similar way, followed by Ádám Kendeffy, János Bethlen, the teacher at Nagyenyed, Károly Szász, Dénes Kemény and others.[2]

These (mostly young) people were active at the county meetings – they had the right to speak in the county in which they possessed an estate, but in many cases, villages or private persons bestowed some land upon them, and in this way, they were able to extend their activities to larger areas (they were called "wandering patriots"). These people struggled not only to alleviate actual grievances but also and particularly for the abolition of serfdom and for agrarian reform, the union with Hungary and the replacement of German by Hungarian as the official language. They fought for the cause of the Constitution against absolutism and for the cause of the Hungarian nation. The absolutist state, represented by Metternich, tried to neutralize these activities; Metternich sent in 1833 baron Ferenc Wlassics to Kolozsvár (Cluj) as a plenipotential royal envoy. Some of the Transylvanian lords wanted to boycott Wlassics, but János Bethlen proposed to entertain contacts with him. The result was that Wlassics finally sent a memorandum to Vienna, in which he stated that the only way to secure peace in Transylvania was to keep the constitution and convoke the diet. He was therefore recalled by Vienna. A series of clashes between the Hungarian population and the representatives of the Emperor followed. Lastly, the diet was convoked in 1834. On this diet, the Liberal party and the Conservative party represented themselves; the debates were on the same high level as those on the diet at Pozsony (German Pressburg, Slovakian Bratislava).[3] However, the discussions in the diet were not, as in other democratic countries, made public. In order to amend this, Wesselényi published mimeographed news bulletins of them, but the authorities confiscated his printing office. In 1835, the diet was dissolved.

---

[1] My beloved Hungarians! We were united, we are united and we will remain always be united, until death will separate us.

[2] Jancsó, 1931, p. 248 - 249.

[3] Ibid., p. 252.

The Rumanian population did not take part in the politics of these times; they developed mainly education and culture. The Hungarian reformist movement had no counterpart among the Rumanians living in Transylvania.

Pascu, p. 182:
> Linguistic unity is evident in the fact that Romanian has been a single language ever since it developed...

Pascu, p. 183:
> It is therefore only natural that the Romanian people should also exhibit cultural unity, which is seen in popular songs, poetry, and tales and in educated lay and clerical writings...

Pascu, p. 184:
> Romania's territorial unity, a reality throughout the ages, should not be understood as some sort of geographic determinism.

1. The pretended linguistic unity of Rumanian was discussed above, p. 112.

2. The basis of a considerable degree of cultural unity was the Orthodox faith. The Reformation movement had no success among Rumanians and also the conversion to the Uniate Church, initiated in Transylvania by the Habsburgs, was of a limited significance.

Between the speakers of the southern dialects and those of Northern Rumanian, there is a great difference in culture since the history of these two branches of the Rumanians was quite different during the last millennium.

Within Northern Rumanian, those living in Transylvania as well as in Moldavia have their own, distinct characteristics, as also those living in Muntenia and Oltenia. It may be mentioned that in Moldavia and Muntenia, people from Transylvania were as late as in the 19th century called *Ungurean* and even the most typical Rumanian folk poem, the *Miorița,* designates the shepherds differently, according to their origin: *muntean, moldovean, ungurean* (those from Transylvania). In the course of history, Moldavia was exposed to influence also from Poland and Russia; Muntenia mainly from the Balkans. The Rumanians living in Transylvania, for centuries within the Hungarian state or independent Transylvania, and in more or less close contact with Hungarians and Saxons, show traces of the influence from these peoples. They also have passed over to their brethren living in the extra-Carpathian territories the considerable influence of the Hungarian language upon Northern Rumanian.

3. The voivodates of Muntenia and Moldavia united in 1859: the new country was then called the United Danubian Principalities. Its status as a kingdom was granted by the Congress of Berlin after the Russian-Turkish war in 1877-78. The political concept of "Rumania", the Rumanian kingdom, exists only from this date on, and consequently, one cannot talk about the "territorial unity of Rumania" before the end of the 1870's . Not even the notion of "Rumania" did

exist before the 19th century; it was, as also mentioned by Pascu (p. 189), first used some years before the 1848 revolution. From the 14th century on, voivodates existed, initially as vassals of the Hungarian kings: Ungro-Vlachia (Muntenia) and Moldavia (Moldova). These voivodates became later vassals of the Turkish Empire. One may assert the territorial unity of these voivodates.

The *geographical unity* of present day Rumania is a fiction. The Carpathian mountains were, during the centuries of Rumanian infiltration to Transylvania, no obstacle for the movements of the shepherd population, but today rather divide than unite the country. In the South, the Danube may be considered a natural border; the river Pruth in the East in a much lesser degree, and in the West, there is no natural frontier at all – the plains to the west of the Transylvanian Alps (Munţii Apuseni, in Hungarian: Erdélyi Érchegység) continue imperceptibly into the Great Hungarian plain.

4. *Economic unity* is also questionable in these circumstances. Trade was in most of the time primitive, barter was used; and while the two Rumanian voivodates had economic connections, such connections were in general more intense with their respective neighbours: with Russia, Poland, the Turkish Empire etc. Braşov was a center of trade not only between Transylvania and Muntenia but also between Transylvania and South-eastern Europe.

Pascu, p. 187:
> The unifying traits of the Romanian nation were clearly drawn, and it should not be surprising that the revolutions in the three Romanian countries in 1848 were very similar.

As pointed out above, Transylvania was not a Rumanian country. The revolutions in the **two** Rumanian countries, Moldavia and Muntenia, were similar, but the aims of the Rumanians in Transylvania were not the same as those of the Hungarians. The Hungarians in Transylvania fought for the same aims as those in Hungary – in fact, it was the same revolution. Idealistic elements predominated here, such as world freedom; it was the revolt of the common people against absolutism, people wanted more power to decide over their lives, etc. These ideas were widespread in Europe in that period. The Hungarians had to fight specifically against the Habsburg rule, for self-determination. In the decades preceding the 1848 revolution, two ways of thought struggled in Hungarian society. According to one, the Hungarians must modernize all aspects of life: develop science (the Hungarian Academy of Science was founded in this period), build up industry, modernize agriculture, build roads and bridges, etc. The chief protagonist of this opinion was count István Széchenyi. According to another view, the country should first liberate itself from the rule of the Habsburgs and then, all the above activities would be much easier. In the circumstances of the period, with revolutions in several European capitals, this last mentioned opinion won the support of the masses in Hungary. The leader of this battle was Lajos Kossuth.

The Hungarians had to struggle for centuries with the Habsburg kings and in this connection, a very important circumstance must be pointed out here: Hungary had an ancient feudal constitution: the *Aranybulla,* the Golden Bull [*bulla*] of Hungary, 1222, and Werbőczy's *Tripartitum.* (The English *Magna Charta* preceeded the *Aranybulla* only by eight years.) It contained the paragraph of entailment and that of resistance – the king was no absolute ruler but could only rule together with the nobility. On the basis of this ancient constitution, the Hungarians demanded that Hungary and Transylvania should not be treated as other territories within the Habsburg empire. The common king was considered a provisionary solution, until the right to elect a king was returned to the Hungarian feudal nation. The war waged by the Hungarians against the Habsburgs in 1848 – 49 showed to Vienna that this claim must be fulfilled, i.e., that the Habsburgs must come to terms with the Hungarians. This is the cause why the Hungarians (collectively) were often accused of defending an old system, opposing progress. The ideas which dominated almost the entire Europe of the period – abolition of absolutism, etc. – were represented in Muntenia and Moldavia by the Rumanian revolutionaries; in Transylvania, by the Hungarians. There, the Rumanians fought on the side of the absolutistic Habsburg empire against the revolutionary Hungarians. Thus, a more adequate description of the situation would be to say that the activity of the Transylvanian Rumanians in 1848 – 49 was very different from the revolutionary activity of those living in the two Rumanian countries.

Pascu, p. 191. **The revolution of 1848**
p. 191:

> Moreover, the Romanian serfs were further threatened by various decrees made by the Hungarian-dominated diet in 1842 and 1847. These called not only for the forced introduction of Hungarian in all Romanian schools and, after a certain time, in Romanian churches as well, but also further usurpations of peasant land and an increase in feudal-style obligations.

On the diet of 1842, a proposal for the extension of the use of Hungarian was made. It was directed against the central power and some old-fashioned elements of the feudal system; the aim was to replace Latin with Hungarian in the juridical system and other areas in which it has been used since centuries. There were also proposals that in a near future, the Orthodox priest-seminars should use Hungarian as the teaching language. However, after the protests of the Rumanians, as well as on the advise of several Hungarian liberals, these

proposals were not taken up in the definitive proposals, sent back to Vienna.[1]
Two decades later, Gheorghe Bariţiu, who was one of those Rumanian
intellectuals who took part in the debates, could write the following:

> [...] we should acknowledge, without regard to nationality, that the fight with the pen was
> justified [...] and natural, the fight of human nature for existence. Such chivalrous fights,
> mind against mind, will always, as long as the world exists, win their worthy value and
> award.[2]

Pascu p 192:

> In the three Romanian countries, the winds of freedom also were blowing. Events were
> discussed in large meetings and plans for the future were forged. This does not mean that
> the revolution was, as it were, borrowed. Rather it was expanded; internal conditions were
> primarily responsible for preparing the way, but there were certain outside influences.

Rregarding the revolution in Transylvania, Pascu gives an idealised picture
about the activity of the Rumanians. He does not mention that the people were
incited by a small number of Rumanian chauvinists: priests of the Orthodox
Church, and some intellectuals. These people fostered massive hatred against
all non-Rumanians, particularly against the Hungarians. The result was that
masses of uneducated peasants were indiscriminately massacring Hungarians,
killing women and children (for example in Abrudbánya [Abrud]), setting fire
onto entire villages and towns (for example Nagyenyed [Aiud] and Zalatna
[Zlatna]) (cf. Pascu p. 204). The Austrian army and the authorities killed also
Rumanians, but, as it also appears from what Pascu says, their victims may be
reckoned in dozens, while the Rumanians killed several thousands of Hungarians.

Thus, the Rumanians in Transylvania considered the 1848 revolution as a
new opportunity to attack the Hungarians. This **hostile attitude was not,
however, an inevitable necessity.** The historical records from the first decades
of the 19th century tell us about a friendly atmosphere between Rumanians and
Hungarians in Transylvania. Most of the Rumanian intellectuals followed with
sympathy the Hungarians' struggle for reforms; they read, in Rumanian as well

---

[1] One of the liberals, Dénes Kemény declared on the diet: "We do not want to compel the
Rumanian nation to use our language, but we want to make them possible to learn it, as the language
of state administration." *Beszédtár. Záradékul az 1841/2-ik országgyűlési Jegyzőkönyvhöz.* II.
Kolozsvár, 8. l. 1842. január 27-i ülés [Collection of Speeches. Additional Clause to the Protocol of
the Diet of 1841-1842. Kolozsvár, p. 8; session on January 27, 1842]. Quoted by *Erdély története*
[The History of Transylvania], red. B. Köpeczi, Budapest, 1986, III, p. 1300.

[2] G. Bariţ, "Limbile oficiale" [The Official Languages], *Gazeta de Transilvania*, 1860, Nr. 32;
quoted by *Erdély története*, red. Köpeczi, 1986, p. 1302.

118

as in Hungarian schools, the writings of Széchenyi, Wesselényi and other reformists.[1] Széchenyi gave economic help to the first Rumanian periodical. Many Rumanian intellectuals studied in Hungarian schools, learned the Hungarian language by their own will and also used it. In the late 1820-s, Hungarian was in vogue at the Blaj school, in spite of the fact that Latin was to be used in the schools. Also the Orthodox priests used extensively the Hungarian language. The extent of this is shown by Bogdan-Duică, a literary historian, who after the first World War wrote an article entitled "The Hungarisation of Blaj." [2]   G. Barițiu called this custom "the disease" (morbulu) of the Hungarian speech. It was usual that Rumanians – priests and laymen – wrote their letters to the bishop in Hungarian and many church protocols were written in Hungarian. It must be emphasized that all this happened without any external pressure. A century later, the fact that bishops corresponded with the government in Hungarian, was called "intellectual nullity" (nulitate intelectuală).

This situation changed gradually, beginning with the 1840s. Among the causes of this change, there is the fact that after the appearance of the weekly magazin *Gazeta de Transilvania*, created by Gheorghe Barițiu, Barițiu and later also other young Rumanian intellectuals, many of whom had attented German schools (Gheorghe Lazăr and others), get in close contact with the political leaders in Muntenia: Barbu Știrbei, later voivode, Eliade Rădulescu, Ioan Maiorescu, Ioan Cîmpineanu etc. From 1838 on, these leaders spent their summer holidays regularly at health-resorts in eastern Transylvania, together with local Rumanian intellectuals.[3]   They discussed all aspects of an anti-Hungarian policy both within and outside the Parliament. Mostly upon the influence of their Transylvanian brethren, many of whom also settled in the Rumanian kingdom, Cîmpineanu and others started an irredentist movement, whose aim was the unification of all Rumanians in a single, independent, Rumanian state. This movement gained then momentum and strength also in Transylvania. The resolution of the meeting at Blaj on May 15, 1848, (cf. Pascu p. 196 - 197) was brought about by the pressure from these irredentists and written in a way which was totally unacceptable by the Hungarians; it was intended as a provocation.

The Hungarians considered that they had the right to use their language instead of Latin and German in the entire Hungarian state. This was opposite to

[1] István Kocsis, *Történészek a kereszten. A magyar-román viszony elmérgesedésének története* [Historians on the Crucifix. The History of the Embittering of the Hungarian-Rumanian Relation], Budapest, 1994, p. 315.

[2] Ibid., p. 316.

[3] Ibid., p. 317.

the three hundred years old policy of the Habsburg government; Metternich used the different ethnic groups with the aim of fighting the use of Hungarian. In Transylvania, it was not difficult to make the German-speaking population of the Saxons allies in the struggle for German cultural supremacy in Eastern Europe.[1] Stephan Ludwig Roth published in 1842 the pamphlet *Der Sprachkampf in Siebenbürgen* in which he summarized the demands of the Saxons, giving a German character to Saxon politics. This was not new, because the Saxons have always had lively contacts with Germany and Vienna was a natural link in these contacts. In 1844, a juridical high school was opened in Hermannstadt (Nagyszeben, Sibiu). The professors of this institution taught in a German-Austrian and anti-Hungarian spirit. This academy played an important political role; it contributed significantly to the attitude of the Saxons: the majority of them turned against the revolution in 1848.

The Hungarians, particularly the Szeklers, wanted the union with Hungary, because in this way, a stronger country could oppose Vienna.[2] Also, the menace against both Hungarians and Saxons from the large number of Rumanians was pointed out. The Saxons were divided – in Kronstadt, they were for the union, but the other party, in Hermannstadt, which was against it, won. The Rumanians opposed the union, although not unanimously; the *Gazeta de Transilvania* argued that the union with Hungary made possible for the Rumanians of Transylvania to have closer contact with the Rumanians living in eastern Hungary.[3] It was Simion Bărnuţiu who, under the influence of the Saxons of Sibiu, turned the attitude of the Rumanians against the union with Hungary. (Bărnuţiu showed also later loyalty for the Habsburg dynasty.)

It is significant that on both sides, there were moderate personalities, who thought in wider aspects and realized that **peace between Rumanians and Hungarians was a historical necessity.** They considered that – even if they did not formulate it in this way – the two peoples are historically dependent upon each other, the result of objective circumstances. Cooperation could strengthen both peoples and make them richer, while hostility only weakens them. An early Rumanian transylvanism could have emerged; but, unfortunately, the adherents of the opposing concept, that of confrontation and striving for exclusive power for the Rumanians were stronger. Only the Viennese Camarilla realized the fact that a cooperation between Transylvanian Hungarians and Rumanians would be dangerous for Austria and acted accordingly.

---

[1] Jancsó, 1931, p. 258.

[2] Ibid., p. 263.

[3] Ibid., p. 265.

Pascu, p. 199:

> A large number of Hungarian and Saxon serfs mingled confidently with their Romanian
> counterparts at Blaj...

There were practically no Saxon serfs. The *Universitas Saxonum*, going back to the *Andreanum*, treated all Saxons as belonging to a political order. Also the number of Saxon peasants was very low, and these were mostly wine-growers. The overwhelming majority of the Saxons were town-dwellers and worked with the trades.

In the description of the development of Rumanian national consciousness, Pascu does not mention the influence from outside, which was very important, if not decisive, in this process. A very narrow social stratum introduced from above ideas which they received in several western countries.

The description of the 1848 revolution does not belong strictly to the theme of this book, but an important aspect should be mentioned. The most ardent fighters of self-defence and for independence from Austria were the Szeklers, especially in Háromszék, where furnaces and other factories were in a short time changed to produce guns, gunpowder and ammunition. This was led by Áron Gábor, who also directed his guns in battle (he died in a battle on July 2, 1849). In the face of the common danger, the nobles, the free soldiers, and the bondsmen (who were promised liberation) decided to act together. They also explained to the Saxon and Rumanian populations living in south-eastern Transylvania that they did not want to fight them; to the contrary, all nationalities shall be freee and equal. The Szekler regiments fought many successful battles against heavy odds.

11. AFTER THE REVOLUTION (pp. 209 – 226)

The revenge by Vienna hit the Hungarians hard. Seventy-two officers were condemned to death, as well as 25 civilians. These were, however, not executed but put into jail, with 64 other civilians, for long terms.[1] The Szeklers were punished most severely and collectively, because their resistence delayed considerably the occupation of Transylvania by the Austrian army. The Saxon Franz Salmen and the Rumanian bishop Andrei Şaguna, on the other hand, received medals for their help in defeating the revolution.

General taxation was introduced, with many new taxes. But the presence of

---

[1] B. Köpeczi, red., *Erdély rövid története* [A Short History of Transylvania], 1989, p. 465.

the large army in the country caused also great damage and much suffering to the population. German was systematically introduced into the administration down to the village level.[1] Cultural control was introduced: newspapers could appear only with the authorization by the chief police of the Empire and the permission of the authorities was necessary even for theatre pieces to be performed, etc.

The Saxon autonomy, however, did not fit into the centralized state that Vienna planned to create; the Saxon seats were reorganized into counties in such a way that several Rumanian areas were attached to them and at the same time, some areas inhabited by Saxons were put to counties inhabited mostly by Rumanians. This was another expression of the divisive policy of the Habsburg government.

The Rumanian army units were dissolved. Rumanian clerks were sought but in the beginning, they were few; in 1860, only at most 300 sufficiently educated Rumanian civil servants existed in Transylvania.

The Hungarians were those who had suffered most in the post-revolutionary period. Immediately afterwards, two thirds of the Hungarians of Transylvania were either conscripted as common soldiers into the imperial army, were in jail or had emigrated. The liberal petty nobility was passive, and the urban population and the peasants followed their example. This was true also of the Rumanian public functionaries in areas where both Hungarians and Rumanians lived side by side. (A characteristic region in this respect was the county *Beszterce-Naszód [Bistriţa-Năsăud]*). Many Hungarians believed that a new revolution will liberate the country, and such plans were really forged: the Makk (a former colonel) – Horváth – Gál (the government commissioner of the county Háromszék in 1848) conspiracy against Austrian rule in 1851. The authorities discovered it and the conspirators were executed.

During the revolution of 1848, the serfs were liberated, and 70 – 80% of the peasants became owners of a small or medium-sized land plot. It is true that several landlords tried to get back some parts, particularly forests, but this did not change the general trend: the situation of the peasants became much better.[2] It is estimated that in Transylvania and in the Partium, 78% of the serfs were liberated with compensation given to the landlords by the state. There were totally 974.846 people, who have received 921.430 hectares (2.295.500 English acres), the majority of all arable land. **80% of this land became the property of Rumanian peasants.** (5.158 landowners received from the state 38,348.748

---

[1] Jancsó, 1931, p. 304.

[2] Köpeczi, 1989, p. 473.

122

Florins as compensation,[1] but the economic situation of the landlords after the defeat of the revolution was so bad, that a large part of this money was used to pay debts.) The proportion of those peasants who were themselves obliged to compensate the landlord was much higher in the Szekler land.[2]

The Charter of October (1860) reconstructed the local autonomy. The empire was centralized. The counties of Năsăud and Făgăraş had Rumanian administrations, and two other counties had Rumanian Lord Lieutenants. For the first time in history, Rumanians were permitted to reach a leading position in the Saxon "Kings territory" (although there were only four of them at this time). There, the Gubernium, where Hungarians played an important role, helped the Rumanians.

Pascu 211:
> In the overwhelming majority of cases, however, the amount of land owned was totally inadequate to support a family.

This is not a correct description of the situation.

A radical change in the life of the Rumanians living in Transylvania occurred in 1848, with the liberation of the serfs. It was the middle nobility who forced this reform, which thus was realized in Transylvania earlier than in Russia (1861) and in Moldavia and Muntenia (1864). As stated for example by Petre Suciu:[3] after 1848, "the economic situation of the Transylvanian peasantry was tolerable, in certain areas even prosperous." The political setting contributed to this: in cases of dispute, the Austrian authorities judged regularly against the Hungarian middle nobility and in favour of the Rumanians, because they were on the Austrian side during the revolution.

---

[1] Jancsó, 1931, p. 316.

[2] Köpeczi (red.), 1989, p. 474.

[3] Petre Suciu, *Probleme ardelene* [Transylvanian Problems], Cluj, 1924, p. 37; quoted by S. Bíró, *Kisebbségben és többségben. Románok és magyarok (1867 - 1940)*, [In the Minority and in the Majority. Rumanians and Hungarians /1867 - 1940/], Bern, 1989, p. 9. – Sándor Bíró (1907-1975) studied theology and general history at Cluj University and at the Sorbonne in Paris. In 1942, he received *summa cum laude* a doctor´s degree in East-European history at Budapest University, where he in 1948 became a private docent; he worked for several years there as an assistant lecturer. His main area of interest was the situation of the Hungarian folk group in Great Rumania. Born in Transylvania and living there until the age of 38, he had personal experience of this. The work we refer to – his main achievement – is based on a thorough study of the laws and regulations of the state, as well as pertinent Hungarian and Rumanian literature and newspapers. It could not be published in Communist Hungary.– We use the first part; the second part, regarding the period between 1918 and 1940, does not belong to the theme of the present book, but it should be mentioned as one of the best accounts of the situation of the oppressed Hungarian folk group in Great Rumania.

In certain territories, the Rumanians were able to build up, in one or two decades, rich farms: around Arad, in the areas of the former frontier guards (these were dissolved in 1851); around Brassó and Nagyszeben. The situation in northern Transylvania was worse because, among other things, there were more big estates there. But even there, the Austrian authorities helped much more the Rumanian peasants than the Hungarians in *Kalotaszeg* or the Szeklers, because of the above mentioned reasons.

According to Ioan Slavici (Rumanian author,1848–1925), the Rumanian peasantry was quite strong at the time of the creation of the monarchy. They did not bother much about politics but were mainly interested in acquiring more land and a better living standard. It was essentially the same for them whether Transylvania remained autonomous or united with Hungary.[1]

On pp. 220 – 221, Pascu describes the Transylvanian diet in Sibiu in 1863. This diet cannot be considered as a Parliament of the Transylvanian Rumanians. It was rather a means for the goverment in Vienna in its endevour to get information about how the nationalities would relate to certain parts of a possible agreement with the Hungarians.

Pascu talks about the autonomy of Transylvania in the period in question in categorical imperative. This is not correct, since Vienna ruled over the country directly, but considered it tacitly as a region belonging to Hungary. This is shown by such measures as the integration of the system of the counties in Hungary to that of the Transylvanian system, and the transformation of the Szekler seats into counties. With the agreement of 1867, Vienna accepted the union with Hungary.

By elevating the Transylvanian Orthodox bishopric to an archbishopric, the Hungarians contributed to the detachment of the Rumanians from the Serbian Church, and helped the creation of an autocephal, Rumanian Orthodox Church.

The period between 1870 and the beginning of the 20th century was very prosperous for the Rumanians. Economy developed, many Rumanians gained their fortune during this time.

Pascu, p. 211:
> Emigrants were especially attracted to Moldavia and Ţara Românească, where living conditions were better. In 1870, of 16.458 passports issued in Transylvania, 15.867 were for those areas and only 591 for other countries. In any case, most left illegally, without passports. In 1862, roughly 10.000 Szeklers emigrated to Moldavia and Ţara Românească from the seats of Ciuc and Trei Scaune in southern Transylvania alone.

---

[1] Ion Slavici, *Politica naţională română* [The Rumanian National Politics], Bucharest, 1915, p. 27; quoted by Bíró, 1989, p. 11.

The number of passports issued is not the same as the number of emigrants. This appears also from the sentence, referring to the Szeklers, where Pascu uses the word "emigrate": these Szeklers did really emigrate. Passports were in that time issued without any difficulty; one did not even need to explain the reason of asking for a passport.

The Szeklers fought most ardently for the revolution and were punished by Vienna in several ways. Thus, they did not receive the right to use the forests in the territory of the Szekler frontier guards – which the emperor gave to the Rumanians in the Banat and in Năsăud county. A large part of the Szekler territory lacked industry and also a railway, which was one of the reasons that the realization of the forests was more difficult there. The poorest among the Szeklers did not have wood and had no pastures, which was the cause of the emigration of many Szeklers.[1]

The situation of the great forests is interesting. After 1867, the Hungarian government could have made the vast forests in the territory of the former frontier guards state-owned, since most of the forests in Naszód (Năsăud) were, in 1861, declared to belong to the state of Austria. However, after the representatives of the local Rumanians asked to resolve the issue in favour of them, the Hungarian government declared, in 1872, its resignation from these forests in favour of the Rumanian school-establishment.[2] This made possible the building of the Rumanian grammar-school in Naszód, in which the well-known Rumanian poet Gheorghe Coșbuc (1866 - 1918), and the writer Liviu Rebreanu (1885 - 1944) were educated.

The difference between the policy of liberal Hungary and that of the Rumanian state after 1919

The Private Properties of the Szeklers in Ciuc (*Csíki Magánjavak*) were created in the same time as those of the Rumanians in Naszód and Karánsebes and were by the Hungarian state after 1861 handled in the same way. However, the Rumanian state, after 1919, was not as magnanimous as the Hungarians were. According to the law in 1921, the properties of the Rumanians around Naszód (Năsăud) were **not** nationalized and this was later extended also to the properties around Karánsebes (Caransebeș). At the same time, of the Private Properties of the Szeklers in Ciuc, 27.000 *hold* (15.390 hectares) of forests and pastures were confiscated. The directors of the Private Properties appealed against this totally illegal decision, but the state ruled, in 1923, that **all** these lands be confiscated. The explanation given was that the Szeklers had not

---

[1] Bíró, 1989, p. 11 and 14.

[2] Ibid., pp. 12 – 13.

owned these lands but used them only by usufructuary right which they, moreover, had lost by their "unfaithful revolt" in 1848 (!). The lands were thus the property of the Hungarian state after 1861 and the Rumanian state being the legal successor of Hungary, owns them today. – This outrageous infringement of lawful rights was first brought to the Rumanian Parliament but without any result. It was lastly brought to the United Nations, where the right of the Szeklers, after several years, was recognized. In spite of this, the Rumanian state did not give back the lands to their legal owners, the Szekler peasants.[1]

In 1884, a Rumanian priest wrote in the *Tribuna* that the Hungarian peasants in the central area, *Mezőség (Câmpia Transilvaniei)* were very poor, and the Rumanian peasants often gave them help to live from one day to the other.[2] In the mountains of Maramureş, however, the Rumanians too were poor, although many of them were able to supplement their revenue by grazing sheep.

In 1872, the bank *Albina* was created, with the aim to help Rumanian peasants to buy land. In the following two decades, another 50 Rumanian banks were founded. They worked according to national principles, i.e., they furthered the economy – especially by bying land – of the Rumanians by lending money at a very low interest. According to Slavici, "the land owned by Rumanians in the kingdom of Hungary was ten times as much in 1900 as in 1850."[3] They also gave financial assistance to the Rumanian irredentist associations *Astra* and, later, the *Liga Culturală Românească*.

The Austro-Hungarian Central Bank, as well as a number of banks in Budapest supported the Rumanian banks with granting loans at "prime rate", which enabled these institutions to offer low cost loans to Rumanian peasants. If these banks had not done this, – for example because of national prejudice or anti-Rumanian sentiments, – the Rumanian banks would have become incapacitated. The credits given to Rumanian banks were often twice as high as their entire capital.[4]

Towards the end of the century, buying of land by Rumanian peasants weakened and a number of farms were declared bankrupt. But this was not caused by the policy of the Hungarian government. According to Suciu:

Many well organized farms disappeared mostly because of two sins: alcoholism and

---

[1] Bíró, 1989, pp. 312-314.

[2] *Tribuna* (Sibiu), January 18-30, 1885 [Nr. 14], quoted by Bíró, 1989, p.16.

[3] Ion Slavici, *Românii din Ardeal* [The Rumanians of Transylvania], Bucharest, 1910, p. 32; quoted by Bíró, 1989, p. 17.

[4] Bíró, 1989, pp. 39 – 40.

126

senseless squandering. These and many other sins, but particularly the lack of rational management have deeply and ruthlessly undermined the basis of our farms.[1]

Similar statements may be read in a booklet written about the causes of the phenomenon. In this booklet, however, as in many others, the Rumanian authors also used antisemitic agitation, asserting that the Jewish innkeepers cheated the Rumanian peasants and took their goods, etc.[2] In the second half of the 19th century, such agitation was very frequent in the Rumanian press; often connected with an appeal to boycott the Jewish merchants and innkeepers. In the above mentioned booklet, this is summarized as follows: "Beware of the Jewish swindlers and of the foreign banks." In this kind of chauvinistic propaganda, the Rumanians were said to be "the only really honest" people.

In the first decade of the 20th century, the buying of land by the Rumanian peasantry, with the efficient financial help of the Rumanian banks, increased. The old Hungarian estates disappeared successively. According to a study made in 1913, out of those 16 counties of Transylvania, the Rumanian peasants bought most land in 14 of them.[3]

All this would not have been possible without the total indifference of the Hungarian state. It did not raise any obstacle in the way of free buying of land. Moreover, it helped effectively the peasantry in increasing their knowledge, in order to achieve better farming results. The economic committees in the counties were ordered to instruct the peasants in modern ways of management; and in areas of the nationalities, this instruction was to be given in the language of the respective nationality. The state also provided free animals of high quality, fruit-trees, etc. to individuals, societies and villages. According to a list from 1910, six counties, most of them with a Rumanian majority, received in that year animals worth 407.834 crowns. In a Rumanian book about the annexed territories of Hungary, published in 1920, it is stated that "During the last ten years, the breeding of cattle showed considerable progress, not so much quantitatively but as regards quality. One may say that the value of the animals rose by 50%."[4]

---

[1] Suciu, *Probleme ardelene*, [Transylvanian problems], 37; quoted by Bíró, 1989, p. 17.

[2] *Cărţile săteanului român*. Cluj – Gherla, 1903; "Păcatele noastre" de Petre Suciu, p. 15 – 16. [The books of the Rumanian village inhabitant. "Our sins", by Petre Suciu, p. 15 – 16] quoted by Bíró, 1989, p. 18.

[3] Bíró, 1989, p. 19 – 20.

[4] Ion Enescu & Iuliu Enescu, *Ardealul, Banatul, Crişana şi Maramureşul din punct de vedere agricol, cultural şi economic* [Transylvania, the Banat, Crişana, and Maramureş, from the agricultural, cultural, and economical viewpoints], Bucharest, 1920, p. 70 – 74; quoted by Bíró, 1989, p. 23.

127

The picture of the Hungarian landlord invariably as an usurper and exploiter, given by Pascu, does not correspond to reality. There were many landlords who helped the Rumanian peasants more than Rumanian landords did. This was also mentioned in the Rumanian press, which caused great concern among strongly nationalistic Rumanians. Thus, a newspaper in Brassó (Braşov) specified in 1909 that the Rumanian peasants in Máramaros (Maramureş) hated the Rumanian lord, while they often stated: "There is no better lord than the Hungarian" (*Domn mai bun ca Ungurul, nu-i*).[1]

At the same time as the economic situation of most of the Rumanian peasantry became much better, areas remained in which there were many poor villages. The contemporary Rumanian leaders asserted that this was caused by the Hungarian state. However, the picture is not as simple. Several Rumanian publicists expressed that other factors were also important or even primary. The weekly magazine *Revista Bistriţei* [The Magazine of Bistriţa] stated in 1903:

"The first cause of our poverty is the immoderate use of spirits."[2] The second cause was, according to the same publication, luxury, particularly as regards clothing. Dionisie Longinu, a Rumanian lawyer, held a similar opinion and also stated:

> The negligence of the peasant, his aversion for learning, the lack of practical instructions and models, the criminal lack of confidence in the intellectuals, the abuses of intellectuals against the people and their indifference to the peasants, the unlimited trust of the people in foreigners, the lack of following advice, alcoholism, laziness, hatred against each other and the many litigations, loitering, the irrational loans, their senseless use, the interests and the luxury... These are some examples of the cause of emigration to America.

A comparison of the proportion of day-workers (the poorest of all working people) may throw some light upon the situation of the Rumanians as compared to the Szeklers: In 1900, the proportion of day-workers in Hungary was 25.2%. In the Rumanian areas, it was only 19.7%, while among the Szeklers, 30.7% were day-workers.[3]

---

[1] *Revista Bistriţei* [The Magazine of Bistriţa], Nr. 9, 1909; quoted by Bíró, 1989, p. 27. – Much later, in the 1950s, a Rumanian peasant in Brâncoveneşti (Marosvécs) said the following about a Hungarian nobleman: *Domnişorule, pe vremea domnului Kemény, baronul, puteam tăia lemne în pădurile lui, cât ne dorea sufletul. Acum, de când pădurea e a statului român, nu putem aduna nici vreascuri, că altfel pădurarul ne împuşcă.* [Young man, at the time of baron Kemény, we were allowed to cut down as much timber in his forests as we wanted. Now, since the forest belongs to the Rumanian state, we cannot even collect brushwood, for if we do, the forester will shoot us].

[2] *Revista Bistriţei*, January 18 – 31, 1903, Nr. 3; quoted by Bíró, 1989, p. 28.

[3] Bíró, 1989, p. 29.

The situation of the peasants in Transylvania as compared to the Rumanian lands

The strongly biased and deceptive presentation by Pascu and his frequent reference to "national oppression" in Transylvania gives a fundamentally false picture about the real situation of the Rumanian peasants there. They were not exploited in a higher degree than other peasants; and the Rumanian landlords in Muntenia and Moldavia (Moldova) oppressed their own peasants in a much harsher fashion. There, as mentioned above, the serfs were liberated 16 years later. The independence war of 1877 ruined several tens of thousands of peasants.

Giurescu (1975) gives the following account of the situation of the peasants in Rumania in the period in question:

> Although the agrarian production increased much in the last decades (between 1886 and 1906 by 100%), and the prices of the products increased considerably, the peasantry was in a difficult situation, with a very low living standard. The chief cause of this was the lack of land, the wrong distribution of ownership: while 4.171 landlords owned 3,787.192 hectares, 1,015.302 peasants had only 3,319.596 hectares, thus, about three hectares each of them. The rest of the agrarian class (between 10 and 100 hectares) owned a total of 816.414 hectares of land.
>
> To this comes the unfortunate system of leasing, – very many owners of big estates did not work themselves the fields but gave them to the lessees, a considerable part of whom were strangers, whose interest was to draw as much profit as possible. This resulted in an inhuman exploitation of the peasants, whose working days were bought cheap but who were forced to pay usurious rent for the money advances given for food, increasing their dijmă [metayage] (up till one in two), and often, unjust measurements. The local administration, sharing a joint interest with the lessees, was on their side.[1]

Peasant revolts broke out in several counties in the years 1888, 1889, 1892, 1894, and were put down by the army, with many casualties among the peasants. After a transient improvement, brought about by the parcelling of a part of the land owned by the state and better conditions for loans, the situation deteriorated again. After 1900, the value of the land rented rose from 25 lei/hectare to 40, later to 60 or even 80 lei, and big trusts of lessees were organized, whose main aim was to increase profits.[2]

In the early 20th century, about 70% of the large estates were hired to lessees, who paid usually the rent for 5 years. There were lessee trusts, of which the largest, that of the Fischer brothers in northern Moldavia handled, in 1904, 76 large estates with a total amount of land of 236.863 hectares (2.368 square

---

[1] C.C.Giurescu & D.C. Giurescu, *Istoria românilor* [The History of the Rumanians], Bucharest, 1975, p. 648.

[2] Zoltán Szász, *A románok története* [The History of the Rumanians], Budapest, [1990], p. 100.

kilometers).[1] Because of the short terms of the lease, the lessees were not interested in the development and improvement of agriculture; their aim was to extort as much profit as possible. The lessees leased the land, divided it into small parcels, passed them to the peasants, for money and for material returns; which meant a very high degree of exploitation. About 300.000 peasants lived in huts dug in the earth, and diseases caused by malnutrition and bad living conditions were widespread.[2]

The unbearable burdens caused a peasant revolt in Botoşani county in 1907, (in the village *Flămânzi;* the word means "those hungry"), against Fischer's lessee-trust, which paid 20 lei for one hectare to the landowners and took 50 – 70 lei from the peasants who worked on the fields.[3] The main demand of the peasants was to lease one hectare for 25 lei. The revolt spread rapidly practically to the entire Moldavia and Muntenia. According to *Istoria României. Compendiu*, 1969 (p. 314), it was a natural continuation of the

> centuries old peasant revolts for land and for freedom, against suppression and social injustice. Having socio-economic causes, the revolt is explained by the general evolution of Rumania at the end of the 19th and the beginning of the 20th century.

The most frequent method used by the peasants was attacks on and burning down of the houses of the landlords and of the lessees, as well as attacks on the parish-halls.[4] The politicians tried to explain the exploitation of the peasants by accusing the Jews, since there were a number of Jews among the landlords and the lessees. The prefect of the county Botoşani, Vărescu, stated: "I would not give a single Rumanian for a million Jews." Stere Constantin, professor at the university of Iaşi, publicist and newspaper editor, was one who described the misery:

> Our peasants are in a constant state of hunger, because of the agrarian situation here. In the north of Moldavia, 88% of the peasants have no animals at all and cannot give milk to their children, of whom 40 – 50% die before age 5 years because of malnutrition.[5]

The conclusion of this article is as follows:

> The agrarian population in the free Rumanian kingdom is living in much more miserable economic conditions than those of their oppressed brethren in Hungary, Bucovina, or even

---

[1] Giurescu & Giurescu, *Istoria românilor,* 1975, p. 656.

[2] Ibid., p. 100.

[3] Ibid., p. 100.

[4] *Istoria României. Compendiu,* 1969, p. 316.

[5] *Tribuna poporului* [The People's Tribune], (Arad), March 11, 1907, Nr. 24: "Cuvântul profesorului universitar dela Iaşi C. Stere în chestia ţărănească" [The opinion of C. Stere, professor at Iaşi university on the agrarian question], quoted by Bíró, 1989, p. 31.

130

Bessarabia.
The great peasant revolt of 1907 was suppressed brutally by the army. Mass-executions, mutilations, torture were usual; often carried out by the landlords or the lessees themselves, who "tortured or killed with their own hands the former rebels."[1] Against about 20 villages, guns were fired, and entire villages were wiped out. Approximately 11.000 peasants were killed in this civil war of the Rumanian upper class against the Rumanian peasants. After the revolt was put down, hundreds of peasants were condemned to life-time hard labour. According to Nicolae Iorga, the authorities made sentences that "surpassed all limits of the law and of decent humanity, and which bring shame on us." The peasants are now exposed to the "class- and personal vengeance of the landlords and the lessees" – added Iorga.

The Rumanian press in Hungary was of course also affected by these events. It was no longer evident that Rumania was the country of dreams, that "for all Rumanians, the sun rises in Bucharest."[2]

One of the leaders of the Orthodox Church in Nagyszeben (Hermannstadt, Sibiu) expressed his view in a Bucharest newspaper in 1911 as follows:

> The economic situation of the Rumanian peasants in Hungary is by far better than that of those living in Rumania. Among the causes of this, there is our cultural situation, which cannot be compared with that of the peasants living in Rumania. Almost all of our peasants can write and read, and they are living in quite good hygienic standards.[3]

* * *

The class of Rumanian craftsmen developed mainly under Saxon and Hungarian influence. Of great influence upon the cultural development of the Rumanians in Transylvania were the merchants. Many Arumanian and Greek merchants immigrated to Hungary; their children grew up as Rumanians and had in general the financial means for studying. These young intellectuals then reached high posts within politics and economics. There were no limitations of commerce in Hungary; if there were clashes on the basis of nationality, they were organized by Rumanians against Jewish innkeepers and merchants. Similarly, only the Rumanians propagated the idea that Rumanians should only buy from Rumanians (not from Jews, Hungarians or Saxons).

Before 1867, there were very few Rumanian merchants in the towns; but thereafter their numbers increased significantly: in Brassó (Braşov), there lived

---

[1] *Istoria României. Compendiu*, 1969, p. 318. – This peasant revolt is the theme of one of Liviu Rebreanu's major novels: *Răscoala* [The Revolt], Editura Adevărul, Bucharest, 1932.

[2] *"Soarele pentru toţi români la Bucureşti răsare"* – one of the slogans of the Rumanian nationalists in Hungary; formulated in 1884 by Ion Slavici in *Tribuna*. Cf. Bíró, 1989, p. 33.

[3] Bíró, 1989, p. 34.

in 1870 110, in 1895, already 200; and in Nagyszeben (Sibiu), their number increased fivefold during the same period of time.[1]

The Rumanian intellectuals were, until 1867, chiefly priests and teachers. There were no restrictions on entrance to the middle schools or to the universities, and those who wanted to study were also helped by scholarships from the *Gojdu-fond,* as well as by the *Astra* and other Rumanian institutions and societies. The result was summarized in 1912 by a Rumanian author as follows:

> Beyond doubt, it is the merit of Transylvania to have provided a safe basis for the middle classes, particularly the small industry and the middle landlords. Understanding the spirit of the times, we have reached in this respect as far as to be able to say that we are represented in the same proportion as the other co-inhabiting nationalities in some parts of Transylvania and in the Banat of Timiș, but especially in the Saxon "Kings territory." And not only numerically but also as regards quality. In this respect, future promises even more.[2]

As mentioned above, a significant number of Rumanian civil servants were employed in the state and county administration beginning with the period after the 1848 revolution, when they took the place of many Hungarian civil servants, who resigned (passive resistence). During the period of absolutism (1850 – 1867), Transylvania was practically laid under Rumanian rule; even in counties with a Rumanian minority, the administrators were often Rumanian. They even introduced Rumanian as the official language in a number of such districts.[3] After the 1867 agreement between the Hungarians and Vienna, Transylvania was united with Hungary, and the Transylvanian governorship was abolished, its role having been taken over by the Hungarian state. However, in the counties, which were autonomous and not affected by the change of constitutional law, the Rumanian civil servants remained in their positions. Nobody thought of their dismissal. The only exception to this was in the Saxon territories.

It was the radical Rumanian movement, fighting for the annexation of Transylvania and the Banat by Rumania, that caused some concern among the Hungarian leaders. Beginning with the 1880-s, Hungarians and Saxons were put to control the Rumanian leaders of the counties, the Lord Lieutenant was thus Hungarian or Saxon, while the county chief next to him (*alispán*) and most of the rest of Rumanian civil servants remained in their office.[4]

---

[1] *Gazeta Transilvaniei*, Brașov, January 4 – 16, 1896, Nr. 3. Quoted by Bíró, 1989, p. 39.

[2] Ibid., (Bíró 1989), p. 43.

[3] Ion Slavici, *Lumea prin care am trecut* [The world which I have gone through], Bucharest, 1930, p. 33; quoted by Bíró, 1989, p. 44.

[4] Bíró, 1989, p. 49.

Rumanians in leading positions, civil servants, in Hungary, used their power and influence to spread irredentist proclamations, often from Rumania. The *Irredenta Manifesto* from 1885, written in Bucharest, instigated the Rumanians living in Hungary **to take to arms "against their Hungarian oppressors" and kill all of them.** In spite of the knowledge of these facts by the Hungarian authorities, these civil servants were almost never dismissed from their office.

It should be remembered that in contemporary Europe, the situation was very different. Neither the Germans, nor the Russians were generous in this respect: in Bessarabia, with the majority of the population Rumanian, the number of Russian civil servants was overwhelming.

There were, however, many Rumanian intellectuals in Transylvania who had a cause to complain. The number of Hungarian petty nobles, ruined economically, was quite large; and many of them sought positions in public administration. Because of political influence, many places were filled with such people and the Rumanian candidates were ignored. The policy of the Hungarian state was also restrictive in this respect because of the fear of Rumanian irredentism, which endangered the integrity of the country. Thus, a vicious circle was created. Those frustrated intellectuals who could not find a position according to their qualifications, were the chief propagators of irredentism. This is the explanation of the discrepancy between the real situation of the Rumanians in Hungary and the fierce accusations of oppression being constantly put forward in the Rumanian press. Many of them went to Muntenia and became there the chief agitators against Hungary and for the annexation of Transylvania.

The policy of the Hungarian governments was in general based upon a liberal ideology. This explains also a number of obvious mistakes. As an example, the Hungarian embassy in Bucharest may be mentioned. In 1894, when the *Memorandum* was put forward, the Hungarian government sent a Rumanian-born diplomat to Bucharest as its ambassador. When the translation-section was created there, a Rumanian was appointed to press-referee. He decided what the members of the Hungarian government, most of whom did not understand Rumanian, should know about the Rumanian press in Hungary and in Rumania, what was said in the Rumanian Parliament, etc. In 1893, for example, a debate took place in Bukarest, in which the aims and methods of Rumanian irredentism in Hungary were discussed. The press-referee decided not to translate and send this debate to his Hungarian employers; as a result, the Hungarian government did not receive adequate information about the strength of this movement.

In Rumania, the employment of people in the service of the state was dependent upon their ethnic origin. The chief question was, whether the supplicant was a born Rumanian (*român din naștere*).[1] This was the case even when stipends for students were distributed. – Professor Loebell was the most distinguished disciple of the known Rumanian physician Victor Babeș. He moved with Babeș from Budapest to Bucharest; later, he moved to Iași and taught pharmacology at the University there. He asked for a permanent employment, but the government refused this, because of his Jewish origin. In spite of the solidarity of his colleagues on the Iași university, the government did not change its mind; to the contrary: they requested Loebell to resign, because they wanted to appoint a Rumanian in his place.[2]

The liberal economical policy of the Hungarian state favoured the Rumanian peasants. While no foreigner was permitted to buy land in Rumania or in Russia, anybody could do this in Hungary.[3] With the increasing amount of land acquired by Rumanians and the increasing number of Hungarian peasants emigrating to the USA, the Hungarian government planned to give some support to the peasants. This activity, however, was not considered as a main priority, as shown by the following figures: between 1881 and 1914, 21 settlements were created on state-owned estates and on land bought with money of the settlement-fund. During 20 years, about 2000 people received land in this action. In 1914, the Hungarian settlement fund owned 700.000 crowns, and had 7 millions of debts. This should be compared with the settlement policy of other countries: in Germany, 900 millions, in Great Britain, 2400 millions, in France, 100 millions and in Denmark, 57 millions were assigned to the same purpose.

As a consequence of these circumstances, many Hungarians in Transylvania were assimilated to the Rumanians. This was particularly frequent in villages with a mixed population. While the Rumanians helped each other, the Hungarian, liberal government did nothing to save these people for the Hungarian nation. These Hungarians had only the Rumanian bank to ask for loan, and this bank did not help non-Rumanians. Between 1850 and 1900, 309 initially mixed, Hungarian – Rumanian villages became purely Rumanian.

The international press wrote at the same time about the "oppression of the Rumanian population by the Hungarian state."[4]

---

[1] After the annexation of Transylvania, in the 1920´s, the school-law of Anghelescu contained the racist directive that only *român de sânge* ("Rumanian by blood") is permitted to teach the Rumanian language and literature.

[2] Bíró, 1989, p. 56.

[3] Ibid.,p. 65.

[4] Ibid.,p. 63.

134

12. THE CONSOLIDATION OF CAPITALIST SOCIETY
(pp. 227 – 254)

Pascu, p. 239: **The Austro-Hungarian Dual Monarchy and Romanian Political Autonomy**

Pascu, p. 240:

> The Hungarian dominant classes wanted a law that would wipe out the economic, social, cultural, and political distinctions between the various provinces that had been incorporated into Hungary.

This serves only to bolster Pascu's assertions about the nationality law of 1868. He wants to convince the reader that it was made in order to suppress the nationalities. But the talk of more or less irresponsible journalists or politicians is not relevant for a judgment about the official policy of a state. The law itself must be analysed, and then it will be seen that it was neither forcible nor inequitable.[1]

The law of the nationalities, 1868:XLIV was the first law in Europe which codified the rights of ethnic groups in a country. It was based on democratic and liberal principles; much more so than the rules that defined the relation between the majorities and the minorities in contemporary Europe. **It contained juridical guarantees and it departed from the principle of collective rights.**

This law prescribed in 29 paragraphs the use of the languages of the nationalities. The official language of the state was Hungarian. The laws were to be translated and published in the languages of the nationalites (paragraph 1). According to paragraph 6, the clerks of the municipal authorities were obliged, as far as possible, in official contacts with the villages, congregations, societies, institutions and private persons, use the language of these. The law secured the use of the nationality languages in court; defined the situation of these languages in education, as well as in the villages and on village meetings. Paragraph 20 stated that the village meetings were free to choose which language to use and paragraph 21 stipulated that "the village administrators must, in their contacts with the inhabitants, use their language." The law also declared that starting of schools in which the languages of the nationalities are used was free, and that such schools had the same rights as similiar state schools. Paragraph 27 stated that when deciding who will be taken as a civil servant, the only condition

---

[1] Bíró, 1989, p. 69 – 72; G. Gratz, *A dualizmus kora – 1867-1918*, I, [The Period of Dualism – 1867-1918], Budapest, [1934], ed. 1992, p. 82. – Gusztáv Gratz, 1875-1946, was an economist, politician, expert on Political Science, historian; a member of the Hungarian Academy of Science. As an active politician, he was in the first decades of the 20th century the eyewitness of events in Central and Eastern Europe. His book on the history of Hungary between 1867 and 1920, in 3 volumes, is thus based, besides a rich bibliography, on personal experience.

should be personal abilities. To belong to a nationality should be no obstacle, – on the contrary, the government wanted to strive for employing several persons from the nationalities in posts as high judges and administrators, particularly as Lord Lieutenant. Rumanians attained high positions, becoming even members of the Supreme Court of Cassation.

The deeply democratic and liberal character of this law was also noticed by a number of French, English and German authors. Bíró quotes Eisenmann, who wrote that this law shows "a generous spirit and a sincere desire for truth, and that it is very liberal" (très libérale).[1]

A problem is, of course, how this liberal law was complied to in practice. Representatives of the nationalities in Hungary have sometimes affirmed already before the war that it was not kept; after 1918, this opinion became unanimous. One weakness of the law was that it lacked sanctions if violated, which may be explained by the liberal spirit in which it was formulated. The use of "as far as possible" should have been replaced in many cases by a positive prescription.

Thus, the implementation of this liberal law was to some extent dependent on the Hungarian officials being law-abiding; as well as on their good will regarding the nationalities. However, this in its turn was to a very high degree determined by the behaviour of the nationalities. One of the conditions of the implimentation of this liberal law would have been that the nationalities too accepted it as a legal ground. By not doing this, they weakened the law, making transgressions much easier.[2] Thus, if the law was not totally implemented, one cannot blame exclusively the Hungarian administration.

In the year in which the law of nationalites was created, only 2 decades have passed since 1848, when the Hungarian people suffered serious losses because the Rumanians in Transylvania took the part of the Habsburgs, considered by all of Europe a reactionary empire. After the defeat of the Hungarians' fight for freedom, absolutism with Austrian – German – Czech domination followed, a period in which the nationalities, particularly the Rumanians, were considerably strengthened to the detriment of the Hungarians (cf. above, pp. 120 - 123).

In 1867, when the Habsburgs, after 17 years of absolutism, normalized their relations with the Hungarians, the representatives of the Rumanians went to

---

[1] Louis Eisenmann, *Le compromis austro-hongrois de 1867*; Paris, 1904, p. 551; quoted by Bíró, 1989, p. 70.

[2] Gratz, [1934] ed. 1992, I, p. 87. – Imre Mikó, in *Nemzetiségi jog és nemzetiségi politika* [Nationality Law and Nationality Politics], Minerva, Kolozsvár, 1944; 550 pages, devotes several chapters to the presentation of this law. Mikó (1911-1977) was a Doctor of Laws, assistant Professor at Kolozsvár University. We refer to his main work, a scholarly account of the rights of national minorities in Hungary in the 19th century and up to 1918, the situation of the Hungarians in Transylvania between 1920 and 1940, the nationality policy of Hungary up to 1944, etc.

Ferenc Deák and asked him to take into account the Rumanian interests in Transylvania.[1] They referred to the status of Croatia; however, there was only one nation, while in Transylvania, there were three. Therefore, **the exclusive domination of the Rumanians, which they demanded, could not be accepted there.** (In a declaration at Blaj, 1868, they demanded the restauration of the situation before 1867 – when the Hungarians were maltreated. This was also unacceptable by the Hungarians.) When the nationality law was debated in the Hungarian Parliament, the Rumanians made a counter-proposal, which would have placed all Hungarians, with the exception of those living between the Danube and the river Tisza, under the domination of the nationalities (in Transylvania, the Rumanians). A Rumanian author, Ioan Cavaler de Puşcariu, stated about this:

> This seemed impossible under the situation which the Hungarians reached by their successes. Because of this, neither the Saxons in Transylvania, nor the Germans of Hungary, but not even the Slovaks joined the proposal; and the Rumanians of Transylvania should have insisted on the language laws of Sibiu instead of the counter-proposal of the nationalities, which did not suit them.[2]

The nationality law was practically totally implemented during the first decade of its existence. The *Tribuna* wrote in 1885, that during the first years of dualism, the Rumanians of the Hungarian crown lived in a situation which was "more or less favourable" for the interests of their national progress. Education of the Rumanian youth was, under the protection of the Church, not influenced by the government; in the villages, Rumanian was the official language, at court, Rumanian was used extensively, etc. This was confirmed by Slavici after the war, in his memoirs.[3]

The Rumanians had a *de facto* autonomy, whose main backing was provided by the Orthodox Church, with a net of schools on all levels except a university.

Pascu, p. 249:

> ...the "citizens" of Romania exposed the policy of denationalizing the Romanians in the Austro-Hungarian Empire, a policy backed by school laws, political associations, the Magyarization of names, resettlements, and trials of journalists and newspapers.

These accusations were propagated widely in Europe. Most Western journalists and politicians were not sufficiently familiar with the situation in

---

[1] Bíró, 1989, p. 71.

[2] Ioan Cavaler de Puşcariu, *Notiţe despre întâmplările contemporane* [Notes about contemporary events], Sibiu, 1913, p. 125; quoted by Bíró, 1989, p. 72.

[3] Ion Slavici, *Lumea prin care am trecut* [The world which I have gone through], Bucharest, 1930, p. 64 – 65; quoted by Bíró, 1989, p. 73.

south-eastern Europe and it is understandable that they believed in the vigorous Rumanian propaganda. The Hungarian government did not bother to initiate a counter-propaganda or at least relevant information campaigns.[1] These circumstances explain the many statements and protests in favour of the "suppressed Rumanians" quoted by Pascu (p. 246 – 250).

However, the real situation was different. The use of the Rumanian language was guaranteed by paragraphs 20 – 24 of the Nationality law.[2] County and communal autonomy assured that in Rumanian districts, Rumanians were elected as officials; these used of course Rumanian in their contacts with the people. Where the communal meeting decided that Rumanian will be the official language, no one raised any obstacle to this. This was the case in areas with a large Rumanian majority. The use of the mother tongue in written texts became problematic, particularly after 1875, in those villages in which the members of the meeting did not care about or were not aware of their rights, or where the non-Rumanian leaders were ill-disposed. This was the case also in villages in which the other nationalities were opposed to the use of Rumanian. It also happened that the Chief Lieutenant wanted the use of Hungarian because he did not understand Rumanian. It is important to emphasize that during the entire period of Austro-Hungarian dualism (1867 – 1918), **the Rumanians used their mother tongue in their contacts with the village administrators, even if these were not Rumanians.**

In many places, the documents were written in both Rumanian and Hungarian, in order to make possible the understanding by the Chief Lieutenant (*főispán*), who usually did not know Rumanian. But many people considered that this had caused too much work and therefore, some of them decided to use only Hungarian. Thus, purely practical considerations sometimes resulted in the use of Hungarian. The description by Slavici throws light upon the situation:

> It was in this way that the Rumanian language was taken away from public administration, so that one could say that it was not the Hungarian government which prescribed the Hungarian language but the Rumanians themselves have abandoned their rights to use

---

[1] G. Gratz gives an interesting account of the possible causes of this peculiar policy: "Hungarian public opinion does not seem to have been aware of the perils for Hungary of this action." This may be explained, continues Gratz, by the belief in the strong position of Hungary within the Monarchy, and the widespread reluctance to think of disturbing events and circumstances. Moreover, it was a general belief that the Rumanian agitation would not be taken seriously by the West-European countries, if it is ignored in Hungary. This was, of course, a great mistake; in the opinion of Gratz, Hungarian society – intellectuals, politicians – should have informed their colleagues in Europe about the real situation, thus counteracting the severe distorsions of the Rumanian irredentist propaganda.(Cf. Gratz, *A dualizmus kora*, I, p. 382.)

[2] Bíró, 1989, p. 76.

138

their own language.[1]

In the counties with a Rumanian majority, such as Hunyad (Hunedoara), Szeben (Sibiu), Brassó (Braşov), Fogaras (Făgăraş), Beszterce-Naszód (Bistriţa-Năsăud), Krassó-Szörény (Caraş-Severin), Arad (Arad), and Bihar (Bihor), requests written in Rumanian were accepted during the entire period. In several places, the authorities organized instruction in the Rumanian language; for example in Temeş county, the county leaders held a five-month course in 1906, on which 40 county administrators took part.[2]

On the county meetings and at the town offices, the situation was as follows (according to a Rumanian magazine):[3] 1. In the counties of Beszterce-Naszód, Brassó, Nagyküküllő (Târnava Mare), and Szeben, people used their own mother-tongue; 2. In Hunyad, Krassó-Szörény, Arad and Alsó-Fehér (Alba) counties, "the Rumanians have already partly secured the use of their language". 3. In counties where the Rumanians were in a small minority, the question of what language to use was of no major importance.

In the local administration – from the meetings of the village councils to the highest level of local government – the Rumanian language was used practically in all areas where the Rumanians were in the majority. Hungarian was used only in cases that were in the sphere of activity of the parliament.

The passivity of the Rumanians after 1867 in political life was also a cause for the oblivion of the right to use Rumanian on county meetings. On the meetings in Déva and Dés (in the counties Hunyad and Szolnok-Doboka [Dăbâca]), the Rumanians used for many years their mother tongue. However, later, when the Rumanian members did not come to the meetings, Rumanian was not used and the right to speak that language was forgotten. (This passivity in politics may partly be explained also by the preoccupation of the Rumanians with economics, the strengthening of their own economic potential.)When they changed their tactics and started to take part in political life, they also wanted to use their mother tongue, and, in spite of the protests from some Hungarian members, they finally succeeded to secure their right to speak Rumanian.[4] The situation was similar in the town meetings. Moreover, in the towns with a Rumanian majority, – as for example in Balázsfalva (Blaj) or Naszód, – the Hungarian deputees were obliged to speak Rumanian, and the Hungarian

---

[1] Slavici, *Lumea...*, p. 72; quoted by Bíró, 1989, p. 78.

[2] Bíró, 1989, p. 83 - 84.

[3] *Libertatea* [The Freedom], Orăştie, January 12 – 25, 1902: "Lupta în comitate" [The fight in the counties]; quoted by Bíró, 1989, p. 87.

[4] Bíró, 1989, p. 87.

inhabitants had to forward their petitions in Rumanian.

In the elementary schools, middle schools and higher education of the Orthodox and the Greek Catholic Church, the teaching language was Rumanian. For one decade after 1867, Hungarian was not even taught as a foreign language in these schools. In 1879, Hungarian was introduced **as a foreign language** to be taught in the elementary schools, and in 1883 also in the middle schools.[1] In the theological faculties, however, which were receiving significant amounts of state money, Hungarian was never obligatory. The Apponyi-law in 1907 increased the number of hours for teaching Hungarian, but did not change the teaching language, which continued to be Rumanian. Also the school protocols were even thereafter written in Rumanian.

State schools made out about 25 – 30% of all schools. In these, in spite of the law, the teaching language was mostly Hungarian. This was one of the greatest mistakes made by the Hungarian governments in the period in question. However, since the majority of the Rumanian children and youth frequented church schools, this injustice affected only a smaller part of them.

Thus, the Rumanians living in Hungary were to a very high extent able to use their mother tongue also in public life. There were misuses, but people could get help from law and most often from the liberal Hungarian authorities. Compared to the situation of some national minorities today in the most civilized, democratic countries of Europe, – for example that of the Swedes in Finland or the German-speaking population in Tyrol (Italy) – one finds shortcomings. However, such a comparison is not relevant. An adequate basis of comparison must refer to the period in question.

The situation of the national minorities in Serbia, Russia, and Rumania in the decades before the first World War

In **Serbia**, about a quarter of million of Rumanians lived. They were not allowed to use their mother tongue in public places, and not even in their churches, where the use of Serbian was obligatory. The authorities organized evening courses in which Rumanian youth were taught the Serbian language and Serbian songs. Episcopal decree ordered the Rumanian Orthodox priests to change the Rumanian names to be more like Serbian, and the same was done in the schools and in offices: Sandu became Sandulovic, Iancu – Iancovic, etc.[2]

---

[1] The European press wondered, how it was possible that the language of the state was not obligatory in the schools of the nationalities in Hungary – that it was taught only as a foreign language, as if the state had spontaneously given up, in extreme tolerance and liberalism, one of its important roles.

[2] Bíró, 1989, p. 100.

In **Russia,** (in the province of Bessarabia), about one million Rumanians were living.[1] They were not permitted to use Rumanian in the church services, except some words on the occasion of funerals. According to Ion Nistor,

> ...in 1867, the Moldavian language [Rumanian] was abolished in all public schools of Bessarabia. From that time on, all schools, driven by the Church, the *zemstvo* [a kind of peasant community, with local autonomy of the landowners, which also had an administrative function] or the state, were Russian schools, with the Russian language, and with a Russian spirit.

Nistor quotes an official Russian text, in which it is stated:

> If we want Bessarabia to melt entirely together with Russia, then we must, by the use of the schools, in a short time make at least half of the Bessarabian peasants Russian. This is the aim of the system of public education recently adopted by the government.

In 1912, 56 middle schools existed in Bessarabia. "In none of these institutions were the Bessarabian students taught Rumanian, not even as a foreign language." Nistor adds that a few Rumanian students continued their studies at Ukrainian and Russian universities, and only very few in Iaşi or in Bucharest.

> In the same spirit of intolerance and hostility against all what is Rumanian was also the 'Public Library' in Chişinău conducted, created by public subscription in 1832. In 1899, this library had more than 20.000 volumes among which Mister Zamfir Arbore could not find a single Rumanian publication. And it could not have been otherwise, since no publication from Rumania could pass the river Pruth, no magazines, literary books or scientific works, no Rumanian political magazines.

In Rumania, it is difficult to find data about the proportion and number of the non-Rumanian nationalities. The official publication about the 1900 census[2] gives the following data: total population: 5.956.690, of these, 5.489.296 were Rumanian citizens and 278.560 (5%) "had no citizenship", of whom 256.488 (92%) were Jews. However, with the use of other sources, it may be discerned that there were almost one million (about 16%) non-Rumanians: 129.217 inhabitants were living in Dobruja (recently annexed), of whom the publication says: "foreign settlers", who "became Rumanian after the annexation of the area". (Most of these were Turks, others Bulgarians, Russians, and Greeks.) In

---

[1] The following data about the situation of the Rumanian population in Bessarabia (Basarabia) in the epoch between the mid-19th century and the first World War are taken from Ion Nistor, *Istoria Basarabiei* [The history of Bessarabia], ed. 1991, Chişinău (after the third edition published in 1923 in Cernăuţi), p. 253 – 257.

[2] Bíró, 1989, p. 101.

Moldavia, there were about 50.000 Tchangos (a Hungarian population, the descendants of those Hungarians who remained in that territory east of the Carpathian mountains when the great majority of the Hungarians settled in the Carpathian basin. In the course of time, a number of Szeklers settled in the same area.) The Tchangos were severely suppressed by the Rumanian state. In the schools, including the priest seminaries, the teaching language was exclusively Rumanian and there was no question of teaching Hungarian even as a foreign language. Most of the priests did not know Hungarian, but even those who did, were forbidden by the Rumanian bishop in Iaşi to speak that language. They were not even allowed to speak Hungarian privately with their congregation. The bishop permitted after some hesitation that confession could be made in the mother tongue. Religious publications in Hungarian, which some priests rarely had procured, were confiscated by the authorities; and the texts on grave stones were to be written in Rumanian. The placenames were accepted only in the Rumanian version and if somebody wrote also the Hungarian name in brackets, the letter was not forwarded by the Rumanian postal service. Also the family names were Rumanized: Bartók became Bartoc, Baka – Boacă, etc.[1]

The Rumanian press in Hungary approved this chauvinistic policy of the Rumanian governments. While they vehemently attacked the Hungarian government and authorities even for minor injustices against Rumanians, they agreed to the total suppression of the non-Rumanian languages – Hungarian, Turkish, etc. – as well as to the persecution of the Jews **in Rumania.** There were, of course, people who discovered this contradictory behaviour:

> It seems that our brethren [the Rumanians in Transylvania] have two different standards: one for the outside world and one for their own use. They condemn chauvinism in their country but accept it here in Rumania.[2]

* * *

Pascu, p. 242:

When discussing the reaction of many Rumanians upon the declaration of independence after the war in 1877 – 1878, Pascu quotes sentiments that suggest an attitude not far from racism: "The appeals made by the various committees invoked 'blood ties,'" the Rumanians are bound "'by close ties of blood' which 'will never be broken but by death itself,'" "Impressive national solidarity was

---

[1] Ibid., p. 103.

[2] From an essay by Radu Ciomag in *Nouă Revistă Română* [New Rumanian Magazine]. Bíró, 1989, p. 103, quotes a commentary (a fierce rejection) of this essay in *Românul* [The Rumanian], Arad, October 25, 1911, Nr. 234.

seen among all in whose breast beats an impassioned Romanian heart,'" etc.

Pascu p. 239:

> [About the Blaj *Pronouncement:*] The product of a long debate among the Transylvanian Romanian political leaders, it expresses the basic ideas of the struggle of a Romanian bourgeoisie from 1848 to 1867, and is a vehement protest against the forced incorporation of Transylvania into Hungary. It was developed at a meeting in Blaj on 15 May 1868, which was attended by roughly 60.000 peasants from most parts of Transylvania. The *Pronouncement* was a mass protest, demonstrating that the great majority of the population of Transylvania considered the forced union with Hungary a historic injustice.

The *Pronouncement* was the work of a Rumanian anti-unionist elite. However, there existed a significant Rumanian group which wanted to preserve the Austro-Hungarian dualism, but with a much wider cultural and linguistic autonomy for the Rumanians in Transylvania and Hungary. This grouping was, numerically, at least as significant as the group against dualism, but lacked the necessary political means to express its opinion. The politicians in this group were of less calibre; some of them sympathized openly with the Hungarians. This shows that the relation between the two peoples in the period in question was by far as hostile as Pascu suggests. Hungarian-friendly sentiments were certainly augmented by the passive resistance showed by the Hungarians in the Bach-Schmerling era (1850 – 1867).

During that time, the Rumanian bourgeois class was very small. In general, its members would approve the union of Transylvania with Hungary.

However, the anti-union group was historically first and had a rich tradition; it was able to gather the best men among the Rumanians. A representative member of this movement was bishop Andrei Şaguna, who always was loyal to the Imperial Court; he received for his services the title of baron. (This is the only example that a Rumanian Church person has received such a high lay distinction.) Şaguna was active also in the period when the dominating Rumanian attitude was passivism.[1]

Pascu, p. 243 – 244:

> ...[the 100th anniversay of Horeas uprising was] an occasion to recall a century of suffering and to resolve to put an end to it. In the service of this idea, the newspaper *Tribuna* [Tribune], founded by Ion Slavici, began publication in Sibiu in April 1884. It was to distinguish itself through its steadfast and courageous defense of the Romanian national cause, of national culture, economic development, and national

---

[1] Keith Hitchins, *Orthodoxy and Nationality. Andrei Şaguna and the Rumanians of Transylvania 1846 – 1873,* London, 1975.

unity.

This newspaper played an important role in the spiritual preparation of the *Memorandum* because it planned,beginning in September 1884, the formulation of a purely political document, which would be a comprehensive synthesis of the allegedly anti-Rumanian policy of the Hungarian government.

Pascu 244:

> The press devoted considerable attention to the *Memorandum* in France, Belgium, and England. Student organizations in Paris, Brussels, and other French and Belgian cities discussed it eagerly and guaranteed it a wide audience, while the English politicians William Gladstone and Edmond Fitzmaurice, a former foreign secretary, responded favorably.

Pascu exaggerates the sympathy shown by those two English politicians. In public opinion in England in that time, the sympathy for the Hungarians, aroused by the speeches of Lajos Kossuth about the fight of a small nation for freedom and independence, were still alive. On the other hand, the English – French alliance existed already and considered the small Rumanian kingdom as an enemy, since this, in 1883, concluded a secret treaty with the Austro-Hungarian monarchy, a potential ally of Germany.

It should be added that Kossuth, according to the principle of "the enemy of my enemy is my friend", a continuation of the politics of prince Ferenc Rákóczy II, strived to find friends among the enemies of the Habsburgs. In the same way as Rákóczy was the ally of the French king Louis XIV, Kossuth wanted to make friends in England and in the entire Anglo-Saxon world. This was the beginning of the Anglo-Saxon orientation of Hungarian politics.

Pascu, p. 244:

> The League for the Cultural Unity of All Romanians, founded in Bucharest in December 1890, played an important role in preparing both Romanian and foreign public opinion.

In spite of its euphemistic name, this league was a political organisation; its members were predominantly emigrants from Transylvania. They continued an irresponsible anti-Hungarian propaganda, which later became a part of the "nation-unifying" policy driven by all Rumanian governments before the first World War. An important aspect of the activity of this league was the propaganda in the Western press, securing a wide publicity for the Rumanian cause.

The presentation of the Memorandeum to the Viennese court was very well timed; it acted as a counter-balance to the millennium of Hungary.

Pascu, p. 245:

> The press law, stricter in Transylvania than in Hungary, sought to throttle free written expression...

If this would have been the case, the text of the *Memorandum* could not have been published in Transylvania.

Pascu, p. 245:

> The unequal treatment of the nationalities was also evident in economic life. Hungarian landowners and bourgeoisie attempted by every means to eliminate or limit as much as possible the participation of non-Magyar peoples in the economy of the country...

As shown above, it was exactly this period of time when a large number of Rumanian peasants received land and increased significantly their living standards.

Pascu does not mention that those who sympathized with the *Memorandum* were only Rumanians. The Hungarian public opinion was aware, at that time, of the real aim of the Memorandum-movement: the annexation of Transylvania by Rumania.

Pascu, p. 246:

> The Romanian socialists declared their solidarity with the Romanians in Transylvania, "brothers with the same origin and the same language."

It may be concluded that the Memorandum-movement proved that even for the Rumanian socialists, the national ties were decisive, far above social aims and demands.[1]

A similarly nationalistic spirit characterized *Contemporanul*, the weekly of a leading socialist, Dobrogeanu-Gherea. This trend prevailed also in the policy of the Rumanian Communist Party after the second World War, when this party was in power, and is extant even today. In the question of national aims, the different social and political trends showed most of the time the same attitude.

The Memorandum-movement indicated that the nationalistic Rumanian circles knew about the inner weaknesses and contradictions of the Monarchy. At the same time, this movement signalled the birth of the Rumanian nation. A significant part of this process took place in a foreign country and in a surcharged atmosphere.

Pascu, p. 251:

> When, late in 1897, the diet in Budapest passed a law Magyarizing place names, public protest meetings were organized in many Transylvanian cities...

---

[1] This attitude was so strong within the Socialistic movements in Rumania that as late as in 1945, Lucreţiu Pătrăşcanu, the minister of justice in the government of Gheorghiu-Dej, could declare: "*Eu sunt în primul rând român, şi numai în al doilea rând comunist.*" [I am in the first place a Rumanian and only in the second place a Communist.]

There was **no question of a general change** ("Magyarization") of the place-names. For about 30 years, each nation used its own names privately as well as in public or in the contacts with the authorities.[1] There were, however, certain placenames, such as Rumanian Săcel or Săliște, Hungarian Szentmiklós or Szentkirály, which appeared in several places. This caused practical problems, among other things, for the post offices. The law sought to amend the situation, by requesting that each village may have only one official name. This was to be determined by the Ministry of Interior, "after listening to the village meetings" – "taking into consideration, as far as possible, the wish of the villages in question". This name was then obligatory in official documents, signboards, etc. However, in paragraph 5, it was stipulated that "the name different from this may be written in brackets".

There were also **cases** of Magyarization of Rumanian placenames. Thus, in 1912, in Sibiu county, the Ministry of Interior decided that the Rumanian and German names, written in their Hungarian forms, should be official: Rebrișoara became Kisrebra, Ampoița – Kisampoly, etc. However, it must be emphasized, that this procedure was not general, the Rumanian names became official in many areas.

As regards the use of placenames in newspapers or books, the Hungarian politicians and authorities did not interfere at all.[2] The same was the case with the family names. In contrast to practice in Russia and in the Balkan peninsula, the Rumanian family names were freely used in Hungary.

Pascu, p. 252:

[To the 40th anniversary of the kingdom] Throngs of intellectuals and peasants from Transylvania, the Banat, and Bukovina went to Bucharest to express their support for unity, both by their mere presence and by the many demonstrations that took place in the capital during the jubilee [in 1906].

Pascu, p. 253: [at the general meeting of the Astra in 1911],

Thirty thousand delegates from the various branches all over Transylvania were present, as well as intellectuals and politicians from Transylvania, Bukovina, and Romania.

This demonstrates a fact of fundamental importance: the tolerance and liberal spirit of the Hungarian authorities; there was no obstacle to the flow of people across the frontiers – even masses could pass without any difficulty in both directions.

---

[1] Bíró, 1989, p. 97.

[2] Ibid., p. 98.

Pascu, p. 252:
> Gyula Andrássy proposed a bill to introduce Hungarian as the training language in all military units, while Albert Apponyi's school law sought the introduction of Hungarian in the nationalities' religious schools.

After a severe struggle, the Hungarian government succeeded to introduce Hungarian instead of German in the **Hungarian units** of the army. It is important to emphasize that this referred exclusively to the Hungarian units; the other nationalities were not concerned.

In the church schools, the *lex Apponyi* from 1907 increased the number of hours in the teaching of Hungarian as a foreign language; but the **teaching language remained also after this, Rumanian.**

The artificially instigated revolt against this law succeeded to persuade even persons to react who did not even know what it really contained.

13: THE BIRTH OF UNIFIED ROMANIA (pp. 255 – 288)

Pascu, p. 256:
> However, Romania did not yet enter the war on either side. The Crown Council, meeting in Sinaia on 3 August 1914, decided that Romania should follow a "policy of national instinct" – a period of neutrality and subsequent cooperation with whichever powers recognized Romania's right to rule the provinces of the Austro-Hungarian Empire inhabited by Romanians.

This was the policy to bide one's time. Scarcely a normal postponement, this tactical reaction was the expression of a typical Rumanian political strategy. They simply waited to choose sides until it became obvious which part would win the war.

Pascu, p. 259:
> Thus an agreement was reached on Romania's territorial demands, and on 17 August a treaty of alliance was signed by Romania, Russia, France, England, and Italy. [...] **The signatories also agreed not to conclude any separate peace...** (emphasis added).

It must be pointed out that in the summer of 1916, as also mentioned by Pascu (p. 259), it was to be expected that the Allies would win the war. The clause not to conclude a separate peace was soon violated: the German army drove out the invading Rumanian army from Transylvania and entered Bucharest on December 6, 1916. Rumania concluded at first an armistice, later (in May 1918), a separate peace with the Central Powers. Pascu p. 266:

The peace of Bucharest, by which the country's riches and a good part of its territory was taken over by the Central Powers, was signed on 7 May.

Pascu, p. 263:

...the great victories over the German army commanded by the storied Marshal Mackensen in Mărăşti, Mărăşeşti, and Oituz.[...] The battles of summer 1917 and the historic victories of the Romanian troops can be compared to the great encounters of Verdun, Marne, Isère, and Isonzo...

The army of Mackensen was demoralized and retreating. It was attacked from the back by a Rumanian army of peasants, who used axes and scythes. They cruelly killed even the wounded. In Rumanian history writing, in the future, it always was described as "the symbol of national bravery and heroism" (*simbolul vitejiei şi eroismului naţional*). This was the only confrontation between the German army and the Rumanians; it had the same function in later Rumanian history writing as the battle at Posada with the Hungarian army of Carol Robert in 1330.

Pascu, p. 265:

Union with Bessarabia

This question does not belong to the history of Transylvania, but to that of Great Rumania. Pascu is, however, consistent, since this book, in spite of its title, to a considerable extent treats the history of the creation of Great Rumania[1].

Pascu, p. 267:

Legions of Romanian-American volunteers began to organize to participate in the fight against the Central Powers. Through such activities and editorials in their newspapers [...] the Romanians in America succeeded in winning over American public opinion and such large and prestigious newspapers as the *Washington Post* and the *New York Times*. Many congresmen, too, joined their forces, including the former president Theodore Roosevelt...

The propaganda spread in the Western countries by Rumanian nationalists was really vigorous. It was also, as all political propaganda, onesided and lacked objectivity. In the absence of any counter-propaganda from Hungary, many Western journalists and politicians believed even the most obviously incorrect assertions.

---

[1]This is also pointed out by Pál Bodor, in *A hisztéria szükségállapota. Kellemetlen kézikönyv Romániáról* [The Emergency State of Hysteria. An Unpleasant Textbook about Rumania], Szabad Tér Kiadó, Budapest, 1990, p. 206. – P. Bodor, author and publicist, who belongs to the Hungarian folk group in Transylvania, was the chief of the Hungarian-language television-programs in Bucharest. At the end of the 1970´s, he emigrated to Budapest. In this volume, he discusses the situation of the Hungarians in Rumania, giving much attention to the role of the writing of history in present day politics.

148

In spite of these circumstances, the attitude of the Western Powers as regards Rumania and its territorial claims was by far as unanimous as asserted by Pascu. Thus, Charles Danielou, the referee of the Trianon peace treaty, stated in his report to the French Parliament: "There was also another option: to preserve the Habsburg empire. Many people are of the opinion that a divided Germany and a preserved Austro-Hungarian monarchy is in the interest of France, in which case, of course, the monarchy should have granted some autonomy for the nationalities as well as give to the Czech and the Croatian territories the same political status as that of Hungary. To this aim, it had been sufficient to transform the ancient provincial diets in Prague and in Zagreb into Parliaments. This solution, by **preserving a centuries-old framework, would have reduced the causes of hostilities in Central Europe. It is certain that in France, this option would have received the majority of votes**" (emphasis added).[1]

Also Woodrow Wilson, the president of the United States, wanted, until the spring of the year 1918, to preserve the economic and political unity of the Austro-Hungarian Empire, changing it to a confederation of autonomous nations.[2] Even at the Paris peace conference, the American delegation (after Wilson had left Paris), tried to oppose the exaggerated territorial demands of the Rumanians, Serbs and Czechs, supported by Clémenceau. Wilson's standpoint was based upon the democratic principles which prevailed in his country; he tried to introduce these to eastern Europe. Unfortunately, Wilson possessed no sufficient knowledge about the many different peoples living in Central and Eastern Europe, and about their history. Most of them were for centuries living under the reign of great powers: the Turkish Empire, Russia, and the Habsburg Empire. It was only after the first World War that they had an opportunity to acquire independent statehood. Soon after the United Sates joined the war, Wilson created an Inquiry Committee, in which experts would make proposals and ideas for a just order after the war. The president of the Committee was House, who had the same opinion about Austria-Hungary as Wilson. Also the 14 points of Wilson about the independence of all nations were formulated with the collaboration of this Committee. A member of the Committee, Charles Seymour, later member of the American peace delegation in Paris, submitted a plan about the federalization of Austria-Hungary. As shown on map 11, the proposed confederation would contain six countries: Bohemia, Austria, Hungary,

[1]Charles Danielou: "Le traité de Trianon", report for the French Parliament, quoted by G. Gratz, *A forradalmak kora – 1918-1920* [The Period of the Revolutions – 1918-1920], Budapest, 1935, ed. 1992 pp. 288, 343.

[2] Magda Ádám: "Egy amerikai terv Középeurópáról, 1918." [An American plan about Central Europe, 1918]; *História* (History), Budapest, 1987, Nr. 4, p. 16.

Poland-Ruthenia, Transylvania, Croatia and Bosnia ("Yugoslavia").The explanations to the map were dated May 25, 1918.

The Rumanian government, with Brătianu as prime minister, had to persuade to support the union not only the Americans but also a major part of the Rumanians living in the USA, who did not want the union.

President Wilson was forced to change his opinion about the preservation of the Austro-Hungarian Monarchy in May 1918. This was because further

Map 11. – An American proposal (Charles Seymour) for the federalization of Austria-Hungary, May 1918. (From Magda Ádám, "Egy amerikai terv Közép-Európáról, 1918" [An American Plan concerning Central Europe, 1918], in *História* [History], 9, 4, 1987, p. 19.)

discussions about a separate peace with the Monarchy were made impossible since Clémenceau published Emperor Karl's willingness to conclude a separate peace with the Allies.

Regarding the resolution of the assembly of the Transylvanian Rumanians in Alba Iulia, December 1, 1918, Lansing, the American foreign minister stated in a letter to president Wilson that the delegates represented only a certain stratum of the population, and the juridical value of the resolution was therefore questionable. Lansing considered that Rumania could not decide the problem, this was a task for the peace conference.

In her research in the Wilson Center, Magda Ádám found also that Andrew, the American *chargé d'affaires*, reported in a confidential memorandum that the demands of the Rumanian government to annex Transylvania are groundless, since

> ...in Transylvania, the proportion of the Rumanians is 60 to 65%, but only a quarter or half of them wants a union with Rumania. The Rumanian invasion in Transylvania was welcomed only by a small part of the population.[1]

It should be added that the assembly at Alba Iulia did not consider the opinion of the other nationalities living in Transylvania, not even the two largest: the Hungarians (about 32%) and the Saxons (about 8%). Such an arbitrary decision could only be taken at the end of a long war, with the Hungarian part exhausted. The Alba Iulia decision was in fact only an attempt at the late legitimization of a decision already made earlier on the basis of power.

Wilson's idealistic notions could not be realized, since the victorious powers accepted the Rumanian demands. The result was that large areas with purely or overwhelmingly Hungarian population were annexed by Rumania, – a flagrant violation of Wilson's principles.

Pascu, p. 278:

> In Paris, the National Council for Romanian Union firmly demanded the dismemberment of Austria-Hungary into independent national territories, on the principle of self-determination of peoples.

Pascu, p. 279:

[The Rumanians in Transyvlania sent an ultimatum to the Hungarians, demanding that the Central Rumanian National Council should rule over all institutions in regions with Rumanian majorities; the rejection of this ultimatum would imply that] ...the Romanian people had been prevented from exercising its right to determine its own destiny...

It is obvious that the principle of self-determination of peoples should have been applied also to the other nationalities, who made up almost half of the population (the proportion of the Rumanians in the entire territory to be annexed by Rumania was 53%). If the Rumanians demanded self-determination for the territories in which they were in the majority, the same should have been accorded to the Hungarians where they were in the majority: in the Szekler counties, in Kalotaszeg, and in several counties with a Hungarian majority in the western part of the territory; as well as to the Saxons (mainly in southern Transylvania).

---

[1] Magda Ádám, op. cit., in *História,* 1987, p. 17.

151

In any case, the fact that only one of the three folk groups living in Transylvania were represented on the assembly in Alba Iulia, makes its decisions, according to international law, null and void.

Pascu 281:
> Not only were there delegates from all institutions and social classes, but the selection of Alba Iulia was extremely appropriate.

Not even the Rumanians were represented equally from the viewpoint of social status: In an earlier version of Pascu's history of Transylvania,[1] published in Rumanian and Hungarian, Pascu also gives the number of delegates: 1228. This text mentions in the first place the Orthodox Rumanian Churches' heads: "the bishops, the vicars, deans, the episcopal consistoria"... Most of the delegates belonged to this category. They made out the influential stratum also in the Cultural League and in the Rumanian Central National Council; it is reasonable to assume that they also played the major role in chosing the other delegates. The main principle in this selection was that the delegates must be "good Rumanians", i.e., they should accept the union of Transylvania with Rumania. The largest social group among the Rumanians – the peasants – had no representatives on this meeting. In no other country of contemporary Europe were such kind of meetings organized.

Pascu, p. 284:
> Full national liberty and equal rights were granted to all coinhabiting nationalities, including the right to education, administration, and justice in their own language; to belong to legislative bodies and to participate in the government of the country in proportion to their numbers; to full religious liberty for all faiths; to a strictly democratic regime in all spheres of public life;...

These principles were also laid down in the peace treaty of Trianon in June, 1920. – Reality was, however, very much different. The first major violation of these promises was revealed in the 1923 Constitution, which lacked all these items. In 1923, the power of Rumania over the newly acquired territories was consolidated and secured. In these conditions, the Rumanian government did not consider itself obliged to adhere to promises given a few years earlier.

5. Unified Romania

pp. 285–286: Taking a realistic view of the situation, the national minorities – the Germans in Bessarabia, the Poles and the Germans in Bukovina, and the Saxons, Swabians, Slovaks, Szeklers, and some of the Hungarians and Ruthenians in Transylvania – saw

---

[1] *Mit jelent Erdély?* [What means Transylvania?], Bucharest, 1984, p. 229; a translation of Ştefan Pascu, *Ce este Transilvania?* [What is Transylvania?], Cluj-Napoca, 1983.

that they would have to come to terms with the new social and political situation.

All ethnic groups in the new Great Rumania were at the mercy of the Rumanian army and state apparatus. These exerted in different ways a very strong pressure upon all non-Rumanians to give a declaration of faith. Thus, there can be no question of any voluntary declaration. There were, however, differences between the situation of the different nationalities. The Transyvlanian Saxons were during their 800 years history always a separate group, with their own autonomy given to them by the early Hungarian kings; they stuck to their privileges (granted to them by the *Universitas Saxonum* and the *Diploma Andreanum*). In these conditions, the union with Rumania implied for them a change from Hungarian to Rumanian rule.

The situation of the Hungarians was different. The Hungarian community did not accept the union. This appears also from the formulation given by Pascu: p. 286: ..."**some of the Hungarians** and Ruthenians in Transylvania – saw that they would have to come to terms with the new social and political situation" (emphasis added). Also *Istoria României. Compendiu*, 1974 (p. 354) writes about "some circles of the Hungarian public opinion" and gives the names of two persons, who have "understood the fight of the Rumanians for unification and its historical necessity." This does not mean that they welcomed the union.

Pascu, p. 287:

> This assembly wanted to show the world that "it is a question first of all of the categorical desire of the unanimous assembly that the Swabian people be united with the Romanian people, whose civilization is superior, whom the Swabians love and respect, and to whom the Swabians feel bound by the origin of many of their sons of common Latin origin."

The source of these statements is not given. In the Hungarian version of his *History of Transylvania*, p. 235, Pascu refers in this connection to *Revista Institutului Social Banat – Crişana*, 1943, p. 420, where the following is found:

> Coinhabiting during the centuries has taught the Swabians to appreciate the Rumanians "according to their real value", [...] the experience of recent times only strengthened the Swabians in their conviction that "only the union with Rumania may provide the necessary guarantees for their existence and progress."

The reference to a "common origin" is nonsense – the Swabians are a German population and their origin is entirely different from that of the Rumanians. Pascu quotes a source from 1943 on the declaration of the Swabians given in 1920; – the original source remains obscure.

When it was supposed that every nationality in Transylvania should express their loyalty to the Rumanian state, the situation of the Jewish community was

153

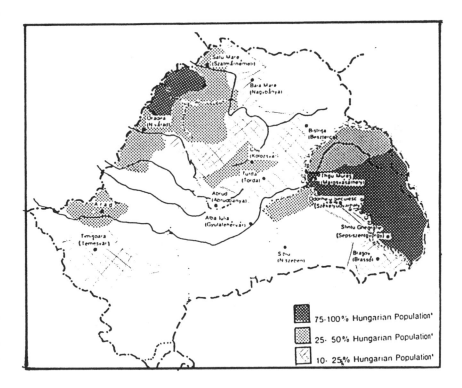

Map 12. – The Hungarian population in Transylvania, according to *Anuarul Statistic al RPR*, Bucharest, 1959, 1961, 1969 (modified from: *Transylvania. The Roots of Ethnic Conflict*, ed. Cadzow, Ludanyi, & Elteto, Kent State University Press, 1983, p. 224.)

perhaps the most difficult. Their refined sense of danger and instinct of self-conservation helped them also to get over this historical moment: On 31st of March, 1919, the representatives of the Transyvlanian Jews in Bucharest subscribed the declaration of loyalty to the Rumanian state. This declaration was perhaps the mostly desired declaration of loyalty by the Rumanian leaders. It must be added, that the delegation stressed the necessity of granting the freedom of their cultural and religious traditions. As in the case of the other national minorities, the Rumanian leaders promised also the Jews all these rights. However, while the former have been granted Rumanian citizenship automatically, the Jews had to ask for it individually and not all of them were given citizenship. But the real value of these promises were shown two decades later,

154

in 1941, when Marshal Antonescu ordered "ethnic and political purification."[1]

Pascu, pp. 287–288:

> Thus, by late 1919, more than 80 percent of the Transylvanian population had agreed to the unconditional union of Transylvania with Romania. The resolutions of union and support, freely made in popular assemblies, invested the act of union with a plebiscitary character.

This is not correct. The proportion of the population which agreed to the union was much less. As mentioned above, Andrew, the American *chargé d'affaires*, estimated that only at most half of the Transylvanian Rumanians wanted the union with Rumania. This means at most 30 – 33% of the total population even if one would accept the proportion of the Rumanians given by Andrew (60 – 65%). Out of the other nationalities, the Hungarians rejected the union; their proportion of the population was about 32%. Thus, even if all of the Saxons and the Swabians would have agreed to the union, those who rejected it were in the majority (62 – 65%). However, it is obvious that also the resolutions of the German-speaking populations were made under pressure. It may therefore be stated that the great majority (much more than two thirds) of the population of Transylvania rejected the union with Rumania.

A note may be necessary here about the Rumanian population of Transylvania. It would be erroneous to imply that all Rumanians living there automatically wanted the union with Rumania. That many of them did not want it has been stated also by Aldo Dami in 1932:

> The frontier decided in Trianon has left outside Hungary a Hungarian area, and in addition, territories inhabited by other peoples whose interests are to such a high degree common with those of Hungary that their choice cannot be doubted if they had been consulted. The frontier is thus not based on the ethnic situation, nor on the sentiments of the population,

---

[1] Already in July 1940, a pogrom was organized in Dorohoi; a massacre among Jews in Iaşi took place on the order of Marshal Antonescu in June; and in the "hell named Transnistria", more than 300.000 jews were killed, starting in 1941. Cf. *Martiriul evreilor din România 1940 - 1944* [The Martyrdom of the Jews in Rumania 1940 - 1944], red. S. Stanciu, Bucharest, 1991. – On July 3, 1941, Antonescu sent instructions to the civil servants sent earlier to Bessarabia and Bucovina, from which we quote: "ETHNIC AND POLITICAL PURIFICATION. – We are in the great and most favourable historical moment for a total ethnic unfettering, for a national revision and for the purification of our People of all those elements, foreign to its soul, who have grown as mistletoe, to darken its future. **So that we do not loose this unique moment, we must be inexorable**" [*The Martyrdom...*, p. 139]. – In this context, it may also be mentioned that in February 1944, Antonescu proposed to Hitler the occupation of Hungary, even offering Rumanian troops for such an action. When Hitler, after the occupation of Hungary in March, 1944, called Antonescu to Klessheim, he told the Rumanian dictator that Germany was no longer the guarantee of the Vienna decision from 1940, which gave back northern Transylvania to Hungary.

nor on their own interestes – which only they can know.[1]

Also the Slovaks and the Croatians were more or less forced into the new states of Czechoslovakia and Yugoslavia: when a Slovakian delegation led by R. P. Hlinka and Jehlicka arrived in Paris in order to demand of the Peace Conference a referendum for Slovakia, Beneš got the French police to expel it from France by force. – As for Yugoslavia, Yves de Daruvar states: "The Croatian Parliament (*sabor*) decided in October 1918 on separation from the Austro-Hungarian Empire, but not its fusion with Serbia. This fusion was the result of a veritable act of coercion (*fusion qui fut le résultat d'une véritable action de force*).[2]

Pascu, p. 288:

> Faced with this undeniable reality, the rest of the Hungarian population gradually modified its stance concerning the Alba Iulia resolutions, especially as the principles of equal rights for national minorities approved in Alba Iulia were put into effect.

The first part of this statement is correct: also the Hungarians had no other alternative than to accept the changes brought about by forces that were stronger than they.

Pascu does not mention that also the Hungarians held a meeting in December 1918. About 50.000 participants gathered in the center of Kolozsvár (Cluj), the delegates of 28 counties uttered their opinion, which was formulated by the president, professor Imre Apáthy, as follows: "We must acknowledge that we have been defeated by the numerical superiority of our enemies. But this does not mean that any other nation would have the right to rule over us."[3]

The resolutions made in Alba Iulia regarding the rights of the non-Rumanian nationalities were subsequently forgotten. As mentioned above, this was also the case with the international peace treaty concluded two years later in Versailles (Trianon), which contained 14 paragraphs of minority protection. These were not included in the 1923 Constitution of Rumania, and the national minorities were in the new Great Rumania exposed to oppression.

---

[1] Aldo Dami, *La Hongrie de demain*, Paris, 1932, p. 133.

[2] These data are taken from Yves de Daruvar, *Le destin dramatique de la Hongrie*, Paris, 1970, p. 96 and 159, respectively.

[3] Imre Mikó, *Huszonkét év. Az erdélyi magyarság politikai története 1918. dec. 1-től 1940. aug. 30-ig* [Twentytwo years. The political history of the Transylvanian Hungarians from December 1, 1918 to August 30, 1940], Budapest, 1941, p. 12.

Pascu, p. 288:
(The union was achieved) ..."on the basis of contemporary legal principles."

One may ask: which law was in force in that territory in 1919 – 1920? Pascu's text seems to imply that this was the Rumanian law. This is, however, very questionable, since the territory was not yet juridically a part of Rumania.

14. GREAT ROMANIA (pp. 289 – 298)

Pascu, p. 289: **The Paris Peace Conference**

> The so-called World Parliament that met in Paris for the peace conference of January 1919 struggled to find equitable solutions for a war-torn world, new, fairer arrangements to protect it from a new catastrophe.

This World Parliament aimed, similarly to the Congress of the Holy League a century earlier, at securing the peace of Europe for all time, by the solution of the most difficult problems.

Today, after more than seven decades, it is obvious that this aim was not reached. To the contrary, the peace treaties in Paris of 1920 lay the foundation for new catastrophes, such as the second World War, because the noble principles of peoples' self-determination were not realized. Another sinister consequence of the Paris peace treaties (specifically, the creation of multi-national Yugoslavia) was the war waged on the Balkan peninsula in the first half of the 1990-s, which was not less than a catastrophe.

It may be added that the League of Nations was unable to resolve any litigious problems and to enforce and to put into effect its own principles, recommendations and resolutions. Its total fiasco was obvious for the whole world already after a decade of its existence. It must be stated, with sorrow, that its spiritual successor, the UNO, is not more successful.

Pascu, p. 291:
> Romania, for example, which had suffered material losses of 31 million gold lei in addition to an enormous human toll, was to receive 1 percent [of the war damage paid by the Germans].

This low amount suggests that in spite of their declarations and the treaty of August 1916, the allied powers did not recognize Rumania as an equal part neither in the war effort, nor in the peace talks.

Map 13. – Proposals of the Western Powers for the Hungarian-Rumanian frontier (1919). It appears that there was considerable difference between the four countries: the Italians and the USA wanted to preserve purely or predominantly Hungarian areas in Hungary, which, at the final decision in Paris (1920) were given to Rumania. (After V.V. Tilea, *Acţiunea diplomatică a României Nov. 1919 – Mart. 1920* [The Diplomatic Activity of Rumania November 1919 – March 1920], Sibiu, 1925, map 1).

Proposals of experts from

Italy — — —	USA —·—	France — —·	England ······

frontier according the treaty of 1916: —•—•—•—
frontier determined in Paris, 1920: ⊢⊣ ⊢⊣⊱⊣
frontier of Transylvania in the 19th century: —————

Pascu, p. 291:
> ...certain clauses which would mean outside interference in Romania's internal affairs. Among these were measures set by the Great Powers to protect the national minorities [...] The Romanian delegation protested and refused to accept such terms, promising to grant the national minorities equal rights with the Romanian people...

One may ask, if the Rumanian government was so sure to grant equal rights to all its citizens, why were measures to control its policy unacceptable? The control of promises is always indispensable. In any case – at present, the problem of national minorities is not considered an internal affair of the country in question but one of the most important problems to be solved in Europe.

Pascu, p. 292:
> .. the authors had made a profoundly serious effort to understand the Central European situation, to weigh impartially the demands of the nationalities and Hungary's rights. [...] ...the decisions incorporated into the treaty were made "after examining documents of all kind that might be cited in support of the Hungarian position."

However (p. 293): The nature of the peace treaties of 1919 and 1920 is sometimes disputed.

Pascu also quotes Ch. Seymour's statements about the Trianon Treaty being in favour of Hungary, and in conformity with the ethnic distribution of the population.

The Paris Peace Treaty caused more problems than it solved

Discussing the decisions made at Versailles, it is impossible to evade a sharp critique of them. Consider only the principle declared before the peace treaty: each people shall live in freedom in its own country – and the results. These were neither just, nor impartial. The frontiers were **not** drawn in conformity with the ethnic distribution of the population, and with insignificant exceptions, no plebiscites were held.

On the peace treaties after the First World War, the Western Powers created two new states: Czechoslovakia and Yugoslavia, and approximately doubled the territory of Rumania. The population of these states was then as follows:[1]

Czechoslovakia:

Total population:	14.085.000	
of which Czechs:	7.200.000	– 51.1%
Slovaks:	2.000.000	– 14.2%
others:	4.885.000	– *34.7%*

---

[1] The following figures were taken from J. Galántai, *Trianon és a kisebbségvédelem* [Trianon and the Protection of the Minorities], Edit. Mecenas, Budapest, 1989, pp. 25-26.

Yugoslavia:

Total population:	12.012.000	
of which Serbs:	5.000.000	– 41.6%
Croatians:	3.500.000	– 29.1%
Slovens:	1.025.000	– 8.5%
others:	2.487.000	– *20.7%*

Rumania:

Total population:	18.000.000	
of which Rumanian:	12.815.000	– 71.2%
others:	5.185.000	– *28.8%*

These figures show that (1) in all these countries, the proportion of ethnic minorities was high, in two of them around one third of the entire population, and (2) in Czechoslovakia and Yugoslavia, the "majority" was constituted by two, respectively three different nations. One of these had the power in each of these new countries, with only 51.1% and 41.6% of the population in Czechoslovakia and Yugoslavia, respectively.

Two historical currents were the basis for this unfortunate arrangement: the strong nationalistic movements among the intellectuals of the different peoples living in the Austro-Hungarian monarchy, and the Western Powers' need for allies in South-East Europe.[1]

This may explain why monstrous lies were accepted as truth. One of these was the assertion by Beneš, that the Slovaks feel themselves to be Czechs and want to belong to Czechoslovakia. (Masaryk, along with Beneš the founder of the Czechoslovak state, stated in a book published before the war that the Slovakian nationality is different from the Czech.[2]) The Czech leaders also affirmed that the Hungarians living south-east of Pozsony (Bratislava, Pressburg), in the *Csallóköz*, were earlier Slovaks who have been magyarized. (There is no evidence whatsoever for this assertion.) Several lies were put forward about the number of Hungarians to be incorporated into the new state of Czechoslovakia: against 650.000 Hungarians, 450.000 Slovaks would remain in Hungary; later, the French expert Laroche declared that "according to Beneš", this number would be 638.000. (The real numbers were: more than one million Hungarians,

---

[1]Cf. Zsuzsa L. Nagy, "Peacemaking after World War I: The Western Democracies and the Hungarian Question", in *The Hungarians. A Divided Nation*, red. Stephen Borsody; Yale Center of International and Area Studies, New Haven, 1988, p. 47.

[2]*Zur russischen Geschichte und Religionsphilosophie*, I, pp. 259 and 263, quoted by Gratz, *A forradalmak kora*, [1935], ed. 1992 pp. 290 and 343.

most of them along the new frontier, were forced to live in Czechoslovakia while only 140.000 Slovakians remained in Hungary.)[1]

A circumstance in the following years aggravated the situation: although the Peace Conference ruled that provisions regarding the rights of the national minorities should be incorporated in each country´s Constitution, this was not done in any country. Instead, chauvinistic politicians oppressed those who did not belong to their (the majoritary) nationality. The development of severe internal tension was inevitable in these artificial states.[2]

Naturally, when this was made possible by the international political situation, the major subdued nations revolted. During the 2nd World War, Croatia and Slovakia became independent, and, similarly, after the fall of Communism in 1989, the oppressed populations put down the domination of the Serbs and of the Czechs, respectively. The creation of Yugoslavia and of Czechoslovakia after the First World War was a political absurdity.

Of all people, the Hungarians suffered − in relation to their number − most of the unjust and inhuman Paris Peace Treaties: out of about 10.000.000 Hungarians in 1910, almost a third, 3.100.000 were forced by these treatises to live under foreign rule .

Along the new Hungarian-Rumanian frontier, large areas with a purely or predominantly Hungarian population: the region of Szatmár (Satu Mare), part of the Körös-region (Crişana), and the surroundings of the town Arad were given to Rumania.[3] Also north of the new Hungarian-Czechoslovak frontier, an

---

[1] Some delegates at the conference asked whether it would be possible to draw the frontier in a way which would force a lesser number of Hungarians to live in Czechoslovakia? The Czech delegation answered that the plains were necessary for the Slovaks, because many of them, living in the industrialized mountainous territory, went in the summer to the plains to work in agriculture, where they could earn an important part of their yearly income. This was a distorted argument. It was true that many Slovaks did travel, in the summer, towards the south, but not to the strip of territory in question but to Budapest and to the Great Hungarian plain. This was, however, left unsaid, since it demonstrates the economic unity of the Slovak area with the Hungarian territory south of it. − Cf. Gratz, *A forradalmak kora*, 1934, ed. 1992, p. 290-292.

[2] ..."the transformation of the Danube region within the framework of the Versailles peace system could lead only to further tensions and conflicts. The new order not only worsened interstate relations, but spoiled the political and intellectual climate of the entire region, thus engendering all kinds of vicious forms of nationalism. Ultimately, it paved the way to a situation in which Hitler´s Germany was able to set the successor states of the defunct Habsburg Empire against one another and subdue them all" (Zsuzsa L. Nagy, in Borsody (red.), *The Hungarians. A Divided Nation*, 1988, p. 48.)

[3] In order to change this demographic situation, a large-scale policy of settlement of Rumanians into these territories was started and continues in our days; thus, around Nagyszalonta (Salonta),

almost purely Hungarian strip of land was given to Czechoslovakia and the situation was similar in the south, in the Vojvodina.

The largest Hungarian area, the Szekler country, in southeastern Transylvania, without a direct contact with the rest of the Hungarian territory, also became a part of Rumania. In this compact Hungarian area, the different Rumanian governments have always made efforts to change the demographic situation. Thus, during the Communist rule, they industrialized the Szekler counties, which meant that factories were built in which the workers were imported from the trans-Carpathian territories of the country.

All in all, the Paris peace treaty forced at least 1.6 millions of Hungarians and 800.000 of Germans to live in Great Rumania. Compared to this, the number of Rumanians left in Hungary was negligible (their number today is 28.000, but only 15.000 really consider themselves Rumanians). At most five villages (in the Körös valley and in the county of Békés) had a Rumanian majority. The only purely Rumanian village was Méhkerék (Micherechi).

In this context, also the conference at Rapallo in 1922 must be mentioned, which was convoked with the aim of revising some of the most conspicuous injustices of the Paris peace treaties, in the first place between Germany and Soviet Russia. For Hungary, its result was that this conference ordered a plebiscite for the town Sopron and its surroundings.

Pascu, p. 295:
> More than a million people died...[...] The economic losses, however, were recouped within the surprisingly short period of three years.

Almost half of these, about 400.000 people, were non-Rumanians.

As for the short period of recuperation, it is by no means surprising, because with the material riches found in Transylvania, it was not difficult to repair the damages caused by the war and to eliminate the deficit in the balance of payments and the state budget, bring inflation under control etc. (Also Pascu recognizes that Transylvania alone contributed about 48% of Great Rumania's total output in mining and metallurgy.)

Pascu, p. 296.
> Private estates and state lands – about 6 million hectares – were distributed among the peasants without regard to nationality...

This is wrong. In reality, not only the estates of those Hungarian landowners who moved to Hungary were expropriated, but also many poor Hungarian peasants were, under different pretexts, deprived of their small plots. They were

---

Rumanians were still in the early 1990-s settled from northern Moldavia (Moldova).

thus forced to seek other means of existence. The land-reform of the Rumanian kingdom was in general designed to damage the nationalities, especially the Hungarians.

Before the first World War, the proportion of small estates in Europe was, after Bulgaria and Belgium, the highest in Transylvania: 70%. The proportion of medium estates was 11.6% and that of the large estates, 18.5%.[1] Moreover, only a third of the large estates belonged to private persons, the rest was the property of the state, the villages, the Churches, schools and of the compossessorates. The land reform in Transylvania was different from that in Muntenia and Moldavia. In Transylvania, the land to be confiscated was determined first. A smaller part of this land was then divided between those who asked for it; the larger part was retained as a state reserve (*rezervă*). The state organs and also private persons then speculated on a large scale in these estates.[2] Many members of the local committees created to carry out the land reform lacked the necessary knowledge and bribery was usual. Because of this, they were very often changed. Only after having bribed these committees were many Hungarians able to retain their land plot granted by the law.

The land reform was a catastrophe for the Churches, the schools and the foundations. These were deprived of a large part of their economic basis when their lands were expropriated. The Hungarian Churches in Rumania owned, before the land reform, 211.820 acres of land, of which 179.100 acres, i.e., 84.5%, were expropriated.

The ancient lands, forests, and pastures, owned by the Szekler communities, were over several centuries essential for the economy of a large number, particularly of poor, Szeklers, who were dependent upon their animals. As mentioned above, p. 124-125 , these were also confiscated and part of them was then distributed among rich Rumanians. Thus, for example, out of the land of the common ownership in Borszék (Borsec) made state-owned ("for national aims"), 150 building plots for villas were given to Rumanian dignitaries (including three ministers, one prefect and five deputies of the Parliament).[3]

---

[1] Mikó, 1941, p. 28. – Mikó also mentions that in Muntenia and Moldova (Moldavia) the proportion of the small estates was 48%.

[2] Ibid., p. 29.

[3] Ibid., p. 34.

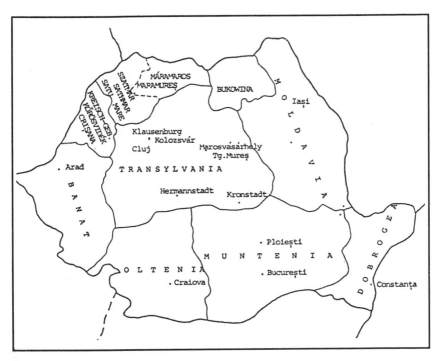

Map 14. – The provinces of Rumania.

Pascu, p. 298:
> [the unification of the national state] could nevertheless not have been fully completed without international support, specially on the part of the European peoples and the Americans.

The propaganda of the Rumanian diplomacy, supported by Rumanian emigrants and solidarity movements, was designed to make possible the creation of Great Rumania.

164

CONCLUSIONS

1. What is historical truth? This is a difficult question and it may be maintained that it is impossible to write a thoroughly impartial and objective history. "The historian might pursue its course on the lines dictated by his own curiosity, skill, and ability, eventually arriving at whatever approximation of the truth that these provide him."[1] When Pascu writes, for example, about the economic situation of Transylvania towards the end of the 19th century, he may be said to pursue the course dictated by his own curiosity and arrives at an approximation of the truth. – However, there are circumstances and events, often simple, which are obvious for everyone familiar with the subject in question. There are also elementary rules of describing the past, which should not be violated. Thus, for example, quotations should not be torn out of their contexts. Pascu quotes Auxentius Durostorensis in a way which is false by all standards. He quotes certain sentences chosen in order to be able to draw the desired conclusions. It is sufficient to read the relevant text **in its entirety** to confirm this and state that the real conclusion is the opposite of what Pascu pretends (see above, pp. 34 – 35). Another example of unacceptable methods is the way Pascu writes about presumed Rumanian districts (*ţări*) in Transylvania before the arrival of the Hungarians. As shown above, p. 32, in *Voievodatul Transilvaniei*, he indicates that **the many "ţări" he enumerates are only assumed to have existed,** in Rumanian: *vor fi existat.* In the English version this is omitted, so that the reader is left with the false information that a large number of politically organized Rumanian districts existed in Transylvania in the 10th – 11th centuries.

2. A serious weakness of this treatise is the **lack of references.** Assertions are made which, upon checking, are shown to be entirely without a material basis. This is the case, for example, with Pascu's assertion that on the eve of the Tartar invasion, out of the population of Transylvania, "roughly 65 percent were Romanian" (cf. above, p. 56).

3. Although Pascu certainly knows them, he evades to mention important juridical categories of the state and the constitution, which could explain the internal differences between the Hungarian state and the young Rumanian kingdom. Through the entire presentation of the period between the 10th and the 19th century, Pascu disregards the contemporary social conditions in Europe and reflects back present day nationalistic ways of thinking into the past. This causes a biased view and a basically false writing of history. This is the more remarkable as Pascu is a Transylvanian himself, thus, he should know the great

---

[1]Paul E. Michelson, in the Foreword to Pascu's *History of Transylvania,* pp. X–XI.

difference between the feudal nation and the concept of the nation in its modern sense. However, this attitude must be intentious, – otherwise it would not be possible to present the thousand years old Hungarian state as a historical interlude. The history of Transylvania before 1918 is an integral part of the history of Hungary.

4. Pascu's *History of Transylvania* is not really a scientific treatise but rather directed at laymen; and the author seems to reckon with the relatively scarce knowledge of the non-professional reader. The book is in its contents one-sided, tendentious and distorted, written in the spirit of extreme nationalism and the structure of the work is designed singularly from this viewpoint.[1]

5. The book was written in the most tense period of the Hungarian-Rumanian relations, when Ion Lăncrănjan published his essay "*Cuvînt despre Transilvania*" [Essay about Transylvania], Bucharest, 1982; a literary work conceived in an intolerant, extremely chauvinistic spirit.[2] As stated by Andrew Ludanyi:[3]

> Rumania's assertion that Transylvania is the communal property, sphere of interest, and inheritance exclusively of the Rumanian people makes the existence of Hungarians and other minorities an inconvenience that must be overcome in some fashion, via emigration, assimilation, exclusion, or deportation.

About at the same time, European historiography started to revise the interpretation of events occurred at the beginning of the century. This did not mean that the conclusions drawn should affect everyday politics. Historical truth may be sought in an objective way and has a value in itself. New interpretations of events were tried also by Hungarian historians. However, Rumanian historiography, dominated by politicians, was not able to free itself from the traditional conditionings and saw in this endeavour a kind of ideological

---

[1] Pascu's *History of Transylvania* seems to have been ordered by a single person; something suggested by the fact that in the Hungarian version (p. 7), a quotation from N. Ceauşescu is found.

[2] Lăncrănjan continued the tradition of those Rumanian politicians who strived to exclusivity for one (the Rumanians) of the three major peoples in Transylvania, totally ignoring the others: "Transylvania is not and cannot be a simple eastern Switzerland, because on both sides of the Carpathians, **one single people, one single will,** (*un singur popor, o singură vrere*) have lived and worked, loved and dreamt, since the most ancient times..." (p. 136; emphasis added). It appears from the present volume that this is not true; the Rumanians started to settle in Transylvania earliest at the beginning of the 13th century, among Hungarians, Saxons, and Slavs. Of course, Lăncrănjan's attitude does not correspond to modern, humane standards, also without regard to history or numerical considerations. – For more details about Lăncrănjan´s essay see the critical survey below.

[3] Andrew Ludanyi, "Ideology and Political Culture in Rumania: The Daco-Roman Theory and the ´Place´ of Minorities", p. 230; in: *Transylvania. The Roots of Ethnic Conflict*, ed. J.F. Cadzow, A.Ludanyi, L.J. Elteto, The Kent State University Press, Kent, Ohio, 1983.

groundwork of politics striving at territorial revision.

6. Pascu describes the history of Transylvania almost exclusively from the viewpoint of the Rumanian population, (which shortly before the union in 1920 with Rumania made out 53%, thus, just above half of the inhabitants). The significance of the Rumanians is grotesquely magnified, while that of the other nationalities is neglected. In reality, these nationalities: the Hungarians (with the Szeklers) and the Saxons played a decisive, leading role in the history of Transylvania. Also the relations between the different Transylvanian peoples are described in a misleading way.

7. Besides its extreme nationalistic preconception, Pascu's book shows also the traces of a conservative Marxistic conception in its terminology and style.This was also pointed out by Paul E. Michelson´s Foreword, p. XIV.

8. The thought system behind Pascu´s writing of history is that of certain Rumanian political circles and aims at creating an ideological basis, a justification, of the present situation by reflecting the present day chauvinistic system of ideas back into the past, in which these could not have existed.

* * *

It was mentioned above that the Rumanian national (irredentist) movement, dominated by an intolerant attitude vis-à-vis the non-Rumanian inhabitants, was only one of the political options of the Rumanians living in Transylvania. It has most of the time been stronger than the moderates and is still today a significant factor in politics. This movement strives for supremacy, for exclusivity in Transylvania, and does not recognize the right to existence of other folk groups (which had been living in the country for more than one thousand years). This ideology is based on an old fashioned, 19th century nationalism. Writing of history in this spirit, as shown in this book by Ştefan Pascu, has always been and is still an important part of this chauvinistic policy. History is transformed in such a way that it explains and justifies the claims for exclusivity of the Rumanians: they were the autochthons, conquered and subdued by the ancestors of the Hungarians, who also have kept them centuries along in servitude.

No real peace and coexistence between the three major folk groups in Transylvania is possible as long as these utterly false concepts are taken as truth by the majority, or even by a significant number of the Rumanians.

In the 20th century, two great wars and several minor ones were fought in Europe. Two totalitarian systems rose and fell in this century, both of which used the falsification of reality (present and past) as a very efficient weapon in their striving for more power. Now that these powers have disappeared, also their spiritual base of lies and falsifications should be eradicated. A radical change in writing of history is therefore a prerequisite of a durable peace. For Rumania, such a change would imply the disposal of the theory of Daco-Roman continuity. This should be substituted by the description of the development of the Rumanian people from the ancient Balkan population who were Romanized during the Roman period there, and their wanderings towards the north-east beginning in the 11th-12th centuries. Also the subsequent history, thus, for example the relation between the different folk groups in Transylvania should be described without prejudice.

There is today some reason to hope that these ideas will, some day, be generally accepted.There have always been and there are even today Rumanian historians and linguists who wanted to do research without prejudice and political considerations: Ioan Bogdan (1864 - 1919), professor of history at Bucharest University, the most important Rumanian slavist; Dimitrie Onciul (1856 - 1923), the founder of the critical school of Rumanian historiography. Radu Rosetti (1853 - 1926) pursued research of the past without idealizing it. Constantin Giurescu (1875 - 1918) distinguished himself from other historians of his period by using a much richer documentation. – Some years after the first World War, historians started to criticize Nicolae Iorga's strongly nationalistic and biased method of writing history. In 1931, a new programme for Rumanian historiography was proclaimed in the *Revista Istorică Română* by Gheorghe Brătianu, Constantin Giurescu, and Petre Panaitescu. They stated that historians should seek the truth without political considerations. To give an example, we refer here only to P. Panaitescu, who studied carefully the documents of the surrounding peoples, (especially those of the Poles,) in order to see the history of the Rumanians objectively and in its context. His monograph on Michael the Brave is a masterpiece of writing history based on facts revealed by careful research (cf. above, p. 92).

Ovid Densusianu (1873 - 1938) wrote the first scientific history of the Rumanian language, based on a vast material, showing its close connections with the Balkan languages. He explicitly warned his colleagues of doing research according to preconceived, nationalistic ideas. Alexandru Philippide (1859 - 1933) concluded his research about the Rumanian language with the thesis that it developed, until the 7th century, south of the lower Danube. Also the history of the Rumanian language by Alexandru Rosetti contains the facts that confirm Densusianu's conclusions, and this may be said also about much of the writings of Ion I. Russu. (It should be remembered that their works appeared mainly in a period when there was no freedom of research and publishing.)

The majority of the Rumanian people in Transylvania, who are living together with or near the Hungarians and Saxons, also want peace between the different nationalities. Also many politicians would like to act according to the traditional Transylvanian spirit of tolerance and cooperation. They know that different folk groups can live in the same state, that they all contribute to the richness of life and culture and that such a situation does not menace any folk group, nor the stability of the state – to the contrary. There are, fortunately, a

168

number of examples of this in Europe.

Clarifying the past is one of the prerequisites of this. We hope that the present book, by disclosing the prejudiced, chauvinistic writing of history, will contribute to a return of Rumanian historiography to its predecessors who sought only the truth, because "the real patriot is not he who wants to falsify reality and to deceive himself, and the scientist forgets his duty if he evades telling the truth, however painful it may be".[1]

---

[1]O. Densusianu, *Histoire de la langue roumaine,* ed. 1975, Bucharest, p. 26.

References.[1]

Ádám, Magda, "Egy amerikai terv Középeurópáról, 1918" [An American Plan about Central Europe, 1918], *História* [History], Budapest, 1987, 4.

Asztalos, M. (red.), *A történeti Erdély* [Historical Transylvania], Edit. Erdélyi Férfiak Egyesülete, Budapest, 1936.

Bârzu, Ligia, *Continuitatea populaţiei autohtone în Transilvania în secolele IV - V. (Cimitirul 1 de la Bratei)* [The Continuity of the Autochthonous Population in Transylvania. The Cemetery No 1 at Bratei], Edit. Acad. RSR, Bucharest, 1973.

Bichir, G., *Cultura carpică* [The Culture of the Carps], Bucharest, 1973.

Bíró, S., *Kisebbségben és többségben. Románok és magyarok (1867 – 1940)* [In the Minority and in the Majority. Rumanians and Hungarians (1867 – 1940).] Edit. Európai Protestáns Magyar Szabadegyetem [European Protestant Hungarian Free University], Bern, 1989.

Bodor, P., *A hisztéria szükségállapota. Kellemetlen kézikönyv Romániáról* [The Emergency State of Hysteria. An unpleasant textbook about Rumania], Szabad Tér Kiadó, Budapest, 1990.

Borsody, S. (red.), *The Hungarians. A Divided Nation,* Yale Russian and East European Publications, 1988.

Cadzow, J.F., Ludanyi, A., Elteto, L. J., (red.), *Transylvania – the Roots of Ethnic Conflict,* Kent State University Press, Kent, Ohio, 1983.

Cantemir, D., *Descriptio antiqvi et hodierni status Moldaviae,* Edit. Acad. RSR, Bucharest, 1973.

Caragiu Marioţeanu, Matilda, *Compendiu de dialectologie română (nord-şi sud-dunăreană),* [Compendium of Rumanian Dialectology (North and South of the Danube)], Edit. ştiinţifică şi enciclopedică, Bucharest, 1975.

---

[1]Abbreviations are mainly constructed by the family name of the author + the year of publishing of the work in question. Where this is not the case, the abbreviation is given following the complete data about the work.

Constantinescu, M., *Daicoviciu*, C., & *Pascu*, Ş., *Istoria României. Compendiu* [The History of Rumania. Compendium], Edit. didactică şi pedagogică, Bucharest, 1969 (first edition).
Abbreviation: IR Compendiu 1969

Daicoviciu, C., *Dacica. Studii şi articole privind istoria veche a pămîntului românesc* [Dacica. Studies and Articles on the Ancient History of the Rumanian Land], Bibliotheca Mvsei Napocensis, Cluj, 1969.

Daicoviciu, C., (red.) *Istoria Romîniei* [The History of Rumania], vol I., Edit. Acad. RPR, Bucharest, 1960.
Abbreviation: IR 1960

Daruvar, Yves de, *Le destin dramatique de la Hongrie*, Editions Albatros, Paris, 1970.

Deér, J., Gáldi, L. (red.), Magyarok és románok [Hungarians and Rumanians], Budapest, 1943.

Densusianu, O., *Histoire de la langue roumaine*, Ed. B. Cazacu, V. Rusu, I. Şerb, Bucharest, 1975.

Dragomir, S., *Vlahii din nordul peninsulei Balcanice în evul mediu* [The Vlachs in the North of the Balkan Peninsula in the Middle Ages], Edit. Acad. RPR, Bucharest, 1959.

Drăghicescu, D., *Din psihologia poporului român* [About the Psychology of the Rumanian People], Bucharest, Leon Alcalay, 1907; new edition: Editura Albatros, Bucharest, 1996.

Du Nay, A., *The Early History of the Rumanian Language*, Edward Sapir Monograph Series in Language, Culture, and Cognition, 3, Jupiter Press, Lake Bluff, Illinois, 1977.

Du Nay, A., *The Origins of the Rumanians. (The Early History of the Rumanian Language.)* Matthias Corvinus Publishing, Toronto–Buffalo, 1996.

Galántai, J., *Trianon és a kisebbségvédelem* [The Peace Treaty of Trianon and the Protection of Minorities], Mecenas, Budapest, 1989.

Giurescu, C.C., & *Giurescu*, D.C., *Istoria românilor din cele mai vechi*

171

timpuri pînă astăzi [The History of the Rumanians from Ancient Times to the Present], Edit. Albatros, Bucharest, 1975.

Gratz, G., A dualizmus kora. Magyarország története – 1867-1918 [The Period of Dualism. The History of Hungary – 1867-1918] vol. I and II. Magyar Szemle Társaság, Budapest, 1934; new edition: Akadémiai Kiadó, Budapest, 1992.

Gratz, G., A forradalmak kora. Magyarország története – 1918-1920 [The Period of the Revolutions. The History of Hungary – 1918-1920]. Magyar Szemle Társaság, Budapest, 1935; new edition: Akadémiai Kiadó, Budapest, 1992.

Gudea, N., "Cîteva observaţii şi note critice cu specială privire la partea istorică a monografiei *Etnogeneza românilor* de I.I. Russu [Some Remarks and Critical Notes with Special Reference to the Historical Part of *Rumanian Ethnogenesis* by I.I. Russu], *Acta Mvsei Napocensis*, XX, 1983, pp. 903 – 916.

Hitchins, K., Orthodoxy and Nationality. Andrei Şaguna and the Rumanians of Transylvania 1846 – 1873, London, 1975.

Hitel – Kolozsvár 1935-1944, II [Credit – Kolozsvár 1935-1944, vol. 2; a collection of studies on Sociology and History] red. Éva Záhonyi, Edit. Bethlen Gábor, Budapest, 1991.

Illyés, E., Ethnic Continuity in the Carpatho-Danubian Area, East European Monographs, CCXLIX, Boulder; Columbia University Press, New York, 1988. 2nd revised edition: Hunyadi Öcs. Mk., Hamilton, Canada, 1992.

Jancsó, B., Erdély története [The History of Transylvania], Minerva, Cluj-Kolozsvár, 1931.

Kiss L., Földrajzi nevek etimológiai szótára [Etymological Dictionary of Geographical names], Akadémiai Kiadó, Budapest, 1978.

Kocsis, I., Történészek a kereszten. A magyar-román viszony elmérgesedésének története [Historians on the Crucifix. How the Relation between Hungarians and Rumanians got worse], Püski, Budapest, 1994.

Kosztin, Á., A dakoromán legenda. Keresztény kultuszhelyek Erdélyben [The Legend of the Daco-Romans. Christian Places of Worship in Transylvania],

Népszava, Budapest, 1989.

Köpeczi, B. (red.), *Erdély története* [The History of Transylvania], vol. I, Akadémiai Kiadó, Budapest, 1986.

Köpeczi, B. (red.) *Erdély rövid története* [A Short History of Transylvania], Akadémiai Kiadó, Budapest, 1989.

Lăncrănjan, I., *Cuvînt despre Transyilvania* [Essay about Transylvania], Edit. Sport-turism, Bucharest, 1982. – 2nd edition: Editura regiei autonome a imprimeriilor, imprimeria "Coresi", Bucharest, 1995.

Maior, P., *Istoria pentru începutul românilor în Dacia* [The Origins of the Rumanians in Dacia], ed. by F. Fugariu, Edit. Albatros, Bucharest, 1970, vol. I.

Meteș, Ș., *Emigrări românești din Transilvania în secolele XIII - XX* [Emigrations of Rumanians from Transylvania in the 13th – 20th centuries], Edit. Științifică și enciclopedică, Bucharest, 2nd edition, 1977.

Mihăescu, H., *Limba latină în provinciile dunărene ale imperiului roman* [The Latin language in the Danubian provinces of the Roman Empire], Edit. Acad. RPR, Bucharest, 1966.

Mihăilă, G., *Studii de lexicologie și istorie a lingvisticii românești* [Studies of Lexicology and the History of Rumanian Linguistics], Edit. Didactică și pedagogică, Bucharest, 1973.
Abbreviation: Mihăilă Studii 1973

Mikó, I., *Huszonkét év. Az erdélyi magyarság politikai története 1918 dec. 1-től 1940 aug. 30-ig* [Twentytwo years. The Political History of the Transylvanian Hungarians from December 1, 1918 to August 30, 1940], Studium, Budapest, 1941.

Mikó, I., *Nemzetiségi jog és nemzetiségi politika* [Nationality Code of Laws and Nationality Policy], Minerva, Kolozsvár, 1944; new edition: Edit. Optimum, 1989.

Nägler, T., *Die Ansiedlung der Siebenbürger Sachsen*, Bucharest, 1979.

Ormos, Mária, *Padovától Trianonig. 1918-1920* [From Padua to Trianon. 1918-1920], Edit. Kossuth, Budapest, 1983.

Papacostea, Ş., "Relaţiile internaţionale în răsăritul şi sud-estul Europei în secolele XIV - XV" [The International Relations in the East and South-East of Europe in the 14th – 15th centuries], *Revista de istorie,* Bucharest, 34, 5, (May 1981), p. 908.

Pascu, Ş., Voievodatul Transilvaniei [The Voivodate of Transylvania], Edit. Dacia, Cluj; vol. I: 1972, vol. II: 1979, vol. III: 1986, vol. IV: 1989.
Abbreviation: Voievodatul I, II, III, and IV, respectively

Pascu, Ş. (red.), *Istoria României. Compendiu* [The History of Rumania. Compendium], 3rd edition, Edit. Didactică şi pedagogică, Bucharest, 1974.
Abbreviation: IR Compendiu 1974

Pascu, Ş., Ce este Transilvania? [What is Transylvania?], Edit. Dacia, Cluj, 1983.

Pascu, Ş., Mit jelent Erdély? [What means Erdély?], (A Hungarian translation of *Ce este Transilvania?*) Edit. Kriterion, Bucharest, 1984.

Pascu, Ş., Rusu, M., Iambor, P., Edroiu, N., Gyulai, P., Wollmann, V., & Matei, Ş, "Cetatea Dăbîca"[The Castle of Dăbîca], *Acta Mvsei Napocensis* V., Cluj, 1968.

Pólay, E., A dáciai viaszostáblák szerződései [The Contracts on the Wax-tablets from Dacia], Közgazdasági és jogi könyvkiadó, Budapest, 1972.

Popović, I., Geschichte der Serbokroatischen Sprache, Bibliotheca Slavica, O. Harrassowitz, Wiesbaden, 1960.

Protase, D., Problema continuităţii în Dacia în lumia arheologiei şi numismaticii [The Problem of Continuity in Dacia in the Light of Archaeology and Numismatics], Edit. Acad. RSR, Bucharest, 1966.

Protase, D., Autohtonii în Dacia [The Autochthons in Dacia], Edit. Ştiinţifică şi enciclopedică, Bucharest, 1980.

Puşcariu, S., "Le rôle de la Transylvanie dans la formation et l'évolution de la langue roumaine", *La Transylvanie,* 1938, p. 41.

Rosetti, A., Istoria limbii române [The History of the Rumanian language], definitive edition, 1986; Edit. Ştiinţifică şi enciclopedică, Bucharest.

Rosetti, A. (red.) *Istoria limbii române* [The History of the Rumanian Language], vol. II; Edit. Acad. RSR, Bucharest, 1969.
Abbreviation: ILR 1969

Rosetti, A. (red.), *Istoria literaturii române* [The History of the Rumanian Literature], Bucharest, 1970.

Russu, I.I., *Limba traco-dacilor* [The language of the Thraco-Dacians], Edit. Ştiinţifică, Bucharest, 1967.

Russu, I.I, *Etnogeneza românilor* [The Ethnogenesis of the Rumanians], Edit. Ştiinţifică şi enciclopedică, Bucharest, 1981.

Schramm, G., "Der rumänische Name der Donau", *Dacoromania* I, 1973, pp. 228 – 236.

Stanciu, S. (red.), *Martiriul evreilor din România 1940 – 1944.* [The Martyrdom of the Jews in Rumania 1940 – 1944], Edit. Hasefer, Bucharest, 1991.

Suciu, C., *Dicţionar istoric al localităţilor din Transilvania* [Historical Dictionary of the localities of Transylvania], Edit. Acad. RSR, Bucharest, vol. I: 1967, vol II: 1968.

Szász, Z., *A románok története* [The History of the Rumanians], Bereményi könyvkiadó, Budapest, 1990.

Tamás, L., *Rómaiak, románok és oláhok Dácia Trajánában* [Romans, Rumanians and Vlachs in Dacia Traiana], Magyar Tudományos Akadémia, Budapest, 1935.

Vékony, G., *Dákok, rómaiak, románok* [Dacians, Romans, Rumanians], Akadémiai kiadó, Budapest, 1989.

SUBJECT INDEX

NAME INDEX

INDEX OF PLACENAMES

184

GAZETTEER
1. Rumanian – Hungarian – German

Abrud – Abrudbánya – Gross-Schlatten

Adjud – Egyed

Aghireş – Egeres

Agrişul Românesc – Olah-Egres

Aiud – Nagyenyed – Strassburg

Alba county – Fehér

Alba Iulia (Bălgrad) – Gyulafehérvár – Weissenburg

Aldorfu see Unirea

Almaş – Almás

Amlaş – Omlás

Ampoiţa – Ompolyica, Kisompoly

Araci – Árapatak

Arad – Arad

Archiud – Erked

Ardeal – Erdély – Siebenbürgen

Ardeova – Erdőfalva

Ardud – Erdőd

Băbâlna – Bábolna

Bălgrad – (see Alba Iulia)

Bârsei, Ţara – Barcaság

Bârzava – Berzova

Band – (Mező)bánd

Beiuş – Belényes

Beclean – Betlen

Bihor county – Bihar

Bistriţa – Beszterce – Bistritz

Benţid – Bencéd

Blaj – Balázsfalva – Blasendorf

Borsec – Borszék

Bran – Törcsvár – Törzburg

Braşov – Brassó – Kronstadt

Bratei – Baráthely – Breitau

Brâncoveneşti – Marosvécs

– Wetsch

Bucur – Bukurfalva

Calata – Kalota

Capâlna – Kápolna

Caşolţ – Hermány – Kastenholz

Caransebeş – Karánsebes – Karansebesch

Caraş-Severin county – Krassó-Szörény

Calvasăr – Hidegvíz – Kaltwasser

Caţa – Kaca – Katzendorf

Căuaci – Kovácsi

Câmpia Transilvaniei – Mezőség

Câmpul Pâinii – Kenyérmező

Câmpulung – Hosszúmező

Cârţa – Kerc – Kerz

Ceheiu – Somlyócsehi

Cetatea de Baltă – Küküllővár – Kokelburg

Chesău – Keszü

Chioar – Kővár

Chiseu – Keszi

Cipău – (Maros)-Csapó

Ciuci – Maroscsúcs

Ciumeşti – Csomaköz – Schamagosch

Cloaşterf – Miklóstelke – Klossdorf

Cluj – Kolozsvár – Klausenburg

Codlea – Feketehalom – Zeiden

Colun – Kolun – Kolun

Comiat – Komját

Copand – Maroskoppánd

Crainimăt – Királynémeti –

Baierdorf

Ineu – Jenő

Criş – Körös
Crişana – Körösvidék
Cund – Kund – Reussdorf

Dăbâca county – Doboka
Dej – Dés – Desch
Demsuş – Demsus
Deva – Déva – Schlossberg,
   Dimrich, Denburg
Dobra – Jófő, Dobra
Dobrin – Debren

Făgăraş – Fogaras – Fogarasch
Feldioara – Földvár – Marienburg

Gârbova – Szászorbó – Urwegen
Gârbău – Magyar-Orbó
Gârbăul Românesc – Oláhgorbó
Ghimbav – Vidombák –
   Weidenbach
Giula – Kolozsgyula
Giulacuta – Gyulakuta
Giulatelec – Gyulatelke
Giuleşti – Máragyulafalva
Giuluş – Gyulas
Gurasada – Guraszáda

Harniceşti – Harnicsháza
Haţeg – Hátszeg – Hotzing
Hăghig – Hídvég
Hălchiu – Höltövény – Heldsdorf
Hălmagiu – Halmágy – Halmagen
Hăşmaş – Hagimas
Hoghiz – Olthévíz – Warmbach,
   Warmwasser
Hunedoara county – Hunyad(vár)

Ilia – Illye (Elye)
Iladia – Illyéd

Lechinţa de Mureş – Maroslekence
Lopadea Veche – Oláh Lapád
Lugoj – Lugos
Luna – Lóna
Lunca – Lonka

Maramureş county – Máramaros
Mărul – Almafa
Madefalău (Siculeni) – Madéfalva
Mediaş – Medgyes – Mediasch
Medieş – Aranyosmegyes
Mestecăniş – Nyíres
Mehadia – Mihályd, Mehádia
Micherechi – Méhkerék (Hungary)
Micloşoara – Miklósvár
Moreşti – Malomfalva
   – Mühlendorf
Mugeni – Bögöz

Năsăud – Naszód
Noşlac – Nagylak
Nucşoara – Nuksora

Oaş, Ţara – Avas
Obreja – Obrázsa
Oituz – Ojtoz
Oradea – Nagyvárad –
   Grosswardein
Orăştie – Szászváros – Broos
Orşova – Orsova

Pianul de Jos – Alsópián,
   Szászpián – Deutschpien

Răcăjdia, Răcăşdia – Rakasd
Răşinari – Resinár –
   Städterdorf, Reschinar
Râşnov – Rozsnyó
Râu de Mori – Malomvize

Râuşor – Rusor
Rea – Gonoszfalu
Rebrişoara – Kisrebra
Ribiţa – Ribice
Ruşi – Rüsz – Reussen
Ruşi – Rusz, (1453: Oroszfalw)
Rodna – Radna
Roşia Abrudului, Roşia de Munte,
    Roşia Montană – Verespatak
Rotbav – (Szász)-Veresmart –
    Rotbach

Salonta – Nagyszalonta
Sarsig – Sárszeg
Satu Mare – Szatmár
Sárkány – Şercaia, Şerpeni –
    Schirkanyen
Sânmiclăuşul (Sânnicolaul) Român
    – Oláhszentmiklós
Sântana de Mureş – Maros-
    szentanna
Sântimbru – Szentimre
Saschiz – Szászkézd (Zaazkyzd)
    – Kaissd, Keissd
Săcădate – Szakadát
Sebeş – Szászsebes
Sfântu Gheorghe – Sepsi-
    szentgyörgy
Sibiu – Nagyszeben – Hermann-
    stadt
Siculeni – Madéfalva
Sighişoara – Segesvár
Silivaşul Săsesc – Szász-Szilvás
Slimnic – Szelindek –
    Stolzenburg
Solnoc-Dăbâca county – Szolnok-
    Doboka
Soporul de Câmpie – Mezőszopor
Streiu – Zejkalva
Stremţ – Diód – Nussschloss
Suplac – Széplak

Şelimbăr – Sellenberk –
    Schellenberg
Şiclău (Arad) – Sikló
Şoimuş – Solymos
Şura Mică – Kiscsűr

Tălmaciu – Talmács
Tămăşasa – Tamáspatak
Târgu Mureş – Marosvásárhely –
    Neumarkt
Târnava Mare county –
    Nagyküküllő
Târnăveni – Dicsőszentmárton
Teliu – Nyén
Teiuş – Tövis
Timişoara – Temesvár
Tohanul Vechi – Oláhteleky
Trăscău, Rimetea – Torockó –
    Eisenmarkt
Turda – Torda – Thorenburg
Turia – Torja

Unirea (Aldorfu) – Aldorf –
    Wallendorf
Ungra – Ungra – Galt

Valcău,Văleni – Magyarvalkó
Valea Sasului – Sóspatak
Veneţia – Venice
Viscri – Szászfehéregyháza –
    Weisskirch
Vladimirescu, Glogovaţ, Glogovăţ,
    – Glogovác, Öthalom –
    Glogowatz
Vurpăr – Borberek – Burgberg

Zarand – Zaránd
Zlatna – Zalatna – Klein-
    schlatten, Goldmarkt

GAZETTEER
2. Hungarian – Rumanian – German

Abrudbánya – Abrud – Gross-schlatten
Aldorf – Unirea (Aldorfu) – Wallendorf
Almafa – Mărul
Almás – Almaş
Alsópián – Pianul de Jos – Deutschpien
Arad – Arad
Aranyosmegyes – Medieş
Árapatak – Araci (Arpatac)
Avas – Oaş

Balázsfalva – Blaj – Blasendorf
Baráthely – Bratei – Breitau
Barcaság – Ţara Bârsei – Burzenland
Bábolna – Băbâlna
Belényes – Beiuş
Bencéd – Benţid
Berzova – Bârzava
Beszterce – Bistriţa – Bistritz
Betlen – Beclean
Bihar county – Bihor
Borberek – Vurpăr – Burgberg
Borszék – Borsec
Bögöz – Mugeni
Brassó – Braşov – Kronstadt
Bukurfalva – Bucur

Csomaköz – Ciumeşti – Scha-magosch

Debren – Dobrin
Dés – Dej – Desch
Demsus – Demsuş

Déva – Deva
Dicsőszentmárton – Târnăveni (Dicio Sînmartin)
Diód – Stremţ – Nussschloss
Doboka county – Dăbâca
Dobra see Jófő

Egeres – Aghireş
Egyed – Adjud
Erdély – Ardeal (Transilvania) – Siebenbürgen
Erdőd – Ardud
Erdőfalva – Ardeova
Erked – Archiud

Fehér county – Alba
Feketehalom – Codlea – Zeiden
Fogaras – Făgăraş
Földvár – Feldioara – Marienburg

Glogovác, Öthalom – Vladimirescu, Glogovaţ, Glogovăţ
Gonoszfalu – Rea
Guraszáda – Gurasada
Gyulafehérvár – Alba Iulia (Bălgrad) – Weissenburg
Gyulakuta – Giulacuta
Gyulas – Giuluş
Gyulatelke – Giulatelec

Hagimas (Hagymás) – Hăşmaş
Halmágy – Hălmagiu
Harnicsháza – Harnicesşti
Hátszeg – Haţeg – Hotzing
Hermány – Caşolţ – Kastenholz

Hidegvíz – Calvasăr – Kaltwasser
Hídvég – Hăghig
Hosszúmező – Câmpulung
Höltövény – Hălchiu
Hunyad county – Hunedoara

Illye (Elye) – Ilia
Illyéd – Iladia

Jenő – Ineu
Jófő, Dobra – Dobra

Kaca – Caţa – Katzendorf
Kalota – Calata
Kápolna – Capâlna
Karánsebes – Caransebeş – Karansebesch
Kenyérmező – Câmpul Pâinii
Kerc – Cârţa – Kerz
Keszi – Chiseu
Keszü – Chesău
Királynémeti – Crainimăt – Baierdorf
Kiscsűr – Şura Mică
Kisrebra – Rebrişoara
Kolozsvár – Cluj – Klausenburg
Kolozsgyula – Giula
Kolun – Colun – Kolun
Komját – Comiat
Kovácsi – Căuaci
Körös – Criş
Körösvidék – Crişana
Kővár – Chioar
Krassó-Szörény county – Caraş-Severin
Kund – Cund – Reussdorf
Küküllővár – Cetatea de Baltă – Kokelburg

Lóna – Luna
Lonka – Lunca

Lugos – Lugoj

Madéfalva – Madefalău, Siculeni
Magyarorbó – Gârbău
Magyarvalkó – Valcău, Văleni
Malomfalva – Moreşti
– Mühlendorf
Malomvize – Râu de Mori
Maroscsapó – Cipău
Maroscsúcs – Ciuci
Maroskoppánd – Copand
Maroslekence – Lechinţa de Mureş
Marosszentanna – Sântana de Mureş
Marosvásárhely – Târgu Mureş – Neumarkt
Marosvécs – Brâncoveneşti – Wetsch
Máragyulafalva – Giuleşti
Máramaros county – Maramureş
Medgyes – Mediaş – Mediasch
Mezőbánd – Band
Mezőség – Câmpia Transilvaniei
Mezőszopor – Soporul de Câmpie
Méhkerék – Micherechi
Mihályd, Mehádia – Mehadia
Miklóstelke – Cloaşterf – Klossdorf
Miklósvár – Micloşoara

Nagyenyed – Aiud – Strassburg
Nagyküküllő county – Târnava Mare
Nagylak – Noşlac
Nagyszalonta – Salonta
Nagyszeben – Sibiu – Hermannstadt
Nagyvárad – Oradea
Naszód – Năsăud
Nuksora – Nucşoara

191

Nyén – Teliu
Nyíres – Mestecăniş

Obrázsa – Obreja
Ojtoz – Oituz
Oláhegres – Agrişul Românesc
Oláhgorbó – Gârbăul Românesc
Oláhlapád – Lopadea Veche
Oláhszentmiklós – Sânnicolaul
   (Sânmiclăuşul) Român
Olthévíz – Hoghiz – Warmbach,
   Warmwasser
Oláhteleky, (1294:Tohou [Tohan],
terra seu villa) – Tohanul Vechi
Omlás – Amlaş
Ompolyica, Kisompoly – Ampoiţa
Orsova – Orşova

Radna – Rodna
Rakasd – Răcăjdia, Răcăşdia
Resinár – Răşinari – Städterdorf
Ribice – Ribiţa
Rozsnyó – Râşnov
Rusor – Râuşor
Rusz (1453:Oroszfalw) – Ruşi
Rüsz – Ruşi – Reussen

Sárkány – Şercaia, Şerpeni –
   Schirkanyen
Sárszeg – Sarsig
Segesvár – Sighişoara –
   Schessburg
Sellenberk – Şelimbăr –
   Schellenberg
Sepsiszentgyörgy – Sfântu
   Gheorghe
Sikló – Şiclău (Arad)
Solymos – Şoimuş
Somlyócsehi – Ceheiu
Sóspatak – Valea Sasului

Szakadát – Săcădate
Szatmár – Satu Mare
Szászfehéregyháza – Viscri –
   Weisskirch
Szászkézd (Zaazkyzd) – Saschiz
   – Kaissd, Keissd
Szászorbó – Gârbova – Urwegen
Szászszilvás – Silivaşul Săsesc
Szászváros – Orăştie – Broos
Szászveresmart – Rotbav –
   Rotbach
Szászsebes – Şebeş – Mühlbach
Szelindek – Slimnic –
   Stolzenburg
Szentimre – Sântimbru
Széplak – Suplac

Talmács – Tălmaciu
Tamáspatak – Tămăşasa
Temesvár – Timişoara –
   Temeschwar
Torda – Turda – Thorenburg
Torja – Turia
Törcsvár – Bran – Törzburg
Tövis – Teiuş – Dreikirchen,
   Dornstadt
Torockó – Trăscău, Rimetea –
   Eisenmarkt

Ungra – Ungra – Galt

Venice – Veneţia
Verespatak – Roşia Abrudului,
   Roşia de Munte, Roşia Montană
Vidombák – Ghimbav –
   Weidenbach

Zalatna – Zlatna – Klein-
   schlatten, Goldmarkt
Zarand – Zaránd
Zejkfalva – Streiu

GAZETTEER
3. German – Hungarian – Rumanian

Baierdorf – Királynémeti – Crainimăt

Bistritz – Beszterce – Bistriţa

Blasendorf – Balázsfalva – Blaj

Breitau – Baráthely – Bratei

Broos – Szászváros – Orăştie

Burgberg – Borberek – Vurpăr

Burzenland – Barcaság – Ţara Bârsei

Desch – Dés – Dej

Deutschpien – Alsópián – Pianul de Jos

Dreikirchen, Dornstadt – Tövis – Teiuş

Eisenmarkt – Torockó – Trăscău, Rimetea

Fogarasch – Fogaras – Făgăraş

Goldmarkt *see* Kleinschlatten

Grossschlatten – Abrudbánya – Abrud

Halmagen – Halmágy – Hălmagiu

Heldsdorf – Hălchiu – Höltövény

Hermannstadt – Nagyszeben – Sibiu

Hotzing – Hátszeg – Haţeg

Kaissd, Keissd – Szászkézd – Saschiz

Kaltwasser – Hidegvíz – Calvasăr

Kastenholz – Hermány – Caşolţ

Katzendorf – Kaca – Caţa

Karansebesch – Karánsebes – Caransebeş

Kerz – Kerc – Cârţa

Klausenburg – Kolozsvár – Cluj

Kleinschlaten, Goldmarkt – Zalatna – Zlatna

Klossdorf – Miklóstelke – Cloaşterf

Kokelburg – Küküllővár – Cetatea de Baltă

Kolun – Kolun – Colun

Kronstadt – Brassó – Braşov

Marienburg – Földvár – Feldioara

Mediasch – Medgyes – Mediaş

Mühlbach – Szászsebes – Sebeş

Mühlendorf – Malomfalva – Moreşti

Neumarkt – Marosvásárhely – Târgu Mureş

Nussschloss – Diód – Stremţ

Reussen – Rüsz – Ruşi

Reussdorf – Kund – Cund

Rotbach – Szászveresmart – Rotbav

Städterdorf, Reschinar – Resinár – Răşinari

Strassburg – Nagyenyed – Aiud

Schamagosch – Csomaköz – Ciumeşti

Schessburg – Segesvár –

Sighişoara
Schirkanyen – Sárkány – Şercaia
Schlossberg, Dimrich, Denburg –
Déva – Deva

Temeschwar – Temesvár –
Timişoara
Thorenburg – Torda – Turda
Törzburg – Törcsvár – Bran

Urwegen – Szászorbó – Gârbova

Wallendorf – Aldorf – Unirea
(Aldorfu)
Warmbach, Warmwasser –
Olthévíz – Hoghiz
Weidenbach – Vidombák –
Ghimbav
Weissenburg – Gyulafehérvár –
Alba Iulia (Bălgrad)
Weisskirch – Szászfehéregyháza
– Viscri
Wetsch – Marosvécs
– Brâncoveneşti

Zeiden – Feketehalom – Codlea

Virgiliu Ştefănescu-Drăgăneşti:

ROMANIAN CONTINUITY IN ROMAN DACIA
LINGUISTIC EVIDENCE
Romanian Historical Studies, Miami Beach, Florida, 1986
A CRITICAL SURVEY

The author presents his ideas in four chapters: 1) Relations between Latin and Gothic; 2) the words *Valah* and *Rumân;* 3) the word *Ardeal;* and 4) Rumanian religious terminology which according to the author was borrowed by the Hungarians before the year 1001 A.D.

1. "Daco-Roman Borrowings in Gothic and their Importance for the History of the Romanian People"
Ştefănescu-Drăgăneşti (ŞD) puts forward the theory that the interactions between the Latin and the Gothic languages took place in Dacia Traiana.
a) The Latin elements in the Gothic language.
After a long introduction, in which the author affirms that a numerous Latin-speaking population remained in Dacia after 275 A.D., when the province was abandoned by the Roman state, it is concluded that the Goths could borrow the numerous Latin elements found in their language "only from the Romanized population which remained in Dacia" (p. 16).

If a Latin-speaking people had lived in Dacia in the 4th century, a Latin influence could have been exerted upon Gothic there. But the author makes a logical error, since nothing indicates that such an influence could **only** have occurred in Dacia. In fact, it can be shown about most of the Latin elements in Gothic that they were **not** borrowed in the territory of Dacia Traiana.

ŞD lists 18 examples of Latin words borrowed by Gothic (p. 18). He forgets, however, the chronological aspect: in what period were these words borrowed? It is possible to show that at least 12 of these 18 words were transferred to Gothic **during the first two centuries A.D.** This is indicated by certain phonetical features: the preservation of the Latin semivowel *u;* as well of the diphthong *ai* (*Caesar* > *kaisar*); loss of the final vowel: Latin *lucerna* > Gothic *lukarn.* It was in this period that most of the Latin elements were borrowed by the Gothic language. Many of these words exist also in modern Germanic languages: *wein* > English wine; *asilus* > English ass, German *Esel;* *kaupon* > German *kaufen,* Swedish *köpa,* etc. **In these centuries, no Goths were living**

in Dacia. Corazza[1] mentions 26 Latin lexical elements in Gothic from this period.

In the 3rd century, at least three of those 18 words listed by ŞD were borrowed (*arka, karkara* [cf. German *Karcer*], and *skaurpio*. Considering that *karkara* also exists in German and that there were no scorpions in Dacia, it is very unlikely that these words would have been adopted by the Goths in Dacia. Corazza mentions 17 words borrowed by Gothic in the 3rd century. Roman – Gothic contact was probably more close in that century than earlier. Words as *militon* "to serve in the army" indicate Gothic soldiers in the Roman empire, and are not restricted to Dacia; as are not such words as *assarjus* "a bronze coin" *unkja* "a measure of land" indicating economic contact (*unkja* appears in several modern Germanic languages). There are words which because of their semantic content must have been borrowed elsewhere than in Dacia: e.g., *ulbandus* "camel", *saur* "Syrian", *saban*, a linen cloth made at Saban, near Bagdad. Not all words show such specific characteristics, but their adoption in Dacia is unlikely, since the Goths lived at most 25 years (in the last quarter of the century) in Dacia in the 3rd century.

In the entire 4th century, Goths were living in the former province of Dacia, so they could have borrowed Latin words if a Latin-speaking population were really living there. However, the number of Latin words adopted by the Goths in the 4th century is insignificant (Corazza mentions six).

Thus, ŞD-s conclusion that Latin loanwords in Gothic prove "a massive Latin-speaking Daco-Roman population" in Dacia in the 3rd – 4th centuries (p. 19) cannot be accepted. (One may add that not a single of the Latin words which were borrowed by the Goths exists in Rumanian.)

Affixes, loan translations, grammatical loans and similarities of the Gothic grammar with Latin indicate relatively close and durable contact between the two peoples, also attested to by the loanwords. They have of course no value in the localisation of contact. (Many loan translations were made by Wulfila.)

b) Assumed borrowings from Gothic by "Daco-Roman"

ŞD mentions eight words "which we think to have been taken by the Daco-Romans from the Visigoths at the same time when the latter borrowed from them the Latin elements shown above".

These hypotheses, considered by ŞD "most probable", ("we think it could have been adopted from Proto-Romanian", etc.) cannot be accepted. Since the assumption that the Latin loanwords in Gothic were borrowed in Dacia was

---

[1]Vittoria Corazza, "Le parole latine in gotico" [The Latin words in Gothic], in *Atti della Accademia Nazionale dei Lincei*, Roma, 1969; VIII, vol. XIV, Fasc. 1.

shown false, this theory is also groundless. But there are also certain circumstances and characteristics that exlude or make a borrowing from Gothic by "Daco-Roman" very unlikely of seven of these eight words. Thus, Rumanian *bucher* "crammer, swot; person who learns something by heart, in a mechanical way" is obviously of Slavic origin, as is also *buche* "the 2nd letter in the Cyrillic alphabet; letter, book, etc." (The Cyrillic alphabet did not exist in the 4th century.) The verb *a găti* exists also in Slavic and in Albanian; *gard* is found in Albanian, *iubi* is found in all Slavic languages. Rumanian *hrană* "food" derives from Salvic *xrana* and is one of those Slavic words which introduced the sound *h* (as German *ch*) into Rumanian.[1] Also *leac* (Old Slavic *lěkŭ* 'remedy') and *sticlă* (Old Bulgarian *sticlo*) derive most probably from Slavic.[2]

ȘD assumes also grammatical patterns found in the Gothic Bible and without parallels in the Romance languages other than Rumanian, to have been borrowed by the "Daco-Romans" in Dacia (p. 26 – 27). These are: the forming of the future tense with the auxiliary *a voi*; colloquial future with *a avea*; and the postposition of the definite article. **These are balkanisms,** (balkanisms are found in Rumanian, Albanian, Bulgarian, Greek, and Serbo-Croatian).[3]

Concluding, it must be stated that the Latin influence upon the Gothic language (and the other Old Germanic languages) was exerted in large parts of Europe, during several centuries of contact between speakers of the two languages. Regarding most of this influence, there are features (pertaining to chronology, sound patterns, and semantics) that indicate that it **could not have been exerted in the territory of Dacia Traiana.** Old Germanic (Gothic) elements in Rumanian are assumed but none of these assumptions stands up for a critical examination.

2."The Historical Significance of the Words 'Valah' and 'Rumân'"

The word *valah* is defined by Breban as follows: "the name given to the Rumanians in the Middle Ages by other peoples".[4]

Ștefănescu-Drăgănești assumes that the Hungarians borrowed the Germanic word *walah* "no doubt before they came to Pannonia". The Hungarian word for *valah* is *oláh*. ȘD argues that this cannot have been obtained from Slavic

---

[1] Rosetti, 1986, p. 288 and 315.

[2] Ibid., pp. 305 and 288, respectively.

[3] Cf. for example K. Sandfeld, *Linguistique Balkanique. Problèmes et résultats,* Paris, 1930; Du Nay, 1996, pp. 85 - 87, 238 - 239; Rosetti, 1986, p. 257 - 258; A. Rosetti, *La linguistique balkanique,* Bucharest, 1985.

[4] Vasile Breban, *Dicționar al limbii române contemporane* [Dictionary of Contemporary Rumanian], Bucharest, 1980, p. 653.

"because in Hungarian there are a lot of words beginning with the consonant *v* (see any Hungarian dictionary) and therefore the pronunciation *Vlah* would have been preserved" (p. 39, referring to a Hungarian-Rumanian and a Hungarian-English dictionary).

The Hungarian language evades consonant clusters at the beginning of words. The consonant *v* existed in its present-day form in Hungarian since the 14th century. Earlier, it was pronounced like English *w,* thus as a bilabial rather than labio-dental *v.* There is no evidence that the Hungarians would have adopted *walah* before the 13th century. It is generally considered to derive from Slavic.[1]

An examination of the designation for the Rumanians in early documents of the Hungarian chancellary, written in the Latin language, shows that *oláh* was not used before the mid-thirteenth century. Those referring to Transylvania contain mentionings of Vlachs beginning with the year 1212. Tamás listed all these documents, as follows:[2] In a document written in 1222, *terra Blacorum* is mentioned, in 1223, *terram ... exemptam de Blaccis,* in 1224, *silva Blacorum et Bissenorum.* The consistent referring to the Vlachs as *Blaccus* suggests that in those decades, a name with a similar sound pattern was used by the Hungarians. In contrast to this, all the documents written after the Tartar invasion (1241 – 1242) designate the Rumanians as *olacis* – which is the Latinized form of Hungarian *oláh.* In 1247, there is *terra Szeneslai Vaivoda Olacorum,* in 1250, *Olacis,* in 1252, *terra Olacorum de Kurch,* in 1260, *valachi* appears in a text describing soldiers fighting in the Hungarian army; uncertain if coming from outside the country or not; in 1262, there is *Olachis,* in 1291 again *Olachis,* in 1292, *Olacorum,* in 1293, *universos Olacos,* and in 1294, *Olachys.* From these data it appears that the Hungarians used initially a word corresponding to "vlach" (in Latin documents, *Blaccus)* to designate the Vlachs, and thereafter, from the mid-thirteenth century on, *oláh* was used. (Before 1212, no documents mention this population in Hungary.)

The connection assumed by ŞD of the name of prince *Ramunc* mentioned in the *Niebelungenlied* with Rumanian *Râmnic* is unacceptable. Rumanian *Râmna, Râmnicul, Râmnicul Sărat, Gârla Râmnicului, Râmnicelul,* etc. derive from Slavic.[3] The Slavic word from which these names derive is *ryba* "fish"; many of

---

[1] Bárczi, G., *A magyar nyelv életrajza* [The history of the Hungarian language], 3rd edition, Budapest, 1975, pp. 50, 119, 138.

[2] Tamás,L., *Rómaiak, románok és oláhok Dácia Trajánában* [Romans, Rumanians and Vlachs in Dacia Traiana], Budapest, 1935, p. 191 - 197.

[3] Iordan,I., *Nume de locuri românești în Republica Populară Română* [Rumanian Placenames in the Peoples´Republic of Rumania], vol. I, Edit. Acad.RPR, Bucharest,1952, p. 73 – 74.

them designate rivers. There is Slovakian *Ribnik* "brook with fishes", Croatian and Serbian *Ribnik,* Ukrainian *Rybnyk.* From Slavic *ryba* derive also Rumanian toponyms, such as *Ribiţa* and *Ribiţioara;* cf. Slovakian *Ribitse.* (ŞD mentions that there are very little fish to be caught in some of these rivers today. This is, of course, irrelevant; the names were given centuries ago.)

The thought that "there was only one Wallachian dukedom at the time of Attila" (p. 42) revives a theory put forward by Petru Maior in the early 19th century; Maior believed that the Huns lived together with "Daco-Romans" in Moldavia and Transylvania. Today it is clear that in the time of Attila, in the 5th century A.D., only the Latin language existed; the different Romance languages (thus also Rumanian) emerged 3 – 4 centuries later.

The term *rumân* has in the course of time acquired the sense of "shepherd" and, later, that of "peasant" and "serf', "thus underlining the continuous presence of the large number of Daco-Romans in former Dacia, bearing the hardships of being ruled by various invaders" according to ŞD (p. 43–44). This kind of reasoning is not new; Diculescu assumed that the sense of "serf' developed during the symbiosis with the Gepidae, because of the subordinated situation of the "Daco-Romans". These are unacceptable assumptions; the sense of "serf' of the word *rumân* developed in the Rumanian voivodates because of the misery and severe exploitation the peasants were exposed to for several centuries there (see above, Pascu, *A History of Transylvania. A critical survey,* pp. 100– 102, 106-108).

Another proof of Daco-Roman continuity according to Ş.D. is the word *bătrân* "old", from Latin *veteranus* "soldier wo had served his time", thus with a changed sense (p. 44). This is also a naive theory; veterans were living in most Roman provinces, the change of sense *veteran* > *bătrân* is not specific to a certain territory but could have occurred anywhere in the Roman Empire.

3. "The Historical Significance of the Word 'Ardeal'"

Ştefănescu-Drăgăneşti affirms that *Ardeal* "has always been used by all Romanians as a second name for Transylvania" (p. 49).

There are two problems with this statement. The designation *Ardeal* is not a second name for Transylvania, but the original and for a long time the only Rumanian name for the province. In other words, it is the popular name, used by the peasants. *Transilvania* is taken from Latin, and is, as will be shown below, the translation of the original sense of the Hungarian name *Erdély.* The other question concerns the word "always" in the above statement. The first known document that mentions *Ardeliu* is from 1432.

According to Ş.D., *Ardeal* derives from the Indoeuropean root *ard-,* which means "high, height, hill, mountain, woody region" (p. 49). ŞD enumerates a large number of toponyms from all over Europe; and states that the root *ard-*

derives from Celtic.

The number of toponyms with *ard-* is really impressive. However, these names have nothing to do with *Ardeal,* the similarity is a simple coincidence. (One could also mention Rumanian *arde* "to burn", or *ardei* "pepper, paprica", [borrowed by some Hungarian dialects in Transylvania: *árdé*] also with a similar sound pattern but totally irrelevant in this context.)

The reasoning given by Ş.D. about Hungarian *erdő* and Erdély is full of serious errors. The word *erdő* "forest" is a Hungarian word and existed at the beginning of the second millennium: it derives from the verb *eredni* "to originate".[1] The Hungarian word *fa* does not mean "a clamp of trees, a little wood" (p. 58) but simply "tree". Thus, the Hungarians did not need to borrow a Rumanian word for "forest" from the Rumanians; (it is also quite absurd to assume that such a word would derive from the name of a province). The assumed form *"erdel"* for Rumanian *Ardeal* (p. 58) is thus wrong, as well as the reasoning after this (p. 58 – 59) .

The Hungarian designation for Transylvania is *Erdély.* Its first known mentioning in a written text is from the end of the 12th century, in the *Gesta* by Anonymus: *siluam igfon que iacet ad erdeuelu:* i.e., *erdő* + *elv(e)*: "beyond the forest". The documents of the Hungarian chancellary were in that time written in Latin, and the translation of this sense appears first: in 1075, *Ultra silvam* is recorded, in 1111, *Mercurius princeps Ultrasilvanus.* In the same century appears the form used later on: *Partes Transsilvanae.* The German translation appears also early: in the 13th century, *Überwald* or *Über Walt* are mentioned.[2] The Germans have, however, their own specific name for the province: *Siebenbürgen.* The Rumanians borrowed Hungarian *Erdély* in the form of *Ardeliu,* attested for the first time in 1432. The *e > a* change is regular in Hungarian borrowings of the Rumanian language: Hungarian *Egyed >* Rumanian *Adjud, Egeres > Aghireş, Egerbegy > Agârbiciu,* as well as *ellen > alean, egres > agriş,* etc. According to Király, "the number of words of Hungarian origin with this change of *e-* into *a-* well surpasses the number of inherited words or imported from other languages which show the same phenomenon."[3]

Toponyms with *"erdő"* appear all over the territory where Hungarian is spoken. In Transylvania, they were borrowed in different sound patterns by speakers of Rumanian. *Erdőfalva* "village of the forest" in Cluj county was borrowed in the form of *Ardeova;* a village with the same name in Hunyad

---

[1] Géza Bárczi, *A magyar nyelv életrajza* [The History of the Hungarian Language], Budapest, 1975, p. 107.

[2] Ştefan Pascu, *Voievodatul Transilvaniei,* I, 1972, p. 22.

[3] Francisc Király, *Contacte lingvistice* [Linguistic Contacts], Timişoara, 1990, p. 126.

(Hunedoara) became *Ardeu* in Rumanian. *Erdőd* (Hungarian *erdő* + the suffix -*d*) in the region of Szatmár (Satu Mare) was borrowed in the form *Ardud*. In documents, these Hungarian names are mentioned beginning with the 13th to the early 16th centuries; the Rumanian names much later.[1] In Rumanian, these names have no sense; and this is the case also of other borrowings of Hungarian toponyms, such as Hungarian *Erősd* (*erős* "strong" + the suffix -*d*) > Rumanian *Ariuşd*, etc.

Rumanian *agriş* "gooseberry" derives from Hungarian *egres*, not the other way around, as asserted by Ş.D (p. 60). This Hungarian word has several sound patterns, such as *egris, egrës*, etc. The original meanings were "unripe grape, gooseberry, the juice of unripe grape, and wild wine". Of these, modern Hungarian has only the second; and modern Rumanian the first and the second. Rumanian has, however, developed three new senses: "a kind of sorrel, red currant and black currant".

Several authors have assumed that placenames of Celtic origin exist in Rumania (G. Weigand, G. Kisch, etc.) None of these theories stands up, however, to a critical examination. Rumanian toponyms: *Galaţi, Grindul Galaţilor, Gălăţeni,* etc. do not derive from Celtic *Gallatae* or *Gallati.* Instead, they may render the personal name found in documents *Galacz,* the South Slavic personal name *Gal,* or even the Hungarian appellative *gálic(kő)* or *galacz(kő)* "vitriol, copper sulphate (stone)". The name of the city *Galaţi* on the shore of the Black Sea may derive from Cumanian *gala(t)* < Arabic *kalhat* "fortress, fortified town".[2] One may agree with Iorgu Iordan, who does not believe in Celtic toponyms in Rumania "because the preservation of a so ancient people (before the Rumanians existed as an ethnic entity), even in the form of some toponyms, seems to me very little probable".[3]

> Ştefănescu-Drăgăneşti, p. 61:
>
> In point of grammar, Hungarian *ellen* is a proposition meaning "against, counter to", while Rumanian *alean* is a noun meaning "affliction, moral pain, distress", a much more extensive meaning expressing the sufferings of a people under foreign occupation and oppressed for centuries on end. The word could therefore be of Daco-Roman origin and borrowed by Hungarian.[...] its adoptation by the Romanians from the Hungarians cannot be sufficiently proved.

ŞD mentions Old Slavic *alinu* and Latin *alienus* as possible sources of *alean.*

---

[1] Suciu, vol. I, 1967, p. 43.

[2] Iordan, *Nume de locuri româneşti în RPR* [Rumanian placenames in the Peoples' Republic of Rumania], 1952, p. 229.

[3] Ibid.

It may be of interest to present the case of Rumanian *alean* in some detail, because it shows how easy it is to find false etymologies which suit to preconceived ideas.

Hungarian *ellen* has 4 different senses: 1) postposition, 2) adverb, 3) noun, and 4) adjective. Rumanian *alean* has the following senses: 1) preposition, 2) prepositional and adverbial locutions, 3) noun. The original sense of Hungarian *ellen* is "before something"; the semantic development was then: "before something" > "against something" > "towards (something)". After the original sense was forgotten, *ellen* became an adverb signifying attack or defence, and this is its main sense today. Rumanian *alean* changed from functions of postposition and of adverb to that of a noun. This is a specific development only in Rumanian, and there are no Hungarian counterparts to the senses developed in this way. However, they departed from a concrete element of the senses of Hungarian *ellen*: "(all kinds of) antipathy" or even more generally "sentiment (connected to negative notions)". Thus, Rumanian *alean* has, as a noun, the following senses: 1) sorrow, sadness; 2) longing; in Transylvania, archaic: "anger, hatred", in Transylvania and Moldavia, "grief, sorrow, melancholy, nostalgy".

As a prepostition, *alean* means in Transylvania "against, in face of".

This word belongs to the old stratum of loanwords from Hungarian; it appears for the first time in *Psaltirea Scheiană* (16th century). It is deeply rooted in the language; with powerful poetical effects, which explains its frequent use in old Rumanian religious texts, as well as its occurence in modern poetry.[1] Rumanian *alean* has also derivatives which are no longer used, but appear in early texts, such as the Dictionary of Anonymus from the Banat: *aleniş* "enemy", from Hungarian *ellenes* "opposed, hostile to"; *alenşig* "enemy", from Hungarian *ellenség* "enemy"; *alenzuiesc* "I am opposed to (something)", from Hungarian *ellenzek*, with the same sense; *alenzuitură* "opposition", from Hungarian *ellenkezés*, with the same sense. These loanwords, with a sound pattern very near their Hungarian counterpart and an identical sense, provide an additional proof to the conclusion that Rumanian *alean* was borrowed from Hungarian.

The case of *alean* is a good example of the risks of etymologies not based upon a thorough knowledge of the circumstances: for example, both the form and the sense of Latin *alienus* "foreign, alien" resemble Rumanian *alean*, but this etymology is nevertheless false.

---

[1] The sense of this word developed through several intermediate senses towards "dozing": cf. the poem of Eminescu: *Freamăt de codru:* "Tresărind scînteie lacul /Şi se leagănă sub soare; /Eu, privindu-l din pădure, /Las *aleanul* să mă fure /Şi ascult de la răcoare /Pitpalacul." [Sigh of the forest. The spark makes the see to quiver /And it swings under the sun; /I, looking it from the forest, /Allow myself a little sleep /And I listen from the coolness /To the quail.]

4. "The Significance of Romanian Religious Terminology Borrowed by Hungarian before the Year 1001"

The theory put forward in this chapter is that the Hungarians borrowed Rumanian words before the year 1001 (their Christianization according to the Roman Catholic Church) which

> appear to be indisputable proofs, on the other hand, of the presence of the Romanians in the plains of the river Thiess [sic] and Transylvania, when the Hungarians came to Pannonia at the end of the 9th century (p. 69).

(The German name of the river in question is rightly Theiss, Hungarian Tisza, Rumanian Tisa.) Ştefănescu-Drăgăneşti asserts that the Rumanian religious terminology was created in Dacia "from Latin language material" (p. 72), whither many Christians fled from Rome, where they were persecuted. (One of those six words given as examples is of Hungarian origin: *lăcaş* "dwelling, home", from Hungarian *lakás*, with the same sense. It is now obsolete, but was frequent in the early religious texts: *lăcaş sfînt* "church".)

The author asserts that the Christians "established important communities which played an important part in Romanizing Dacia..." There is no written source about this, and even less substance is in the assertion of Ş.D. that there was a "uniform religious atmosphere" (p.74) in Dacia Traiana. Archaeological finds unearthed there abound of many Roman and Oriental gods, so even if there had been any Christians, there could not have been a uniform religious atmosphere.[1] That Christians were persecuted in the Empire does not imply that they fled to Dacia, during the Roman era or thereafter.

Ş.D. quotes V. Gr. Chelaru stating that "the Slavic languages south of the Danube borrowed a number of lexical and even grammatical elements from Romanian... (p. 77). This is correct, and the Rumanian adoptions from South Slavic are even more numerous, i.e., the impact of South Slavic upon Rumanian was decisive, this idiom having been the superstratum of Rumanian. This contact is one of the circumstances which indicate that the Rumanians lived in that era south of the Danube.[2] (The Slavic religious terms were, of course, originally borrowed from Greek and Latin.)

Assumed Rumanian borrowings in Hungarian

Ş.D. assumes that four words were borrowed by the Hungarians from Rumanian before the year 1001.

---

[1]Cf. above, pp. 13-14, 16.

[2]Cf., for example, Du Nay, 1996, pp. 110-111 and 240-241.

204

Hungarian *karácsony* "Christmas"
is assumed to originate from Rumanian *crăciun*, with the same sense. ŞD also
believes that this is an inherited Latin word (*creatio*) in Rumanian. None of these
assumptions is correct. Latin *creatio* would have resulted in Rumanian **creciune*
(unstressed Latin *ea* > Rumanian *e*; Latin *-one* > Rumanian *-une*: Latin *tationem*
> Rumanian *tăciune*).[1] The word *kracun, kerecun*, etc. appears in Ruthenian,
Slovakian, Bulgarian and Russian. Rumanian *crăciun* derives probably from
Bulgarian. Hungarian *karácsony* derives also from Slavic,[2] most probably from
Russian *korocjun*, found in the Chronicle of Novgorod from 1143, with the
sense of "time between November 12 and December 24". Today, *karacun* and
korocun have the sense of "December 12".[3] Rosetti also states (1986, p. 558):

> The Slavic populations in the Danubian provinces, which lived together with the
> Romanized local populations, have adopted Latin *creatione* to their mode of pronunciation,
> and the phonetical modification specific to Rumanian was restricted to the change of
> unstressed Slavic *a* to *ă*..

Hungarian *kolinda*
was borrowed by the Hungarians living in Transylvania from the Rumanians,
together with the popular New Year's custom of going in groups to each house
in the village and singing. The assertion of Ş.D., that the Hungarians could not
have borrowed religious words from heretics (p. 85) is nonsense. Similarly to
crăciun, Rumanian *colindă* is not an inherited Latin word but was borrowed from
Slavic. Latin *calendae* > Old Slavic (Common Slavic) *koleda* "New Years day";
is found in practically all Slavic languages.[4]

Hungarian *szent*
derives from Slavic *sfetu*.[5] The initial consonant cluster is regularly changed
in foreign words borrowed by Hungarian. The *n* may be explained by the
Slavic nasal *e*. Rumanian *sînt* is inherited from Latin (*sanctus*), but *sfînt* was
borrowed from Slavic.

---

[1] Rosetti, 1986, p. 556.

[2] Bárczi, 1975, p. 49 and 118. Bárczi believes that this word may have been borrowed from
Russian or Bulgarian before the Hungarians came to the Carpatian basin.

[3] Rosetti, 1986, p. 556.

[4] Ibid., p. 558.

[5] Bárczi, 1975, p. 118.

Hungarian *keresztény*
derives from Slavic.[1] Ş.D. argues that Slavic *hristiianin* would have resulted in Hungarian *kiristiny* (p. 82). This was, in fact, also the case, but the development towards more open vowels, occurring during the first centuries of the second millennium changed *i* to a more open *ë*. This process, which also included *u > o, o > a, ü > ö*, etc., was largely completed in the mid-14th century. The two forms coexisted, however, for long periods of time, as shown by the texts: *kyrist* (pronounced *kirist*) from 1248; *Kerezt* (pronounced *kërëst*) from 1261.[2] Rumanian *cristian*[3] is inherited from Latin, although late, as shown by its sound pattern, with *-tian* preserved. This Latin group disappeared otherwise regularly: Latin *pastionem* > Rumanian *păşune*, Latin *ustium* > Rumanian *uşe*. – Also this word shows a similarity between Rumanian, Slavic, and the Balkan languages: its sense is in Rumanian, Bulgarian, Russian, Albanian, and New-Greek not only "Christian" but also "Jesus Christ" and "man, human being".

A number of Hungarian leaders had become Christian before 1001, establishing contact with the Orthodox Church in Constantinople. Consequently, certain religios customs have been adopted from the eastern Church, but there was no need of Rumanians to achieve this. In the 10th century, it was not yet decided to which of the two Christian centers Hungary would belong.

Ş.D. asserts (p. 84):

> After the year 1001 [...] with the introduction of the practices of the Roman Catholic Church in Hungary and Transylvania, the two populations were separated and the Romanians started being persecuted as heretics.

There is no historical or any other kind of evidence to support this. Rumanians did not live there before the early 13th century.[4] Their number increased especially after the Tartar invasion in 1241–42, – they were also called and settled by the Hungarian king – and they were never persecuted as heretics.

---

[1] *A magyar nyelv története* [The History of the Hungarian Language], ed. Lóránd Benkő, Budapest, 1967, p. 289.

[2] Bárczi, 1975, p. 130.

[3] Rosetti, 1986, p. 346 and 771.

[4] Cf. above, Ş. Pascu, *A History of Transylvania. A Critical Survey*, pp. 51-53; Du Nay, 1996, chapters V and VI.

CONCLUSION

1. There is no evidence of any Latin influence on Gothic having been exerted in Dacia. On the other hand, chronological, formal, and semantic traits exclude the origin from Dacia of most of this influence. The assumption of Gothic elements in Rumanian is based on false etymologies.

2. There is nothing to indicate that the Hungarians borrowed the word "*walah*" from Germanic populations before they settled in the Carpathian basin. The corresponding Hungarian word was in documents first written "*Blaccus, Blacci*," and after the mid-13th century in its later form: *Olacis, Olachys*; corresponding to Hungarian *oláh*. This is in accord with other circumstances which indicate that the Vlachs started to come to Transylvania in the early 13th century. The Hungarians learned their name (vlach) most probably from Slavs, and adapted it during the first half of the 13th century to their own language, i.e., to *oláh*.

The sense of "serf" of the word *rumân* developed in the Rumanian voivodates, where the peasants were for centuries exposed to severe exploitation.

Rumanian *bătrân* "old", from Latin *veteranus* "soldier who served his time" has no value in determining the territories of the ancient Rumanians, the change of sense could occur anywhere in the Roman Empire.

3. The Rumanian popular name *Ardeal* "Transylvania" was borrowed from Hungarian: *Erdély*. (The Indo-European root *ard-* in toponyms has nothing to do with *Ardeal*.) The first written attestation extant of *Erdély* is from the end of the 12th century: *Erdeuelu (Erdőelve)*; its sense is "beyond the forest". Its Latin translation appeared already in 1075: *Ultra silvam*; from the 12th century on, *Transilvania* is used. The German translation (*Überwald*) appeared in the 13th century. The Rumanians borrowed *Erdély*; the first known mentioning being in 1432: *Ardeliu*.

4. Only one of those four religious terms assumed by Ştefănescu-Drăgăneşti to have been borrowed by the Hungarians before 1001 was really borrowed from Rumanian (*colinda*, a popular custom) but much later than assumed by Ş.D. The rest derive from Slavic. Two of these words (*crăciun* and *colindă*) are not inherited Latin words in Rumanian but were borrowed from Slavic.

Thus, contacts between Latin and Gothic (Old Germanic) existed in several areas of Europe, but in spite of what Virgiliu Ştefănescu-Drăgăneşti contends, linguistic evidence indicates that Dacia north of the Danube did not belong to these areas. Remains in Latin and the Germanic languages of these contacts are therefore no proof of Roman-Rumanian continuity north of the lower Danube.

References

Bárczi, G., *A magyar nyelv életrajza* [The History of the Hungarian language], 3rd edition, Gondolat Kiadó, Budapest, 1975.

Benkő, L. (red.), *A magyar nyelv története* [The History of the Hungarian language] Tankönyvkiadó, Budadpest, 1967.

Breban, V., *Dicţionar al limbii române contemporane* [Dictionary of Contemporary Rumanian], Edit. Ştiinţifică şi enciclopedică, Bucharest, 1980.

Corazza, Victoria, "Le parole latine in gotico"[The Latin words in Gothic], *Atti della Accademia Nazionale de Lincei,* Roma, 1969, VIII, vol. XIV, Fasc. 1.

Du Nay, A., *The Early History of the Rumanian language,* Edward Sapir Monograph Series in Language, Culture, and Cognition, 3, Jupiter Press, Lake Bluff, Illinois, 1977.

Du Nay, A., *The Origins of the Rumanians (The Early History of the Rumanian Language),* Matthias Corvinus Publishing, Toronto–Buffalo, 1996.

Iordan, I., *Nume de locuri româneşti în Republica Populară Română* [Rumanian Placenames in the Peoples' Republic of Rumania] , Edit. Acad. RPR, Bucharest, 1952.

Király, F., *Contacte lingvistice* [Linguistic Contacts], Edit. Facla, Timişoara, 1990.

Pascu, Ş., *Voievodatul Transilvaniei* [The Voivodate of Transylvania], Edit. Dacia, Cluj; vol. I: 1972, vol. II: 1979, vol. III: 1986, vol. IV: 1989.

Rosetti, A., *Istoria limbii române* [The History of the Rumanian language], definitive edition, 1986; Edit. Ştiinţifică şi enciclopedică, Bucharest.

Rosetti, A., *La linguistique Balkanique,* Edit. Univers, Bucharest, 1985.

Sandfeld, K., *Linguistique Balkanique. Problèmes et résultats;* Paris, 1930.

Suciu, C., Dicţionar istoric al localităţilor din Transilvania [Historical Dictionary of the localities in Transylvania], Edit. Acad. RSR, Bucharest, vol. I: 1967, vol II: 1968.

Tamás, L., Rómaiak, románok és oláhok Dácia Trajánában [Romans, Rumanians and Vlachs in Dacia Traiana], Magyar Tudományos Akadémia, Budapest, 1935.

How fabricated history is used for political purposes – Ion Lăncrănjan's *Essay on Transylvania.*[1]

This book, published in more than 50.000 copies in 1982, is not a historical treatise but an essay written for the laity, the general reader, whose capabilities to check its contents are very limited. Lăncrănjan[2] departs largely from the theses also presented by Pascu in *The History of Transylvania,* but augments them *ad absurdum.* The main themes are the theory of the Daco-Roman-Rumanian continuity and the alleged autochthoneity of the Rumanians in the territory of what once was Dacia Traiana, as well as the alleged oppression of the Rumanians by the Hungarians during a millennium. The author presents these theses as absolute truth. He then fabricates "proofs" of a Hungarian aggression allegedly threatening the Rumanian state in our days. This kind of propaganda was usual during the Communist era, especially under Ceauşescu, although it was most often made in a more camouflaged manner.

Unfortunately, the chauvinistic trend in Rumanian politics is very strong also after the political change in 1989. It is therefore necessary to present and analyse this essay – one of the best examples of the intolerant, almost racist spirit of this ideology. A second edition of Lăncrănja's essay was published in 1995, in which also several articles about it may be read. Most of them defend Lăncrănjan's reasoning; whose answers to critics also appear here. It must be added, however, that Lăncrănjan's instigation of hatred agaflnst particularly the Hungarians in Rumania was condemned already in the Ceauşescu period, by courageous

---

[1] Ion Lăncrănjan, *Cuvînt despre Transilvania* [Essay on Transylvania], Editura Sport–Turism, Bucharest, 1982. – The volume published under this title contains four essays, all of which address Transylvania. The fourth of these, pp. 121-188, is *Cuvînt despre Transilvania* – All quotations from this text as well as from other Rumanian texts in this survey were translated by the present authors.

[2] Ion Lăncrănjan, 1928–1992, author. Schools: industrial gymnasium, Braşov, school of metallurgy in Câmpina. Vice-editor at *Gazeta literară* [Literary Magazin] 1965–67. His main work is *Cordovanii* [The Cordovan's] in three volumes appeared in 1963, won the Prize of the Society of Rumanian Authors and the Prize of the State. Several essays devoted to Rumania, Communism and N. Ceauşescu. – From *Scriitori români* [Rumanian authors], Bucharest, 1978, we quote (about *Cordovanii*): the life of a village is described, and "the mental processes are extremely wide, marked usually by cosmic phenomena, earth is a mythological projection, a loved and provoking airy vision, the peasants are founders of country and of civilization. Everything is recorded with passion and emotion, the geology of the sentiments and the endless silences, dreaming and the syncopated monologue of hatred, the greatness of tradition, the harsh joy of the present".

Rumanian writers (see below). In the new situation after 1989, many Rumanian intellectuals have raised their voices against the chauvinists.

* * *

The writing of history in the national-romantic style

Writing history in the national-romantic spirit has old traditions in Europe. In the 18th century, when nations in the modern sense of the word were formed, it was usual that German, Scandinavian, Lithuanian, etc. scholars put forward theories about their own nation´s exceptional qualities, ancient origins, augmenting its merits out of proportion and without regard to elementary facts. In Hungary, for example, the theory of the origin from the Huns was popular in the 19th century, and there were authors who asserted that "at the beginning, everybody was Hungarian".

The protagonists of the *Transylvanian School* have propagated similar thoughts. Ştefan Pascu gives the following short characterization of this school:

> The "Transylvanian School" developed the ideas of the great seventeenth-century chroniclers from Moldavia and Ţara Românească, in particular those of Dimitrie Cantemir, a humanist and pre-Enlightenment scholar and prince of Moldavia. The representatives of the school focused their ideas and their scholarly and political work on the most important questions: the origin, continuity, and unity of the Romanian people. Their zealous defense of thier cause occasionally led them to exaggerations – for example, they asserted that the Romanian people were of purely Roman origin, and the Romanian language purely Latin.[1]

A representative work of this school is *Istoria pentru începutul românilor în Dacia,* by Petru Maior (1756 – 1812), from which we quote a few passages in English translation:[2]

> But from where did the name of the Cumans [also called *comani*] come? There is no doubt that the Rumanians, as today, also earlier, have called themselves *romîni*, i.e., *romani*. From the name *romani*, nothing more was necessary than to change the Latin letter r to Greek c, since they are very like each other.[3]

About the cause of the lack of Old German lexical elements in Rumanian:

> ...it was impossible to become related [German with Rumanian] because not a single sound can be, I believe, as harsh and as disgusting for Rumanian ears as is the language of the Saxons in Transylvania.

And about the Hungarian language:

> But the real cause of the fact that there is no relationship between the Rumanian and the Hungarian languages is, that the Hungarian language, being a language of Asia, can not be compared with the Rumanian language, which is a European language and a very near sister

---

[1]Pascu, Ş, *The History of Transylvania,* Dorset Press, New York, 1990, p. 153.

[2]For a discussion of this text in English, see Illyés, 1992, pp. 49–53.

[3] Petru Maior: *Istoria pentru începutul românilor în Dacia*, ed. by F. Fugariu, Editura Albatros, Bucharest, 1970, vol. I, p. 250.

211

of the Italian language, which is the sweetest of all European languages.[4]

Abot Rumanians in the 5th century:

> Otrococius, in part 1, *About the Origins of the Hungarians,* chapter 4, says that the language which Priscus designates as that of the Ausonians, was the Rumanian language. From this it follows that Attila and his boyars, as well as the rest of the Huns, knew the Rumanian language. I am therefore not surprized that the Rumanians were not afraid of Attila and his Huns, but remained gladly together with them, as we have read above, chapter 3, § 5, since the Huns spoke with them in Rumanian and so they understood each other perfectly. It is not surprising that Attila and the rest of the Huns knew Rumanian, because in those times, Attila and the rest of the Huns were usually born and grown up in Dacia, among Rumanians. From which also follows that in those days, a large number of Rumanians lived in Dacia and that there were much more Rumanians than barbarians, because not the majoritary population learns the language of the minoritary population but those who are few [learn the language of] those in the majority.[2]

It is scarcely necessary to point out the utter falseness of these assertions. To find Romans where the chronicles write Cumans is only ridiculous; and similarly ludicrous is the idea of Rumanians in the 5th century. (In that period, no Romance languages and peoples existed, only Latin.)

Ion Luca Caragiale, the distinguished Rumanian author (1852 – 1912) observed this spirit in Rumania and wrote some excellent caricatures of it.

From *Momente și schițe*, by Ion Luca Caragiale:[3]

p. 117:

> Teacher: ... Well; – now: we, Rumanians, must know from where we originate? ...from where?... tell us!
> Student: (energetically) From Trajan, Sir!
> Teacher: (winking at the inspector, who is enchanted) And who was Trajan?
> Student: He was a good man!
> Teacher (excited): Good, the little love! I say, by heaven, good... And against whom did he fight?
> Student (solemnly) Against the Turks!
> Teacher (laughing in good humour): like hell! Where were the Turks in those times in Europe!... Only later were the Turks discovered... (intensely) Against the Dacians! [Rumanian: *cu dacii*].
> Student (more loudly) Against devils! [Rumanian: *cu draci*].

p. 125:

> Teacher:[...] Now, the youngster Ftiriadi! Tell us, that also the illustrious matron, your honoured mother hears it: is it not so that the Earth revolves around the sun for each of three years in 365 days and then, in the fourth, in 366 days?

---

[1]*Ibid,* vol. II, p. 10.

[2]*Ibid.,* vol. I, p. 144.

[3]Ion Luca Caragiale, *Momente și schițe* [Short stories], Editura tincrctului, Bucharest, 1966. – Translation by the present authors without taking the dialectal and somewhat uneducated speech of the teacher into account.

Little Ftiriadi: Yes, Sir.

Teacher (makes an approbing gesture towards Mrs Ftiriadi who, very satisfied, rises from her seat, adjusts the necktie of the boy, kisses him and takes place again) – Now, is it not so that pressure is sufficiently demonstrated by those two hemispheres of Magdeburg?

Little Ftiriadi: Yes, Sir.

Teacher (towards the whole class) – Well, you oxen, see the example of application! (to little Ftiriadi) Well, one more and that will do! Tell us: is it not so that Ioan Corvin of Hunead, and Mathias Corvin, and then all the Hungarian magnates were of our people, Rumanians?

Little Ftiriadi: Yes, Sir!

Teacher: Good! Bravo! Excellent! [...]

p. 102:

"The green Rumanians"

(Caragiale describes the proliferation of different asssociations in his country, stating that he himself is a member of eight. The ninth, which he recently joined,)

seems to me mostly welcome; it accords with a great and ardent national necessity. The reader will readily be convinced how urgent it is to set up our new association.

But we shall let the promoter of the founding of this association talk...

"We, green Rumanians, depart from the following healthy principles of national progress:

It is impossible to love one's own nation if you do not hate the other nations.

A nation's own faults cannot be its enemies; its enemies are exclusively the qualities of other nations.

Therefore, a nation should not lose time by contemplating how to correct its faults and how to further its qualities; it has something more rewarding to do: to remark on the faults and to detract or deny the qualities of others.

Consequently, a nation should always be frightened of the others, because the only condition of the existence of one is the discrediting of the rest.

From this follows the necessity of the most extreme national exclusivism.

The man who has a child with a woman of another nationality, or vice versa, fosters some monsters, who half will love blindly the nation among which they have been born, and half will hate it fiercely.

May the God of our ancestors save any Rumanian man or woman to give birth to such teratologic specimens!

These are the principles which have led us when founding our new society."

...

p. 104: *The Statutes of the society "Green Rumanians"*

...

Chapter II

About the duties of the members of the society in general.

§ 4. – All members of both sexes and of all ages of the society "Green Rumanians" have the duty to hate everything which is alien or derives from aliens, everything that is not green Rumanian and everything that is not from green Rumanians.

A number of articles follow which enumerate in detail what is not green Rumanian and which must be rejected systematically by every member of the society, such as, for example, non-Rumanian sentiments, non-Rumanian art, non-Rumanian ideas and mentality.

Then:

§ 9. – An exception from these rules is non-Rumanian capital.

...

Chapter IV
About the duties of the female members.

§ 40 – The female members of the society must be virtuous as the Roman matrons were.

§ 41 – The female members of the society must become good Rumanian mothers.

§ 42 – They have the duty to give birth to healthy children, according to the ancient advice: *mens sana in corpore sano.*

...

§ 48 – They must nurse their children, nourishing them, together with the milk, with green Rumanian sentiments and ideas, according to the present statutes.

§ 49 – If a member would not have milk or, accidentally, the mamills would not be perforated, or would tickle herself too strongly, an alien wet nurse should not be taken in any conditions, who would give alien milk to the child and give him in the same time alien sentiments and ideas; but she must engage a green Rumanian nurse, preferably an active member of the society.

Recent Rumanian historical and linguistical literature

During the era of Communism, no publication could appear in Rumania in which the theory of Daco-Roman continuity would have been questioned, let alone denied. There are, however, great differences in details in the presentation of these problems by the Rumanian **professional** literaure. The following quotation from a school manual for the 4th grade of the elementary school from 1969[1] gives an idea about how the youngest generation was instructed about Rumanian history:

How was the Rumanian people formed? – After the occupation of Dacia, Trajan filled the villages and the towns with soldiers, functionaries and colonists. The Dacian and the Roman population lived and worked together, the contacts which developed during work, contact with friends as well as family relations brought them near each other successively and the old enmities disappeared. In this way, the Daco-Roman population developed in the course of time. After the retreat of the Roman state, the Daco-Romans continued to live their own life, and succeeded to overcome the difficulties caused by the People' Migration.

In this manual, the Rumanian language is characterized as follows: Of Dacian origin is *Dunăre* and six other words; from Latin, twelve words, among others *om* 'man' are mentioned and of Slavic origin, only four.

This primitive, idyllic description does not contain any truth except that emperor Trajan occupied (part of) Dacia. Dacian words do not exist in Rumanian. The number of lexical elements of Slavic origin is much higher than those inherited from Latin.[2] The evidence for the development of the Rumanian language in the Balkan peninsula is not even mentioned.

Books of history, while adhering to the theory which under the Communist era

[1]D. Almaş, Eleonora Fotescu, *Hazánk története* [The History of our Fatherland; a Hungarian translation from Rumanian], Textbook for the elementary schools, 4th grade, Edit. didactică şi pedagogică, Bucharest, 1969, p. 43.

[2]Illyés, 1992, chapter III; Du Nay, 1996, chapters II and IV-E.

was official, differ significantly with regard to several fundamental problems. Some authors consider only the former province of Dacia Traiana as the territory of the "Daco-Romans", others include the entire territory of present day Rumania. A very old topic of dispute is also the role of the Dacians: while the Transylvanian School denied their importance (or even existence in Dacia Traiana), the official ideology during the last decades was that the Dacians were the main constituents of the "Daco-Roman synthesis".

Treatises of linguistics are more objective. For example, a history of the Rumanian language written for University use,[1] states:

> The theory wich assumed that the Rumanian language and people were formed exclusively north of the Danube (starting with D. Cantemir, P. Maior, B.P. Hasdeu) [...] could not be proved from the scientific viewpoint, because the dialects south of the Danube (Arumanian, Meglenitic, Istro-Rumanian) do not confirm it.

In the *History of the Rumanian language* by Rosetti, this is even more clearly elaborated and the reader may draw his own conclusions from the facts, for example the changes during Late Latin, the presentation of the Albanian connections, the South Slavic influence etc.[2] This is the case also of the *Histoire de la langue roumaine,* 1903, by Ovid Densusianu. Alexandru Philippide denied explicitly the Daco-Roman theory (*Originea românilor* [The Origin of the Rumanians]), I-II, 1923-27, Iaşi. I.I. Russu[3] stated that the "historical-comparative study" of the Rumanian language has a documentary value, while the archaeological finds are not concludent.

All these publications appeared in Rumania, and the treatises of E. Illyés and A.Du Nay are mainly based upon these and other Rumanian works. These have been used in the critical survey of Pascu's *History of Transylvania.* As mentioned above, Lăncrănjan's essay contains many of Pascu's theses. Therefore, references will frequently be made to the above survey, i.e., to pp. 1 – 168 above.

Of course, the analysis should not search for details, or for absolute correctness, because this essay is not a scientific but a literary text. (The author states himself [on p. 161] that he is not a historian.) Therefore, some simplification and digression from reality should be tolerated.

[1] Florica Dimitrescu (red.), *Istoria limbii române,* Edit. Didactică şi pedagogică, Bucharest, 1978, 389 pp. The quotation is from p. 32.

[2] A. Rosetti, *Istoria limbii române,* Bucharest, 1986 (definitive edition).

[3] I.I. Russu, *Etnogeneza românilor* [The Ethnogenesis of the Rumanians], Edit. ştiinţifică şi enciclopedică, Bucharest, 1981, p. 155.

215

About the organization and contents of the essay

It is difficult to discover any structure in this essay of 67 pages, but the following may give a general idea about its contents: After an introductory section, in which it is asserted that the Rumanians have lived in Transylvania for two thousand years and were always in the majority there (the Daco-Roman theory of continuity, re-iterated in the following sections several times), the author writes about the importance of the village in the history of Transylvania; in the following section, the main theme is broschures of hatred spread by Hungarian right wing extremists in the 1930's; then Lăncrănjan states that Transylvania can never be like Switzerland, where four different nations are living peacefully together; then, the unity of Transylvania with other parts of present day Rumania is stressed; in the following section, it is asserted that the Rumanians in Transylvania were exploited to a higher degree than in the Rumanian voievodates; then a parallel is drawn between the Dacian state of Burebista and Great Rumania (the decision at Alba Iulia [paragraphs I to IX] on December 1, 1918 is reproduced, p. 161) and it is denied that any Hungarian culture of importance has ever existed in Transylvania. The domination of the Rumanian Fascists, the Iron Guards " ... appears to us the most dreadful period in the history of Rumania" and "difficult was also the period of Antonescu's dictatorship" (p. 169).[1] However, these were alien to the soul of the Rumanians, because "also in this difficult period, the Rumanian people's attitude was profoundly Anti-Fascistic, anti-Hitleristic and against conquerings", p. 170. On p. 175, Lăncrănjan asserts that the Hungarians receive too much rights (in the 1980's!) and ask for even more. In the following section the Daco-Roman theory is taken up anew, and it is asserted that the Hungarians came to Transylvania mainly after 1526 (p. 180) and have never really succeeded in establishing themselves there. Towards the end of the essay, the words of Nicolae Ceaușescu about equality between nationalities and the building of Socialism are quoted (from the meeting of the Central Committee of the Rumanian Communist Party in October 1968). Lăncrănjan concludes his essay by saying that he did succeed to tell only a small part of all that would have to be told about Transylvania.

CRITICAL REMARKS

Lăncrănjan: "Continuity ... almost has no need of any argumentation"

This essay may be compared with Petru Maior's *Istoria pentru începutul rominilor în Dacia,* written about two centuries ago (see above, pp.210-211).

---

[1] An indication regarding the spiritual climate in Rumania several years after 1989 is that Antonescu is now being rehabilitated (monuments are raised and streets are named after him, etc.)

216

Lăncrănjan uses an inflated, sometimes bombastic style, (extremely long sentences with enumerations, re-iterations etc), in an obvious attempt to appeal to sentiments rather than to objective, critical thinking. It could be a modern poem displayed in prose. Assertions are not argued, or the argumentation is a caricature of any rational reasoning. A characteristic example of this is the following passage (about the peasants who lived in Transylvania, p. 127):

> In the beginning, he was Dacian, afterwards, he was Roman, and later, Rumanian, in a natural continuity, which the archaeological and linguistic investigations will throw light upon from different viewpoints but will never be able to explain it entirely. And this is not because this doubtless continuity would be a mystery or a miracle, but because it is real and natural, bound to these places to such a high degree that it almost has no need of argumentation, being part of the characteristic and essential order of things which are an intrinsic part of the mode of existence of an entire people. It has no sense, for example, to prove that the Mureş is Mureş and that it is the same river from its springs to its confluence with the Tisa and that it had for more than two thousand years the same name.

While the name of river Mureş has probably existed for thousands of years, it was not inherited from Latin but borrowed by the Rumanians from Slavic, and the names of those five other rivers mentioned by Lăncrănjan were also borrowed from Slavic or from Hungarian (cf. above, p.65). This fact is one of those which disprove the point which Lăncrănjan asserts here – Daco-Roman continuity north of the lower Danube.

Significant errors regarding the history of Transylvania
   1. [About the Rumanian peasant:]
> ...the land was no longer his, but he knew that once, in the period of the communities and of the voivodates, it belonged to him. (p. 125).

This is re-iterated on p. 141: [the Rumanian peasants]
> have suffered an enormous amount of pains in the course of those thousand years: they have been robbed, at first, of their lands, in the favour of the newcomers, of the colonists, in favour of some newly made nobles...

p. 152: the situation of the Rumanian peasant was
> in general worse and more difficult than that of his brothers in the Rumanian Principalities

and the Rumanian collectivities were robbed of their lands
> at the same measure as the occupation and colonization of Transylvania was extended and consolidated.

On p. 154, Lăncrănjan even asserts that the Hungarians
> wanted to transform the Rumanians into working animals.

Therefore,
> ...the coming of the Hungarians to Transylvania caused the clock to go backward, from the social viewpoint, keeping things in their feudal petrification, ecoming more and more rigid, more and more reactionary... (p.154).

The Hungarians coming to Transylvania in the 10th century did not find there any Rumanians from whom they could "rob their lands". Later, during the feudal period, the situation of the peasants in the entire continent became difficult, with frequent revolts in most European countries. The situation of the peasants in Muntenia and Moldova was most of the time much worse than in Transylvania (cf. above, pp.106-108, 128-130). This caused masses of peasants to flee in all directions, predominantly to Transylvania and the Banat, particularly in the 17th and 18th centuries.

2. Transylvania was

...a territory in which other nations, such as Hungarians, Germans, Szekelys, came or were brought by colonization, with whom we, the Rumanians, wanted to live in good and useful agreement, our rage having been aroused only when our old rights were suppressed, when an attempt was made on our existence, when it was desired that we should no more exist, that we disappear in favour of others. The scope of the colinizations was not only Transylvania but the entire Country, it aimed at the dispersion, the disruption of a unity which was more than evident (p. 128).

As most of his assertions, Lăncrănjan re-iterates this (p. 152): "it was desired that this people no longer exist".

In the second half of the 13th century, when the Rumanians started to settle in Transylvania, Slavs, Hungarians, Szeklers and Saxons lived there (cf. above, pp. 53, 57, 72-73).

3. The Rumanians had to fight "during one thousand years" against "a policy of de-nationalization"(p. 130).

To talk about such a policy going on for thousand years is anachronistic and false. In the Middle Ages, nations in the modern sense of the word did not exist, religious affiliation and social hierarchy were decisive. As stated by S.B. Vardy, for example:

But most of these problems, which today are often characterized as manifestations of "Magyar oppression" of the national minorities, stemmed not so much from the dominance of the largely Magyar Hungarian nobility over the various nationalities of the Carpathian Basin, but rather from the nature of the prevailing social and economic conditions. The feudalistic and highly stratified social system made the peasant masses – irrespective of their nationality – economically and personally dependent upon the nobility. This phenomenon, however, was not limited to the lands of the Hungarian crown; it was characteristic of the social development throughout much of Central and Eastern Europe. Within this area that encompassed the land of the so-called second serfdom, the peasants of medieval and early modern Hungary were undoubtedly better off than those of Russia or of the Danubian Principalities of Moldavia and Wallachia.[1]

---

[1] *Transylvania. The Roots of Ethnic Conflict.* Edited by J.F. Cadzow, A. Ludanyi & L.J. Eltetö; The Kent State University Press, Kent, Ohio, 1983, p. 148.

4. Transylvania was

a part of something whole, it was a part of the Country (p. 142).

The character of the Rumanians in Transylvania were different from those living in Oltenia, Moldavia or other territories, but:

Only seemingly, because in reality, in those two millennia of existence in these territories, the Rumanian temperament is one and the same in the entire Country, as proved beyond any doubt, by the unity of the language spoken by Rumanians.

Transylvania cannot have been part of "the Country" before this (Rumania) existed, i.e., before the union of Moldavia and Muntenia in 1859 (under the official name *Danubian Principalities*, which was after 1878 changed to *Kingdom of Rumania).* In reality, it became part of this country in 1920. – Rumanians did not exist two thousand years ago since the Neolatin peoples and languages were formed towards the end of the first millennium AD. and before that date, one cannot talk about Rumanians, as one cannot talk about Italians, French etc. (Of course, Lăncrănjan may refer to the **ancestors** of the present day speakers of Rumanian. These lived, until around 1100 AD, in the Balkan peninsula; cf. Duy Nay 1996.)

Regarding the unity of the Rumanian language: there are four Rumanian dialects, of which northern Rumanian is at present spoken mostly north and partly also south of the Danube while the others exist and existed also in the past exclusively south of the Danube, in the Balkan peninsula. Lăncrănjan forgets to mention these southern dialects. The unity of northern Rumanian is not the result of an ancient existence of its speakers in present day Rumania but of a relatively late colonization of this territory. Moreover, Transylvania has no Rumanian sub-dialect; the Rumanians living in the north-east have in their idiom traits from Moldova and those in the south, from Muntenia.[1]

5. Lăncrănjan affirms that because of a policy against all "foreign" elements in Hungary after 1867, many Rumanians emigrated to the USA (p. 140). In this period,

...it was told to the Rumanians, even when their existence was acknowledged, that they were good for working as servants, working for the higher classes, fighting, if necessary, for Austria and for Hungary; they should praize the emperor and the king, forget their language, abandon their faith and spit with disgust at their ancient and really noble traditions. (p. 141).

Large masses have emigrated in that period to the USA. In Hungary, the relative proportion of these was highest among the Slovaks, somewhat lower among the Hungarians and lowest among the Rumanians. The proportion of day-

---

[1] Du Nay, 1996, p. 128.

laborers was (according to statistics from the turn of the century,) 33.6%, 48.4% and 31.5%, respectively. Thus, almost half of the Hungarian working class belonged to this lowest paid category, while less than a third of the Rumanians were in this situation. As shown above, p.127, within Transylvania, the proportion of day-laborers among the Szeklers was much higher than among the Rumanians. The situation of the Rumanian peasants in Hungary after 1867, was very different: In 1848, the peasants were liberated, earlier than in the Rumanian Principalities. They acquired large amounts of land during this period. They had their own schools, press and literature, free contact with Rumania, etc. (see above, pp. 125–127). The living standard of the Transylvanian Rumanians in general was in this period, as also earlier, higher than that of their brethren in the Rumanian Principalities. To this comes that they lived in a constitutional state and that their opportunities to study were much better than those of the inhabitants of Muntenia and Moldavia.

6. One of the most aberrant assertions made by Lăncrănjan in this essay is the following (p. 180):

> The truth is that the penetration in masses of the Hungarian element into Transylvania occurred after [the battle at] Mohács (1526), by the attribution of estates to some nobles, by new colonizations, as also after this, in the period of dualism [1867-1918] and later, in 1940 (for " Northern Transylvania"), with the aim of changing the character of some places...

How can it then be explained that, for example, out of 511 placenames mentioned in the 13th century, 83% are of Hungarian origin and only 3 (0.6%) are Rumanian ? Or that out of 1757 settlements known before 1400 AD, 77% were of Hungarian and only 4.3% (76) of Rumanian origin?[1] Or that the Rumanian names of all rivers of any importance in Transylvania were borrowed from Slavic, Hungarian or German? Or that most of the names also of the "Rumanian districts" were borrowed from Hungarian? (cf. above pp. 84-86).

Lăncrănjan's own data contain additional evidence against his thesis. It is sufficient to check the origin of the placenames and geographical names he mentions while showing Rumanian culture in Transylvania: he enumerates 34 villages from which distinguished Rumanian intellectuals originated. In spite of the fact that these are situated (with one exception) in the areas which became populated by Rumanians already during the 14th–15th centuries and are still today the most typical Rumanian areas, the majority of the names of these villages is **not** of Rumanian origin. Out of those 34, 14 (41%) are of Hungarian origin and only 7 (20.5%) are Rumanian (of which one was first mentioned in 1482 and the rest after 1700). Ten of these names are of questionable origin,

---

[1] Illyés, 1992, p. 331.

probably mostly Slavic.[1]

Lăncrănjan enumerates ten Rumanian districts: *Ţara Haţegului, Ţara Amlaşului, Ţara Oaşului,* etc., of which nine are in Transylvania. Six of these are of Hungarian origin and only *Ţara Moţilor* is a Rumanian name, meaning "the district of the *Moţ*-es".

7. Lăncrănjan finds a connection between the Dacian empire of Burebista in the 2nd century BC and the annexation of Transylvania by Rumania in 1918:

> ...the recognition, even if indirect, of an ancient and natural aspiration, of which it may be said, without any exaggeration, that it came to those who accomplished the Union of 1918 from the time of Burebista, it was as ancient, it was as deeply implanted in the earth outside and inside of the Carpathians, being one with them, being one with the Country. What I say here may appear pathetic or even exaggerated, but if this idea, this aspiration, would not have been so ancient and powerful, I would say and repeat it (I say it and repeat it deliberately), would the whole Country have moved so animated and approving in the period of Michael the Brave when the first union was accomplished? I believe that this would not have been the case (p. 156).

The Dacian ruler Burebista (or Rubobostes etc., several variants of this name appear in the chronicles) has, in the early 2nd century BC conquered a large territory between the river Tisza in the west and the Black Sea in the east; its center was probably in Transylvania.[2] After his death, this empire fell apart. The belief that during those 2100 years that have passed, there existed all the time a striving for a Great Rumania is not only "pathetic and exaggerated" – it is sheer fantasy. It is characteristic of the romantic school of writing history, usual in Europe in the 18th century but abandoned in the rest of the Continent long ago. The anachronistic interpretation of Michael the Brave´s short rule over Transylvania has been discussed above, pp. 89-92.

> ...the "thesis of non-continuity", the arbitrary assumption of an uninhabited territory, is wrong, Transylvania was not a desert, a lowland plain, which any wind could deprive of life (p. 179)
> ...who tried to prove something which has not been proved until then and will never be possible to prove: that Transylvania was desert, when the Hungarians came here... (p. 134)

---

[1]Cf. Coriolan Suciu, *Dicţionar istoric al localităţilor din Transilvania,* vol. I, 1967, vol. II, 1968. See also E. Illyés, *Ethnic Continuity in the Carpatho-Danubian Area,* 1988, second revised edition, 1992, chapter IV, p. 291 (Geographical names).

[2]About the history of the Dacians, see for example *Istoria Rominiei* [The History of Rumania], red. C. Daicoviciu, Bucharest, 1960, chapters 5 and 6; Giurescu, C.C., & Giurescu, D.C., *Istoria românilor* [The History of the Rumanians], Editura Albatros, Bucharest, 1975, pp. 30–78.

On pp. 136–137, the author asserts that the absence of any written record about a Romance population in Transylvania for many centuries after 275 AD is no argument against continuity. In this way, Lăncrănjan gives a false picture of the "non-Dacian" view of the history of the Rumanians: the assumption of an uninhabited territory represents an old thesis, put forward once but abandoned long ago. The silence of historians is considered an argument against continuity, but *ex silentio* arguments can rarely be decisive. The circumstances that exclude the possibility of Daco-Romans are of an entirely different nature.[1]

Lăncrănjan: "not sentimental arguments" but "incontestable truth"

> In fact, our people "argued" their continued existence saying, in the most natural way, that they are "here since the beginning of the world". But these are, will be said to me, sentimental arguments, simple poetic exaltations, and I will answer, taking into account in which circumstances they are talking and the fact that I live and work in a new, Socialistic state, in which the nationalities have equal rights – that the brotherhood to which we strive cannot really be realized but only in case some real and essential data are recognized (and not only formally, out of politeness): our continuity, that the Rumanians were always in the majority in Transylvania and the irreversibility of our great unification being a natural part of these data. Any violation of this incontestable truth, any falsification of these essential data, any undermining of them will produce, in the new circumstances, new forms of irredentism, and irredentism, even subtile and perfide, can only produce confusion *[derută]* and anger *[mînie]*, will push things back, towards the old discords, will favour imperialism, hurting the national interests of the Rumanians and of all those who live and work together with them, in the same free and proud country, which with right was and is called Rumania, from whose body no part may be disrupted, no area, without producing a deep and unforgettable wound, a deep bleeding which will be touching for a long time, as it happened in 1940, as it happened many times also earlier, as it should not happen any more (pp. 127–128).

Lăncrănjan seems to be aware, for a moment, of the spurious nature of his argumentation ("sentimental arguments, simple poetic exaltations"); nevertheless, he evades to prove his theses, and still, he demands blind acceptance of them.

One may wonder whether Lăncrănjan knew about those non-Hungarian authors who also denied the Daco-Roman theory: R. Rösler, G. Weigand, A. Dami, K. Sandfeld-Jensen, G. Stadtmüller, G. Schramm, etc.? Or about Ovid Densusianu and the Rumanian professor at Iaşi University, Alexandru Philippide?

---

[1] Illyés, 1992, Du Nay, 1996.

222

Truncated quotations – falsification of texts

Lăncrănjan: "...later, so called historians made their entrance..."

On p. 132, Lăncrănjan warns the Rumanians not to forget that "revisionistic tendencies still exist". One finds with surprize that this assertion is mainly based on two statements made by the Hungarian Communist Party leader, János Kádár: "The treaty of Trianon was an imperialistic treaty which dismembered Hungary, giving Transylvania to Rumania" and, at the Helsinki Conference: "In our century, after the useless sacrifices made during the first World War, the territory of the loser Hungary was reduced to its third."

One may discuss to what extent the treaty of Trianon was imperialistic; it is also true that many areas of Hungary before 1918 were inhabited by non-Hungarians, but the facts remain, and the above statements are essentialy true. Such statements of historical facts do not imply any thought of a revision of the frontiers. Kádár, during his long rule, has never even mentioned revision.

Lăncrănjan also asserts that in Hungary before 1920, the nationalities were exposed to a "brutal policy of de-nationalization" (p. 132). This is **not** true, cf. above pp. 134-139.

Lăncrănjan then writes about the years between 1940 and 1944, when northen Transylvania was under Hungarian rule and affirms that "tens and hundreds of people" were "tortured and murdered" according to

a "national ideology" which seems to have been most properly synthetized in a pamphlet called Without mercy *[Fără milă]*, written by one Dücsö Csaba... (p. 133)

In a new edition of Lăncrănjan's essay[1] one may find a photocopy of the page of the pamphlet on which this text appears. This makes the comparison of Lăncrănjan's quotation with the original possible. It may then be discovered that Lăncrănjan quotes selected sentences from the Hungarian text, leaving out others, – without indicating this (for example by [...]). We mark, in the translation of the quotation, with numbers in brackets [ ] the omitted sentences and give them below, after the translation of the quotation from Lăncrănjan:

Lăncrănjan, pp. 133-134:

"In this pamphlet, which was part of an entire system of racist propaganda, it was said, through the voice of the *levente*[2] called Torday:[1] "I do not wait for revenge to come. I do not wait. I shall suppress every Wallachian whom I encounter. Every one I shall suppress. There will be no mercy. [2] I shall set fire on the Wallachian villages in the night. I shall put to the sword the entire

---

[1]By Mihai Ungheanu, Bucharest, 1995.

[2]*levente* "member of a paramilitary youth organizationin Hungary between 1928-1944."

population, I shall poison the wells and I shall kill even the babies. [3] I shall destroy in the bud this mean and thievish people. There will be no mercy for anyone. Not even for the babies, not even for the pregnant mothers! [4] I shall eradicate every Wallachian and then there will be no other nation in Transylvania than one single, the Hungarian, my nation! I shall make the future Horea's and Cloşca's harmless. There will be no mercy!"... [5]   All these things belong, it is true, to the past, and it is more than necessary to forget them. But this cannot be done, really and for ever, as long as provocations continue in a certain way and from a certain part, without any brutality, using a more "modern" speech, which suits the present. But not even then they reached ´Fără milă´ at once."

The omitted passages are as follows:
[1] "Yes, you must wait!"
    "I do not wait" – shouted now Levente infuriated. "I do not wait! Because it is always my people, my nation that sheds blood! Always! Hungarian blood was shed throughout history and Hungarian blood is being shed also today!"
[2] "In the same way as there was no mercy for the Hungarians in the time of Horea nd Cloşca and as there is no mercy for them now! In the same way, there will be no mercy for the Wallachians either! I say this, Levente Torday! I will do the same as they do!"
[3] ... in the same way as the people of Horea stabbed to death with scythes the young Hungarians!
[4] There will be no mercy for them because they did not give mercy either. I shell revenge all the massacres committed by Wallachians! Revenge! Ruthless, mercyless revenge! I shall make a nationality policy! There will be no such thing that the Hungarian sheds his blood and the Rumanian multiplies as a house-bug. No, indeed!
[5] Piroska shouted passionately: "Do not say such things, Levente! Think of your conscience!"

    The comparison of the entire text with that quoted by Lăncrănjan reveals the falsification committed by this author. In this way, he was able to present for the Rumanian reader the picture of an enemy – the Hungarian. It appears clearly from the entire text that these horrible threats appear **in a novel,** written by a writer who belongs to the small fry (this, in fact, is also mentioned by Lăncrănjan: *...un oarecare Dücso Csaba, scriitor de duzină...*, "but this does not change the real situation", p. 133). The words are uttered by one of the characters, who is not a Hungarian *levente* but is called Levente Torday, i.e., his Christian name is Levente. It appears also that Levente had in mind all the massacres committed in the course of history on Hungarians by Rumanians and all he uttered here was inspired by his rage over these massacres. However, an other character in this novel, a girl named Piroska, disapproved vehemently all Levente had said.

Lăncrănjan must necessarily have known all this, otherwise he could not have chosen the sentences quoted above, omitting other relevant elements. Therefore, it must be stated that he **deliberately altered facts** in order to be able to assert that the threatenings uttered by a character in a shoddy novel are "the most real systematizing of a 'national ideology' [of Horthysm]" and are "part of an entire system of racist propaganda" (p. 133).

Lăncrănjan has proved with this falsification that his aim is not the defend his own people but to attack specifically the Hungarians. He also has proved, indirectly, that it is not possible to find in reality what he wanted, i.e., a racial ideology among Hungarians which would threaten the Rumanian people. (Otherwise, it would not have been necessary to fabricate a "proof".) Since Lăncrănjan asserts that the Hungarian "national ideology" was (and is) based upon such a text, this is an assault at Hungarians in general.[1]

The aim of Lăncrănjan must obviously have been to block any discussion about decisive questions of Rumanian history. This appears from the passage following the above quotation, in which he proceeds to affirm that the denial of the theory of continuity and the statement that the Rumanians came to Transylvania later than the Hungarians and the Germans (Saxons) – is the first stage in the preparation of massacres among the Rumanians.

> Not even then was *Fără milă* written at once. At first, they spoke about the "unjustice to Hungary" by the Trianon Peace Treaty, without mentioning the Great Popular Meeting at Alba Iulia, by which an entire nation has spoken... (p. 134) – and
> ...later, so called historians made their entrance, who unearthed dead theses, which strived to prove what was not proven until then and will never be possible to prove in the future: that Transylvania was void of any population when the Hungarians arrived here, the Rumanians came later, it is not known when, how and from where, because there is not a smallest trace in their folklore, in their tales, nor in the skies, nor on earth, of this so called coming. After these [...] came the politicians, the representants of the most reactionary cirlces, who wanted to get back their priviliges, and lastly, the killings mentioned above followed (p. 134).

In this way, Lăncrănjan suggests that any mentioning of unjustice suffered by one and a half millions of Hungarians in Transylvania after the first World War as well as any questioning of the theory of Daco-Roman continuity leads

---

[1] No reference is given; the identity of Dücsö Csaba, the editor of the novel, and other circumstances remain obscure. The Hungarian author György Száraz, in his answer to Lăncrănjan (1982), stated that he could not find the novel of Dicső Csaba, although he does not deny that it may have existed. He had a number of pamphlets in his library, written by Rumanian Fascists in the 1930's, in which similar hatred, in the same style, is expressed against the Hungarians. Száraz added that he did not consider that these Fascists represent the Rumanian people in general.

inevitably – to killing of Rumanians.

Who would dare to take up the question of Daco-Roman continuity in a country where it is generally considered that the real intention is not the clarifying of a historical problem but to prepare massacres among Rumanians by racist elements? To judge from the entire spirit of the essay, it is, unfortunately, very probable that another aim of Lăncrănjan with this text was to instigate the Rumanian people against the Hungarian folk group in Transylvania.

He describes the murder and torture of Rumanians in 1940 vividly, in a way which inevitably must raise anger in the mind of every human being and, even more, in the mind of Rumanians. These descriptions do not correspond to reality. They are based upon *Teroare Horthysto-fascistă în nord-vestul României, septembrie 1940 - octombrie 1944,* Bucharest, 1985, red. Mihai Fătu and Mircea Mușat. Most of this publication is a forgery, as shown by falsified photographs etc. The real situation was that the Hungarian troops, when coming to northern Transylvania after the Vienna treaty, were attacked in some villages. According to the laws of any army, the Hungarian army punished those who were guilty of such attacks. The number of people killed in these actions is given by Lăncrănjan in a way typical of this author: "tens and hundreds of Rumanians". The reader may wonder: were they tens, i.e., thirty, or sixty people murdered? – or were they hundreds, in which case there may have been, say, four hundred or even more dead. (In reality, there were at most tens.)

The Hungarian population living in southern Transylvania was, after 1940, exposed to a more intensive terror by the Rumanian authorities than ever before. Lăncrănjan fails to mention this and he also evades to mention the killings committed by the Maniu-guards in the autumn of 1944 in northern Transylvania. They murdered bestially not tens but hundreds of Hungarians in several villages. To this come all the tortures, beatings to death and murders committed by the Rumanian Secret Police, *Securitate,* in the years of Communist rule, for more than 40 years beginning in 1947. The entire extent of these atrocities is not yet known. Thousands of Hungarians were condemned to many years of prison for nothing – i.e., only for being Hungarian. In these decades, the Communist regime persecuted any opposition; also Rumanians were put into jail, such as Cornel Coposu, the former leader of the Peasant Party, and later Paul Goma, Mircea Dinescu, and others, for their courageous opposition against tyranny. But the Hungarians were exposed, besides Communist oppression, also to a nationalistic persecution. The entire Hungarian community was kept in a state of uncertainty and permanent anxiety by harassments, illegal inprisonments, etc.

The "eastern region" – of Hungary or of Europe?

Another example of Lăncrănjan's use of a truncated quotation in order to be able to prove a preconceived idea is the following:

> Transylvania is not, in fact, a simple region, one of 'our eastern parts', as I have read not long ago in a book printed here, in our country, Rumania (I have the volume Destin şi simbol, by Meliusz Joszef [sic] in mind, where the word our has nothing to do with us [Rumanians] ... (p. 135).

It appears in the following that Lăncrănjan asserts that the Transylvanian Hungarian author Méliusz József wrote about Transylvania as "the eastern part of Hungary". Having read only what Lăncrănjan quotes, one may believe this. However, the entire text from which this quotation was taken shows that Méliusz referred to Europe, in whose eastern part he was living:

> I am a prisoner, as so many others, not only on these eastern regions of ours, which are full of sorrow, but everywhere in Europe.[1]

Méliusz answered in an open letter to the magazine *Luceafărul*, protesting against this falsification; but the editors of the magazine did not publish his letter. Later, this false assertion was taken up in several publications as an established fact: In the 2nd edition of *Cuvânt despre Transilvania*, 1995 pp. 165-166, for example, Mihai Ungheanu writes about the essay:

> The author takes up the appearance of imperial hallucinations in contemporary publications, some of them very near us. In the book written by a colleague of Hungarian language, he discovers the expression: 'our eastern regions', where not Moldavia [...] is meant but Transylvania, seen reminiscently as an 'eastern region' of 'great' Hungary. Without the astonishment of such assertions, maybe Ion Lăncrănjan did not have written his book, but the perseverance of some anachronistic theses [...] makes him to state that they need an answer. What does the author discover in this way?

And in another article of the same publication, pp. 223-224, by I Novac:

> The author of *Cuvânt despre Transilvania* found the reflex of a voluntary or involuntary way of thinking according to which Transylvania was treated as the eastern part of what once was Hungary, in the mind of a Hungarian colleague, the inhabitant of Bucharest, member of the same Writers' Association, a book which, published in 1973 [in Rumania], expressed the old irredentist tendency of Hungary and its propaganda.

---

[1] From Méliusz' open letter of protest against Lăncrănjan's essay, quoted (and commented upon) in the second edition of this essay, in 1995, p. 172.

Lăncrănjan: "No eastern Switzerland"

In the following section (p. 135), the aim pursued by Lăncrănjan comes clearly to light.

> Transylvania was not and cannot become Switzerland with its cantons, as some persons have considered once, as others consider also today, persons committed forever to disquiet and aggressivity, without regard where they are, in Europe, in America or in Australia, in fact, on the margins of these continents, because the instigators cannot live but on the margins of evil and in the shadow of revansch (p. 135–136).

Thus, those who desire that the different nations, different languages and cultures in Transylvania should live together in peace, as is the case in Switzerland, are considered by Lăncrănjan "committed to aggressivity", and "instigators living on the margins of evil".

> Transylvania is not and cannot become a simple eastern Switzerland because on both sides of the Carpathians lived and worked, loved and dreamt, from ancient times, **one single people, one single will**... (p. 136, emphasis added).

It would be difficult to express more clearly and concisely the chauvinistic idea of the exclusivity of the Rumanians in Transylvania.

On p. 129, the following assertion may be read:

> ...in the Danube valley, along the Pruth, the Olt and the Murăş, on the Cerna and the [rivers] Criş, **one and the same people** lived from ancient times (emphasis added).

These passages reveal the real aim of this distorted history-writing. **This aim is not to defend a nation** (although this is pretended) **but to oppress other nations.** This situation raises the issue above the controversy between Hungarians and Rumanians into the sphere of general interest. Representatives of the international community have repeatedly declared that this kind of agitation should not be tolerated because it may be the prelude to acts of ethnocide. If Lăncrănjan would be afraid of aggression, of "Dücső Csaba", of Fascism, one would only criticize him because he seeks these threats where they do not exist. But Lăncrănjan has different aims. What he said in the above passages, indicates that he wants **exclusivity** for the Rumanians. Not to accept the situation of peaceful coexistence among different nations, demanding exclusive rights for one, is the essence of Fascism. It is the same reasoning which was known earlier during the 20th century in the shape of Nazi propaganda: "in this territory (in our *Lebensraum),* only our own nation has the right to live."

228

About Hungarian culture in Transylvania

A Hungarian writer declared that

he was born "into a collectivity which was formed to 99% in the spirit of Hungarian culture", although Transylvania was not formed in this spirit, in this proportion and not even his native village, to localize the problem, has been formed in this spirit (pp. 175–176).

According to Lăncrănjan, the declaration of this writer is based on the thesis of Hungarian cultural superiority:

this "thesis" replaces other argumentations, used when continuity no more can be questioned, when the preponderant proportion and the permanence of the Rumanians in Transylvania no longer may by denied.

There are many villages in Transylvania whith a predominantly or even purely Hungarian original population, as there are many purely Rumanian villages. If the Hungarian author had affirmed that entire Transylvania was formed to 99% in the spirit of Hungarian culture, it would be right to question this. But to deny even one single village its Hungarian character is simply wrong and discloses Lăncrănjan's totalitarian, exclusivistic spirit. (Regarding continuity, this statement of the Hungarian author about his own native village has nothing to do with this theory; it is characteristic of Lăncrănjan to find attacks against the Daco-Roman thesis also where such attacks do not exist. It may be added that continuity not only **can** be questioned, but is proven wrong; cf. Illyés, 1992; Du Nay 1996.)

Another [Hungarian author] told about Oradea [Hung. Nagyvárad] that it was "the second large spiritual centre in Hungaria after Budapest, in that time". (The preface to the volume *The Barons and the Cumanians* by Ady Endre), and other partizans of such proceedings, here or in Hungary, go further, blurring consciously, or ignoring completely the presence of the Rumanian element in Transylvania (as well as in the history of Transylvania, of course) (p.181).

Nagyvárad (Oradea)[1] was before 1920 a city with a predominantly Hungarian population; the great Hungarian 11th century king, Ladislaus the Saint is buried there, it is the seat of a Catholic and a Calvinist Bishopric, the city in which

---

[1]The Rumanian name *Oradea* derives from Hungarian *Várad.* – In many places in south-eastern Europe, old towers gave the name of settlements. In the extra-Carpathian areas of Rumania, these are based on Slavic *grad* or *zamok,* or Rumanian *cetate* < Latin *civitas.* In Transylvania, most of these names derive from Hungarian *vár* 'castle'. When borrowing this name, the Rumanians adapted it to their own sound system in different ways: there are, for example, Hungarian Temesvár > Rumanian Timişoara, Váradja > Oarda (the village in which Lăncrănjan was born), but also Hungarian Várfalva > Rumanian Varfalău, and Várvíz > Varviz, as well as Várad > Oradea (cf. A. Du Nay, "Oriental Latin and 'Daco-Scythia'", in *Forum Linguisticum,* Jupiter Press, LACUS, vol. IV, 3, April 1980, p. 246).

many Hungarian authors, such as Ady Endre, the great poet, were living and working. Stating similar facts does not imply "blurring consciously or ignoring completely" that also Rumanian culture has traditions in Oradea.

Lăncrănjan: "The national minorities have too much rights"

Continuing his argumentation, Lăncrănjan advocates for something which cannot be less than a total assimilation of the ethnic groups living in Rumania. He affirms that they have received too many rights:

. ..certain real, unquestionable rights are extended many times in a forced way, the pretentions and requests increasing all the time, as they are satisfied... (p 175).

This essay was written in the years 1980–1982, when the oppression of the national minorities was severe and increasing; minority rights were not extended but, on the contrary, diminished. (For example, more and more Hungarian pupils were forced to study in Rumanian classes and a few years later, the Communist government ordered that the names of villages and towns in the territory of the country may only be written in Rumanian even in newspapers and other publications of the national minorities, etc.)

Lăncrănjan continues:

but if one day we will be asked, in the possibly most democratic way, to take our rivers on our back and to move from this Country, what will we do, Rumanians, – will we satisfie this request, or what will we do? (p. 175)

Thus, to give any rights to the Hungarian population, means that the Rumanians will be expelled .[1] This reasoning is absurd.

In the rest of this essay, the author returns to the Daco-Roman theory, the "close contact in all times" of Transylvania with "the Country", the alleged policy of suppression exercised by the Hungarians, etc. But the main purpose of the entire essay and of the propaganda in this spirit is expressed in the passages quoted above, p. 227 (Lăncrănjan, pp. 135-136), which means, to put it plainly: those who want to establish peace and cooperation between the different nationalities living in Transylvania, similar to that existing in Switzerland, are aggressors .In Transylvania, there do not exist different nationalities, **only one single nation,** the Rumanians, who have been living there since several thousand

---

[1]One should also note the vivid image, the literary description of this assertion: "to take our rivers on our back". In the 2nd edition of his essay (1995, p. 143), Lăncrănjan mentions that when writing these lines, he had in mind the last lines of a poem by Octavian Goga, *Oltul* (which contain approximately the following: collect our earthy remains and all your rivers – we should move to another country!). – The rivers of Transylvania belong as much to the Hungarians and Germans as to the Rumanians. Historically, they belonged only to the former two nations, as shown by their names (cf. above, pp. 65–66).

years. The Hungarians who (in spite of the above statements) are living in Transylvania should not have any human rights, because this would lead to the killing or the expulsion of the Rumanians.

This is the face of Fascism in Europe at the end of the 20th century.

The emotional effect of Lăncrănjan´s *Essay on Transylvania*

The situation in Rumania after 1989 is more hopeful than it was under Ceauşescu. Now, mass-media may inform the population about circumstances in other countries and give diverse opinions in all fields of human thinking. Unfortunately, those who want radical changes in many of these fields have to work in a very hard climate and to struggle with very great difficulties. Among the masses, the emotions fostered before 1989 still are vivid: too many people believe that the non-Rumanian folk groups threaten the security of the Rumanians and agree with chauvinistic propaganda in, for example, that these folk groups should be oppressed. It is totally understandable that the Rumanian hates the Hungarians, if he or she believes that the Hungarians made his ancestors

> to suffer an enormous amount of pains in the course of thousand years ... and robbed their lands...
> the Rumanian was good as a servant ... should forget his language, abandon his faith and spit with disgust at his ancient and really noble traditions;

the Hungarian national ideology is based on Dücső Csaba, who wanted to

> kill every Wallachian...

and that during the course of history, Hungarians always oppressed and killed Rumanians, – without having any idea about the real situation.[1]

Critical voices from Hungary and Lăncrănjan´s reaction to them

In the Hungarian press published in Rumania, no mention of this essay has been made, but in Hungary, several critical articles appeared.[2] Lăncrănjan has commented upon these, showing a total absence of understanding of the objections presented by these authors. Thus, in his answer to the criticism put

---

[1] Although there is no excuse for any killing, the fact is that, for example in 1784-85 (Horea´s revolt), in 1848-49, and in 1944, much more Hungarians were killed by Rumanians than vice versa.

[2] Száraz, Gy., *Egy furcsa könyvről* [About an odd book], Magvető kiadó, Budapest, 1983; also published in the volume by the same author: *Történelem jelenidőben* [Contemporary history], Magvető kiadó, Budapest, 1984, pp. 670–733. – Köteles, P., "Gondolatok egy torzkép előtt" [Thoughts in the face of a caricature], in the magazine *Tiszatáj*, Szeged, 9, 1982.

forward by Köteles Pál in *Tiszatáj* (Szeged, Hungary),[1] Lăncrănjan pretended that his aims were morally high, namely, to express his infinite love for Transylvania and to increase understanding between the different populations living in Rumania.

On p. 161 of the same volume (*Vocaţia constructivă*), Lăncrănjan asserted that this book was

> ...a book of my soul, a book of sincere and pathetic love, love which does not mean anger against others, as it was understood, as some present day inquisitors have forced themselves to understand it, old and wicked partizans of quarrels. I do not insist because I have told this before: to love your natal places, to love your Country until self-sacrifice does not imply that you have to hate other places and other countries.

And:

> I don't know what the destiny of my other books will be ... but I would like that this book lived after me, it is to such a high degree justified ... its message is so clear and inflexible as its expression is composed.

It does not make sense to go into more details, because nothing new appears in this answer written on twenty pages (a third of Lăncrănjan's original article).

A new edition of Lăncrănjan's essay appeared in 1995, in which besides Lăncrănjan's answers to critics, articles defending this author were published. To this edition, Lăncrănjan has written an epilogue *(Postfaţă,* pp. 147-152), in which he affirms: "*'Cuvânt despre Transilvania'* was not and is not an anti-Hungarian book, but it was, and it is, anti-revisionistic, its polemics are aimed at those who have militated and militate in favour of tearing apart Rumania into pieces."

The Rumanian Writers' Association condemned Lăncrănjan

In the years after the publication of this book, the Rumanian Writers' Association discussed it repeatedly. The essay as well as its author were unanimously condemned by distinguished authors: Eugen Jebeleanu and Mircea Dinescu (who later was inprisoned because his resistence against the Communist regime of Ceauşescu). The conclusions were, in the words of I. Novac (in the 2nd edition, p. 229): "János Kádár should not be attacked, the Hungarians are friends with the Rumanians, Hungarian revisionism is an invention, Lăncrănjan's book is a fallacy, and its author lacks knowledge of history and politics and has no talents."[2]

---

[1] In a collection of articles *(Vocaţia constructivă* [Constructive Vocation] 1983, pp. 98 - 118.

[2] I. Novac disproves strongly the condemnation of Lăncrănjan and affirms about Eugen Jebeleanu, that he is an "old supporter, without reservations, of Hungarian revolutionism [*sic,* probably erroneously for revisionism] and of the Hungarian historical theses, in whose name

Concluding remarks

This would make the mentioning of Lăncrănjan´s essay unnecessary. If we have discussed it in some length, it is because it makes part of a very strong spiritual tendency in Rumania, which is manoevered by certain politicians by a propaganda similar to that contained in Lăncrănjan´s essay, based also on the interpretation of history according to Ştefan Pascu. This indicates that Pascu´s writing of history has a well defined practical political significance.

Above, it was shown how Lăncrănjan **fabricated** consciously "proofs" of "revisionists" who "want to tear Rumania apart": by truncated quotations. It is obvious that all his talk about "a book of sincere and pathetic love", "not anti-Hungarian" is camouflage. He also pretended that Transylvanian Hungarian authors who wrote about Hungarian culture for example in Nagyvárad (Oradea) or in a village in central Transylvania are at least not friendly against the Rumanians or, in some cases, openly inimical, and even "revisionists". All this only because they mentioned obvious facts about Transylvanian Hungarian culture – **without** attacking any other nationality. What remains of being Hungarian if one is not permitted to describe one´s own village or to refer to a town with intimate binding to Hungarian culture?

After the political change in December, 1989, and the death of Lăncrănjan, the falsifications of this author are still being spread. Thus, in the 2nd edition, a page from a novel is reproduced (se above, pp. 222-224), and in spite of the fact that it appears clearly from the text on this page that it is part of a novel, the editor of the 2nd edition of Lăncrănjan´s book commented upon it as follows: "Black on white: page 156 from the Horthyst programme of the extermination of the Rumanian population in Transylvania, the pamphlet 'Without mercy'".

Since most Rumanian readers do not understand the Hungarian text, they get the message that it is proved ("black on white") that there existed a programme of "horthysts"[1] aiming at the extermination of millions of people!

In such circumstamces, the clarifying of the questions of history is not only a scientific necessity but also a practical one.

---

he has brutally maltreated *Cuvânt despre Transilvania* as well as Ion Lăncrănjan."

[1]The use of Miklós Horthy´s (1868-1957) name in this context contains a flagrant lie in itself, fabricated by the Communists. Horthy was an admiral in the Austro-Hungarian navy. In the summer of 1919, he joined the new, anti-Communist government that was being organized in Szeged, and succeeded in building up a new Hungarian army which in the autumn of the same year defeated the Communists. He then was elected as the regent of Hungary. In contrast to many other politicians, he did not use his power in order to become rich; thus, for example, his estate in 1944 was the same size as in 1919. He and his son saved many Jews in the summer of 1944; in October, he was forced by the Fascist F. Szálasy to abdicate. His son was put in the concentration camp at Malthausen. Horthy died in exile in Portugal. (Cf. P. Gosztonyi, *Miklós von Horthy. Admiral und Reichsverweser*, Musterschmidt, Göttingen-Zürich-Frankfurt, 1973).

233

References

Almaș, D., *Fotescu,* Eleonora, *Hazánk története* [The History of our Fatherland; a Hungarian translation from Rumanian, textbook for the elementary schools, 4th grade]; Editura didactică și pedagogică, Bucharest, 1969.

Cadzow, J.F., Ludanyi, A., Elteto, L.J. (red.) *The Roots of Ethnic Conflict,* Kent State University Press, Ohio, 1983.

Caragiale, Ion Luca, *Momente și schițe* [Short stories], Editura tineretului, Bucharest, 1966.

Du Nay, A., *The Early History of the Rumanian Language,* Edward Sapir Monograph Series in Language, Culture, and Cognition, 3, Jupiter Press,Lake Bluff, Illinois, 1977.

Du Nay, A., "Oriental Latin and 'Daco-Scythia'", in *Forum Linguisticum,* Jupiter Press, LACUS, vol. IV, 3, April 1980, pp. 246–267.

Du Nay, A., *The Origins of the Rumanians – The Early History of the Rumanian Language,* Matthias Corvinus Publishing, Toronto – Buffalo, 1996.

Dimitrescu, Florica (red.), *Istoria limbii române* [The History of the Rumanian Language], Editura didacticăși pedagogică, Bucharest, 1978.

Gosztonyi, P., *Miklós von Horthy. Admiral und Reichsverweser*, Persönlichkeit und Geschichte, Band 76/77; Musterschmidt, Göttingen – Zürich – Frankfurt, 1973.

Illyés, E., *Ethnic Continuity in the Carpatho-Danubian Area,* East European Monographs, CCXLIX, Boulder, Columbia University Press, New York, 1988. Second revised edition: Hunyadi Öcs. Mk., Hamilton, Canada, 1992.

Köteles, P., "Gondolatok egy torzkép előtt" [Thoughts in the face of a caricature], in *Tiszatáj,* Szeged [Hungary], 9, 1982.

Láncrănjan, I., *Cuvînt despre Transilvania* [Essay about Transilvania], Editura sport – turism, 1982.
Second edition with *Addenda,* by Mihai Ungheanu, Editura regiei autonome a imprimeriilor, Bucharest, 1995.

234

Lăncrănjan, I., *Vocaţia constructivă* [Constructive vocation], Editura cartea românească, Bucharest, 1983.

Maior, P., *Istoria pentru începutul românilor în Dacia* [The History of the Origins of the Rumanians in Dacia], ed. by F. Fugariu, Editura Albatros, Bucharest, 1970.

Rosetti, A., *Istoria limbii române* [The History of the Rumanian Language], definitive edition, Editura ştiinţifică şi enciclopedică, Bucharest, 1986.

Russu, I.I., *Etnogeneza românilor* [The Ethnogenesis of the Rumanians], Editura ştiinţifică şi enciclopedică, Bucharest, 1981.

Suciu, C., *Dicţionar istoric al localităţilor din Transilvania* [Historical Dictionary of the localities in Transylvania], vol. I, 1967, vol. II, 1968. Editura Acad. RSR, Bucharest.

Száraz, Gy., *Egy furcsa könyvről* [About an Odd Book], Magvető kiadó, Budapest, 1983.

APPENDIX.

From: David Prodan: *Memorii* [Memoirs], Bucharest, 1993.[1]

David Prodan (1902 – 1992) was, according to *Enciclopedia istoriografiei românești* [The Encyclopedy of Rumanian Historiography], red. Ştefan Ştefănescu, Bucharest, 1978, p. 275: "A historian of the Middle Ages, specialist of international reputation. He has made basic research on the social structure of medieval Transylvania." He was also a member of the editing committee of *Istoria României*, vol. III, 1964.

Prodan wrote his memoirs over a very long time, beginning in 1965 and writing the last sections in the 1980-s and early 1990's. These last sections include articles abut N. Iorga, C. Daicoviciu and Ştefan Pascu. About Pascu, there is a "sketch of a portrait" (pp. 172 – 176) and "Ştefan Pascu, career in sciences" (pp. 176 – 218).

We abstain from quoting Prodan's characterization of Ştefan Pascu, but consider it interesting to show how he judged Pascu in his quality of a historian. We do this by quoting, in English translation, some relevant passages from Prodan´s autobiography.

> Ştefan Pascu started his career in sciences with not less than with "The History of Transylvania" (1944), (in the same year with "Petru Cercel"), in its entire extension. If somebody begins his career in sciences with a work of synthesis, which normally should conclude it, it is clear: he lacks responsibility. The more so as the history of Transylvania was one of the most difficult subjects, and least studied.
>
> From where comes this science? It is simple: from the special course of the history of Transylvania held by his professor Ioan Lupaş for several years, certainly with the thought of [once] publishing it. It is a copy of the course made on the basis of notes taken, with a doubtful own accent (?) which should make it a "personal" work. The second trait of his début is the falsification of the work of others. Thus, the two main traits of his entire scientific career are found there from the beginning.
>
> But we may say that this is a sin which also others have committed. The man will think about it and better himself. Nothing of that. The lack of scruples, superficiality, continues and even worsens, his basic schooling having been superficial.
>
> After August 23, even he changed his countenance. After he first set himself up for being the secretary of Iuliu Maniu's guards, he plunged into the Social-Democratic party (p. 176 in D. Prodan´s *Memorii*).

---

[1] David Prodan, *Memorii* [Memoirs]. Text îngrijit şi adnotat, cu o postfaţă de Aurel Răduţiu. Editura enciclopedică, Bucharest, 1993; 240 pages.

Pascu has accomplished the necessary change of countenance also in his science. He has even overbid this, – he was even more of a historical materialist, a revolutionary than it was necessary. In the work "*Peasant revolts in Transylvania. I. The Period of the Voivodate*" (1947), he discovered in the Middle Ages even more peasant revolts than have really occurred. He retained, however, superficiality. With great ease, he places **in the 14th century** images as follows:

"The serf was forced to work for the owner of the land 4 to 6 days a week; to give him the nineth and the tenth of the harvest, *quinquagesima* of the sheep; of porks and of beehives usually the half, other gifts *[daruri]* three times a year etc." (p. 176).

Prodan states that the reference given by Pascu about these circumstances does not contain anything about the question. But Pascu reiterates these assertions on the following (13.) page:

"When their land was not **taken away from them,** the serfs were exposed to extremely harsh **fiscal** (!) (emphasis added) obligations. The serf was forced to work for the **feudal lord 4 to 6 days** a week; he was also forced to give the landlord the gift of land (*terragium*), then a nineth and a tenth part of his harvest (*nona* and *decima*); a sheep with lamb out of fifty (*quinquagesima ovium*) *half* of the porks and the beehives and other gifts three times a year" (now according to A. Kurz, *Magazin*, II, p. 368). One looks after there; it is the text of the second agreement with the peasants in 1437. Nothing but the payment of 1 Florin, three gifts, **one day of work a year,** the trial of the serf.

Flagrant confusions between fiscal, feudal, and pertaining to the Church, which continue also in the rest, severe anachronisms across centuries, for which the student of grade 2 is failed without mercy (p. 177).

In *Din Istoria Transilvaniei* [About the History of Transylvania], 1st edition, p. 187, Pascu wrote:

"In the foundry of guns in Alba Iulia, **204 smiths, 47 locksmiths, 84 carpenters, 80 wheel wrights, and about 1300 auxiliary workers worked in 1645 – 1646.**" What a factory in that age! And in seven months, only 10 large guns were made! Considering this production, what could so many smiths, locksmiths, carpenters, wheelwrights, so many auxiliary workers do? Going to the source, we find that there were so many **working days** achieved by the smiths, locksmiths, carpenters, etc. toghether! (p. 179).

Prodan shows in detail, with many examples, that Pascu's presentation of the obligations of the peasants as well as the demographical situation of Transylvania is full of mistakes, miscalculations, and inconsistencies, making his results and conclusions largely worthless.

About Pascu's assertion that the Hungarian name of Transylvania (*Erdély*) is a translation from Latin (*Ultrasilva, Transsilva*) (*Voievodatul Transilvaniei*, I, p. 21, see above, p. 46), Prodan is of the following opinion:

How – the Hungarians, when they came, have named it in Latin and then, later, they translated it for themselves in order to understand it, into Hungarian! From where comes this monstruosity? Simply from the appearance in the chronicles, which were written in the Latin language, of the Latin name first and only later the appearance of the Hungarian name. This happened also with Siebenbürgen, translated (by the Saxons) from Septem Castra (p. 22) (Prodan 179).

Pascu writes about the ethnic structure of Transylvania in *Voievodatul Transilvaniei*. From Prodan's comments on this section we quote the following:

> The effort to reconstruct "The Ethnic Structure of Transylvania" is praiseworthy, something very difficult for the historian with the help of existing documents. Nothing is more difficult than to quantify the population and then it is even more difficult to state the proportion of the nations. We appreciate all efforts, with the condition that it must be, just because of this, as correct as possible.
> The work tries to achieve this with "statistical" and "documentary", "ethno-toponymic", "onomastic or antroponymic", and "toponymic" arguments, and reaches the conclusion: In view of these ethno-demographic realities, could an objective investigator question the absolute majority of the Rumanians in entire Transylvania and their great majority **in very numerous regions?**
> The data are conclusive even if fragmentary, as they were preserved or as they are known. Very good! If the demonstration would be invulnerable. But God forbid a specialist examination! (p. 202).

In the following, Prodan shows how Pascu argues: he translates the Hungarian name of a number of villages into Rumanian and writes these names with capital letters, giving the impression that they in reality could have been named in that way, e.g. Hungarian Aranymező: "Cîmpul Aurit" (the real name being Băbeni), Hungarian Egerbegy: "Şorecani" (real name: Tămăşeşti; Pascu's name is erroneously based on the word *egér* "mouse", but it is *éger* "alder"); Hungarian Nagylak: Rumanian Lacul Mare (Hungarian *lak* "dwelling", not lake!), Hungarian Árpás: Grînari (but Hungarian *árpa* "barley", not wheat) etc. (pp. 203–204).

Writing about how Pascu treats the toponymy of Transylvania, Prodan remarks:

> Only a personal assertion, of great significance: "the names of many villages derive from personal names. Those with the suffix -*eşti* [...] are of Thracian origin and so are also those with the suffixes -*ni.*" Maybe the Thracians named them as we have them before they were Rumanians!? (p. 203).

Pascu

> uses without any scruples the absence of a historical criticism [in Communist Rumania], **the weak knowledge by our historians of the history of Transylvania,** the immunity assured by his offices, the fear among people, ... (p. 206, emphasis by Prodan).

Pascu

> is today the most often quoted Rumanian historian; he has succeeded to imprint the stigma of shame of his ethics far and wide, degrading with his level an entire historiography.
> Such a performance is only possible in the conditions of our times, with our lack of control, with our lamentable ethics. Certainly, our Hungarian colleagues jubilate, with fits of laughter, on such a performance of Rumanian historiography (p. 209).

238

Contents

* Pascu's chapters 1 – 14 are given, followed by some of their main topics (headings in Pascu's text). The more detailed presentations, written by the present authors to provide a background and explanations to certain circumstances and events are printed in italics in this list. Of these, those which lack a special heading in the text, are written in brackets.

239

Appendix.

List of maps

List of tables

PART

II

NOTE

THIS BOOK IS NOT FOR SALE

FREE DISTRIBUTION ONLY TO:

LIBRARIES, HISTORIANS,

RESEARCH INSTITUTES,

GOVERNMENTS

AND OTHER INTERESTED PARTIES

ÁRPÁD KOSZTIN

THE DACO-ROMAN LEGEND

Cristian Cultic Places in Transylvania

MATTHIAS CORVINUS PUBLISHING

HAMILTON - BUFFALO

PRINTED WITH THE HELP OF

MARIKA BUTTY

IN MEMORIAM:

GYULA BUTTY

THE ORIGINAL HUNGARIAN TITLE:

A DÁKOROMÁN LEGENDA
KERESZTÉNY KULTUSZHELYEK ERDÉLYBEN
(ISBN 963 322-000-000)

THE   FIRST ENGLISH EDITION

BY SPECIAL PERMISSION:

MATTHIAS CORVINUS SOCIETY

CONTENTS

Appendix

I

The Foundation of Christianity,

Cultic Places

Christianity as a world-religion was founded by Jesus Christ. Due to the tireless work of the Apostles, it spread rapidly. It came into being in Palestine during the first half of the first century.

The early, oldest Christian congregations made contact with the Jews living in Diaspora beyond the borders of Palestine during and after the years of the Jewish wars (66-70 A.D.). After the unsuccessful Jewish uprising and the devastation of Palestine in 70 A.D., the Jewish-Christian religious communities suffered great losses and diminished in numbers.

The dispersed people were looking for and took refuge in the eastern provinces of the Roman Empire. At this time, numerous Jews lived outside of Palestine, mainly in the commercial centres, like Damascus, Antioch, Athens, Corinth, in the larger towns of the costal district of Asia Minor as well as in Rome.

By crossing the borders of Palestine, Christianity had to break with the Judaic roots in order to avoid becoming a small Jewish sect. At the same time, pagans joined them in growing numbers. The first stage of Christianity, i.e. the Early Christianity lasted from the founding of the first Christian congregations until the emergence of Paulinism.

Paulinism made a radical change in the lives of the first Christians. It also determined their further destiny. The bases of the united Christian Church came into being.

It was almost impossible to build Christian cultic places during the times of persecution of Christians, at the time of early Christianity. Their religious ceremonies were performed in their underground cemeteries and catacombs, which also served as their hiding-places. While avoiding the dangers of threatening conflicts, they lived by their spiritual values by withdrawing into themselves and helping each other. By locking themselves into their family homes and avoiding showy formalities, they celebrated the mystery; they were one in prayer and in Mass or Communion, as it was assigned by Christ [1].

The believers of the new faith, which spread in the world of the Jewish Diaspora, got together in the home of a wealthy co-religionist, usually on the upper floors. It happened sometimes that the whole building served the community. The best examples of the early Christian places were found under the cathedral of *San Giovanni e Paolo* in Rome, or in Dura-Europos, in Syria, where a dwelling house-church (*domus ecclesiae*) was found under the ruins of a city devastated by the Partuses in 265 [2].

Constantine the Great, the Greaco-Roman Emperor (247-337 A.D.), recognizing the power and opportunity in the foundation of Christianity, reached an arrangement with the Christian Church in 313 A.D. He officially recognized, and guaranteed the freedom of the Christian Church. In his famous Milanese Ordinance (*rescriptum*), the Emperor ordered that all the places where Christians used to gather, and all the goods belonging juridically to the folds (*ecclesiae*) were to be handed back to the Christian communities without any payment or compensation.

A huge amount of money was put at the bishops' disposal for the purpose of church building. According to the new law, the former pagan temples and estates of the holy places were given to the Christian Church. The edictum (ordinance issued by the emperor) started the building of Christian churches on the whole territory of the Roman Empire.

Christian temples were built everywhere. Constantine built the first Christian cathedral in Rome. This building was later named *San Giovanni Cathedral*. The construction of the *Saint Peter Basilica* started in 325 over the tomb of Peter the Apostle. The sacred place remained the centre of Christianity until the times of Pope Julius II. (1503-1513). By the end of the third century, the number of congregations has increased considerably.

At the beginning of the fourth century half of the population was Christian in Asia Minor, Armenia and Ciprus. A significant number of Christians lived in Syria (Antiochia), Egypt (Alexandria and Thebes), Rome, South and Central Italy, Africa, on the Iberian peninsula, on the northern part of Italy, in Gaul and in the provinces along the Danube river.

Theodosius (346-395), Holy Roman Emperor from 381 A.D., made Christianity the official state religion and started to suppress the pagans. Christianity left its catacomb life once and for all in the fifth century A.D. The church building of Constantine continued. The cathedral was the main form of churches built.

With the death of Theodosius in 395, the Holy Roman Empire was finally divided into two parts, the Western and the Eastern Empires. After that year, the Eastern-Roman Empire (Byzantium) lasted for more than one thousand years as an independent historical formation.

The Western-Roman Empire came to an end during the years of the Great Migrations due to the endless attacks of barbarians. The Empire was devastated by the Huns in the fifth century, and the southward movements of the Slavs immediately begun from the territories of present day Poland. They managed to reach the Elbe River in the west, the Danube in the southwest. During the sixth century they got into Pannonia, Thrace and Macedonia.

The Western-Roman Empire was gradually replaced by the newly founded Christian feudal states. As the consequences of the division of the Roman Empire, the Greek-Catholic (Orthodox) Church took shape in the east, and was strongly intertwined with the state. At the same time, the Papal supreme power was developed in the Western Church.

Christianity, as we have seen, used to be a persecuted religion. The northern banks of the Danube River known by the name Dacia Traiana (part of later Transylvania, and Oltenia) were the only exceptions to the persecutions after

271 A.D., when Aurelianus withdrew his legions and colonuses (settlers) from those territories. The exception lasted for a couple of decades, until the first flocks of migrating people, the Goths, appeared.

If there had been a Romanized population on these territories, the houses of congregations (*domus ecclesiae*) or cathedrals of theirs would have been built. However, there are no buildings or even traces of these to be found. Neither do we have any documents or other data proving their existence, even though - it is needless to say - after the withdrawal of the Roman legions in 271, until the appearance of the first barbarian people, the Goths, Christianity could spread free of pressure of any kind and persecution by the Roman administration in Dacia Traiana.

When discussing the theory of Daco-Roman continuity, it is necessary to investigate the situation also south of the lower Danube, in the Balkan Peninsula. Let us give a broad outline of the Byzantine Church Architecture and the architecture affected by the Byzantine style in the 4th-12th centuries in addition to works of art and other paintings parallel to the spread of Christianity.

We have already referred to the first Christian Churches built by Constantine and Theodosius. The Byzantine art's most outstanding architectual work, the monumental *Hagia Sophia* (532-537), was built in Constantinople during the reign of Justinianus, Eastern-Roman Emperor (482-565). The construction of the *San Vitale Cathedral* in Ravenna, financed by a rich Syrian banker, Julianus Argentarius, started before 532 and ended in 547.

The Bulgarians adopted Christianity in 865. According to a Greek source from the 11th century, their reigning Prince Boris I. (852-889) ordered the building of seven churches already in the same year, i.e. in 865. The era's biggest church, the *Great Basilica* is the most important art work of the Bulgarian architecture from the 9th-10th centuries. The *John the Baptist Church* in Nesebar, on the shore of the Black Sea, was built in the tenth century. The most monumental and most imposing relic of the Bulgarian architecture, the monastery of Rila was built between 927 and 942 in a small basin on the southern slope of the Maljovica. The second oldest monastery built in 1070, can be found in the environs of Tirnovo.

At the beginning of the 10th century there were no other states in the area which would have been able to compete with the strength and power of the Bulgarian state. The state's main goal was the full conquest of Byzantium. However, after the death of Tsar Simeon and the long military campaigns, the country's economical and military power became so weak that the State's internal order could not be restored. The Bulgarian State totally collapsed in 1018. The once great Bulgarian Empire became one of Byzantium's provinces. A considerable part of the monasteries were destroyed – especially in the surroundings of Pliska and Preslav, by the endless attacks of the raiding barbarian tribes from the North.

The *Saint Demeter Church* was built in Tirnovo, the capital, in 1186. After the foundation of the second Bulgarian Empire (1185), the tradition has it that the *Saint Peter* and *Paul Monastery* was also built during the second Bulgarian Empire on the Arbanas Mountain. According to the legend the Saint Elias monastery of in Plakovo was also built during the second Bulgarian State. In Skripu near Athens, in Greece, another monastery, originated from 873-874, can be found.

According to an early Russian chronicle, Vladimir, great reigning Prince of Kiev (980), entrusted ten scientists to travel around other people's territories and survey the great religions such as the Muslim, Christian and Greek- Catholic. The scientists gave accounts to the Prince of the monumental Hagia Sophia's fascinating beauty in Constantinople [3]. According to a chronicle, the great reigning prince converted – on the scientists´ recommendation – to Greek-Catholicism with his people. The Russians had already known Christianity, since the *Saint Nicholas Cathedral* in Kiev has been mentioned since 882.

Vladimir ordered all his subjects to embrace Christianity in 988-989. Under the reign of his son, Jaroslav the Wise, 1019-1054, the *Hagia Sophia Cathedral* was erected in Kiev. The Saint George Cathedral was built between 1119 and 1130, while the construction of the *Saint Demeter Church* in Vladimir-Suzdal lasted from 1194 to 1197. Building of additional churches was prevented by the Tartar conquests.

After the Byzantine style church architecture, let us examine the Byzantine art, which exerted a considerable influence on remote territories of the earth.

Byzantine masters made the mosaics of the *Hagia Sophia Church* in Kiev between 1037 and 1061. The frescos in Vladimir were painted around 1195. The Norman kings of Sicily built their churches with Byzantine masters between 1143 and 1200. The *San Marco Cathedral* was patterned after the Hagia Sophia in Constantinople. Its earliest mosaics from the 11th century are also Byzantine masters' work. The gold and enamel Pala d'Oro of the high altar is also an art work from Constantinople. Fresco painting at the end of the 12th century met very high standards in Cyprus under the Byzantine governors' reign [4].

We have to go deeply into the question of the Byzantine church architecture and works of art, because their trend setting spread to the Balkan Peninsula. We will have to look for Vlach (Rumanian) church constructions. We have to look for the Vlach Orthodox chapels and churches of the 7th-12th centuries along the southern and northern banks of the Danube River. If we accept some Rumanian statements, the Rumanian cultic places shall also be found in Transylvania. We have to look for these cultic places especially from the first half of the 9th century.

Prince Krum, Bulgarian ruler, captured some bishops, priests and Christians sometime around 812. He forcibly relocated them to the left bank of the Danube, where they converted a lot of Bulgarians to orthodox Christianity. Around 870, Dacia Traiana and a part of Transylvania also were placed under the authority of Boris who ruled Bulgaria. If Daco-Romans (Rumanians) had lived there, they would have had to yield to the brutal Bulgarian force used against them and convert to Orthodox Christianity. However, we cannot find any contemporary traces of Vlach church architecture, neither on the Balkans nor in Transylvania. The historical sources do not mention the "Romanized Dacians" or the Rumanians in Dacia until the 12th century, although numerous sources talk about the Vlach people on the Balkan Peninsula since the 10th century (976).

Considering the monumental paintings of the Byzantine Empire in the "successor" states, such as Serbia, Bulgaria and Trapezunt, it can be said that there is no mention of the artistic impact of those paintings on the territories north of the Danube. This would not have been imaginable, if the Rumanians, as native people, had lived in Dacia Traina and the other areas in question during the 11th-12th centuries. As the influence of Byzantine art had reached Hungary, for example Szekszárd, it undoubtedly should have reached Dacia Traina also.

The state founding Magyars had some contacts with the Christians before they settled in the Carpathian Basin. The fact, that they did not devastate the cultic places can be explained by their good relationship with the Christians. If the Magyar conquerors had found such Daco-Roman cultic places in Transylvania, those cultic places with their Christian followers would have survived the original invasion of the Magyars as they did in Hungary. These circumstances indicate the Balkan link to the orthodox clerical organizations of the Rumanians; the Bulgarian-Slav liturgical language and the language of the Royal Chancellery; and several features of the early Rumanian culture referring to the close Bulgarian-Slav relationship [5].

The first Rumanian state organizations were founded several hundred years later than those of the surrounding peoples: Wallachia in the second half of the 13th century, and at the beginning of the 14th century; Moldavia at the beginning and the middle of the 14th century.

The Hungarian conquerors took possession of a territory having considerable artistic tradition [6]. The ruins of the Roman province and the art of the Slavs living within the boundaries of the Hungarian State increased the artistic culture of the Hungarians. The same can hardly be said about the Vlachs. The oldest Rumanian Orthodox church was built in the 13th century, it can be found in Demsus. According to Károly Kós "...it is a primitive Rumanian art-work of Byzantine style" [7]. László Kőváry said: "It is probably a crypt raised over an early Christian church, the Longinus' ruins...Considering its size it is very small even for a Vlach church [8]. It is one of the most marvellous and oldest buildings in our country [historical Hungary]. Its steeple originated from the 10th century. Some of our historians think that it is a Roman church, while others believe it is of Gothic origin."

The church, as we have mentioned, was built in the 13th century. This in accordance with the fact that a Hungarian document, which mentions a Rumanian population in Southern Transylvania for the first time, originated from 1210 [9]. The late date of the building of the first Vlach church indicates that there were no Vlach inhabitants in Transylvania in the period of the Hungarian settlement, and that the first Vlachs could not have appeared in the area before the 12th century.

Neither the Roman society and its institutions, nor the settlements' continuity can undoubtedly be determined. In the one-time Roman cities, where traces of German and Avar settlements can be found, cemeteries and different buildings are providing proof that people used up parts of the ruined cities as building material for their houses [10].

Mircea Păcurariu, professor of the Theological University in Nagyszeben (Sibiu) [11], states, "In Doboka (Dăbîca), near Kolozsvár, some Christian churches that originated from the 10th-11th centuries, were newly discovered." He did not state, what kind of churches are in question. Since he considers that these churches were built in the 10th-11th centuries, they must in all likelihood have been Hungarian churches. Păcurariu would probably talk about the churches in greater details, if he could consider them of Rumanian origin.

The Vlach churches between the 14th and 17th centuries, following that of Demsus, were built by the Moldavian and Wallachian voivodes, vassals of Hungary, on the estates in fee granted to them by the Hungarian kings and the Hungarian voivodes in Transylvania. (We will talk about them later in chapter VII.)

Nicolae Stoicescu writes [12] that Christian cemeteries, originating from the time before the Árpád's conquest of Hungary, were found in Dacia, in a part of present day Transylvania. Such tombs might have been found, but this does not necessarily mean that they belonged to Rumanians, since there were Christians among the peoples of the Great Migration, and they were buried as Christians. Objects, indicating their Christian belief, were placed with their bodies.

II

Dacia;

Daco-Roman Continuity

Hungarian historians, like Benedek Jancsó, who dedicated his life to the intensive study of the theory of Daco-Roman continuity, consider that the territories of Dacia included Krassó-Szörény, Hunyad, Alsófehér and Kolozs Counties, the southern part of Szolnok-Doboka County, Torda-Aranyos and Nagyküküllő Counties, – thus, the southwestern and central part of Transylvania. (Its influence and impact could be felt also in neighbouring areas.) According to Jancsó, it never included the Székely territories east of the Hargita Mountains and north of the Feketeügy (Râul Negru) River. Moldavia, Bukovina, Máramaros, and Szatmár, Bihar, Zaránd counties never belonged to Dacia. North and East of the above mentioned territory there were mainly uninhabited lands, not or only loosely connected to the Dacian state [13].

Dacia was attacked by the Romans for the first time in 101 A.D. Traian, crossing the Danube through the Vaskapu (the Iron Gate) of Hunyad County, marched and attacked the Dacian capital, Sarmizegetusa, with his legions. The contemporary centre of King Decebal was found near Várhely, a small village in Hunyad County. One of the Roman leaders, Lusius, crossed the Danube at Orsova and invaded Sarmizegetusa through the Volcano Pass. Decebal asked for peace.

Under the terms and conditions of the peace treaty, Decebal became vassal of the Roman emperor. Traian left a Roman garrison in Sarmizegetusa and returned to Rome with honor and glory. The leader of the garrison was Longinus, who was mentioned by us while discussing the Roman Orthodox Temple of Demsus.

Decebal, however, did not intend to honor the peace treaty. He used the time of peace to rebuild the devastated fortresses and fortifications. He also attacked the Jazygians who were allied with Traian. Decebal also welcomed to Dacia Roman deserters (there were Christians among them) and sent some of them to Rome with the commission to kill Traian. He arrested and held in captivity Longinus, Traian's personal representative. He sent his emissaries to Rome with the message that he will not let Longinus free, unless he gets back the occupied territories plus reimbursements for his military expenses. Longinus poisoned himself in captivity, and the Roman Senate declared Decebal an enemy.

Traian personally lead his legions against Decebal in 105 A.D. Sarmizegetusa was taken and occupied by the Romans. Decebal was captured while trying to escape. (According to the legends, he tried to escape to the north, and fell upon his sword at Kolozsvár.) Traian finished the full conquest of Dacia in 106 A.D. and returned to Rome.

Dacia was made a Roman province; it was named *Dacia Traiana* after its conqueror. According to Roman historians like Dio Cassus and Eutropius, Traian killed off the whole male population in Dacia. He replaced them with new settlers of all nationalities from the whole Roman Empire. The Roman inscriptions in Transylvania, that originated in later centuries, suggest that in addition to the new dwellers, Dacia had Dacians as well as other nationalities living in its territories.

Historical sources tell us that Dacians, living outside the province, raided several times the flourishing new provinces. Between 180 and 190 A.D. Governor Sabinianus made twelve thousand free Dacians settle down with the aim of pacifying them. These Dacians got back to their Fatherland after one hundred years of exile. This was the first time they had contact with the Roman administration, therefore the Romanization could not have taken place before this time, if ever.

The Roman armed forces stationed in Dacia were multinational [14]. Only the commanders and civil servants were from Italy. The newly settled people were not purely native Latin speakers [15]. [Compare the situation in India. After a long period of British rule, only the upper and middle classes learned the English language. The vast majority of the inhabitants of the Indian Subcontinent, or any other colony for that matter, never really mastered it (translator's note)]. Writings, inscriptions, archaeological findings prove that they were urban, miner and merchant people, from Syria to Gaul, who could not speak Latin or spoke it badly [16]; on the inscriptions which were not made by the Roman authorities, names of Oriental Gods abound [17]. These people should have been Romanized before they, intermarrying with the native population, could have been the ancestors of a Neo-Latin people, (the Rumanians). Thus, there were not many native Latin speakers among the settlers. (The number of native Latin speakers radically dropped in Italy too. Therefore, Traian had to issue an order, to stop the dangerous outflow of settlers from Italy.)

Believers of the Continuity Theory are frequently referring to the Latinizing impact of the Roman legions and merchants stationed in Dacia. Participating in the Latinization of Dacia, members of the legions should have been natives from Italy. The legionaries were Roman citizens, but they were recruited from the western and other primarily multinational, non-Latin provinces.

Only two Roman legions were stationed in Dacia, approximately twelve thousand people. Compared to the alleged large population in the territory, they would not have been successful in the Latinization, even if they had been native Latins from Italy and had no other duties to perform. Only the officers were from Rome in the auxiliary troops;

approximately 500-1000 people, who did not live in cities. Since they were stationed along the borders in fortified camps, which were mainly uninhabited areas, they did not have anybody to Latinize. There were only a few Romans among the merchants, therefore they could not have taken part in the Latinization.

The Roman legions had to give up Dacia in 271 A.D. due to the relentless attacks of barbarians. It was robbed and plundered by the Goths, the Sarmatians and other people allied with each other. Emperor Aurelian[1] "...Being convinced that the province with its diminished population could not be kept under control, gave it up and withdrew his troops under organized circumstances. In 271 the army's still remaining units were withdrawn and the population was transferred into Moesia" [18].

From our point of view, it is important to know that along with the withdrawal in 271, historiography commemorates two Dacias, Dacia Traiana and Dacia Aureliana. The first included part of present day Transylvania and Oltenia. The second was situated south of the Danube, bounded by the Skopje-Sofia-Niš triangle. We have to emphasize this, because Rumanian historians, according to their own interest, usually keep silent about Dacia Aureliana.

The giving up and evacuation of Dacia, as well as the transfer of the people was fairly well organized. Naturally, the action did not happen overnight. A significant part of the civil population had already left the province. It is possible that the evacuation was not complete, although there are no reliable data to support this assumption. The number of those who did not leave was most probably insignificant[19].

The Roman reign in Dacia lasted only about 170 years. Later, Dacia became booty of the barbarian peoples. Six hundred dark years followed in this era. It is certain, however, that Transylvania was subject to the rule of the Goths until the beginning of the 5th century. As we can see, Aurelian let them conquer Dacia in 271. Their empire, where Christianity also spread, was destroyed by the attacks of the Huns. Even the Goths became divided into two parts: Western and Eastern

Goths. The Huns conquered Transylvania with their devastating attacks, but after the collapse of their empire the area became the property of the Gepids, later the Longobards.

In the second half of the 6th century Dacia was conquered by the Avars. Their empire existed until the end of the 8th century A.D. Charlemagne, outstanding member of the Carolingian dynasty, defeated them in several battles in the year of 791 and conquered their territory to the Tisza River. The invading Hungarians found a considerable number of Avars, who remained there after the collapse of their empire; they intermarried with the Hungarians. The Avars have left a large number of tombs in which rich material relics were found.

In the 6th century A.D. a new people, different from the other nationalities, started to emerge in greater and greater numbers from the north and the north-east from the Sarmata lowlands to the middle, eastern and southern part of Europe. They were the Slavs. They were peaceful settlers, who earned their living from a primitive form of agriculture. People of the Great Migration would rather have treated them with consideration than harm them. They were considered servants, and their only task was to provide plenty agricultural produce for the country. Their number increased considerably, and they encroached on even larger and larger territories. In the 5th and 6th centuries, they were present not just in the Balkan Peninsula but in Central and Eastern Europe also. To Transylvania, the Slavs started to move probably during the Avar rule in the 6th century. They have absorbed those small ethnic groups who remained there after the devastations of the Great Migration. We have sources about every single ethnic group who lived in Transylvania after the Roman withdrawal in 271. We do not know, however, what happened to the Dacians and the Celts. Accordingly, the remaining fragments of the Dacians could have blended into the people following each other during the years, the same way as the Eastern Celts vanished without a trace.

In the 9th century, only Slavic people lived in small

numbers in Transylvania. The conquering Hungarians could have found only Slavs in the area. This Slavic population lived without any organized state, under the leadership of the head of the clan; gathered around earthworks which served for some sort of defense. The origin of these earthworks can hardly be viewed as Dacian. Especially those, which were dug up recently by the Rumanian historians in that part of Székely land which did not even belong to the territories of Dacia. It is probable that Southern Transylvania and several parts of the Great Plain were subject to Bulgarian rule when the Hungarians arrived. Considering the reports of the Hungarian chronicles concerning the beginning of the 11th century, it is possible that the Bulgarian reign survived until the first decade of the new millennium. It seems that the Hungarians did not have to share the political power, making an allowance for the small Bulgarian territory, with any other people. At the beginning of the 10th century only the Hungarians had political organizations in the Carpatian Basin although this organization was based on the confederation of tribes [20].

We have to stress the fact that there already were some Christians among the Roman conquerors of Dacia, as well as the settlers they transferred here. Christianity was spreading rapidly. In the middle of the 2nd century A.D., even the farthest provinces of the Roman Empire had Christian congregations [21]. Christians must have appeared in Dacia. They did not only care for their religion, but they carried on some missionary activities for the sake of spreading Christianity. There could have been some Christians among them who had been converted to Christianity directly by the apostles and became Latin Christians.

Around the 3rd century, there were several one-time Roman soldiers among the Christian martyrs [22]. This was also professed by Tertulianus Quintus Septimus Florens (152-222 A.D.), a North African Christian Church leader. According to him, Christianity penetrated into the territory along the left bank of the Danube before the Roman legions' withdrawal. This is also believed by D. Pippidi, Rumanian historian (and on the basis of his opinions by several other Romanian historians) [23].

Nicolae Stoicescu, the Rumanian historian mentioned above, stated [24], that the religious freedom of the Christians was not acknowledged at the time of the Roman withdrawal from Dacia Traiana (it was refused recognition until 313 A.D.). Thus, the withdrawal of the Roman administration made the spread of Christianity easier in the former province. This may be correct; however, the following circumstances should be considered:

- If spreading in Dacia, Christianity could not have many followers at the very beginning;

- presumably, the Dacians were not Christians. The new religion could hardly, only as an underground movement, spread before 271 due to the pursuit of the contemporary pagan Roman administration;

-the conversion and exercise of Christianity must have been considered secondary in a situation of endless attacks of the free Dacians;

- after the withdrawal of Dacia Traiana's population to the territories south of the Danube in 271, there had been so few Christians left, that they could not have remained a considerable factor in the survival and propagation of Christianity. (The Christians, considering themselves really Romanized, must have been among those who were most willing to leave the province when the Roman administration left it;)

- after the withdrawal of the legions and the population, Aurelian left Dacia to the Goths. We have very little data about their reign regarding whether Christian religion could have existed in Dacia Traiana;

- the "late Roman" culture does not have any authentic marks in Transylvania referring to an isolated, local population from the era of tetrarchy.[2] Traces of the people living here for an uncertain time can only be found in Baráthely, on the southern banks of the river Nagy-Küküllő. Therefore, there was not anyone the new religion could have spread among.

If Christianity had still existed in Dacia, what kind of cultic places would have borne witness to it? As we have already mentioned, we do not know much about the history of Transylvania for six hundred years, until the Magyar conquest of Hungary. It is probable that during the Peoples' Migration, the population living in Transylvania after the Roman withdrawal was decimated and those who survived were assimilated to other peoples.

This is proven by the destiny of the contemporary Dacian capital, Sarmizegetusa (Grădişte, Hungarian: Várhely). The city where the palace of the Augustanians, the forum, several baths, a temple, sanctuaries, public and private buildings were located, totally perished. In 279 A.D. it was entirely uninhabited. Its stones were carried away for building of houses and the nearby castle. Such a collapse could have happened on the whole territory of Dacia.

What is the significance of the fact that writers of the Clergy, who mentioned so much data about a Christian religious life in the territories south of the Danube, did not write anything about such things in the regions north of the river? Rumanian historians assume that people lived more undisturbed in the mountains, but how did they do it without priests, bishops and clerical organizations?

As shown above, no remains of Christian Churches or Christian cultic places were found in Dacia Traiana from the time of the Roman occupation. During the 2nd and 3rd Centuries the majority of the Dacian population – people in the villages – were still pagan.

If Christians lived in former Dacia Traiana, they could have performed the conversions of the yet non-Christian Daco-Romans and barbarians who settled there. In the early Christian communities every member could preach and the member in question could be his or her own "doctor". [25] It may be asked: why was it then necessary to send missionaries to this territory?

Stoicescu (1980, p. 149) assumes that the withdrawal of the Roman administration in 271 made the spread of Christianity more easy – there was no one who persecuted the believers of the new faith and the cult of the Roman emperor disappeared. Cultic places could have been built freely – however, there are no material remains to show that this would have been the case.

Stoicescu refers to Auxentius Durostorenis, (p. 150): "the bishop named Ulfila[3] was preaching in the Gothic and the Latin languages". Stoicescu then quotes Moga (*Transilvania*, 74,3, 1943, p. 15) who asked: "To whom could this bishop preach in the Latin language if not to the Romanized and Christianized Dacians?"

The answer to this question is as follows: **Ulfila preached in the Latin language in the Roman Empire, south of the lower Danube**. The quotation from the text written by Auxentius Durostorensis is incomplete and therefore misleadning. Reading the entire text, it appears that Ulfila preached for the Goths north of the Danube for seven years; then a persecution of Christians started and the bishop was forced, with part of his congregation, to flee to the Roman Empire – there, he preached for thirty-three years, of course, in Latin, the language of the liturgy among the Roman population (see also Du Nay & Du Nay, 1997, p. 35).

Stoicescu assumes (p. 149) that the Christianization of the Daco-Romans who remained north of the Danube was partly achieved by missionaries coming from the south. He mentions, however, the opinion of P.P. Panaitescu, who believed that their aim were the conversion of barbarians, not that of the already Christian Daco-Romans. Panaitescu also asserted that their Christianity was a natural consequence of the continuity of the Empire in the 4th-6th Centuries north of the Danube [27]. Let us take some points into consideration:

- During the time of the Roman administration, between 106 and 271 A.D. – as we have already mentioned – there were only a few Christians in Dacia Traiana. Their religion could hardly spread. If Christianity did expand it was only moderately successful.

- When the Romans evacuated Dacia Traiana, the first to leave the province must have been the Christian believers among the settlers. The spread of Christianity slowed down, was forced back or even stopped.

- If the Daco-Romans, living north of the Danube were converted to Christianity by the Romans then they would live there as devoted Christians. Why didn't their own preachers convert the barbarians to Christianity? Again; who converted the Rumanians to Christianity in Dacia Traiana ? This question is not new. It was discussed by Petru Maior[4] who believed that Christianity had been brought by the colonuses, and, consequently, there was no need of missionaries, apostles etc. That is why the exact date of conversion is unclear; it is not linked to anybody's name.

This is contradicted by the fact that the official religion in Dacia Traiana was the worship of the emperor, besides the cult of Jupiter and Mars, and already in the mid-second century, the Mithras-cult became widespread,[5] which was an alien, non-Roman cult. One may add, that the territory between the Adria and the Black Sea, and the Balkan territory south of the Danube was intensively Romanized, much more than Dacia Traiana. By the 5th century Illiricum[6] and Moesia were the most advanced provinces as regards the organization of the Christian Church.

The fundamental notions of the Christian faith in the Rumanian language are of Latin origin: *biserică* < latin *basilica, Dumnezeu < Domine Deus, înger < angelus*, etc. Stoicescu asserts (150) that this proves that the Daco-Romans were Christianized in the period "in which the Rumanian people was formed". However, these words are not specific to Dacia Traiana but were also used by the Christians living south of the Danube.

Stoicescu (150) mentions that Dobruja remained for a longer time under Roman rule and was thus exposed to an earlier and more intense Christianization as compared to the other Rumanian provinces. He mentions that a bishopric existed in Tomis[7] (today's Constanța) in the 4th - 6th centuries. This was by A. Ghimpu-Bolșacov called "the first metropolitan seat [*mitropolie*] [8] of our country" [29]

Stoicescu mentions several discoveries of contemporary basilicas, inscriptions of a Christian character, tombs and crypts in this area. However, Dobruja is located south of the Danube – the point is that such remains of a Christian religious life were not found in Dacia Traiana.

Stoicescu also mentions a number of archaeological discoveries of an ancient Christian character also from the territory of former Dacia Traiana, which would prove the presence of the Christian religion there already in the 4th century. These are, for example, a gem found in Torda (Turda), an ex-voto bearing the monogram of Christ and the inscription "*Ego Zenovius votum posui*", found at the village Biertan (see below), – both in Transylvania ; as well as Christian cemeteries of the Ciumbrud-Blandiana B type from the 9th-10th centuries, also in Transylvania.

We do not dispute the results of archaeological research, as we do not dispute the existence of the discovered Christian tombs. We cannot accept, however, the theories put forward by Stoicescu (and others), that the Romanian people were converted to Christianity on the territory north of the Danube, including Dacia Traiana. The difference in this respect between Dobruja and the territories north of the lower Danube is striking: **in Dobruja**, there are remains of several Christian churches, crypts built on tombs of Christian martyrs from the 3rd century, more than 200 inscriptions of a Christian character, many of them on sarcophags from the 4th-7th centuries, etc. All these provide material proof for the statement that in Dobruja, intensive religious, Christian life – clerical organizations, monasteries and episcopacies – must have existed beginning with the 4th century.

If the ancestors of the Rumanians, who adopted Christianity already in the 3rd - 4th centuries, had lived in that period in the territory of Dacia Traiana, there should be similar material remains also there. Christian people of this time could not live, not even temporarily, without buildings and places, such as chapels, meeting-houses, temples etc., serving their worship.

However, nothing of this kind exists north of the lower Danube, as shown also by M. Păcurariu, the above mentioned professor of theology. He listed six relics in his reference book (p. 29-30) but was unable to find any cultic place or any other trace of early Christian organizations in Transylvania.

The above mentioned striking difference between the territories north, respectively south of the lower Danube regarding early Christian churches etc. have been discussed by Rumanian historians. The fact that in the south, – in Dobruja and in Moesia – there were churches and episcopacies in an early period caused several historians to assume that such buildings must have existed also among the Daco-Romans living in the North. This is, however, a dangerous reasoning, writes Auner Carol, historian of the Church. This is because it can be asked: how it is possible that parallel to the strong documentation about the existence of the churches in the neighborhood territories, intensive investigations, going on for decades, could not find similar contructions in the territories north of the lower Danube?

It is well known that emperor Justinian raised the Episcopacy of his birthplace, Tauresium, to the archbishopric rank with the name *Prima Justiniana*. In his second documentary he listed all the episcopacies posted under this archbishopric. In this document, one castle and two fortresses located on the northern shore of the lower Danube are described, but no episcopacy, nor any cultic place, or other religious organization is mentioned north of the river. This completes the picture given by the archeological finds mentioned above.

A few remarks about the *ex voto*, with the inscription "*Ego Zenovius votum posui*" (I, Zenovius made this donation) considered by Stoicescu as one of the most significant proofs of the existence of a Daco-Roman Christian community in Southern Transylvania in the 4th century: It was found in the vicinity of Berethalom (Biertan). On the basis of the letters used and the initials, style scientists determined that it originated from the 4th century. Stoicescu (1980, p. 153):

"The fact, that the inscription is in the Latin language proves that its owner was a Daco-Roman, who talked to his contemporary companions in a language which they understood. At the same time, it is an undeniable proof of the Daco-Roman Continuity Theory, as well as a conclusive proof of the ancient age of Daco-Roman Christianity". (Stoicescu, 1980, p. 153).

As shown above, finds of such objects, in the absence of cult places etc., are not sufficient to prove the existence of Christians and even less that of a Latin-speaking population in the area in question.

The Rumanian language is of Latin origin and the religious terms show that the ancestors of the Rumanians were Christianized in an environment where Latin was the language of liturgy. This must have occurred at an early age, before the Slavic contact.

The Latin form of Christianity was first introduced by the archbishopric of Prima Justiniana, which exercised decisive influence on the life of the Latin-speaking population of the Balkans in the 5th century. However, the scattered, therefore hardly organizable population could not resist the Slav conquests in the 6th-7th centuries. The native people assimilated into the Slavonic culture, and even the shepherd people of the mountains could not keep themselves from the Slavic influence.

This was the Ancient Rumanian or Common Rumanian population. This people, who originally spoke a uniform language (*română comună*), started to migrate in different directions after about 1000 A.D. Some of them migrated to the west, and settled down on the territory of Istria, surrounding the Monte Maggiore. They are the Istro-Rumanians. Others went to the South. Their descendants, the today's Arumanians, or Cincars, live mainly in Macedonia, while the Megleno-Rumanians settled down in Thessaloniki and its surrounding areas.

Another branch of this Ancient Rumanian population moved to the North. They crossed the Balkan Mountains and settled down in the woodlands of the Danube and its northern tributaries, such as the Argeș, the Ialomița and the Dâmbovița. These territories were very suitable for shepherd life. Consequences of the migrations are that we cannot find any Roman cultic places neither on the Istrian Peninsula nor in

Macedonia or the surrounding territories of Thessaloniki.

We have to agree with Ferenc Levárdy, who wrote the following (about the Carpathian basin) [32]:

"The devastations of the migrating peoples, following one after another, wiped out almost every mark of Roman life. Only ruins demonstrate the one-time flourishing Christian life. Due to serious ordeals of the war events, we can hardly talk about any continuity of life. According to the short stories of Saint Jerome,[9] the Carpathian Basin was far and wide blackmailed, robbed, devastated by Goths, Sarmatas, Kvads, Alans, Huns, Vandals, Markomanns. Temples were ruined and the martyrs´ bodies were thrown out; the whole Roman world was crumbling! Most of the time the ones who just recently arrived likely camped among the hewn stone ruins (ruin continuity)."

Naturally, there are some exceptions. During the times of Constantine the Great, an early Christian basilica was raised in Pannonia at Fenékpuszta. It even survived the times when the old Germanic peoples escaping the Huns evacuated Pannonia. The other example is the Transylvanian early Christian temple from the 4th century at Demsus, if it had been a temple at all.

Returning to the question of the migrations of the Rumanians, we can state that they brought their religion with them from the Balkans. An old Rumanian anonymous chronicle [33] tells us that the first conquest of the Vlachs happened in the 7th century from the southern part of the Danube through Oltenia under the reign of the Basarab Dynasty. (We note that the founder of this dynasty, Basarab, was born at the end of the 13th century.) The impact of the Roman Rite Archbishopric, the Prima Justiniana was completely swept away, without a mark, by the Slav invasion. The archbishopric's role was overtaken by an orthodox metropolite, subaltern of the Patriarch, who was residing in Ohrida. Therefore, when they migrated and settled down in Hungary, more specifically in Transylvania, which then was an organic part of the country, the Rumanians had been wholehearted believers of the Eastern Church for centuries.

III

Árpád's Conquest of Hungary;

Conversion to Christianity

Around 830 A.D, a large group of Hungarians appeared in the territories next to the Black Sea between the Don and the Dnester, in Levedia. They lived there until 889 A.D. The Hungarians giving way to the pressure coming from the East, moved to Etelköz, which would be located in today's Moldavia and Bessarabia (the Republic of Moldavia).

The Hungarians get in close contact with Byzantium already in Etelköz (Atelkuzu). They were allied forces during the Bulgarian-Byzantinian Wars, in 894. The Byzantines got to know the Hungarians better, and they managed to receive more detailed information about them. Hungarian links strengthened with the Byzantines. The Byzantine world exerted a significant cultural influence upon the Hungarians. This is proved by the fact that in the contemporary tombs, also Byzantine impact can be found among Sassanide, Arab, Norman and other influences. In the tombs from the 10th century we can often observe objects of Byzantine origin or showing Byzantine characteristics. The findings are often accompanied by money of the Byzantine Emperors. Several objects with Greek inscriptions were found in the tombs. The best example is the silver-button of Piliny [34].

During the two decades after the Hungarians settled down, Hungarians remained faithful to the Byzantine Empire. They also knew that one of the main conditions of the new state's maintenance was Byzantine goodwill and recognition. This point of view was also reasonable, because they sought Byzantine aid to neutralize the German influence. The new Hungarian land belonged to the Byzantine range of influence, even though earlier it had been an organic part of the Holy Roman Empire. That is to say, the knowledge of Roman unity was still alive in Byzantium. The West-Roman Empire's territories occupied by the barbarians were always considered by the emperor's court as belonging to the Byzantine Empire. The lands of Hungary, even after the Hungarians settled down there, were viewed as belonging to the Byzantine zone of interest. The Hungarians also faced these facts. They did not oppose Greek-Catholicism (the Eastern Orthodox Church) neither during the years of settling down nor later.

On the territories of their new homeland, Hungarians found only one people in considerable number, the Slavs. They are not to be mistaken with the Slovaks. In the first half of the 10th century, the Carpathian Basin was not inhabited by the Slovaks but by the Slavs, who lived everywhere on the boundaries between the plains and mountains.

The Hungarian - Slav contact did not take place in the interior of the country. The two peoples met on the confines of the mountainous district, such as the south-western part of Transdanubia; the slopes of the Mecsek, Mátra and Bükk Mountains; the territories along the Tisza and Szamos, the Kraszna Valley and in Transylvania in the area of Gyulafehérvár. The lands lying between this area and the natural boundaries were considered of little value from the Hungarian economical point of view, and served defensive purposes because they were largely uninhabited [35].

The conquering Hungarians settled most densely in Transdanubia. Large parts of the area east of the Tisza river and Transylvania remained uninhabited for a while, since people were afraid of the attacks of their eastern neighbours. Transylvanian findings of the contemporary equestrian tombs prove that "...Central Transylvania: the middle and lower reaches of the Szamos and Maros; and the lower reaches of the two Küküllős were occupied by the Hungarians. No other contemporary equestrian tombs were found outside of this region, which fact is serious enough to presume that no other territories were occupied at that time" [36].

The subjugated Slavs – as was the case also with the Slavs of the Elba-Odera territories, who were assimilated to the surrounding German population, – were after two or three centuries totally assimilated into the Hungarians. Many Slavic words became part of the Hungarian language by this time; words used in state and church organization, trades, and more advanced agricultural methods [37].

Only the Avars, who are mentioned by the sources before Árpád's conquest of Hungary, left significant marks on the area, along with the Slavs. Charlemagne (724-814) ordered their transfer, by their own request to the area between Szombathely and Deutsch-Altenburg (Carnuntum) in 804. The sources still mention them in the decades before the arrival of the Hungarians.

The Hungarians' ancestors were pagans. Christianity was introduced to them by Byzantine missionaries before their state founding (38). They found direct contact with Christianity in their new homeland by the way of the conquered Slavs and the captives taken during the frequent military campaigns in the West. According to Gyula Pauler, "... the pastors of the conquered managed to find the easiest way to the ears of the conquerors. The memento of these apostles was not kept by historiography but by the language. Words pertaining to the Christian religion, such as *Christian, pagan, baptism, confirmation, bishop, priest, monk, saint, angel,* and *altar,* were borrowed from the language of the Slavs (the Slovens). None of them is of German origin [39].

According to Ferenc Levárdy, the Hungarians found some ruins of the old Roman buildings at the time of their conquest of Hungary. They even found temples and priests in Pannonia and in the Szerémség [40]. Archaeological material left by the Hungarians show some Christian influence. The Christian cross appears on a few objects. Almost one dozen tombs, mainly children's burial places were found, with engraved bronze and silver crosses and necklaces. It is a fact that several Hungarian aristocrats, acting from political consideration, converted to Christianity already in the 10th century. According to Ioannes Skylitses, Byzantine historian "Bulcsú ostensibly was baptized into the Christian religion, Constantinus became his godfather, and he was honored by Patrician rank and a lot of money before returning to his homeland. In 952 Gyula, another reigning Prince of the Hungarians, went to the emperor's city, received baptism, and enjoyed the same distinctions. He returned with a pious monk, named Hierotheos, who was by Theofylaktos ordained bishop of Turkia (Hungary). He drove many people out of the barbarian straying to Christianity." Consequently the first Transylvanian bishop started his work in the 10th century and used Greek-Christian rites [41].

The Magyars took the Greek-Christian religion and used its rites. By the time of the Hungarian defeat at Augsburg (Lech Field) in 955, a Greek-Christian bishop was functioning in Hungary. The leaders, commanders and part of the nation were formally baptized.

The alliance between Constantine Porfyrogenithos (903-959) and the Hungarians was made stronger by annual taxes and "gifts" paid by the emperor. The emperor however got so much hostile and disdainful information about the Hungarians – the news of the sorrowful defeat of Bulcsú's army – that he ended the paying of such "gift-taxes". Instead, Olga, the Russian Great reigning Princess put in a claim for the "gift-taxes", after her baptism. Constantine thus managed to acquire Russia for the Greek-Christian Church. Hungary, however, turned from it. Byzantium lost its military alliance against Bulgaria, as well as the influence of the Greek-Christian Church in Hungary.

The Byzantine-Hungarian relationship became so hostile, that Taksony (son of Zoltán, Hungarian leader; 947-972) asked for a bishop from Rome to continue the spread of Christianity. Liuprand, Secretary of the Holy Roman Emperor, Otto I., said: "The Pope ordained a bishop for

Hungary in the winter of 961-962." A Hungarian envoy of Bulgarian origin, by the name of Salk, was sent to Rome. The Pope sent Zacheus with a bulla to Hungary to be bishop there. The delegation, however, was captured in Capua by the followers of Otto. This action was supposed to accomplish the conversion of the Hungarians into the Christian organization by Otto's own bishop. The Hungarian great reigning princes were ready to build up the Christian Church's organization in the 950's and 960's. It was no fault of theirs that the attempt turned out to be unsuccessful [42].

The trend towards Christianity also meant political change. It was expressed by the mission, consisting of twelve Hungarian representatives, who in 973 A.D. were sent to emperor Otto, in Quedlingburg. The Emperor was there accepting the salutations of small populations who belonged to the German Empire's range of interest. By this way, the hostilities between the Hungarians and the German royal court ended. Bruno, the missionary bishop baptized Géza and his son Vajk, who received the name Stephen after the first martyr and patron saint of the church of Passau. However, the new religion did not take root in Géza. According to a later born legend, he considered himself rich enough to serve two gods at the same time.

Until the glory of the battles lasted, the Hungarians did not care much about the conquered territories. It is well known, that a part of the Hungarian army was badly defeated at Augsburg (Bavaria) in 955. Undoubtedly, that great misfortune forced those tribes of the nation, who led their raids on the West during the earlier decades, as well as in 955, to discontinue the attacks. For those who regularly raided the South, the defeat at Augsburg did not bring change. Only the severe defeat at Arcadiupolis in 970-971, ended the marauding on the South.

The intelligent and experienced voivod Gyula, who married Sarolta, Géza's daughter, was Géza's good advisor. With his great influence on the reigning prince, he suceeded in convincing him that there were two tasks to be solved involving the nations' future destiny: Peace must be ensured between Hungary and Germany, and a way must be found for Christianity to capture the soul of the nation.

The first converter's name was Wolfgang. He was followed by Piligrim, who sent a letter to Pope Benedict VII. around 974, in which he informed the Pope that the priests and monks had already converted five thousand Hungarians to Christianity. There was peace between pagans and Christians. Almost the whole nation was willing to embrace the Holy Faith [43].

Géza often had to resort to force to ensure the spread of Christianity. The consequence was discontent and open revolt in some parts of the country. He tried to compromize, and appeased the diehards by also offering sacrifices to the traditional gods. After the marriage of his son, he died with the knowledge that in addition to the homeland, he acquired for his nation strong ties to Europe by the adoption of Christianity.

The work of conversion was led by Archbishop Astrik.[10] There is only one source about the conversion and the organization of the new Church: the biography of Szent Gellért (Saint Gerardus). This source mentions that the first converters were Benedictine monks.

The first truly Christian King, *Szent István* (Stephen I, 997- 1038), wanted to tie Hungary to the Roman-Catholic Church along with the Western Roman-German cultural community, even though he had the opportunity to choose between the Roman and the Byzantine Churches. He helped to secure the Western type Roman-Catholic Christianity for his nation, but he did not make it unique. The former Bishop Gellért of Marosvár (today Csanád, Rum. Cenad) could admit Greek-Christian communities to his diocese. The king made possible the exercise of Greek rites and ceremonies in the Greek language. He provided rich donations to the Greek convents (basilicas) in the Veszprém Valley. Consequently, the Greek-Christian Church continued to live in Hungary undisturbed also after the millennium. It is also an important fact, that king Stephen, being an ally of the Byzantine Emperor while occupying Ohrida, did not bother to take expensive presents for him. Instead he took the relics of the martyr Saint George, much revered by the adherents of the Greek Christian Faith.

King Stephen, following in his fathers footsteps, "...who tyrannized over his own people, but was merciful and generous to the foreigners, especially the Christians", took the view that, "The guests and newcomers are yielding such a large profit, that they deservedly can stand on the sixth place on the honour roll of the king, since the unilingual country with one custom is weak and fallible." As a consequence, he ordered his son, Imre, to benevolently support and cherish the newcomers, "therefore they preferred to stay at his court, rather than living somewhere else" [44].

King Stephen "Often consoled the serfs of the temples, the monks, and priests with alms and donations. All of his available income was spent on pilgrims, widows and orphans. He often made donations through his envoys to the monasteries of provinces abroad" [45].

At the beginning of the 11th century, the Byzantine Emperor, Basilios II. attacked and subdued the Bulgarian kingdom. King Stephen forged an alliance with him for reasons pertaining to both internal and foreign affairs. His troops - as we know from the information of Fundatio Sancti Albani Namucensis - were fighting alongside the Byzantine troops, in the battles against the Bulgarians in 1004. After the conquest of Bulgaria in 1018, the borders of the Byzantine Empire reached the lines of the Danube and the Sava rivers and coincided with the southern borders of Hungary. This direct vicinity required that the good relationship between the two countries should not deteriorate with discrimination against the Eastern Christian Church. The Byzantine influence had to be counted in the state affairs also. It is enough to mention that the double cross of the Hungarian coat of arms is of Byzantine origin.

In the light of these historical facts, Stoicescu's theory about the adaptation of the Slavonic language by the Church of the Rumanians living in Transylvania before the Hungarians settled there, cannot be accepted. Stoicescu argues that "this important religious reform could not have been accomplished under the sceptre of Saint Stephen's Apostlic Crown."

The period is the 10th and 11th centuries, when the Slavic liturgy spread, penetrating also into Russia (46). As we have shown above, King Stephen and his predecessors did not just tolerate, but farsightedly supported the newcomers, thus also the representatives of the Greek-Christian Church and their cultic places. King Stephen was occupied with the conversion of the pagan Hungarians, and had no reasons to persecute his already Christian subjects.

There are also Rumanian authors who contradict Stoicescu in this matter. Petru Maior was of the opinion that Stephen the Saint did not fight or hinder the Rumanians' religion in Transylvania – on the contrary, they even had some privileges given by the first king of the Hungarians. In a footnote to Maior's text, Manole Neagoe remarks: "The two Churches were separated in 1059, it is therefore logical that the Rumanians were not oppressed due to their religious belief by Stephen I." (P. Maior: *Istoria pentru începutul romînilor în Dachia*; critical edition by Florea Fugariu, Bucarest, 1970, vol. I, p. 192) [47].

Stoicescu asserts, referring to P.P. Panaitescu, that Stephen the Saint wanted to spread Christianity because of national interests. This theory could not have been appropriate, even though he would have been reigning during the time when the civil nation's ideas occurred along with feudal and national motives. Saint Stephen's wisdom is a historical fact. He could have been wise; he could not, however, have gone ahead of his time.

Might Stoicescu not have known that there was no antagonism between different nations, nor intolerance of people because of their language at that time? After the Hungarians entered the Carpathian Basin, its ethnic picture changed: "The ethnic picture of the Carpathian basin became extraordinarily colorful, where the Finno-Ugric, Turk, Iranian, and Slavic peoples were living next to each other, on varying levels of the historical evolution" [48].

According to the law of Stephen the Saint, groups of ten villages were obliged to build a temple. If the conquering Hungarians had found temples or churches, King Stephen would not have been forced to order the "ten villages - one temple" law. The issuing of such order proves beyond all question that in Transylvania, even the pagan cultic places could have survived only in small numbers. If they had survived, Stephen would have made them – if only temporarily – Christian temples.

Moreover, if Stephen had been such a king as Stoicescu says, referring to P.P. Panaitescu, he would have used "Rumanian temples" by force for his recently converted people. However, there are no legends nor chronicles about such actions. We do not have any data either that the Hungarian state or clerical leadership, accepting the Western Church's liturgy, forced it on another, non-Hungarian people, for example on the Rumanians. In this case the resistance would have reached such a high level that it would not have passed unnoticed, without a trace in history.

The Hungarian relationship with Byzantium did not slacken until the end of the 11th century, when the Serb principality and Bulgaria, again independent, got wedged in between Hungary and Byzantium. On the other hand, Byzantium declined after the reign of the Komnenoses,[11] and in 1204, it fell to the Western conquerors. In 1261, the Palailogoses[12] restored the Greek Empire, but it could only be a shade of the Byzantine Empire. Regarding the friendly relations between Hungary and Byzantium up to the end of the 11th century, the Hungarians had a political interest in supporting the Transylvanian Greek-Catholic (Orthodox) Rumanians – or in any case, not oppressing them – if they had existed there. We do not have any data or references about this question, nor about such a population.

It is a very important historical fact that the Greek and Latin Churches were not divided until 1054. That is why we have stated above that the orthodox religion in Hungary was not exposed to persecution neither by the state politics nor by another Church. There was nothing to prevent the allegedly "native" Transylvanian Rumanians from building their own cultic places or having their own clerical organizations.

King Stephen got his crown from Sylvester II. (999-1003). As an independent, ordained Hungarian king, he rightly founded episcopacies, abbacies and the archbishopric of Esztergom. Unfortunately, the contemporary church documents did not survive. It can only be suspected, that the first Hungarian archbishopric's deed of foundation was dated in Ravenna in 1001. According to György Győrffy "The foundation-stone of the Hungarian Church organization was laid in April of 1001" [49]. From our point of view the foundation of the bishopric of Gyulafehérvár is particularly important. As György Győrffy says, it was founded in 1009. The Transylvanian Bishop got hold of the territories of Kraszna and Szatmár counties, in addition to the "Seven castles, namely Siebenbürgen" counties: Hunyad, Fehér, Küküllő, Torda, Kolozs, Doboka, and Dés. There is no mention, however, of any existing Greek-Christian Rumanian Church, episcopacy or bishop.

It is not by the chance that we left the discussion of Anonymus' *Gesta Hungarorum* to the end of this chapter. The *Gesta* talks about the people found by the Hungarians in Transylvania by the time of their settling down: they were, among others, Blacks and the "shepherds of the Romans". Historiography identified the Blacks as the ancestors of the Rumanians, and came to the conclusion that making the Rumanians appear on stage in Transylvania during Árpád's conquest of Hungary is a serious anachronism. The Rumanians did not settle in Hungary before the 13th century, thus the good monk, Anonymus retroprojected the ethnic situation of his own era to the times of the Árpáds.

According to the notes of Roger (Rogerius) Bacon (1214-1294), "...the Blacks came from ʹold Byzantiumʹ, which was located next to old Hungary and Bulgaria (i.e., Hungary and Bulgaria along the Volga). They live between Constantinople, Bulgaria and ʹnew Hungaryʹ". Hungarian historians showed that the Black people had lived close to the Hungarians' Baskirian Fatherland before they got into Central and Southern Europe. While they attached themselves to the Bulgarians, they still used their own name in the 13th century. It may therefore be that Anonymus did not commit an anachronism. He probably did not talk about Rumanians, but about a people of Turk or Bulgarian origin, in ancient contact with the Hungarians; most probably on the basis of the ancient Gesta [50].

According to Köpeczi,[13] Anonymus got acquainted with the Blacks through Nestor's *Russian Chronicle* from the 12th century. As Nestor says; "The conquering Hungarians found Volohs (Volohi) and Slavs in the Carpathian Basin. They expelled the Volohs and subjugated the Slavs," ..."and from that time on, the land was called Hungarian (*magyar; ugorszka*)". Nestor meant French by the Volohs, in reality the Trans-Danubian Franks, in a wider sense every people speaking a Romance language, or those who belonged to the Holy Roman Empire.

The French crusaders met the Rumanians in the Balkans and pronounced their Greek and Slavic name as *Black,* even though it was spelled *Blach* and pronounced *Vlach* by the native people. The French form was used by the Hungarian chancellery, and declined as Latin words (*blacus, blacci, blacorum*). In the Hungarian documents written up to 1247, the French form: *blak* appears. The Hungarian colloquial form: "*oláh*", came into use after that year. It probably derived from the Greek and Slavic form "*vlach*", through an intermediate "*volach*".

Anonymus placed the Rumanians in Transylvania on the basis of Nestor. His work proves therefore that in his era Rumanians did not live in northern Transylvania.

Anonymus's work does not give any data to find out what kind of people the Hungarians could have found in Transylvania. Modern archeology proves the presence of Slavs. Rumanian material remains from the 10th century, distinctly separable from that of the Slavs, were not found [51].

IV

Transylvania from the

Árpád's Conquest of Hungary

until the Mongol Invasion of the Country

The Church played a very important role in the life of Transylvania before the devastation of the Mongol invasion in 1241-42. We already mentioned that Saint Stephen founded an episcopacy in Gyulafehérvár. It is a very important circumstance, that there were some congregations on the Transylvanian Diocese's Territory, which did not belong to the Bishop's clerical sphere of influence and authority. These congregations belonged to the abbacy of Kolozsmonostor, the abbacy of Kerc, founded by King Béla III. (1172-1196) and to the provostship of Szeben. For a certain period the churches of Barcaság belonged to the Moldavian Catholic bishopric, located in the city of Milcov. These were not Greek-Catholic churches.

Maria Holban deals in detail with the argument [52] which took shape between the Transylvanian Bishop and the Provost of Szeben, who was supposed to fulfill the provostship's position, which recently had become unoccupied. At this time, the Teutonic Knights migrated to South Transylvania and occupied the territories of Barcaság in Brassó County under the leadership of Salza Herman.

The Transylvanian Bishop considered the provostship's foundation in Szeben as a transgression against his sphere of authority. His power would have been further damaged by the wish of the King, who was willing to make the provostship of Szeben an episcopacy and subordinate it to the authority of Kalocsa's Archbishopric. The provostship of Szeben would have gotten hold of all the Saxon dwellers, including those who had belonged to the Transylvanian episcopacy before.

The Transylvanian Bishop immediately sent an envoy to the Pope to protest against the plan. Finally, the Pope refused the foundation of the new episcopacy. The Transylvanian Bishop's sphere of authority was in every way exposed to danger by the immigration of the knights. At this time such an argument with the Rumanians did not take place. Also this fact suggests – among other things – that Vlachs did not live at that time in Transylvania.

Before discussing the question of the settlement of Vlachs in Transylvania, we have to mention briefly the reports about this population in the Balkans. There, written sources record Vlachs (the ancestors of present day Rumanians) since 976 A.D. They are described as nomad or transhumant shepherds, and as conscripted soldiers in the Byzantine Army. They were the ones who led the Cumanians, breaking into Byzantine territories through the passes of the Balkan Mountains in 1094.

At the end of the 12th century, several Serb documents (deeds of gift) mention the shepherd Rumanians, who lived in the mountainous district between the Drina and Morava rivers (see, for example, Du Nay, 1996, pp. 26-39).

It is not possible to state the exact period of time when the first Vlachs shepherds came to Transylvania. Small numbers might have come in the 11th century, but the first document which mentions this people there refers to 1208. The absence of cultic places, as well as the testimony of the geographical names and the place-names indicates that before the end of the 13th century, Transylvania had no significant Rumanian population.

According to a document dated 1223, the land of the Rumanians living along the Olt was donated to the Abbacy of Kerc in 1208 by Andrew II. In the donated territories, there are no Rumanian geographical or place-names, and besides *Olt* and *Kerc* (of unknown origin), three names appear in the document: Egerpatak, Nagybükk and Árpás (*palus Eguerpatak, fagus Nogebik, rivulus Arpas*) – all Hungarian, which were later borrowed by the Rumanians. Thus, this area was not "owned by the Vlachs from ancient times", but was originally inhabited by Hungarians.

A contemporary document named *Andreanum* (1224), which determined the privileges of the Saxons, gave them the right to use the forests of the Rumanians and Petchenegs. Here the king has taken the Rumanian and Petcheneg ownership into consideration.

In 1231 Salza Hermann, who had been just ousted from Barcaság, stayed in Rome, where he mentioned that Rumanians had their own land, as well as the Székelys, and their own customs authorities, which were independent from that of the Barcaság.

In his writings about his victory over the Hungarian King, Czech King Ottokar II. mentioned the Hungarian King's "inhuman men": Hungarians, Cumanians, Slavs, Székelys, Vlachs (Rumanians), and Petchenegs.

On the basis of contemporary and later documents, we can presume the existence of a "Blakland", located in the highlands behind present day Fogaras and Szászváros. This Rumanian-defended frontier region was organized into an administrative unit presumably around 1200.

The protection of the Southern Border Region was devolved primarily on the fortress of Hátszeg and its district. We are informed about the area's Rumanian population since the so called "frieze lands" were given to a noble by King Stephen the Minor in 1263. The donation did not include the lands of the *kenez*-es Drăgan and Kretoch.[14] The king thus recognized the possessory rights of the presumably Rumanian *kenez*-es over some of the territories in question.

The tradition of building temples and monasteries practized by kings and aristocrats was learned by the clans forming smaller branches and families in the 11th-12th centuries [53]. In Transylvania, the Kácsics clan built the monastery of Harina after the Mongol devastation of Hungary, in the middle of the 13th century. The monastery with three aisles and two steeples is related to the family temples of the Transdanubian area (twin-windowed towers).

The building of sacred places for the clans begun. These cloisters and churches gave shelter to monks swarming out of the larger monasteries. At the beginning, the number of monks could have been around twelve, later it was reduced to three or four. We have no information about such temples or monasteries of Rumanian clans in Transylvania.

In the 12th and 13th centuries, the permanent private property was born in the wake of the noble clans forging ahead. It developed the particular type of family or clan owned churches that represented their strength. There is no report about such a church built by a Rumanian landowner.

In the first decades of the 13th century, right before the Mongol invasion, Transylvania was well developed politically, socially, and clerically. Rumanians, however, were not present in this development since we do not have any relics or data referring to their church organizations or congregations.

In the year 1087, the pagan Cumanian people settled down in Wallachia, south of Transylvania. The new neighbors broke into Hungary, two times through the Eastern, and once through the Southern Carpathians. They were defeated and driven out of Hungary on every occasion by *Szent László* (King Saint Ladislas, 1077-1095). He met the Cumanians at Kerlés (Cserhalom) in 1071, at Bökény (Szabolcs county) in 1081 and in Pogányró on the riverbanks of the Temes in 1091. After a century of peace, the Cumanians attacked the country again. They ravaged, robbed, and burned the Barcaság.

The Pope, as well as all other Popes, had the important

task of converting the pagan people, like the Cumanians, to Christianity. Members of the first Dominican Cumanian Mission were killed by the Cumanians. The second mission, however, proved to be successful. They convinced Bors Membrok, leader of the Cumanians to adopt the Christian religion. Membrok sent his own son to Esztergom with the Dominicans. He asked the Hungarian Primate to come to Cumania and convert the population to Christianity. He also asked for a consecrated Bishop for his people. The Hungarian Primate reported the Cumanian request to the Pope and asked for permission to carry it out. The Pope named the Primate to his legate and invested him with full power to complete the necessary tasks. The Primate, accompanied by the Bishops of Veszprém, Pécs, and Transylvania as well as Prince Béla with a small group of people, departed to the lands of the Cumanians. He baptized the Cumanian people in the city of Milkov, between Wallachia and Moldavia. He consecrated Teodorik as the first Bishop of the Cumanians, and the Bishop of Milkov in 1227. We have three documents to prove this in the Secret Archives of the Vatican. The first letter went to the leader of the Hungarian Dominicans, the second document to the Primate of Esztergom, the third to Prince Béla, son of Andrew II., who was later crowned Béla IV. (1235-1270) [54].

Official documents prove also that the Cumanian Bishop became a member of the Hungarian Episcopal staff and that he attended several episcopal assemblies. (Finally the episcopacy of Milkov was annexed nominally to the diocese of Esztergom by Tamás Bakócz [1442-1521], Archishop of Esztergom.) If an Orthodox Rumanian episcopacy had been functioning in Transylvania, the contemporary documents would have mentioned it, even though the Rumanian Bishop would not have been a member of the episcopal staff. But if such documentary did not commemorate it, the crown office should have mentioned Rumanian episcopacies or other smaller clerical organizations. If they had existed, the Hungarian kings would have tried *them* to convert to Catholicism and would have turned their attention to

Wallachia, Moldavia, and the Balkans, only after they had suceeded in Hungary.

Forty thousand Cumanian families asked for and received permission to immigrate to Hungary in 1238. They settled down between the Danube and the Tisza. They and the people of the Teutonic Knights who remained there survived the devastations caused by the Mongols in 1241. Their religious life was, however, endangered by the quickly spreading of the Bogumil heterodoxy.[15] As a countermeasure, the Pope fulfilled the Hungarian King's wish and founded the second Catholic episcopacy at Szörénytornya in 1246. The life of the episcopacy can be traced until 1416. Some of their bishops are known by name. When a new episcopacy was founded, groups of Hungarians settled down on the territories of former Cumania. The territories left empty after those forty thousand resettled Cumanians were colonized by the Megleno- and Arumanians, coming from the Balkans. A small number of them reached Transylvania [55]. They, however, did not live in the territory of Cumania with the Cumanians because we do not have any traces of their clerical organizations.

V

Transylvania during the Mongol Invasion

According to János Túróczi,[16] in 1241 the Tatars (Tartars or Mongols) of Genhis Khan marched into Hungary with four armies, 500,000 armed men [56]. The main body of their army marched through the Verecke Pass to the Tisza Valley. The other three armies attacked from Transylvania.

While the Tatars retreated from the Great Plain and the Maros Valley, they devastated Transylvania to a very large degree. They destroyed everything that had got in their way. The Partium and Transylvania suffered the biggest losses and most casualties.

In his memorandum, *Carmen Miserabile* (Miserable Song) Rogerius, of Italian origin, the Dean of Várad, wrote that when he had escaped from Tatar captivity, and had been travelling through Transylvania, he was hardly able to find a man there; he did not see anything but "heaps of ruins" in Nagyenyed, Torda and Gyulafehérvár. "On the Eve of the Tatar invasion the Hungarian armies were fighting on the Balkans serving the interest of the Hungarian aristocracy and the Papacy. The Papacy, however, did not recruit Western forces against the Tatars in 1240-1242... The struggle against the Mongols was strongly hindered, since the German feudal nobles, serving their own interests in Northern and Eastern Europe, in agreement with the Papal State, led their troops against the divided Russians" [57].

Without any allies and also separated from each other,

Hungary and Poland were attacked by the Mongols, who, after breaking the Russian resistance, turned with full force against the two countries.

King Béla IV. (1235-1270) tried to organize the defense of the country, but failed. The King's desperate efforts were seen with malicious joy by the nobles who felt offended due to the strengthening of the King's power. They put their soldiers at the king's disposal with considerable delay and reluctance. The murder of Kötöny, Cumanian leader, turned the Cumanians away from Béla IV., even though the responsibility did not rest with the King. The King could not mobilize an army of satisfactory numbers, until the very last moment, when the Mongols had already broken into the country, and the danger had become overwhelming.

The army of King Béla IV. could not resist the Mongols, whose horsemen swarmed all over the Tisza area. The Tatars and the Hungarian cavalry fought on the battlefield of Muhi, near the Sajó stream in April 11th, 1241. The battle ended with the total destruction of the Hungarian Army. The King escaped with extreme difficulties. His death would have meant the final destruction of Hungary.

After the battle of Muhi the country was in complete ruins. The number of slaughtered people could be counted in ten-thousands. Most of those who survived were hiding in the deep forests and marshes and were waiting for the day of salvation.

Fortunately, the Mongol Chief Khan, Ogotaj died unexpectedly. Since Batu Khan, the Commander in Chief of the Mongol army, now in Hungary, wanted to be present and take part in the power struggle, following the death of the chief khan, hastily withdrew from the country and returned to Mongolia.

At the end of May 1242, there were no Mongols left in Hungary. The work of reconstruction could start.

King Béla's first task was the reorganization of the country's defenses. He realized that the Mongols had not been able to capture the Hungarian fortresses. He organized a castle system on the border zone, and urged his nobles to build more fortified castles. He founded a new capital at Buda with a splendid royal palace and churches on the Castle Hill (part of modern Budapest).

After the Mongol withdrawal, King Béla immediately started to re-build the country, building new fortified castles of stone also (in Transylvania: Dés, Kolozsvár).

The King sent Vajda (Voivod) Lőrinc to Transylvania "...to gather his people, and arrange everything, by using his authority, that he finds useful to his country". Lőrinc tried his very best to fulfill his duty. He transfered ploughmen and soldiers to the depopulated areas from the territories that suffered less. He also encouraged people from abroad to settle in the devastated territory.

In his letter to the King, the Transylvanian Bishop Gallus, wrote that in the year of 1246 it was hard to find people in Gyulafehérvár and the city's surrounding areas. He asked the King to take the people, who lived or were willing to live on the episcopal properties out of the authority of the voivods and county sheriffs. He, the Bishop of Transylvania, would have been in this case their only master. The King fulfilled his wish.

The Mongol invasion decimated the population, therefore foreigners had to be hired to do the reconstruction. What kind of nationality did they have? Where did they come from? The new dwellers, who were brought to the episcopal and unoccupied royal properties, migrated with their flocks from the Balkans. They were Vlachs, ancestors of today's Rumanians [58]. Most of them ran away from the political discords and battles going on in the Balkan Peninsula. They were led by Bulgarian and Serb *kenez*-es.

During the times of Charles the Anjou (Charles I.) (1307-1342), especially in 1335, they were also invited to Transylvania. In 1370 some of their nobles moved, because of political unrest, from Bulgaria, as well as from the western areas of Wallachia, to Transylvania [59].

The Szamos and Maros valleys were Transylvania's main military routes during the Mongol invasions. These valleys were inhabited by Hungarians. Every enemy, marching through the area, ravaged mainly this people. The Saxons found shelter in their forts and fortified towns, while many Székelys were hiding in the forests. The farming people of the undefended villages always became easy prey of the enemy. That is why they could not and did not grow sufficiently in number. That is why they later were forced to welcome foreign settlers.

King Béla, "the second state founder" settled the Johannite (Maltan) Order of Knights between the Lower Danube and the Olt, which teritory also had been devastated by the Mongols. Their presence, from the year 1247, meant defense for the territory.

The Christian churches, devastated earlier by pagan insurgents, were replaced by new ones. Saint Stephen's orders were reissued by Saint Ladislas I. He ordered that the burned out or devastated churches had to be rebuilt by the congregations. "The churches which were ruined because of their old age must be reconstructed by the bishop." These churches were rebuilt by the time of the Mongol attack (1241). It was hard to find a village without a temple. The churches, however, were mostly robbed, burned and destroyed by the Tatars. The cathedrals of Gyulafehérvár and Nagyvárad had to be rebuilt. The village churches also had to be rebuilt from their ruins. Again, we have no information about the reconstruction of any Greek-Catholic (Orthodox) church in this period in Transylvania. There weren't any.

After the Mongol attacks fortified stone and brick churches were built that could have been used for defensive purposes. Their construction was regulated – under the king's inspiration – by the propriety relations. "Every proprietary recognized the mental and material advantages of the patronage's right." The number of parishes in the 13th century exceeded that of the 11th century. We do not know about Rumanian parishes and church building proprietaries. Thus, in the Hungary of the 13th and 14th centuries, particularly in Transylvania, Hungarian churches made earlier of wood and mud were reconstructed because they were completely destroyed by the Tatars. The reason was not that assumed by Radu Popa, Rumanian historian [60]. The brick and stone churches mentioned by him are newer. They are churches re-built after the Tatar devastations. If there were some Rumanian churches made out of bricks or stones after the Tatar attack in Transylvania, it would mean that they were built in that period, – they could not have been built before the Tatar invasion.

VI

Transylvania between the Mongol Invasion

and the

Beginning of the Turkish Menace

Transylvania recovered substantially during the two decades following the Mongol invasion. Its internal order was peaceful. Its situation changed after 1260, when Béla IV. gave it to his son, István. Transylvania suffered on account of the almost endless discord between father and son. Béla IV. died in 1270, and his son ascended the throne as Stephen V.

Stephen ruled only two years, 1270 - 1272. In spite of his short ruling period, he did not forget about Transylvania. He rewarded the Székelys of Kézd for their bravery against the Tatars. They were settled on a depopulated area of Torda County, the surroundings of Torockó.

After his death, he was succeeded to the throne by his son, who was called *Kun László* (Ladislas IV, "the Cumanian"; 1272-1290). Under his reigning period, life in Transylvania was characterized by disorder and anarchy. The royal rule and laws were replaced by the law of the club and despotism.

The cathedral of Gyulafehérvár was attacked and burned down by the Saxons in February 21, 1277. Kun László beat the invading Cumanians at Hódmezővásárhely in 1282. The defeated Cumanians fled to the Nogaj Tatars. While beating a hasty retreat, they devastated Transylvania.

They returned in 1285. The Cumanians got as far as Pest.

They were beaten by the Royal Army again. As a repeat performance, escaping from the king's troops they withdrew with large booty across Transylvania. On their way out they found time to destroy Beszterce and Kolozsvár. At the fortress of Torockó they were caught and badly beaten by the Székelys. The Székelys also destroyed another group, before they could have left Transylvania.

The Cumanian raids did not end despite their defeat by the Székelys. The Pope proclaimed a Crusade against the Cumanians. The decisive battles of the war between the Crusaders and the Cumanians were fought in Transylvania. The anarchy and chaos did not end until the death of Ladislas IV. in 1290.

Ladislas IV's successor, Andrew III. (1290-1301) travelled across Transylvania in 1291. He convoked the Parliament along with the Transylvanian estates at Gyulafehérvár. In a document he reinforced the nobles, the clergy, and the Saxons in their rights.

Andrew published another notable document, in which he mentions the Vlachs along with the nobles, Székelys and Saxons. Several Rumanian historians came to the false conclusion that the Vlachs possessed equal rights with the Hungarians, Székelys and Saxons and were considered an emancipated nation during the House of Árpád's reign, and they participated in the political and constitutional life of Transylvania as well.

The historical facts, however, show that the participating Rumanians in the assemblies were witnesses rather than legislators. They were supposed to testify to whether it was the truth or not, that the properties of Fogaras and Szombathely really belonged to master Ugrin. The assembly in question was not legislative but judicial. In the next year Vlachs were not invited to the Parliament where Transylvanian nobles, Székelys, Saxons, and indeed the Cumanians participated.

The document of Andrew III. dated 1293, casts light upon why the Rumanians were not invited to the Hungarian nor to the Transylvanian Parliaments. "Being forced by the regime's interest, with the agreement of the magnates, we order that all the Vlachs, residing on anybody's property, should be driven back to our royal property named Székes. Exempted are those sixty households, who were authorized to settle down by Ladislas IV, in Fülesd and Énőd, on the properties of the chapter of Gyulafehérvár."

This document shows – without the slightest doubt – that only the king and persons authorized by the king could give the immigrating Rumanians permission to settle down. At this time only the churches and bishops were allowed to colonize. The landowners did not have the right to harbor Rumanian immigrants yet.

On the basis of the above mentioned documents, it may be stated that the Rumanians were very small in number under the House of Árpád's reign. Also because of this fact, they could not be equal to the other three nations of Transylvania, the Hungarians, the Székelys and the Saxons. As we have already mentioned in Chapter 4., Megleno-rumanians and Arumanians came from the Balkans and occupied the area from which those 40,000 Cumanian families were settled in Hungary; they then spread over the entire Cumania.

The recently settled people were Greek-Catholic (Orthodox) with Slavonic liturgy. King Charles Robert founded the voivodship of Ungro-Vlachia in 1324, based on the Cumanians, Germans and resettled Hungarians in addition to the immigrated Vlachs. The name of Ungro-Vlachia changed later to Muntenia, in Hungarian: Havaselve (Havasalföld). The first voivod of the voivodship was Basarab, who was already in 1324 "Wallachia's only great voivod and ruler".

Louis the Great (1342-1382) organized the feudal voivodship by the name of Kara Bogdania, the later Moldavia. It was located on the northern territories of Cumania, between the eastern slopes of the Carpathian mountains and the right bank of the Prut River. By the request of Louis the Great, the Pope founded the third Catholic episcopacy at Curtea de Argeş, in Wallachia, in 1382.

According to the order of January 29, 1322 by King Charles Robert, the abbacy of Kerc 29 was placed under the protection of the king due to the "attacks of the evil".

Maria Holban dealt in detail with the argument, which had taken shape between the Transylvani Bishop and the provost of Szeben. The provost was supposed to fill the provostship's recently vacated position. On pages 262 - 263, Holban explained in detail that the abbacy of Kerc had not been endangered by the peasants nor by the actions of the Rumanian Greek-Catholics. The Transylvanian Archbishop sent an encyclical letter on November 14, 1343, in which he encouraged the people to hand back the abbacy's stolen properties and other goods, and advised them not to interfere in this abbacy's affairs (situated on the farthest border of the Hungarian kingdom). Not even from this letter one may conclude that the Rumanians rioted against the abbacy.

Maria Holban also demonstrated that the abbacy of Kolozsmonostor had been attacked by Rumanian and Hungarian peasants from the neighboring estate, not by those who had been living on the abbacy's property. Why were only the Hungarian Catholic abbacies the targets of riots and peasant revolts? Why were only the abbacies of Kerc and Kolozsmonostor attacked? Why didn't the peasants turn against Rumanian churches, monasteries or abbacies?

Another very important question can be asked. Why did Maria Holban write about the Rumanian-Hungarian, Transylvanian-Rumanian-Hungarian connections of the 13th-14th centuries? Why did she not write about connections, for example, in the 10th-11th or the 11th-12th centuries? This would be more relevant in the efforts to prove the Dacian-Roman Continuity Theory.

On the basis of the 1332 and 1337 Papal Tithe Collector's list, in his work mentioned above, Péter Pál Domokos (p.60) showed the religious composition of the people living in Transylvania on the territory of the Transylvanian Bishopric. By that time, the reign of the Árpád's had just ended with the rise of the Anjou rule. According to these data, 310,000 Hungarian Székelys, 21,000 Saxons and 18,000 Rumanians lived in Transylvania [61]. The low number of Vlachs suggests that they could not have been present among the conquered or surrendered people in the time of Árpád's conquest of Hungary, and could scarcely have any cultic places or church organizations. Even if they had been present, their number would have been insignificant. With the knowledge of these data we have to dispute the statement of the Rumanian historian Radu Popa. He said that during the 11th and 12th centuries "...headquarters, fortified courts, chapels and small monasteries, serving as spiritual centres [62] had been built by Roman *Kenez* families" in Máramaros, Fogaras, Bihar, Bánság and Hátszeg (Hunyad county). The statement's indefensibility was also felt by the author, who added: "...these wooden buildings were rebuilt as stone and brick buildings during the 13th-14th centuries."

As regards Máramaros, any such building is excluded by the fact that the Rumanians did not immigrate there until the last quarter of the 13th century. The old Russian chronicles tell us that Ladislas IV. the "Cumanian", being afraid of another Mongol invasion, asked for help from Rome and Constantinople in 1284-85. After evaluating his request, a large army was sent to him by Constantinople from the Ibar region, (in present day Serbia). These Vlachs, fighting together with the Hungarians, defeated the Mongols in the upper Tisza valley. Since they did not want to return to their homeland, the king settled them in Máramaros.

We know from a document dated 1335, that Mikola's son, voivod Bogdan settled with his Rumanians in Máramaros as frontier guards against the Mongols. They emigrated from here to Moldavia in 1348; moving slowly towards the south, they met the Rumanians living in Wallachia.

Beginning with the early 15th century, they occupied the territories which later (after 1859) were called Rumania (the United Principalities) and became a politically distinct nation. That is the reason why the Rumanian cultic places appeared 2-3 centuries later than the Hungarians'. Radu Popa's statements would probably be true, if he had referred to the Ibar Region in Serbia. It may be enough to refer to

Romulus Dianu's work, in which he said that the monastery in Peri (Körtvélyes) had been built in 1391, at the end of the 14th century, and was a donation of voivod Dragoş [63].

In the same writing of Romulus Dianu, the author mentions that the Transylvanian Greek-Catholics (Orthodox) were considered schismatics – heretics – by the "Papal Princes". "The Bishops of Buda forbade the Rumanians the building of churches in the towns. This sentence of 1279 had a binding force of law until 1848" [64]. It is our duty to stop here, and enlighten Dianu's superficial reasoning and baseless assertions.

It can be determined that Buda did not have any bishops, not even one. Philip of Fermon, Papal legate convoked a council in the Castle of Buda in September, 1279. Dianu might have been referring to this event. The council's primary goal was the correction of the life and morals of the Polish-Hungarian churchmen and laymen, "...in order to protect the Catholic faith and clerical freedom" [65].

Dianu sarcastically condemned the "Papal Princes" and the "Bishops of Buda". The plain truth is that Philip was Bishop of Fermont, therefore he did not live in Hungary, nor was he a Hungarian. He was neither "Papal Prince" nor "Bishop of Buda". The council's verdict "...dealt mainly with the third estate, its tasks and the observance of the church services." Paragraph No. 126. deals really with the schismatical priests and the authorization of the houses of prayer and chapel buildings they wanted to erect, but not in the form as presented by Dianu. He wrote that "the Bishop of Buda had forbidden the Rumanians to build churches in the cities." Such a resolution was not passed by the council. The resolution did not say a word about the Rumanians. It simply ordered that a schismatical priest should not be allowed to "deliver divine service" in the Catholic Church, and that the schismatics could only build their temples with the authorization of the diocesan bishop. There is no word of Rumanians, cities or prohibition of church buildings. The resolution disposed of the building of houses of prayer and of chapels, not churches. According to Dianu, the resolution had binding force of law until 1848. If this had been true, "schismatical" Rumanian churches could not have been built – for example – in Kolozsvár in 1797, in Marosvásárhely in 1811-1814, etc.

VII

Transylvania During the Times

of the Turkish Expansion

During the reign of *Nagy Lajos* (Louis the Great, 1342-1382), a menacing power appeared on the Balkans, the Ottoman Turks. Turks endangered Hungary as well as the whole Central Europe. Realizing the danger, the king paid special attention to Transylvania. He stayed there from April to August 1366. He strengthened the Charters of the seven Saxon Seats. He visited every important place in the Székely territory.

Under the reign of Louis the Great, the number of Vlachs increased considerably. He permitted the Vlachs to settle not only on the royal, episcopal and prebendal properties, and ruled that also the cities and the landowners should have the right to settle down immigrating Vlachs.

In July of 1366, the Parliament gathered in Torda.[17] According to the royal document, which summarized the orders of the Parliament, the public security was in constant jeopardy. The public law and order were extraordinarily bothered by the Vlachs, living in chaotic circumstances. He allowed free hands to kill off the "evil-doers".

The king visited Transylvania in 1377 for the last time. He convinced the Saxons in Brassó to reconstruct Törcsvár, [18] and to always take care of the fort's defenses. In return, he transferred the authority over the villages of the Barcaság from the Székely sheriff to Brassó. He donated Erdőfelek (Feleacu) with its Vlach dwellers to the city of Kolozsvár. He took all these actions knowing that Transylvania was the south-eastern stronghold of the Hungarian Empire, the supporting pillar of the Hungarian power politics towards the Balkans. After the death of Louis the Great, his oldest daughter, the eleven-year-old Maria inherited the Hungarian throne, but the king's widow, Elizabeth ruled. She was killed by some aristocrats, who were dissatisfied with her rule.

Maria, fiancee of the Prince of Luxembourg, was imprisoned. Zsigmond led his armies to free his fiancee. In 1387, he was crowned the Hungarian king by the nobles, faithful to Maria (1387-1437).

These events prompted the Wallachian voivod Mircea and the Moldavian voivod Peter to break away from the Hungarian kingdom and surrender to the Polish king (1380). One of Zsigmond's tasks was to get the voivods back in line. Mircea surrendered on his own, while Ştefan, who followed Peter as the Moldavian voivod, was forced back.

The period of Zsigmond's reign was critical in the history of Transylvania. During the first decade of his reign, the Turks conquered the Balkans. A little later, the Turks started to threaten, and then annexed the Vlach voivodhsips.

After the Battle of Rigómező (Kosovo), (1389) the Bulgarian, Serb and Bosnian rulers, still cooperating with the Hungarians, had to realize that their power and country could be saved only if they maintained good relations with the Turks. The neighboring Rumanian voivodships also had to engage in the way of equilibrium politics. The Turks first annexed Wallachia, and somewhat later Moldavia. This circumstance led to further deterioration in the relation between the Rumanian voivodeships and Hungary.

In 1396, in the battle of Nikápoly, Zsigmond's army of 90.000 men was defeated by Sultan Bajazid's army. After this battle, the Rumanian voivods showed more willingness to maintain better relations with the Turks than the Hungarian king – because of religious reasons. The Turks required only political submission, taxes, loot and in case of war, troops to support. They did not attack the religion of the voivodship's people. They did not want to convert them to Mohammedanism. The proviso of the Hungarian king's assistance and aid was all the time the conversion to the Roman-Catholic Church. The Hungarian Anjou kings' diplomacy always sharply opposed the Greek Orthodox religion. Louis the Great's every effort tended towards the conversion of the Greek-Orthodox Vlachs, in a peaceful way if possible, to recognize the Papal authority and unite them with the Roman-Catholic Church.

The Hungarian kings committed themselves to the spread of Roman-Catholicism so deeply, that Catholicism was considered a "Hungarian religion" by the people of Eastern-Europe and the Balkans, at least after King Imre's reign (1196-1204) [66].

In order to gain their goodwill, the Vlach voivods turned the Turks' attention to Transylvania. The first Turkish army broke into Transylvania in 1420, under Dan, Wallachian voivod's inspiration. The Székelys and the Saxons resisted, but were defeated by the Turk's numerical superiority. The Turks destroyed Brassó and ravaged the Barcaság and Háromszék. (The Barcaság was inhabited by Saxons, Háromszék by Székelys.)

The Hungarians started to take precautions against the Turks in the period that came after the Battle of Nikápoly. They have fortified the southern borders. At the news of the Turkish approach the forts' significance, primarily the ones capable of harboring large groups of people, grew among the defending Székelys and Saxons. Where there were few forts, a whole range of Székely and Saxon church fortresses formed a defense line [67]. There are no reports about Vlach churches having been included among these.

The fortified castles and churches saved the material possessions of the village people in addition to the protection of their lives. Within the walls, the defending families had their own chambers where they could put their valuable goods and food in a safe place.

Although the presence of Vlachs was a fact at the

beginning of the 13th century in the Southern-Carpathian area, there are no data regarding fortification of Vlach churches or castles. It all points to the fact that the small number of Vlachs, who had just recently became farm hands, were used only as soldiers for defending the castles of the landowners.

The appearance of the Turkish Army on the southern borders of Hungary brought about different kinds of fortresses (royal, noble, and peasant). The fortified churches and castles played an important role in the country's defense. Thick, high, stone walls, bastions and towers were built around the churches, turning them into real fortresses. The building of Transylvanian forts, and the fortification of the stone churches meant defense for the Vlach voivods, too. They were given a chance to increase their strength. Among the owners of castles in Transylvania, we can also find several Wallachian and Moldavian voivods. As vassals of the Hungarian kings and the Transylvanian voivods, several of them were given castles in Transylvania, as will be shown in the next chapter.

VIII

Transylvanian Fiefs of Vlach (Rumanian) Voivods; Rumanian Cultic Places

In the 13th-16th centuries, the voivods of neighboring Wallachia (Havaselve) and Moldavia were vassals of the Hungarian king, sometimes also of the Transylvanian *vajda,* with shorter or longer interruptions. (Transylvania, before it developed into a Principality, was governed by Hungarian royal clerks, *vajda*-s [voivods]). In the Feudal System the lord gave an estate to his vassal who enjoyed the benefits of it as long as he fulfilled the obligations of the relationship. The feudal lord was counting on the vassal's services in peace, as well as in wartime. The vassal was obliged to give military service in addition to the mandatory hospitality and taxes, paid mainly in agricultural products and animals.

We have to survey the contemporary history of Wallachia and Moldavia to get more information about the allegiance between the Vlach voivods and the Hungarian kings.

The Mongol invasion in 1241 basically changed the political conditions in south eastern Europe. The Tatars entrenched themselves in the western and north-western coastal districts of the Black Sea, in the former principality of Kiev, in Moldavia, and in the eastern territories of the second Bulgarian Empire. They swept away the Cumanians, and destroyed most of Hungary. After they settled down in the territories mentioned, they kept raiding their neighbors, Hungarians and Vlachs alike [68].

Béla IV. tried to keep the Mongols far from the borders of

Hungary. In Transylvania, he reorganized the Székely borderguard units. He built strong fortresses, and made efforts to strengthen the southern borders. In Szörény, the power of the *bán* (warden of the southern approaches of Hungary) proved to be weak in keeping the Tatars away. That is why the king donated the Banate of Szörény,[20] with its neighboring territories, to the Johannite Order of Knights, and considered the whole of Wallachia to be his fief. The papacy agreed with the Hungarian king's southern expansion. With the Hungarian expansion, the Pope cherished the hope of further Roman-Catholic gains.

The Turk menace, however, approached. The Turks secured a firm foothold on the Balkan Peninsula, and also endangered the security of Wallachia. The voivods of Wallachia built up family ties and friendly relationships with the Bulgarian and Serb rulers. The Turk expansion could have been stopped only by the South Eastern European people's collaboration. The Papacy and the Hungarian foreign policy – influenced by religious considerations – supporting it, were obstacles of such unity.

Louis the Great's Romanizing foreign policy on the Balkans, with the unquestionable intention towards the political influence behind it, brought only sham results. With his campaigns he only weakened the people of the Balkans and made it easier for the Turks to expand towards the yet free Balkan states, as well as towards Hungary.

Greek-Orthodoxism successfully resisted the Hungarian Romanization. In 1359 the first Greek-Orthodox archbishopry was founded in Wallachia. The Greek Kritopulos Hiakintos was named the head of this, and he called himself the archbishop of Ungro-Vlachia, i.e. of Wallachia. The foundation of the first Wallachian archbishopric was soon followed by the establishment of the Greek-Orthodox episcopacy of Szörény. Orthodox monastery buildings were constructed. Abbay Nicodim, who immigrated from Serbia to Wallachia, founded the monastery of Vodiţa and later the famous monastery of Tismana.

In the 13th century, the northern part of the other Vlach

province, Moldavia developed as part of the principality of Kiev. Later it belonged to the sphere of the principality of Galicia. The Mongols subjugated most of the Russians. Moldavia was also under Mongol dominance, from where the Tatars often broke into and robbed throughout the Transylvanian cities.

In 1345, Louis the Great, whose reign made possible the country's military strengthening, cleaned Moldavia of the Mongols. When the Tatars were ousted, the King organized a military border zone for the defense of Transylvania. The center of the new frontier zone was Baia. Dragoş, the voivod of Máramaros, who participated in the fighting, was placed at the head of it. He was the first voivod of Moldavia under the federal authority of the Hungarian King. Moldavia lived under such authority until 1359, when voivod Bogdan came into power. Bogdan ousted voivod Balk, vassal of the Hungarian King and founded the first independent Vlach principality.

The territory of Moldavia became in this period well defined. The international trade played a very important role in its strengthening. The Hungarian King as well as the Polish King was interested in the security of such trade. The tax income and material interest, related to such commerce, made understandable the ambitions of the Hungarian and Polish kings toward the feudal reign of Moldavia.

Since Poland could enforce its influence because of its geographical location, those in power in Moldavia soon recognized the suzerainity rights of the Polish king. The rulers of Moldavia protected themselves with the well tested methods of Wallachia against the Romanizing ambitions of the Polish kings. They, like the Wallachian rulers, organized the Greek-Orthodox Church. The first monastery was built with the financial assistance of the ruler Peter Muşat (1375-1391) in Neamţ. The construction was carried out by the monks of the Serbian Archbishop, Nicodim, who had already established the basis of the cloistered life in Wallachia. [69]

In both voivodships, the Vlach leadership helped with the

organization of the Greek-Orthodox Church against the spread of Catholicism, and the political influence of the Hungarian and Polish kings, for the defense of their country's independence. They spared neither their monetary nor political assistance. In exchange and recognition, the Church rendered strong assistance against the discordant feudal aspirations and popular movements.

The kenezships and voivodships were united by Basarab, who was already in 1324 "the only voivod and ruler of all Wallachia". He also occupied the Banate of Szörény. He came into conflict with King Robert Charles, who had been the suzerain of his and had supported his wars against the Mongols. The king started a military campaign against Basarab, but was badly beaten in 1330, near the village of Posada. Even though the castle of Szörény remained in Hungarian hands, Basarab's victory ensured the Wallachian independence.

A couple of years later, Basarab could not do anything but join the Hungarian king again, due to the looming Mongol danger. After the death of King Robert Charles, the feudal relationship was restored with the kings' successor, Louis the Great.

During the times of Basarab's grandson, Vladislav, the Hungarian-Wallachian relationship further improved. The king gave the castle of Szörény to Vladislav and donated the estates of Transylvanian Fogaras and Omlás. Vladislav recognized the Hungarian king as his suzerain. At the cost of feudal relationship, the Wallachian reigning prince, even as vassal of the king, gained a foothold into the Eastern part of Hungarian Transylvania with his household; nobles, serfs and slaves.

The development of both principalities was markedly hindered by the Turk advancement and conquests. Almost immediately after the establishment of the states, the fight against the Turk conquests begun.

After their victorious battle of Rigómező (Kosovo-polje) in 1389, the Turks meant the most immediate danger to Wallachia, whose voivod was Mircea cel Bătrân (Old

Mircea). In 1394, a large Turkish army begun to conquer Wallachia under the leadership of Sultan Bajazid. Mircea could not defeat the Turks, but repulsed them in the famous battle of Rovine. Mircea withdrew and escaped to Transylvania, where he formed an alliance with Zsigmond of Luxembourg (1368-1437, Hungarian king from 1387) in Brassó to push back the Turks. Under the terms of the treaty, Mircea recognized Zsigmond and the Hungarian kings in general, as his suzerain.

In the meantime, the Turks annexed Wallachia and enthroned a pro-Turk voivod. Zsigmond, fulfilling the conditions of the treaty, hastened to the help of Mircea. They together defeated the pro-Turk voivod in 1395. Mircea regained his throne.

King Zsigmond gathered an army of crusaders in 1396. He tried to oust the Turks from the Balkan Peninsula, but was badly defeated at Nikápoly[34]. Mircea pulled back his troops north of the Danube and prepared himself to fend off the Turk attack. He was successful. He defeated the Turks two times, in 1397 and 1400.

The Turks occupied two fortresses of Mircea, the fortress of Turnu Măgurele and Giurgiu along the Danube in 1416. In spite of the new Turkish pressure, due to other pressing problems, King Zsigmond neglected his previous alliance. He used all his forces to carry out his Western plans. Mircea made a pledge to pay yearly taxes to the Turks – the independence of Wallachia ended. Turkish raids occurred more frequently along the Hungarian borders. The Turks put their hands on Fort Galambóc in 1428, and Fort Szendrő in 1439.

The Turks now menaced also the other Vlach voivodship, Moldavia. Alexandru cel Bun (Alexander the Good, 1400-1432), and Petru Aron (1451-1457) voivods were fighting the Turks with alternating luck. Finally, voivod Aron declared Moldavia a country under the authority of the Turks. Moldavia too became the feudal principality of the Turks.

Voivod Ştefan cel Mare (Stephen the Great, 1457-1505) did not resign himself to the situation. In one and a half decade, he made Moldavia one of the most important states of southeastern Europe. In his foreign policy, he aimed to ensure Hungarian and Polish help against the Turks [70]. He defeated the Turkish army with Hungarian and Polish assistance in 1475 at Vaslui, but was defeated in 1476 near Războieni. After his loss he marched to the north behind the line of strong Moldavian castles. Facing the united Rumanian-Hungarian army, the Sultan retreated. He even had to give up Wallachia.

Eight years later a war broke out between the Hungarian king, Mathias (1458 - 1490) and the German emperor. Mathias was forced to conclude a peace treaty with the Turks, who profiting from the occasion, immediately annexed the two big trade centers of Moldavia, the cities of Chilia and Cetatea Albă.

Voivod Stephen was still able to destroy two Turkish armies in 1485 and 1486, but he could not achieve more significant results. The forces of Moldavia were not enough to resist the military might of the strengthened Turkish Empire. The ruling prince made efforts to establish an anti-Turk coalition. He started negotiations with king Mathias. Mathias gave him two Transylvanian forts, Csicsó and Küküllővár, flee to in case he was defeated in a battle. Thus another Rumanian ruler, with all his household, nobles, serfs and slaves, won a foothold in the eastern part of Transylvania.

King Mathias died in 1490. The country was in decay. In spite of the Hungarian help, voivod Stephen recognized the Polish king as his feudal lord.

During the times of Stephen's descendants the Turkish pressure increased. There were twenty-six transfers of sovereignty in the principality during a hundred-year period. There were only two extraordinary persons among the rulers. Petru Rareş (1527-1538), ally of János Szapolyai and Ioan Vodă cel Viteaz (voivod John the Gallant), who ruled between 1572 and 1574. John liberated Brăila in Wallachia.

The Sultan, being afraid of an uprising of the Christians living south of the Danube against the Turkish rule, sent 100.000 armed men to Moldavia. After courageous fights, Voivod John was forced to capitulate. Despite the treaty, the Turks massacred the prisoners of war and killed the reigning prince.

We have already have pointed out that Louis the Great donated the properties of Fogaras and Omlás to Vladislav, Wallachian Voivod. Fogaras and Sebesvár were owned by Mircea cel Bătrân. On the basis of the treaty with king Mathias, the owner of Csicsóvár and Küküllővár was Stephen the Great. Later, his successor, Petru Rareș, inherited his possessions.

The Hungarian king János I. (1526-1540) donated the entire Beszterce area with the Radna Valley to Petru Rareș, in addition to the forts of Csicsóvár and Küküllővár. The voivod founded an Orthodox Episcopacy on his fief at Rév. The Bishops came from Moldavia, and governed this Church between 1523 and 1561. – The Rumanian Orthodox Church of Barcarozsnyó (Rum. Râșnov) was built with the help of the Wallachian ruler in the 14th century. Mihai Viteazul (Michael the Gallant, 1593-1601) restored it.

The construction of a stone church began in Brassó in 1495, with the help of Vlad Călugărul, Wallachian Voivod. This church was between 1519 and 1521 enlarged with the assistance of Neagoe Basarab. Aron Vodă, Moldavian ruler, decorated its walls with frescos in 1594. The building, erected in the courtyard of the church, included the old Rumanian School. The school building replaced an older wooden structure, and was built in 1597 with the monetary help of Aron Vodă. The teaching was in Slavonic (the language of the Romanian Orthodox Church) before 1559, then it was changed to Rumanian. The building of Rumanian churches and monasteries continued in Transylvania with the help and financial assistance of the voivodes of the two Rumanian lands.

Finally, we have to remember that István Báthory (1533–1586), Transylvanian ruler, founded the Orthodox Episcopacy of Gyulafehérvár. According to a decree of the

Parliament, the bishop was elected by the Rumanian priests and approved by the ruler. The bishop asked – after having received the approval of the voivod – the Wallachian Orthodox bishop of Târgovişte$_{35}$ to consecrate him. The Rumanian Orthodox Bishop of Gyulafehérvár named himself, after 1577, the Archbishop of Transylvania. Every Rumanian Orthodox priest in Transylvania was placed under his authority.

In the light of these historical facts, it may be stated that the Carpathians did not make out an obstacle between the Rumanians living in Moldavia, Wallachia and Transylvania.

The present day community of Rumanian historians tries to forge an argument for the theory of Vlach continuity in Transylvania from the fact that Rumanian voivods, who were in a difficult situation because of the Tatar and later the Turkish attacks, were helped by the Hungarian kings. This help included most of the time granting of temporary possession of land, in exchange for their services to the Hungarian Kingdom, and safe heaven in times of defeats and temporary setbacks. Rumanian historiography does not shrink back to degrade the two Rumanian states' voivods' well documented vassal relationship with the Transylvanian *vajda*-s and the Hungarian kings, to the level of "political orientation" and "wider trade relationships".

It would be enough to mention only one example to refute this concept. Voivod Mircea cel Bătrân stayed in the Transylvanian city of Brassó as a refugee on March 7, 1395. He wanted to make an arrangement with his superior, the Hungarian King, Zsigmond of Luxembourg, against the Turks. He had a place to which to flee, because the Wallachian voivods have had access to the fiefs of Fogaras and Omlás for more than hundred years. In return of the use of the estates, the voivods, as vassals, had to fulfil several services to their masters. There is no other way to understand this relationship. It is possible that in retrospect, and by using todays' standards, these centuries of Hungarian-Vlach relationship made out a painful period in the history of the Rumanian people, but it cannot constitute the basis or cause for deliberate falsification of history.

Radu Popa refers to excavations in Transylvania carried out in 1964-65 (p. 7.). He states that – although the written sources do not mention Rumanian semi-autonomous kenezships and voivodships until the 13th, and especially the 14th centuries – in Máramaros, Fogaras, Bihar, Bánság and Hátszeg, a feudal Rumanian society had existed. According to Mr. Popa, the objects, discovered in the excavations gave evidence of Rumanian court chapels, and small monasteries from the 11th and 12th Centuries. The construction were supported by the Rumanian *kenez* families' money. In the 13th-14th centuries they were reconstructed by stone and brick like everywhere else in Europe.

Popa, however, did not give any evidence of the existence of these church centres in the 11th-12th centuries. He could not prove that such buildings had been financed by the Rumanian *kenez* families. He did not have any data about the names of the leaders of the church centres. He was unable to name a single place where these supposedly chapel or monastery ruins could have been found, even though he was referring to official documents. If person- and place names did not occur in those official documents – then what would they contain?

Popa´s assumptions serve only one goal: to slip the origin of the cultic places built in Transylvania during the 13th and 14th centuries to the 11th-12th centuries, from which period there are no relics of Rumanian origin. He passes over the fiefs and the senior-vassal relationship between the Hungarian kings, Transylvanian *vajda*-s (later princes), and the Wallachian and Moldavian voivods. However, these well documented historical facts – not the alleged Dacian-Rumanian Continuity – have contributed to the ease with which the Wallachian, Moldavian and Transylvanian Rumanians were able to pass the Carpathian Mountains.

The comparison of construction dates of the Hungarian and Rumanian cultic places presents important evidence against the Theory of Continuity.

314

Let us review the construction dates of the cultic places
(churches) in the Transylvanian cities:
(Rumanian place-names in brackets.)

Place:	Hungarian:	Rumanian:
Arad (Arad)	1139	1865
Beszterce (Bistriţa)	1288	19th century
Bethlen (Beclean)	15th century	19th century
Bonchida (Bonţida)	13th century	18th century
Brassó (Braşov)*	1223	1495
Fogaras (Făgăraş)	16th century	17th century
Fugyivásárhely (Oşorheiu)	13th century	18th century
Gyulafehérvár (Alba-Iulia)	11th century	1600-1601
Kolozsvár (Cluj-Napoca)	12th century	1796-1797
Lugos (Lugoj)	15th century	1759
Marosvásárhely (Târgu-Mureş)	14th century	1750
Nagyenyed (Aiud)	14th century	20th century
Nagyszeben (Sibiu)	14th century	17th century
Nagyvárad (Oradea)	1093	1784
Piskolt (Pişcolt)	14th century	1869
Temesvár (Timişoara)	1323	1936
Tövis (Teiuş)	13th century	17th century
Vizakna (Ocna Sibiului)*	13th century	16th century

Note: the churchs marked with * were built by Moldavian or Wallachian
voivods on their feudal lands in Transylvania.

Several Other Hungarian Church Constructions:

Place:	Built in:
Alvinc (Vinţu de Jos)	13th century
Aranyosgerend (Luncani)	1290
Árapatak (Araci)	14th century
Boroskrakkó (Cricău)	13th century
Bögöz (Mugeni)	13th century
Csíkménaság (Armăşeni)	13th century
Érmihályfalva (Valea lui Mihai)	1284
Gelence (Ghelinţa)	1245
Gernyeszeg (Corneşti)	13th century
Kerc (Cârţa)	1202
Kisdisznód (Cisnădoara)	12th century
Kistorony (Turnişor)	13th century

Kolozsmonostor (Mănăştur)	1059-1063
Magyarvista (Viştea)	13th century
Marosnagylak (Noşlac)	1298
Nagycsűr (Şura Mare)	13th century
Nagydisznód (Cisnădie)	13th century
Réty (Reci)	11th century
Székelyszáldobos (Doboşeni)	13th century
Torda (Turda)	12th century
Vadász (Vânători)	13th century

Other Rumanian Church Constructions in Transylvania:

Place Name	Built in:
Alsolugas (Lugaşu de Jos)	18th century
Bánlaka (Banlaca)	1700
Demsus (Densuş)	13th century
Füzesmikola (Nicula)	1700
Kristyor (Criştior)	1404
Lesznek (Lesnic)	14th century
Lippa (Lipova)	14th century
Nagylupsa (Lupşa)	1421
Oravicabánya (Oraviţa)	1872
Pártos (Partoş)	14th century
Ribica (Ribiţa)	1417
Szelistye (Sălişte)	18th century
Sztrigyszentgyőrgy (Streisânghergiu)	1313
Zeykfalva (Streiu)	13th century

It cannot be uninteresting when the Rumanian churches of Wallachia and Moldavia were built.

WALLACHIA

Place Name	Cultic Place	Built in
Buzău	episcopal church	1500
Căciulata	Cozia-monastery	1388
Câmpulung Muscel monastery	Negru Voda 14th century	
Curtea de Argeş	ruler's church	14th century
Horezu	Varatec monastery	17th century
Piteşti	ruler's church	17th century
Râmnicul Sărat	monastery-church	1691
Snagov	Snagov monastery	14th century
Tismana	monastery	14th century
Târgovişte	ruler's church	15th century

MOLDAVIA

Place Name	Cultic Place	Built in
Arbore	church	16th century
Bacău	church	15th century
Cotnari	church (ruins)	15th century
Dolheştii Mari	church	1450
Galaţi	fortified church	15th century
Putna	monastery	1466-1470
Rădăuţi (Bukovina)	church	14th century
Siret	church	1384
Suceviţa	church	1584
Vaslui	church	1490
Vânător Neamţ	monastery	1375
Voroneţ	monastery-church	1488

On the basis of these data, it can be concluded that the Hungarian Christian churches (monasteries, abbacies) appeared at the beginning of the 11th century in Transylvania. The first church of the Rumanian population – the one in Demsus – was built towards the end of the 13th century, almost three hundred years after the first Hungarian churches.

The oldest Wallachian and Moldavian Christian churches (monasteries) were built in the second half of the 14th century. Numerous structures, however, did not follow the first church buildings until the second half of the 15th, and later centuries. This leads to the conclusion that the Vlachs, infiltrating Transylvania at the end of the 12th century and at the beginning of the 13th century, lived under better, more advanced conditions than those of their brothers living on the northern shore of the Danube. This is also in accordance with the fact that the Vlachs founded their states several centuries later than the neighboring peoples.

*   *   *

Referring the history of the Transylvanian Christian cultic places, we have only pointed out the circumstances that are enough to prove the untenability of the Theory of Continuity. We do not desire to praise nor to disparage anyone or anything. We only want to state and prove that those, who consider Hungarians to be late new-comers, have proclaimed war upon the historical facts. Our work proves that the Hungarians made Transylvania theirs on their own. They fused the people they found there with themselves. We bear out that Saint Stephen was an outstanding ruler. According to the opinion of his times, as well as judged by present day standards, he was a European authority and an apostle of Christianity, which has been embodying progressive conceptions. He was the first European ruler canonized by the Roman-Catholic Church.

The Theory of Dacian-Roman Continuity is untenable and baseless, among other things, because it ignores the basic and decisive question of Christian cultic places in the 10th-12th centuries.

Using the construction dates of the Christian cultic places, the existence, or the lack of them, we wanted to prove the falsehood of such doctrines. These doctrines, born of political considerations, show a totally misconceived idea of the ethnic picture of the Carpathian Basin in the first half of the 10th century. "...they revise the Carpathian basin's political and ethnical relationships in the 10th century by false data and basic errors."   The romantic legend of the Dacian-Roman-Rumanian Continuity serves only political purposes without any scientifically acceptable proof.

APPENDIX

Churches of the Árpádian Age

in East-Hungary

Assembled by János Gyurkó

The following documentation was written independently from Árpád Kosztin's work; it nevertheless supports his statements.

The following Appendix contains the list of the Hungarian Medieval (10th-13th Century) Churches located in the territories annexed by Rumania in 1920. We do not know any early Christian (Roman or Germanic) cultic places from the era before the Árpád's conquest of Hungary, because these places vanished without leaving a trace behind, in the storms of the Great Migrations.

The conversion of Hungarians to Christianity started right in Transylvania in the 10th Century. The first bishop of Hungary, Hierotheos – who had been brought to Transylvania from Constantinople by Gyula, – was working there. The Greek-Orthodox Catholicism did not take root in Hungary. The orthodox Church lost most of its Hungarian followers by the end of the 13th Century.

Géza, the ruling prince called Western missionaries to the country in 972. The conversion work widened under the rule of his son, Saint Stephen. The first Hungarian king ordered "...every ten village to build a church..." (*decem ville ecclesiam edificent*)

Most of the churches, being built after the enactment of the law, were made out of wood or other not durable material, and long since disappeared. This explains the low number of the relics from the 10th-11th centuries. Not only the village churches of lesser importance, but also several well-known, important buildings were made of perishable materials. The Benedictine Abbacy of Szentjobb (Sâniob), where Saint Stephen's right hand was protected from 1083 until the 15th Century, was still a wood building in the 11th century.

At the end of the Árpádian Age in Hungary, excluding Croatia and Slavonia, there were 10,000 - 11, 000 villages. Two thirds of them had a church. It is the peculiarity of the era in question, that sculpture and painting did not yet exist independently from architecture. That is why the whole spatial art can be discovered by studying the historic sacred buildings. The border areas of Hungary are very important in the history of art. Under the Turkish rule, the relics of the Medieval culture almost totally vanished in Central Hungary, but the remnants of historical centres can still be found in upper Northern Hungary (presently in Slovakia), Transylvania, and in the western border zone where the scale of devastation was much smaller. The territories detached from Hungary happen to be the richest in ancient buildings, ruins and relics. Since the loss of the territories in the Trianon Peace Treaty in 1920, Hungarian medieval research has been struggling with outrageous artificial obstacles.

Hungarian historians are often forced to discover the truth behind the unscientific phantasmagorias of the neighboring countries' historians, since they usually do not have the opportunity of local excavations. The best example was the Jesus Chapel at Székelyudvarhely. M. Beldie, Rumanian historian, found a coin of Ferdinand I beside a basement wall. On the basis of this find, she stated in a paper that the building originated from the 16th Century. The chapel was a small temple in Gyárosfalva, a village that no longer exists. In the 16th Century this settlement was already in its declining period, and the tax list of 1567 found only two(!) households capable of paying tax. It is unimaginable that such a weak, disintegrating community would have undertaken temple building. Moreover, such quatrefoil plan chapels are known from the 12th-13th centuries, – that in Székely-udvarhely would be the only one from the 16th century.

In the following list only those relics are listed, from which there is some kind of positive material (we can call it physical), architectual data. Churches mentioned only in documents or contemporary written sources, are left out of the catalogue, because they would have enlarged the size of the book without providing significant data for the history of architecture. Like any other collection, this cannot be complete and perfect either. Since a large part of the subject matter was attained from the literature, it should be augmented with local research.

The examination of the village churches often bring surprising results. The fact that a building that originated from the 19th century contains Medieval parts comes to light only at the time when the covering plaster is removed. This is probably true also in the case of those Transylvanian churches which are considered to have been built in modern times. Systematical protection of monuments and historical architectural excavations have not existed in Rumania since 1977. New findings and observations, being discovered during renovation of local churches, do not get published in the technical journals. The number of discovered or identified Medieval Transylvanian churches would significantly grow if systematic research could be carried out.

Papal tithe collectors rambled all over Hungary between 1332 and 1337. They collected taxes to provide enough money to restart the Crusades to the Holy Land. From their surviving accounts, it can be concluded that they found approximately 1,000 parishes in Eastern Hungary. This high number indicates that the Eastern part of the country was rebuilt during the couple of decades following the Tatar attacks. Rumanian historiography has misinterpreted also these data. In his work titled *Ce este Transilvania?*(What is Transylvania?) – in the Hungarian translation *Mit jelent Erdély?* (1984), Stefan Pascu, academician, wrote on the basis of the Papal tithe collector's list, that in the 13th century two thirds of Eastern-Hungary's population had already been Rumanian.

The author accepted that the places, listed by the tithe collectors with Roman-Catholic parishes, had been populated mainly by Hungarians and Germans. He assumed, however, that only Rumanian Orthodox population lived in every other village. The basis of this distorsion was that Pascu did not pay attention to the outparishes, being on the lowest level of the Church organization which did not have a priest. The organization on the lowest level of the Church was the same as today. Thus, almost every parish had one or two out-parishes belonging to it, where, in many cases, also a church existed. At the end of the Árpádian Age (1301), approximately 2,000 churches existed on the territories in question.

Since the devastations caused by the Turks in central Hungary were much more severe than those in Transylvania, the ratio of the surviving and known relics should be higher in Transylvania than in other parts of the country – so far it is, however, even lower.

Witnesses of the Hungarian history in Transylvania remain silent. A lot of them can be silenced forever. Academician Pascu's primitive confabulation can be disproved by simple counting the listed relics in the Appendix.

70% of the early churches in the observed territories are Hungarian, while 28% German and 2% are Rumanian artworks. Several relics of the Hungarian population survived from the conversion period (for example Csanád.) The German immigration started in the middle of the 12th century, while Rumanians did not immigrate to Transylvania until the beginning of the 13th century, as proven also by our documentation. No Orthodox Rumanian Church built before the 13th century exists – and never existed – on the territory of today's Rumania.

Daco-Roman-Rumanian Continuity, the "two-thousand -year-old dream" vanishes in the daylight of undeniable facts.

CHURCHES OF FORMER EASTERN HUNGARY

Hungarian name	Rumanian name	Built in
Abafája	Apalina	13th century
Abrudbánya	Abrud	13th century
Ákos	Acaş	13th century
Albis	Albiş	13th century
Alcina	Alţina	12th century
Algyógy	Geoagiu de Jos	13th century
Almakerék	Malicrav	13th century
Alvinc	Vinţu de Jos	13th century
Aranyosgerend	Luncani	13th century
Aranyospolyán	Poiana	13-15th
Árkos*	Arcuş	13th century
Asszonyfalva	Axente Sever	13-15th
Baca*	Baţa	12-13th
Bádok	Bădeşti	13th century
Bálványosváralja	Unguraş	13th century
Bályok	Balc	13th century
Bánffyhunyad	Huedin	13th century
Bányabükk	Vâlcele	13th century
Barcarozsnyó-Vár	Râşnov	12th century
Barcaszentpéter *	Sîmpetru	13th century
Belényesszentmiklós		
	Sânnicolau	13th century
Beszterce	Bistriţa	13th century
Bibarcfalva	Biborţeni	13th century
Bihar	Biharia	13th century
Bihardiószeg	Diosig	12th century
Bodonkút	Vechea	12th century
Bögöz	Mugeni	13-14th
Bokajalfalu	Băcăinţi	13th century
Bonchida	Bonţida	13-18th
Borbánd	Bărăbant	13th century

Hungarian name	Rumanian name	Built in:
Borosjenő	Ineu	12th century
Boroskrakkó	Cricău	13th century
Botháza	Boteni	13th century
Brassó-Cenk	Braşov-Tâmpa	12th century
Brassó-Szt. Bertalan	Braşov	13th century
Brulya	Bruiu	13th century
Cege	Ţaga	13th century
Csernáton-Szentkert	Cernat	12-13th century
Csicsókeresztúr	Cristeştii	13-15th century
Csíkdelne	Delniţa	13-15th century
Csíkrákos	Racu	13th century
Csíkszentdomokos	Sândominic	13th century
Csíkszentkirály	Sâncrăinei	13th century
Csíkszereda-Somlyó	Miercurea Ciuc	13th century
Csomakőrös	Chiuruş	13th century
Csomaköz	Ciumeşti	13th century
Dálnok	Dalnic	13-16th
Dés-Óvár	Dej	13th century
Déva*	Deva	13th century
Doborka	Dobârca	13th century
Dolmány	Daia	13th century
Domokos	Dămăcuşeni	13th century
Egeres	Aghireşu	13th century
Egres	Igriş	12th century
Egrestő	Agrişteu	13th century
Érábrány	Abram	13th century
Erdőfűle-Dobópuszta	Filia	13th century
Erked	Archita	13-14th
Feketehalom	Codlea	13-16th
Felek	Avrig	13th century
Felmér	Felmer	13th century
Felsőboldogfalva	Feliceni	13th century
Felsőtök	Tiocul de Sus	13th century
Firtosváralja-Vár	Firtoşu	13th century
Földvár	Feldioara	13-14th
Fugyivásárhely	Oşorhei	13th century
Garat	Dacia	13th century
Gelence	Ghelinţa	13-15th
Gidófalva	Ghidfalău	14th century
Gogánváralja	Goganvarolea	13-15th
Guraszáda	Gurasada	13th century
Gyergyószentmiklós	Gheorgheni	13th
Gyergyóalfalu	Joseni	13-18th
Gyulafehérvár	Alba Iulia	11th century
Gyulafehérvár	Alba Iulia	11-13th

Hungarian name	Rumanian name	Built in
Hajó	Haieu	13th century
Halmágy	Halmeag	13th century
Harcó	Hărţău	13th century
Harina	Herina	13th century
Hegyközszentimre	Sântimreu	12th century
Hegyközújlak	Uileacu de Munte	13-18th
Holcmány	Hosman	13-18th
Höltövény	Halchiu	13-19th
Homoród	Homorod	11-18th
Homorodalmás	Mereşti	13th century
Homoróddaróc	Drauşeni	13th century
Homoródjánosfalva	Ioneşti	13-14th
Homorodszentmárton*	Martiniş	13th
Ikafalva	Icafalău	13th century
Jára-Alsójára	Iara	13th century
Kaca	Caţa	13-15th
Kajántó	Chinteni	13th century
Kakasfalva	Hamba	13-16th
Kalotadámos	Domoşu	13-14th
Kaplony	Căpleni	12-19th
Káposztásszentmiklós	Nicoleşti	13th
Karacsonyfalva	Crăciunel	13th century
Kecsed	Aluniş	13-15th
Kerc	Cârţa	13th century
Keresztényfalva	Cristian	13-15th
Kereszténysziget	Cristian	13th century
Ketesd	Tetişu	13-15th
Kézdiszentlélek-Perkő		
	Sânzieni	13th century
Kide	Chidea	13th century
Kiscsűr	Şura Mica	13-15th
Kisdisznód	Cisnădioara	13th century
Kisenyed	Sângatin	13th century
Kiskászon	Casinu Mic	13th century
Kispeleske*	Pelişor	13th century
Kispetri	Petrincel	13th century

Hungarian name	Rumanian name	Built in
Kisprázsmár	Toarcla	13th century
Kistorony	Turnişor	13th century
Kökös	Chichis	13-16th
Kolozs*	Cojocna	13th century
Kolozspata	Pata	13th century
Kolozsvár-Centrum	Cluj-Napoca	11-13th
Kolozsvár-Monostor		
	Cluj-Napoca	11-13th
Kolozsvár-Óvár	Cluj-Napoca	13-15th
Komlód	Comlod	13th century
Köröskisjenő	Ineu	13th century
Köröstárkány	Tarcaia	13th century
Kozárvár	Cuzdrioara	13th century
Krasznacégény	Teghea	13th century
Krasznarecse	Recea	13-15th
Küküllővár	Cetatea de Baltă	12-13th
Kürpöd	Chirpar	13th century
Leses	Dealu Frumos	13th century
Magyarborzás	Bozieş	13-15th
Magyarderzse	Dârja	13th century
Magyarfenes	Vlaha	13th century
Magyargyerőmonostor		
	Mănăstireni	13th century
Magyarkapus	Căpuşu Mare	13th century
Magyarkiskapus	Căpuşu Mic	13-16th
Magyarlapád	Lopadea Nouă	13-15th
Magyarpéterfalva	Petrisat	13th century
Magyarrégen	Reghin-Sat	13th century
Magyarsárd	Şardu	13th century
Magyarszentpál	Sânpaul	13th century
Magyarvalkó	Văleni	13-17th
Magyarvista	Viştea	13th century
Magyarzsombor	Zimbor	13th century
Maksa*	Moacşa	13th century
Malomfalva	Moreşti	12th century
Malomvíz-Kolcvár	Râu de Mori	13th century

Hungarian name	Rumanian name	Built in
Maroscsapó	Cipău	13th century
Marosfelfalu	Suseni	13th century
Maroskoppánd	Copand	13th century
Marosnagylak	Noşlac	13th century
Marossárpatak	Glodeni	13th century
Marosszentanna	Sântana de Mureş	13th century
Marosszentgyörgy	Sângeorgiu de Mureş	13-18th
Marosszentimre	Sântimbru	13-15th
Marosszentkirály	Sâncraiu de Mureş	13th century
Marosujvár	Ocna Mureş	13th century
Márpod	Marpod	13-15th
Mártonhegy	Şomartin	13-16th
Méra	Mera	13th century
Mészkő	Cheia	13th century
Mezőkeszü	Chesău	13th century
Mezőkölpény	Culpiu	13-15th
Mezőtelegd	Tileagd	13-16th
Micske	Mişca	13th century
Miklósvár*	Micloşoara	12-13th
Morgonda	Merghindeal	13-15th
Nádpatak	Rodbav	12-13th
Nagyapold	Apoldu de Sus	13th century
Nagybáród	Borod	13th century
Nagybaromlak	Valea Viilor	13-15th
Nagycsűr	Şura Mare	13th century
Nagydisznód	Cisnădie	12-16th
Nagygalambfalva	Porumbenii Mari	13-15th
Nagykakucs	Cacuciu Nou	13th century
Nagypetri	Petrindu	13-16th
Nagyrápolt	Rapoltu Mare	13th century
Nagyselyk	Şeica Mare	13-19th
Nagysink	Cincu	13-15th
Nagyszeben	Sibiu	12th century
Nagyszeben-Ispotály	Sibiu	13th century

Hungarian name	Rumanian name	Built in
Nagyvárad-Vár	Oradea	11th century
Néma	Nima	13th century
Nyárádszentanna	Sântana Nirajului	13-14th
Nyárádszentimre	Eremieni	13-17th
Nyárádszentlászló	Sânvasii	13-14th
Nyárádszentmárton	Mitreşti	13th century
Nyomát	Maiad	12-13th
Okiánd	Ocland	13-16th
Oltszakadát	Săcădate	13th century
Őraljaboldogfalva	Sântamaria Orlea	13-14th
Ördöngősfüzes	Fizeşu Gherlii	13th century
Oroszfája	Orosfaia	12-13th
Őscsanád	Cenad	10th century
Őscsanád*	Cenad	13th century
Öthalom	Vladimirescu	12th century
Ottomány	Otomani	13-14th
Páncélcseh	Panticeu	13th century
Pankota	Pâncota	12th century
Páva	Pava	13th century
Pelbárthida	Părhida	12-14th
Pele	Becheni	13-19th
Péterfalva	Petreşti	13th century
Petres	Petriş	13th century
Pókakeresztur	Păcureni	13-14th
Prázsmár	Prejmer	13th century
Pusztaszentmárton	Martineşti	13th century
Radna-Óradna	Rodna	13th century
Réty	Reci	11-13th
Roszcsűr	Rusciori	13th century
Rugonfalva	Rugăneşti	13-15th
Sajószentandrás	Şieu-Sfântu	12-13th
Sajóudvarhely	Şieu-Odorhei	13th century
Sálya	Şoala	12th century
Sárvár	Şaula	13th century
Segesvár-Kolostor	Sighişoara	13-15th
Segesvár-Várhegy	Sighişoara	13-15th

329

Hungarian name	Rumanian name	Built in
Sellenberg	Şelimbăr	13th century
Sepsikilyén	Chilieni	13-18th
Sepsikőröspatak	Valea Crişului	13-17th
Sepsibesenyő	Beşineu (Pădureni)	13-16th
Siter	Şiştirea	12-13th
Somlyóújlak	Uileace Şimleului	13th century
Sövényfalva	Corneşti	13-15th
Szamoscikó	Ţicău	13th century
Szamosfalva	Someşeni	13-15th
Szamosújvárnémeti	Mintiu Gherlei	13-14th
Szarvaskend	Corneşti	13th century
Szászfehéregyháza	Viscri	12-13th
Szászhermány	Hărman	13-14th
Szászkeresztúr*	Criţ	13th century
Szászkézd	Saschiz	13-15th
Szásznyíres	Nireş	13th century
Szászorbó	Gârbova	13th century
Szászpián	Pianu de Jos	13-17th
Szászsáros	Şaroş pe Târnava	12th century
Szászsebes	Sebeş	12-15th
Szászszentlászló	Laslea	13th century
Szászújfalu	Nou	13th century
Szászveresmart	Rotbav	13th century
Szászvolkány	Vulcan	13-19th
Százhalom	Movile	13-16th
Szebenrécse	Reciu	13th century
Szék	Sic	13th century
Székelyderzs	Dârjiu	13-16th
Székelykeresztúr	Cristuru Secuiesc	13-15th
Székelyszáldobos	Doboşeni	13th century
Székelyszentmiklós	Nicoleni	13-15th
Székelyudvarhely	Odorheiu Secuiesc	13th century
Székelyudvarhely-Vár	Odorheiu Secuiesc	13th century
Székelyvaja	Valenii	13-17th
Szentágota	Agnita	13-15th

Hungarian name	Rumanian name	Built in
Mănăstirea	Szentbenedek	12th century
Szenterzsébet	Gusteriţa	12-13th
Szentjob	Sâniob	11-15th
Szentlélek	Bisericani	13-15th
Szerdahely	Miercurea Sibiului	13-15th
Szilágyborzás	Bozieş	13-18th
Szind	Sănduleşti	13th century
Sztrigyszentgyőrgy	Streisângeorgiu	13th century
Tamáshida	Tămasda	13th century
Tompaháza	Rădeşti	13th century
Torda-Ótorda	Turda	13-15th
Tóti	Tăuteu	13-17th
Tövis	Teiuş	13th century
Türe	Turea	13-17th
Ugra	Ungra	13th century
Újváros	Noiştat	13-19th
Váralmás	Almaşu	12th century
Várfalva	Moldoveneşti	13-17th
Várhegy	Chinari	13th century
Vérd	Vărd	13-14th
Veresmart	Roşia	13th century
Vessződ	Veseud	13th century
Vidombák	Ghimbav	13th century
Vízakna	Ocna Sibiului	13-15th
Vurpód	Vurpăr	13th century
Zabola	Zăbala	13-15th
Zalán	Zălan	13-14th
Zeikfalva	Strei	13th century
Zsuk-Alsózsuk	Jucu de Jos	13th century

(*): demolished

FOOT NOTES

1. Aurelian, Lucius Domitius (212-275), Holy Roman Emperor from 270; He   withdrew his legions from Dacia, and placed them south of the Danube, in Moesia (creating two new Dacias: *Dacia Ripensis* and *Dacia Mediterranea*).

2. Form of government in the Asian states of ancient times; such states lived under the rule of four reigning princes.

3. Ulfila (Ulfilas, Wulfila, 311-383), bishop of the Goths. Founder of the Gothic writing. He translated the Bible into Gothic.

4. Maior Petru (1760 or 1761-1821), monk, teacher, later Greek-Catholic Rumanian clergyman in Szászrégen. He was named censor of the Royal Press at Buda in 1808. Convinced propagator of the continuity theory.

5. Cult of the Sun deity

6. Illiricum (Illyria), Balkan area along the Adriatic sea. In 168 A.D. Roman province, 1809-1813 French territory, from 1815 it belonged to Austria, from 1919 Yugoslavian province.

7. Today's Constanţa, Ovidius (43 B.C. - 17 A.D.), Roman poet was exiled there.

8. *Metropolit* is the second highest clerical dignity of the Greek-Catholic Church, following the dignity of patriarch. Originally, name of the Roman-Catholic bishops (or exarchs, patriarchs, primates, archbishops) residing in the capitals of the Roman provinces (*metropolis*). *Metropolie* is the corresponding administrative unit of the Orthodox Church, under the patriarchate but above the bishopric.

9. Father of the Church (342-419), patron saint of writers and scientists.

10. The first archbishop of Kalocsa. Benedictin monk. He came to Hungary as convertor friar during the times of Géza's reign. He led Saint Stephen's mission to ask Pope Sylvester II. for a crown.

11. Dynasty of emperors in Byzantium, until 1158 A.D.

12. The last dynasty of emperors in Byzantium (1259 - 1453).

13. Fertile lowland and mountainous district located along the Olt and Barca rivers, surrounded by the Transylvanian Carpathians.

14. *Kenéz* meant head of the clan; originally, the *Kenéz*-s were colonizing contractors, who received uninhabited lands from the Hungarian King to colonize and populate it. He and his descendants could settle judicial affairs of smaller significance.

15. John Túróczi (1435-1490), Hungarian chronicle writer. Prothonotary (a professional judge of the federal Court of Appeal) in king Mathias' court. His work is the *Chronica Hungarica*.

16. A heretical religious movement, started in the 10th century in Bulgaria. After the 15th century their followers converted to Islam.

17. City in Torda-Aranyos county. The oldest city in Transylvania.

18. Village in Fogaras county (Rum. Bran). Pass between Transylvania and Wallachia. Its stone castle was built in 1377 with the authorization of Louis the Great.

19. Part of Wallachia, located west of the Olt River. Its name is Oltenia today. The area belonged to Hungary before the Turkish reign.

20. Capital of Wallachia in the 14th-16th Centuries, seat of the voivod.

333

REFERENCES

1. Levárdy, Ferenc: *Magyar templomok művészete* (Art in Hungarian churches). Szent István Társulat. Az Apostoli Szentszék Könyvkiadója, Budapest, 1982, p. 19.
2. Szentkirályi, Zoltán: *Az épitészet világtörténete*. II. kötet (World History of Architecture, vol. 2.). Képzőművészeti Alap Kiadóvállalata, Budapest, 1980, p. 7.
3. Szentkirályi, Zoltán: op. cit., p. 52.
4. Faludy, Anikó: *Bizánc festészete és mozaikművészete* (The History of Byzantine Painting and Mosaic). Ed. Corvina, Budapest, 1982. p. 4.
5. Biró, Sándor: *A román nép története* (manuscript) (The History of the Rumanian People). Eötvös Lóránd Tudományegyetem Bölcsészettudományi Kara. Edit. Tankönyvkiadó, Budapest, 1976. p. 23.
6. *Művészeti kislexikon* (Short Encyclopaedia of the Arts) (Ed.: Lajta), Edit. Akadémiai Kiadó, Budapest, 1973. p. 353.
7. Kós, Károly: *Erdély.* (Kultúrtörténeti vázlat) (Transylvania - Culture-Historical Sketches) Erdélyi Szépműves Céh. Kolozsvár, 1934. p. 48.
8. Kőváry, László: *Erdély régiségei* (The Antiquities of Transylvania). Pest. 1852. Tilch János tulajdona. Kolozsvár, p. 17-18.
9. Jancsó, Benedek: *Erdély története* (The History of Transylvania). Cluj-Kolozsvár. Minerva Irodalmi és Nyomdai Műintézet Rt. 1931. p. 42.
10. *A művészet története Magyarországon* (The History of Art in Hungary). (Szerk.: Aradi Nóra.) Gondolat Kiadó, 1983, p. 10.
11. Păcurariu, Mircea: *Istoria Bisericii Ortodoxe Române*. (The History of the Rumanian Orthodox Church).

Sibiu, 1972, p. 47.

12. Stoicescu, Nicolae: *Continuitatea românilor.* (The Continuity of the Rumanians). Editura Ştiinţifică şi Enciclopedică, Bucureşti, 1980, p. 155.

13. Jancsó, Benedek: op. cit., pages 21 and 363.

14. László, Gyula: *Emlékezzünk régiekről!* (Let us Remember the Old Times!) Móra Ferenc Ifjúsági Kőnyvkiadó, Budapest., 1979, p. 57.

15. *Erdély története.* (The History of Transylvania) red.: Köpeczi, Béla. Akadémiai Kiadó, Budapest, 1986. vol. I, p. 58.

16. Karácsonyi, János: *Történelmi jogunk hazánk területi épségéhez.* (Our Historical Right to our Country's Territorial Integrity.) Szent István Társulat, Budapest., 1921, p. 38.

17. Jancsó, Benedek: op. cit. p. 366.

18. Erdély története, op. cit. p. 98.

19. Erdély története, op. cit. p. 103.

20. Kristó, Gyula: *Az augsburgi csata.* (The Battle at Augsburg.) Akadémiai Kiadó, Budapest, 1985. p. 58

21. Helmuth von Glasenapp: *Az öt világvallás.* (Five World Religions.) 4th ed. Gondolat Kiadó, Budapest. 1984, p. 283.

22. Păcurariu, Mircea: op. cit. p.47.

23. D. Pippidi: *Contribuţii la istoria veche a României.* (Contributions to the Ancient History of Rumania.) 2nd ed.Bucureşti 1976; pages 481-496.

24. Stoicescu, op. cit., p. 149.

25. Gergely, Jenő: *A pápaság története.* (The History of the Papacy.) Kossuth Kiadó, Budapest, 1982, p.17.

26. Auner, Carol: *Câteva momente din începuturile bisericii române.* (A Number of Episodes from the History of the Rumanian Church.) Tipografia Seminarului Archid. Gr. Cat. Blaj. Balázsfalva, 1902, p. 21.

27. Stoicescu, Nicolae op. citt. p.149, note 5.

28. Karácsonyi, János: op. cit. p.42

29. A. Ghimpu-Bolşacov: Organizarea bisericii din Scythia Minor în secolul al VI.-lea. (The Organization of the Church in Scythia Minor in the 6th century.) *Glasul bisericii,*

1969, 11-12, pages 1223-1225.

30. Stoicescu, Nicolae: op. cit., p. 151.

31. Maior, Petru: *Istoria pentru începutul romînilor în Dachia* (The History of the Origins of the Rumanians from Dacia). Pesti Magyar Egyetem Királyi Nyomdája, Buda, 1812. Forword by Manole Neago. Publisher: Albatros, 1970, p. 125.

32. Levárdy, Ferenc: op. cit., p. 19.

33. *Istoria Țării Românesci de când au descalecat pravoslavnicii creștini* (The History of Wallachia since the Settlement of the Orthodox Christians).

34. *Archeológiai Közlemények* (Archaeological Papers) 9/1873, p. 22. A Magyar Történelemtudomány Kézikönyve (The Handbook of Hungarian Historiography). Ed. Bálint Hóman, Book 1, 6/b. A Magyar történet bizánci forrásai. Magyar Történeti Társulat (The Byzantine Sources of Hungarian History. Hungarian Society of Historians). Budapest, 1934, p. 128.

35. Kristó, Gyula: op. cit., p. 58.

36. Jancsó, Benedek: op. cit., p. 30.

37. Eckhart, Ferenc: *Magyarország története* (The History of Hungary). Kádor Könyvkiadó, Budapest, 1935, p. 19.

38. Dummert, Rezső: *Az Árpádok nyomában* (In the Trails of the Árpád Dynasty). In the Panorama, 2nd edition. Gondolat kiadó, Budapest, 1977, p. 126.

39. Pauler, Gyula: *A Magyar nemzet története az Árpádházi királyok alatt* (The History of the Hungarian Nation during the Age of the Kings from the Árpád Dynasty). Budapest, 1899. Book 1, p. 18.

40. Levárdy, Ferenc: op. cit., p. 44.

41. Bakay, Kornél: *A magyar államalapítás. Magyar História* (The Foundation of the Hungarian State). Gondolat kiadó, Budapest, 1978, p. 133.

42. Győrffy, György: *István király és műve* (King Stephen and his Achievement). Gondolat kiadó, Budapest, 1982, p. 17.

43. Horváth, Mihály: *A kereszténység első százada Magyarországon* (The First Century of Christianity in

336

Hungary). 6/7. Fejer Cod. dipl. I., p. 260.
44. *Gondolkodó magyarok. István király intelmei*
(Thinking Hungarians. The Admonitions of King Stephen).
Magvető kiadó, Budapest, 1982, p. 17.
45. *Gondolkodó Magyarok. István király intelmei*, p. 49.
46. Stoicescu, Nicolae: op. cit., p. 156.
47. Maior, Petru: op. cit., p. 39.
48. Kristó, Gyula: op. cit., p. 65.
49. Győrffy, György: op. cit., p. 178.
50. Földes, Péter: *Ha az ősi krónikák igazat mondanak.
A honfoglaló vezérek nyomában* (If the Ancient Chronicles
Tell the Truth. In the Trails of the Leaders of the Original
Settlement in Hungary). Móra Ferenc Ifjúsági kiadó,
Budapest, 1982, p. 185-186.
51. Erdély története: op. cit., p. 242.
52. Maria Holban: *Din cronica relaţiilor româno-
ungare în secolele XIII-XIV* (On the History of the Rumanian
- Hungarian Relations in the 13th-14th centuries). Editura
Academiei Republicii Socialiste România. Bucureşti, 1981, p.
13.
53. Levárdy, Ferenc: op. cit., p. 66.
54. Domokos, Pál Péter: *Édes hazámnak akartam
szolgálni* (I Wanted to Do a Service for my Country). Szent
István Társulat, Budapest, 1979, pages 35-40.
55. Domokos, Pál Péter: op. cit., p. 41.
56. Thuróczy, János: *Chronica Hungarorum* (translated
by János Horváth), Európa könyvkiadó, Budapest, 1980, p.
196.
57. *Magyarország története* (The History of Hungary).
Ed. Erik Molnár, Gondolat kiadó, Budapest, 1967, p. 81.
58. Jancsó Benedek: op. cit., p. 42.
59. Karácsonyi János: *Magyarország egyháztörténete
főbb vonásokban 970-től 1970-ig* (The History of the Church
in Hungary from 970 to 1970). Könyvértékesítő Vállalat,
Budapest, 1985, p. 28.
60. Popa, Radu: *"Descălecări" Transilvănene şi
"Întemeieri de Ţară" între tradiţie istorică şi dovezi materiale*
(Transylvanian "Colonizations" and "Foundings of Country"

between Historical Tradition and Material Evidence). *Transilvania* 80/8, p. 7.

61. Domokos, Pál Péter: op. cit., p. 60.

62. Popa, Radu: op. cit., p. 7.

63. Dianu, Romulus: "Transilvania eterna". *Transilvania,* 80/8, p. 61.

64. Dianu, op. cit., p. 60.

65. Pauler, Gyula: op. cit., II, p. 357.

66. Beller, Béla: "Nagy Lajos és a pápaság" (King Louis the Great and the Papacy). *Vigilia,* vol. 49, I, p. 7.

67. B. Nagy Margit: *Várak, kastélyok, udvarházak, ahogy a régiek látták* (Towers, Castles, and Manor Houses, as Seen by our Ancestors). Kriterion, Bucureşti, 1973, p. 20.

68. Bíró, Sándor: op. cit., p. 19.

69. Bíró, Sándor: op. cit., p. 27.

70. Bíró, Sándor: op. cit., p. 53.

71: Kristó, Gyula: op. cit., p. 64.